Anatomy for the Artist

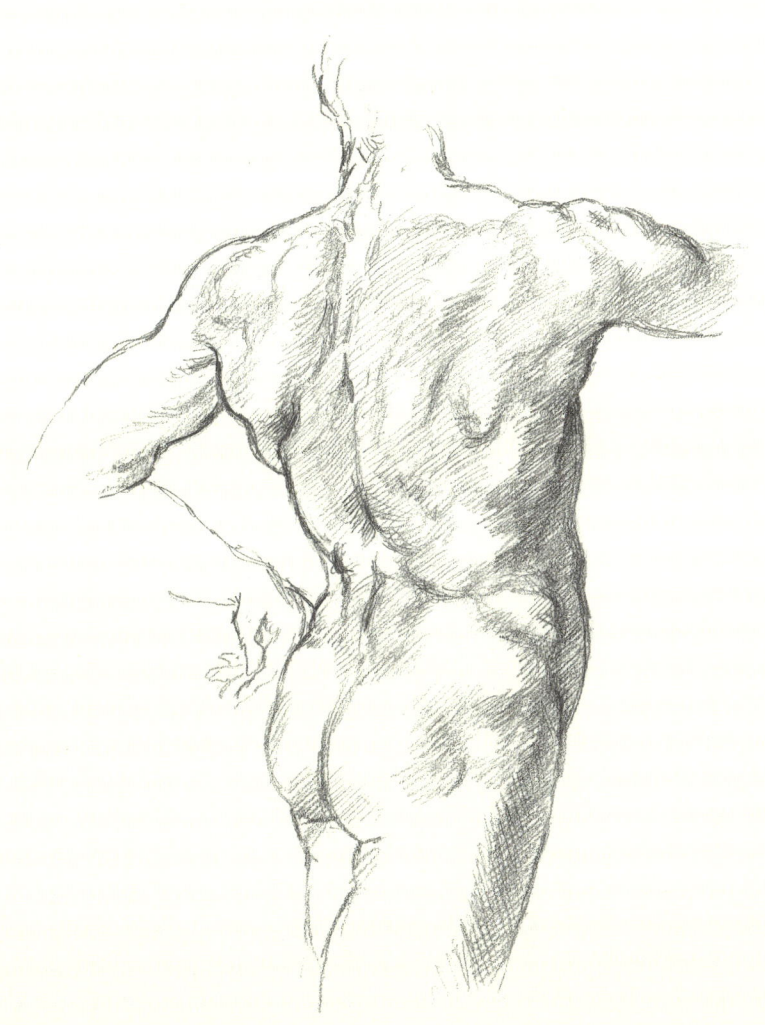

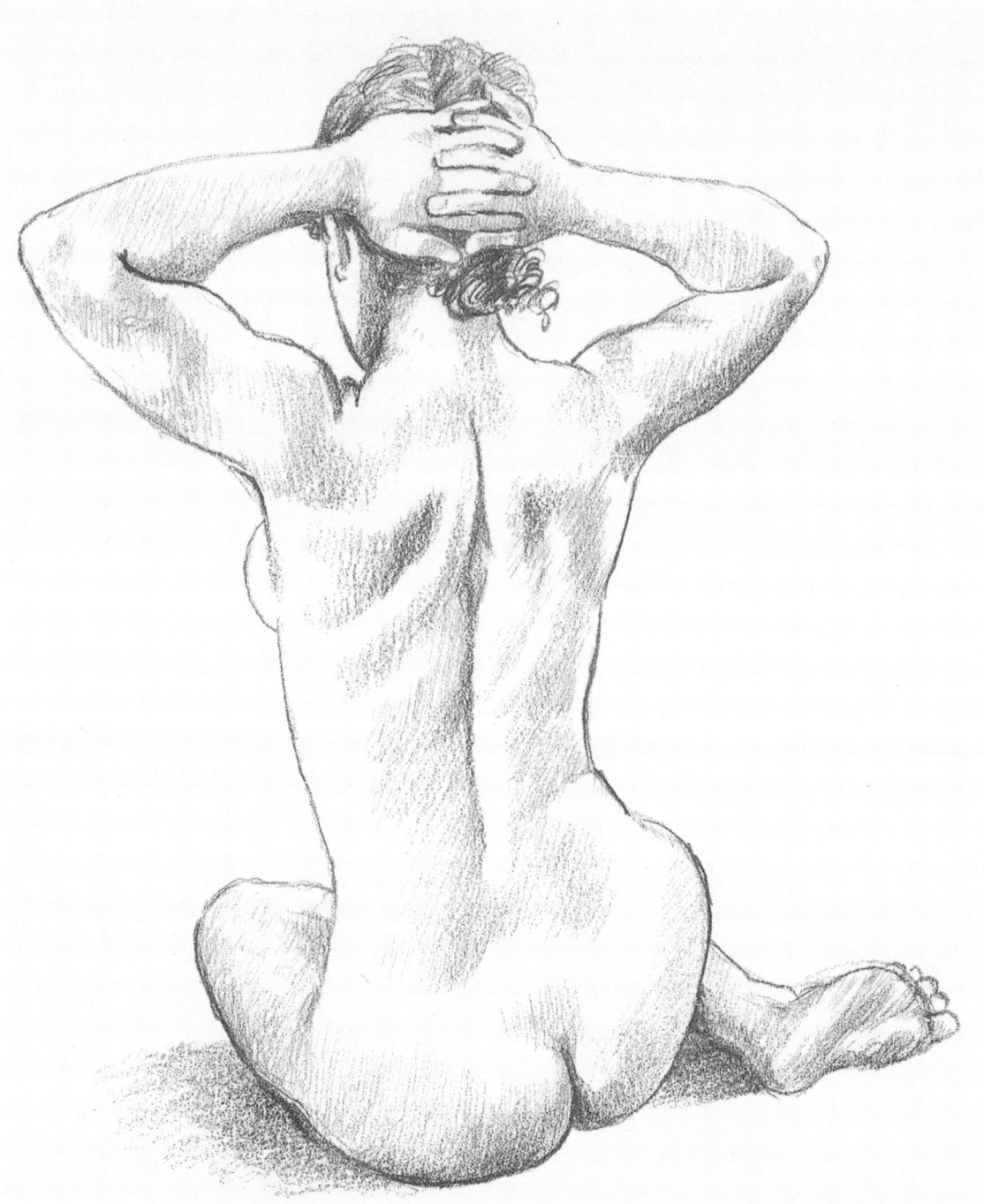

Anatomy for the Artist

BARRINGTON BARBER

ARCTURUS

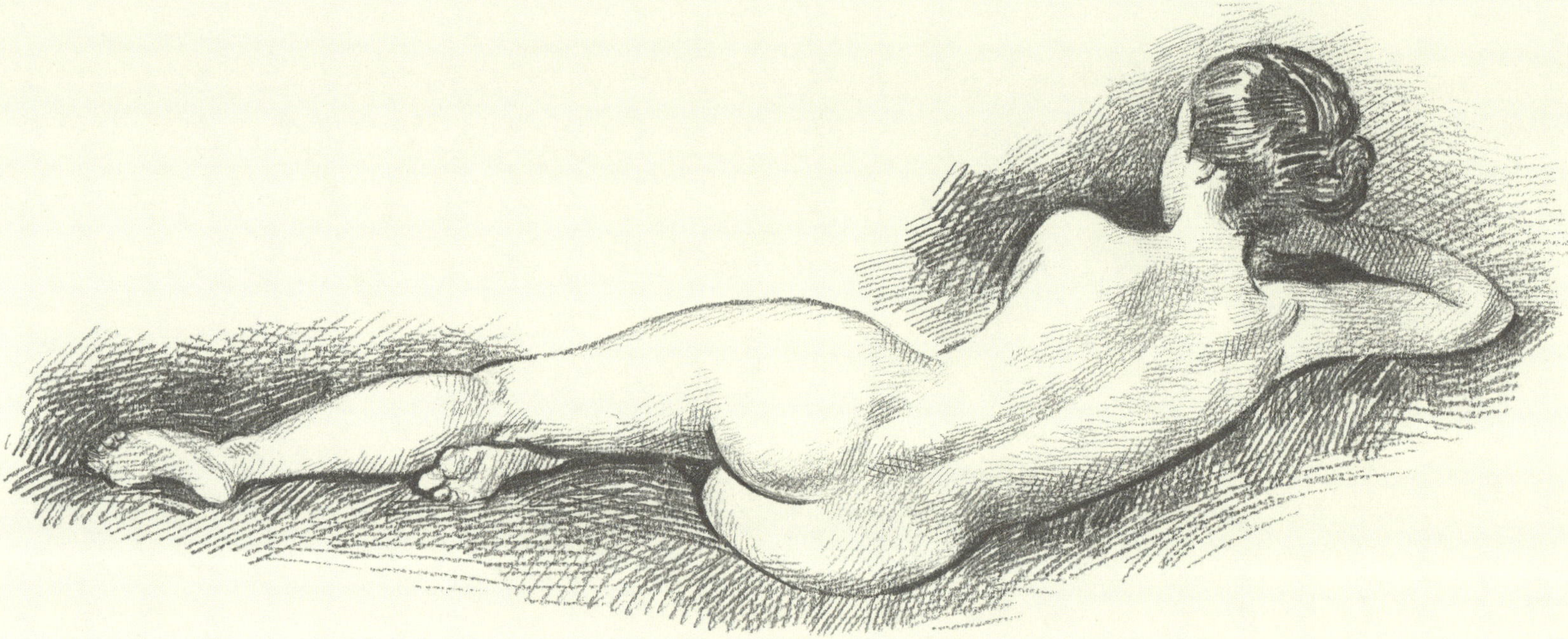

ARCTURUS

This edition published in 2024 by Arcturus Publishing Limited
26/27 Bickels Yard, 151–153 Bermondsey Street,
London SE1 3HA

Copyright © Arcturus Holdings Limited/Barrington Barber

All rights reserved. No part of this publication may be reproduced, stored in a retrieval system, or transmitted, in any form or by any means, electronic, mechanical, photocopying, recording or otherwise, without prior written permission in accordance with the provisions of the Copyright Act 1956 (as amended). Any person or persons who do any unauthorised act in relation to this publication may be liable to criminal prosecution and civil claims for damages.

ISBN: 978-1-3988-4008-9
AD012087US

Printed in China

CONTENTS

Introduction 6
Technical introduction 8
Drawing materials 14
Working in color 17

Chapter 1: Structure and Proportions of the Body 18
The skeleton 20
The muscles 23
Differences between the male and female skeleton 26
Proportions of the figure 28
Proportions in perspective 32

Chapter 2: The Head in Detail 34
Proportions of the head 36
The head from different angles 39
The skull 42
Muscles of the head 46
Muscles of the neck 49
Surface of the head showing the muscles 51
Facial expressions 54
Features of the face 58
The effects of age 66
Draw a head in proportion 68
Draw a tilted head 70
Portraits: different approaches 72
Lighting the head 78
A portrait in steps 80

Chapter 3: The Torso in Detail 84
Skeleton of the head and torso 86
The vertebral column 89
The pelvis 90
Muscles of the trunk and neck 91
Muscles and bones of the torso 94
Views of the torso 101
Views of the torso after master artists 108

Chapter 4: The Arms and Hands in Detail 120
Views of arms and hands 122
Skeleton of the arm and hand 124
Muscles of the arm and hand 126
Muscle and bone structure of the upper arm and shoulder 130

Muscles of the lower arm 138
Flexing the whole arm 142
Skeleton of the hand 144
Muscles of the hand 146
Muscle and bone structure of the hand 148
Surface of the hand 150
The hand in movement 152
Surface views of arms and hands 156
Arms and hands drawn by master artists 158
Draw your own hand 166
Experiment with different materials 167

Chapter 5: The Legs and Feet in Detail 168
Views of legs and feet 170
Skeleton of the leg and foot 172
Muscles of the leg and foot 174
Muscles of the hip and thigh 178
Gluteal muscles 182
Knee joint movement 184
Muscles of the lower leg 186
Muscle and bone structure of the foot 189
Surface views of the foot 192
Surface views of legs and feet 194
Legs and feet drawn by master artists 202
Practice perspective views of legs and feet 208
Experiment with different materials 209

Chapter 6: Drawing the Body 210
Life drawing 212
Dynamic poses 216
Changing ends 220
Working at speed 222
Describing form 224
Form in movement 230
Body language 234
Lighting the model 236
Light and dark tones 242
Life drawing step by step 244
Examples by master artists 246
Practice: the 'Rokeby Venus' 254

Index 256

Introduction

Anatomy books are essential for figure artists, but many are published for medical purposes and tend to give too much information. For example the inner organs of the body are interesting to know about, but not relevant for drawing.

What is important for the artist or art student is to learn the structure of the human form, based on the skeleton and the musculature. There have been a number of good and useful books on this subject. Some are a little out of date, not so much in the information that they give but often in the way it has been presented. Other well-produced, contemporary books are mainly photographic.

My task has been to produce a comprehensive anatomy book that has all the information necessary for an artist, using drawings and diagrams presented in an easy-to-follow format; and I also wanted to put into it everything that I have found useful in my own drawing practices.

In the first part of this book, I deal with the full figure, followed by a chapter on the anatomy of each major part of the body. Each section shows the skeleton from different viewpoints; then the muscles on top of the bone structure; and finally, the surface form of the human body.

Of course, not all human bodies are perfectly formed and proportions do differ from person to person. Throughout the book I have used well-proportioned, fairly athletic figures. This means that you become acquainted with the shapes of the muscles at their best, although you will probably draw many people who do not have well-toned bodies like these.

In the technical introduction immediately after this, you will find an explanation of descriptive terms as used in medical circles, followed by a detailed list of Latin terminology. This is worth reading, because understanding anatomical terms will help you follow the annotations in the book. It may take a little time to remember all the names you need, but after regular use of these terms, you usually remember enough to describe what you are looking at.

I have omitted any description of the brain, heart, lungs and other viscera because these items are housed within the cranium, the ribcage and the pelvis, and it is the bony parts that dictate the surface shape for figure-drawing purposes. I have also left out details of the male genitalia, because the differences in size and shape are too variable.

Throughout history, artists have looked at our bodies and shown their beauty, force and distortions. I have used the best possible references to draw these pictures, including my own life studies, but have not drawn from dissected corpses, as Michelangelo or Leonardo da Vinci did. Artists have contributed a lot to the study of anatomy, both for artistic and medical purposes. In drawing, the practicing artist wants to capture the form of this complex bodily machinery, but first he or she needs to know how it works.

Technical introduction

This section is intended to give you some initial detail about the human anatomy before starting to draw. I have described the properties of bones, muscles, tendons, cartilage, skin, fat and joints, as well as showing diagrams of the different types of joints and muscles. There is also an introduction to anatomical terminology: you will find this useful as certain terms are used throughout the book.

BONES

The skeleton is the solid framework of the body, partly supporting and partly protective. The shape of the skeleton can vary widely. It will affect the build of a person and determine whether they have masses of muscle and fat or not.

Bones are living tissue supplied by blood and nerves. They can become weaker and thinner with lack of use and malnutrition, or heavier and stronger when having to support more weight. They are soft and pliable in the embryo, and only become what we would consider hard and bone-like by the twenty-fifth year of life.

Humans have 206 bones, but a few fuse together with age and it is possible to be born with some bones missing or even having extra ones. We each have a skull, ribcage, pelvis and vertebral column, as well as arm, hand, leg and foot bones. Most bones are symmetrical. The bones of the limbs are cylindrical, thickening towards the ends. The projecting part of a bone is referred to as a ***process*** or an ***eminence***.

Highly mobile areas of the body, such as the wrists, consist of numerous small bones. Other bones, like the scapula (shoulder blade) can move in all directions, controlled by the muscles around it.

The bones of the cranium (skull) differ from all others. They grow from separate plates into one fused vault to house the brain. The mandible (jawbone) is the only movable bone in the head.

The long bones of the arms and legs act like levers, while the flat bones of the skull, the cage-like bones of the ribs and the basin shape of the pelvis protect the more vulnerable organs such as the brain, heart, lungs, liver and the abdominal viscera.

MUSCLES

The combination of bones, muscles and tendons allows both strong, broad movements and delicate, precise ones. Muscles perform our actions by contracting or relaxing. There are long muscles on the limbs and broader muscles on the trunk. The more fixed end of the muscle is called the ***head*** or ***origin***, and the other end – usually farthest from the spine – is the ***insertion***. The thick muscles are powerful, like the biceps; and the ring-shaped muscles (sphincters) surround the openings of the body, such as the eye, mouth and anus. Certain muscles grow together and have two, three or four heads and insertions. Combined muscles also have parts originating in different places.

The fleshy part of a muscle is called the *meat*, and the fibrous part the *tendon* or *aponeurosis* (see below).

Striated (voluntary) muscles operate under our conscious control. The 640 voluntary muscles account for up to 50 per cent of the body's weight and form the red flesh. Organized in groups and arranged in several layers, these muscles give the body its familiar form. The following drawings show the various different types of striated muscles, with the tendons at each end. Note the distinctive shape of the sphincter muscle on the far right.

Smooth (involuntary) muscles are confined to the walls of hollow organs, such as intestines and blood vessels. They function beyond our conscious control.

Cardiac (heart) muscles are both striated and involuntary, with a cell structure that ensures synchronic contraction.

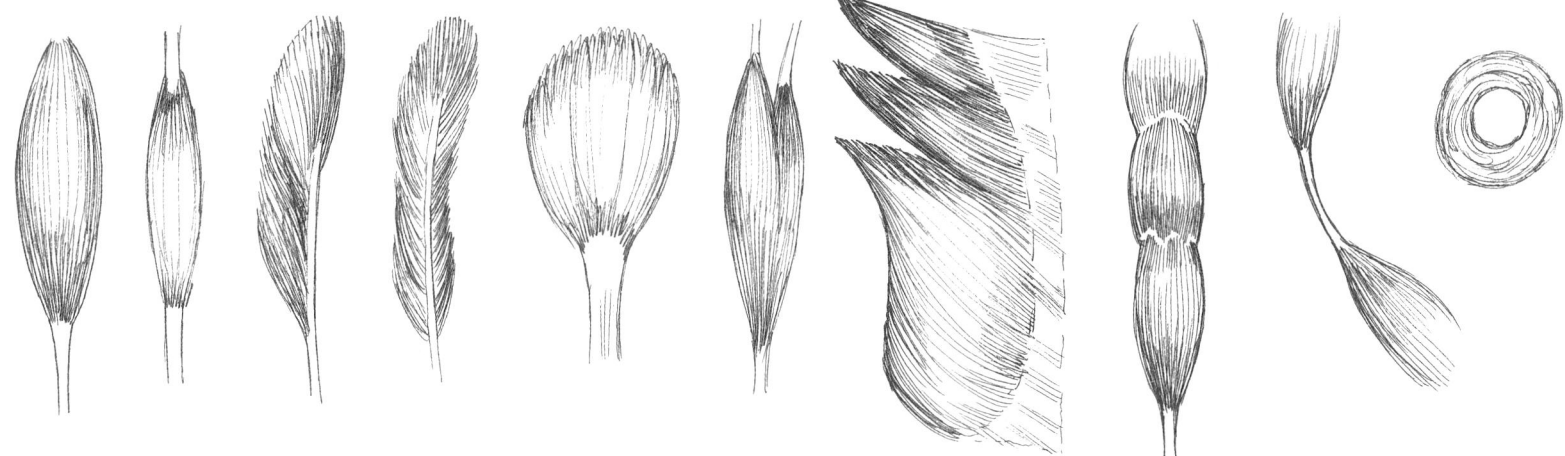

TENDONS

The tendons are fibrous structures that attach the ends of the muscles to the bones at protruding points called *tubercles* and *tuberosities*. Some muscles are divided by intervening tendons (see illustration above, second from right). Tendons may be round and cord-like, or flat and band-like, consisting of strong tensile fibres arranged lengthwise. They are inextensible, allowing the muscles to pull hard against them. Many are longer than the muscles that they serve, such as in the forearm.

APONEUROSES

These are broad, flat, sheet-like tendons, a continuation of broad, flat muscles that either attach to the bone or continue into the *fascia*.

TENDINOUS ARCHES

Fibrous bands connected with the fasciae of muscles.

FASCIAE

Fibrous laminae of various thicknesses, occurring in all parts of the body, enveloping all muscles, blood vessels, nerves, joints, organs and glands. They prevent friction between moving muscles.

LIGAMENTS

Fibrous, elastic bands situated at joints where articulated bones connect, or stretched between two immobile bones.

CARTILAGE

Cartilage is connective tissue composed of collagen (a protein). Fibrous cartilage forms the symphysis pubis (the joint between the pubic bones) and invertebral discs. Elastic cartilage gives shape to the outer flap of the ear. Hyaline cartilage – the most common form – covers the *articular* surface of bones (the ends near the joints); forms the rings of the trachea (windpipe), also the bronchi (airways) of the lungs; and gives shape to the lower ribcage and nose.

SKIN

A tough, self-replenishing membrane about 2 mm thick, which defines the boundary between the internal and the external environments. Human skin is thickest on the upper back, soles of the feet and palms of the hand; it is thinnest on the eyelids. Not only the body's largest sense organ, the skin also protects the body from abrasions, fluid loss and the penetration of harmful substances. And it regulates body temperature, through perspiration and the cooling effect of surface veins.

EPIDERMIS

The skin's top layer with the dermis beneath, a thicker layer of loose connective tissue. Beneath this is the hyperdermis, which is a fine layer of white connective fatty tissue, also called the ***superficial fascia***.

FAT

Fat is the body's energy reserve. Its layers soften the contours of the skeletal-muscular frame. Fat is primarily stored around the buttocks, navel, hips, inner and outer thighs, front and back of knees, beneath the nipples, on the back of the arms, in the cheeks and below the jaw.

JOINTS

Joints form the connections between bones. In fibrous joints, such as sutures in the skull, there is no appreciable movement. There is limited movement in the cartilaginous joints. The most mobile are the synovial joints such as the knees, where the bones are not fixed.

The principal movements of the joints are ***flexion***, which means bending to a more acute angle; ***extension***, straightening; ***adduction***, which means moving towards the body's midline; ***abduction***, moving away from the midline; and ***medial*** and ***lateral rotation*** (turning towards and away from the midline).

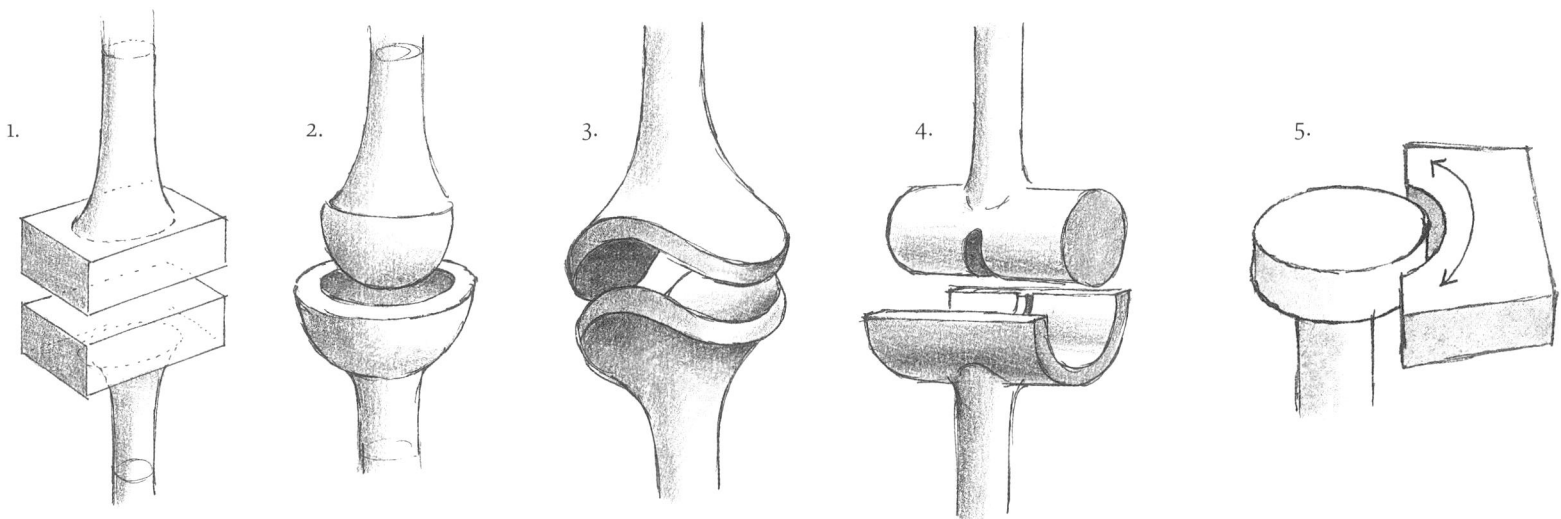

1. PLANE JOINT
Formed by flat or slightly curved surfaces, with little movement, such as the instep.

2. BALL AND SOCKET JOINT
The spherical edge of one bone moves in a spherical excavation of another, like the hip joint.

3. SADDLE OR BIAXIAL JOINT
Allows limited movement in two directions at right angles to each other, like the thumb.

4. HINGE JOINT
Bending and straightening movement is possible on one plane only, such as in the knee, the elbow and the finger.

5. PIVOT JOINT
One bone moves around another on its own axis, such as the radius and the ulna.

UNDERSTANDING ANATOMICAL TERMINOLOGY

To those who have no knowledge of Latin, the Latin names of the muscles and bones may be rather off-putting and hard to grasp. However, once you understand that, for example, an **extensor** is a muscle involved in the process of extension, that **brevis** is Latin for 'short' and that **pollicis** means 'of the thumb', the position, attachment and function of the **extensor pollicis brevis** muscle become much easier to remember.

But even English anatomical vocabulary may not be familiar to everyone who sets out to draw the human body. For this reason, the main technical terms used in this book, both English and Latin, are explained overleaf.

Some technical terms in English

DEEP	far from the body surface
SUPERFICIAL	near to the body surface
INFERIOR	lower
SUPERIOR	upper
ANTERIOR	relating to the front surface or part
POSTERIOR	relating to the back surface or part
LATERAL	farther from the inner line of the body
MEDIAL	of or closer to the median line down the centre of the body
DISTAL	farther from the point of attachment to the trunk
PROXIMAL	nearer to the point of attachment to the trunk
PRONE	(of the arm or hand) with the palm facing down
SUPINE	(of the arm or hand) with the palm facing up
RADIAL	on the thumb side of the arm or hand
ULNAR	on the little finger side of the arm or hand
FIBULAR	on the little toe side of leg or foot
TIBIAL	on the big toe side of leg or foot
ALVEOLAR	of the gums or tooth ridge
COSTAL	of the ribs
DORSAL	of the back; of the back of the hand or top of the foot
FRONTAL	of the forehead
HYPOTHENAR	of the mound of muscle on the little-finger side of the palm
LUMBAR	of the loins
MENTAL	of the chin
NUCHAL	of the nape of the neck
OCCIPITAL	of the back of the head
ORBITAL	of the area around the eye
PALATINE	of the roof of the mouth
PALMAR	of the palm of the hand
PLANTAR	of the sole of the foot
SUPRAORBITAL	of the area above the eye
TEMPORAL	of the temple
THENAR	of the ball of the thumb
THORACIC	of the chest

BONES

CALCANEUS	the heel bone
CARPUS	the wrist
CLAVICLE	the collarbone
COCCYX	the four fused vertebrae below the sacrum
CONDYLE	a knob at the end of a bone
COSTAE	the ribs
EPICONDYLE	a knob on or above a condyle
FEMUR	the thigh bone
FIBULA	one of the lower leg bones
HUMERUS	the upper arm bone
ILIUM	one of the hip bones
ISCHIUM	one of the hip bones
MALLEOLUS	a hammer-shaped prominence of a bone (e.g. in the ankle)
MANDIBLE	the lower jawbone
MAXILLA	the upper jawbone
METACARPUS	the bones of the palm of the hand
METATARSUS	the bones of the front part of the foot, except the toes
OLECRANON	the elbow bone
PATELLA	the kneecap
PHALANGES	the finger and toe bones
PROCESS	a projecting part (also EMINENCE)
PUBIS	the pubic bone, part of the hip bone
RADIUS	one of the arm bones
SACRUM	five fused vertebrae near the end of the spine
SCAPULA	the shoulder blade
STERNUM	the breastbone
TARSUS	the ankle, instep and heel bones
TIBIA	one of the lower leg bones
ULNA	one of the arm bones
VERTEBRA	one of the bones of the spine
ZYGOMATIC BONE	the cheekbone

Many bones are named from their shapes: PISIFORM (pea-shaped), CUNEIFORM (wedge-shaped), SCAPHOID (boat-shaped), etc.

MUSCLES

As outlined on pages 10-11, among the movements of the joints are *flexion* (bending to a narrower angle), *extension* (straightening), *abduction* (movement away from the midline of the body) and *adduction* (movement towards the midline). The muscles involved in such movements are FLEXORS, EXTENSORS, ABDUCTORS and ADDUCTORS. There are also ROTATORS.

Other muscles named from their functions are LEVATORS and DEPRESSORS, which respectively raise and lower some part of the body. A TENSOR tightens a part of the body and a DILATOR dilates it. The CORRUGATOR is the muscle that wrinkles the forehead above the nose (think of 'corrugated iron'!).

Muscles come in various sizes and the relative size is often indicated by a Latin adjective:

LONGUS	long	Similarly with regard to position:	
BREVIS	short	INTEROSSEI	between bones
MAGNUS	large	LATERALIS	lateral, of or towards the side
MAJOR	larger	MEDIALIS	medial, of or towards the middle
MAXIMUS	largest	ORBICULARIS	round an opening
MEDIUS	middle	PROFUNDUS	deep (opposite to SUPERFICIALIS)
MINOR	smaller	(For ANTERIOR, POSTERIOR, INFERIOR and SUPERIOR, see the	
MINIMUS	smallest	English terms opposite.)	

LATIN FORMS THAT INDICATE 'OF THE ...'

ABDOMINIS	of the abdomen	LABII	of the lip
ANGULI ORIS	of the corner of the mouth	LUMBORUM	of the loins
AURICULARIS	of the ear	MENTALIS	of the chin
BRACHII	of the arm (also BRACHIALIS)	NARIS	of the nostril
CAPITIS	of the head	NASALIS	of the nose (also NASI)
CARPI	of the wrist	NUCHAE	of the nape of the neck
CERVICIS	of the neck	OCULI	of the eye
DIGITI	of a finger or toe	ORIS	of the mouth
(DIGITI MINIMI of the little finger or toe; DIGITORUM of the fingers or toes)		PALMARIS	of the palm
		PATELLAE	of the kneecap
DORSI	of the back	PLANTAE	of the sole of the foot
FASCIAE	of a fascia (see below)	PECTORALIS	of the chest or breast
FEMORIS	of the femur	POLLICIS	of the thumb
FRONTALIS	of the forehead	RADIALIS	of the radius
HALLUCIS	of the big toe	SCAPULAE	of the shoulder blade
INDICIS	of the forefinger	THORACIS	of the chest
		TIBIALIS	of the tibia
		ULNARIS	of the ulna

OTHER PARTS OF THE BODY

FASCIA	a sheet of connective tissue (pl FASCIAE)
FOSSA	a pit or hollow (pl FOSSAE)

Drawing materials

Before you start drawing, consider your choice of materials. There are many possibilities and good specialist art shops will be able to supply you with all sorts of materials and advice. However, here are some of the basics to start with.

Pencils, graphite and charcoal

Good pencils are an absolute necessity, and you will need several grades of blackness or softness. You will find a B (soft) pencil to be your basic drawing instrument, and I would suggest a 2B, 4B, and a 6B for all your normal drawing requirements. Then a propelling or clutch pencil will be useful for any fine drawing, such as copying anatomical diagrams, because the lead maintains a consistently thin line. A 0.5mm or 0.3mm does very well.

Another useful tool is a graphite stick, which is a thick length of graphite that can be sharpened to a point. The edge of the point can also be used for making thicker, more textured, marks.

An historic drawing medium is, of course, charcoal, which is basically a length of carbonized willow twig. This will give you marvellous smoky texture, as well as dark heavy lines and thin grey ones. It is also very easy to smudge, which helps you to produce areas of tone quickly.

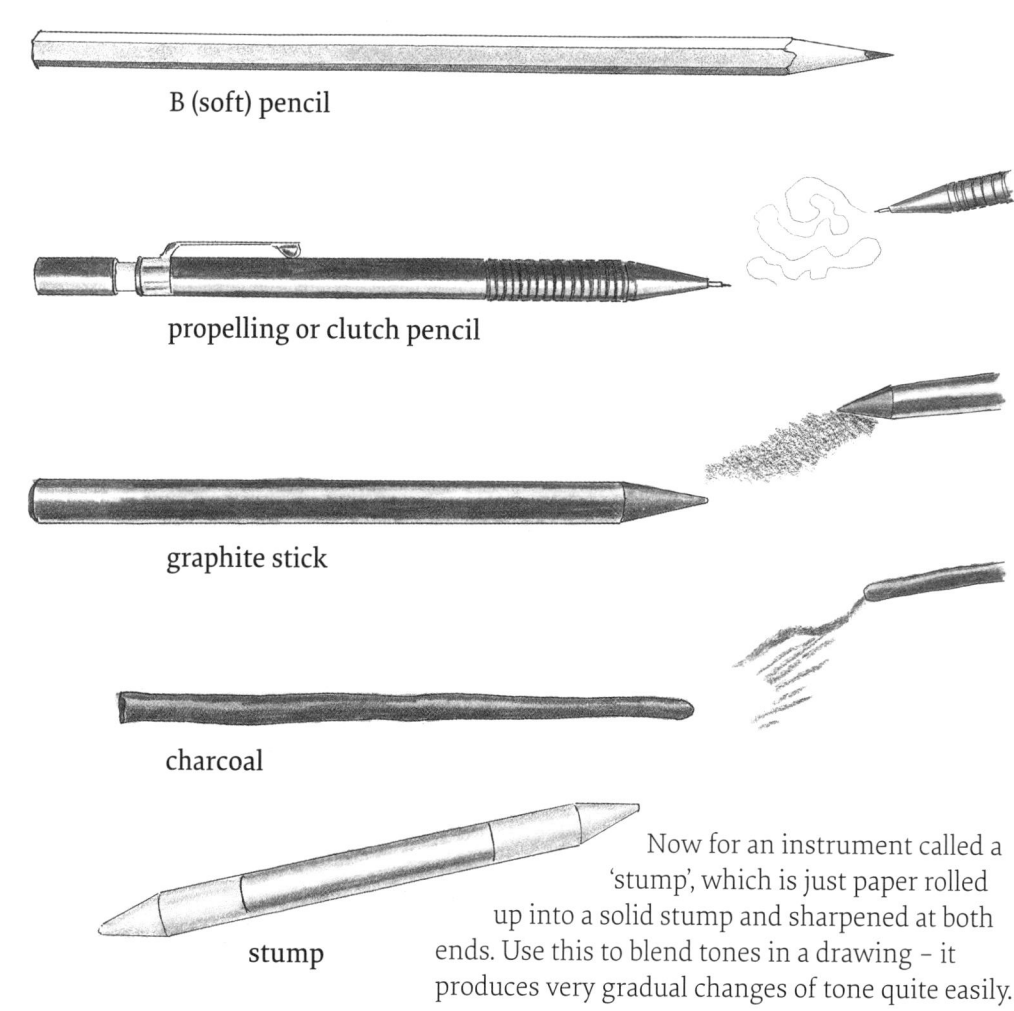

B (soft) pencil

propelling or clutch pencil

graphite stick

charcoal

stump

Now for an instrument called a 'stump', which is just paper rolled up into a solid stump and sharpened at both ends. Use this to blend tones in a drawing – it produces very gradual changes of tone quite easily.

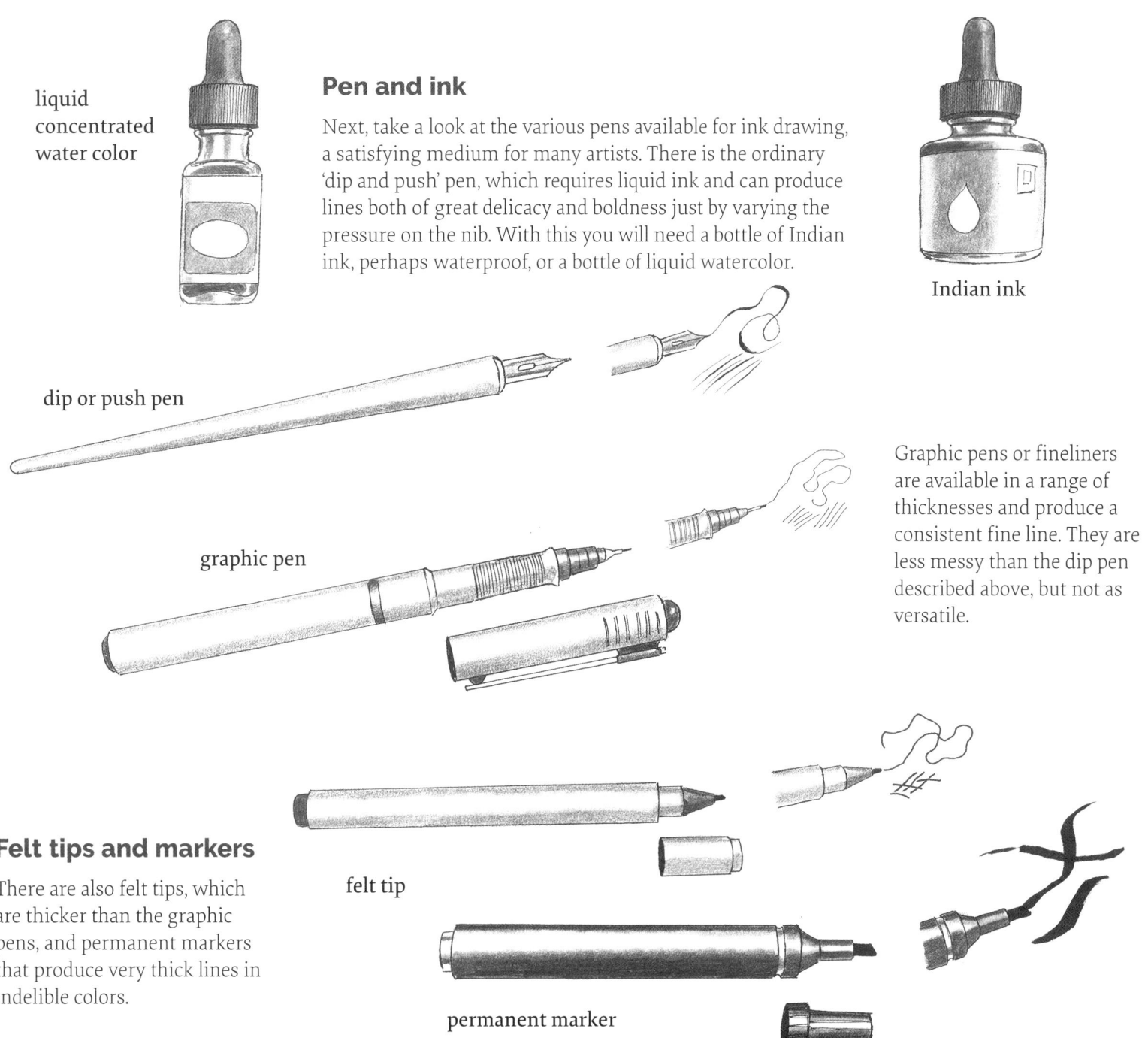

liquid concentrated water color

Pen and ink

Next, take a look at the various pens available for ink drawing, a satisfying medium for many artists. There is the ordinary 'dip and push' pen, which requires liquid ink and can produce lines both of great delicacy and boldness just by varying the pressure on the nib. With this you will need a bottle of Indian ink, perhaps waterproof, or a bottle of liquid watercolor.

Indian ink

dip or push pen

Graphic pens or fineliners are available in a range of thicknesses and produce a consistent fine line. They are less messy than the dip pen described above, but not as versatile.

graphic pen

Felt tips and markers

There are also felt tips, which are thicker than the graphic pens, and permanent markers that produce very thick lines in indelible colors.

felt tip

permanent marker

INTRODUCTION 15

Brushes

If you wish to work in brush and wash, you will need a couple of brushes of different thicknesses; I find that Nos. 2 and 8 are the most useful. The best brushes are sable hair, but some nylon brushes are quite adequate. Use your brushes with a liquid watercolor as shown on page 15.

No.2 sable or nylon brush

No.8 sable or nylon brush

craft knife

scalpel

Erasers

When using pencil you will almost certainly want to get rid of some of the lines you have drawn. There are many types of eraser, but a good solid one (of rubber or plastic) and a kneadable eraser (known as a 'putty rubber') are both worth having. The putty rubber is a very efficient tool, useful for very black drawings; used with a dabbing motion, it lifts and removes marks leaving no residue on the paper.

soft rubber eraser

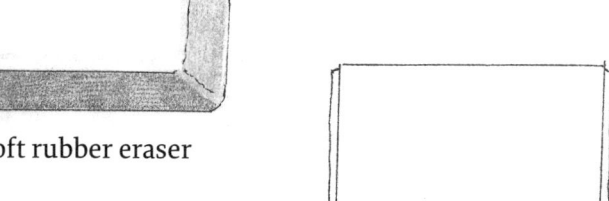

putty or kneadable eraser

Sharpeners

Don't forget you will need some way of sharpening your pencils frequently, so investing in a good pencil-sharpener, either manual or electric, is well worth it. Many artists prefer keeping their pencils sharp with a craft knife or a scalpel. Of the two, a craft knife is safer, although a scalpel is sharper.

INTRODUCTION

Working in color

Color can add an extra dimension to your work. If you enjoy working in color, experiment with some of the options shown here.

Felt tip pens and illuminators

These pens allow thick, solid areas of color to be put on quickly and are useful for larger drawings.

Colored pencils

Don't concern yourself too much with the brand, although some are better than others. Go for as many variations in color as you can find. Thinner pencils can be of superior quality but that is not always the case. Try them out and make your own judgement. Watercolor pencils are similar to ordinary colored pencils but you can use a brush with water to spread their color over larger areas. There are several brands available.

Fineline graphic pens

These pens are good for drawing and behave similarly to a colored pencil but with a more intense color value.

Soft pastels

These come in a wide range of colors and are very useful if you want to spread or smudge your marks. However they are very expensive and tend to get used up quickly.

Hard pastels

Also known as conté crayons, these are essentially the same material as the soft ones but bound together in a compressed form. Hard pastels are square in section whereas the soft ones are round. They last longer and are easier to manipulate. The range of colors is again enormous.

Liquid watercolor (concentrated)

These colors are just like ink but may be diluted with water. They can be used with a pen or a brush.

Watercolor box

Watercolors are easiest to use from a box but they can be bought in small tubes as well.

Chapter One

STRUCTURE AND PROPORTIONS OF THE BODY

In this first section we look at the body as a whole, introducing first the skeletal structure and then the major muscles.

The bony skeleton is rather like interior scaffolding, around which the softer parts of the body are built. Of course, flesh and bone are not separate since the whole lot grows in the womb together, but the skeleton provides the rigid framework that supports the mass of muscles and viscera. It is important for the artist to know which bits of the skeleton show on the surface of the body because, when drawing, it helps to relate the fixed points of the figure to the appearance of the more fleshy parts. Understanding the structure of the skeleton is the basic requirement for accurate figure drawing.

When you draw the human body, you cannot see exactly where the muscles start and end. However, if you know something about the configuration, you'll find it makes it easier to indicate the main shape of any muscle more accurately in your drawing.

Following the full-figure diagrams of bone and muscle structure, we look at the proportions of the human figure, including the differences between men, women and children. Of course there is huge variation in body types, so these proportions are just a guide. Finally we'll consider how your viewpoint can alter the appearance of body proportions – an effect known as foreshortening.

The skeleton
Front view

Here we show three simple views of the skeleton: the front, the back and the side view (also called the anterior, the posterior and the lateral views). I have kept the number of bones named here to a minimum, since we will be going into greater detail when looking at the parts of the body in close-up.

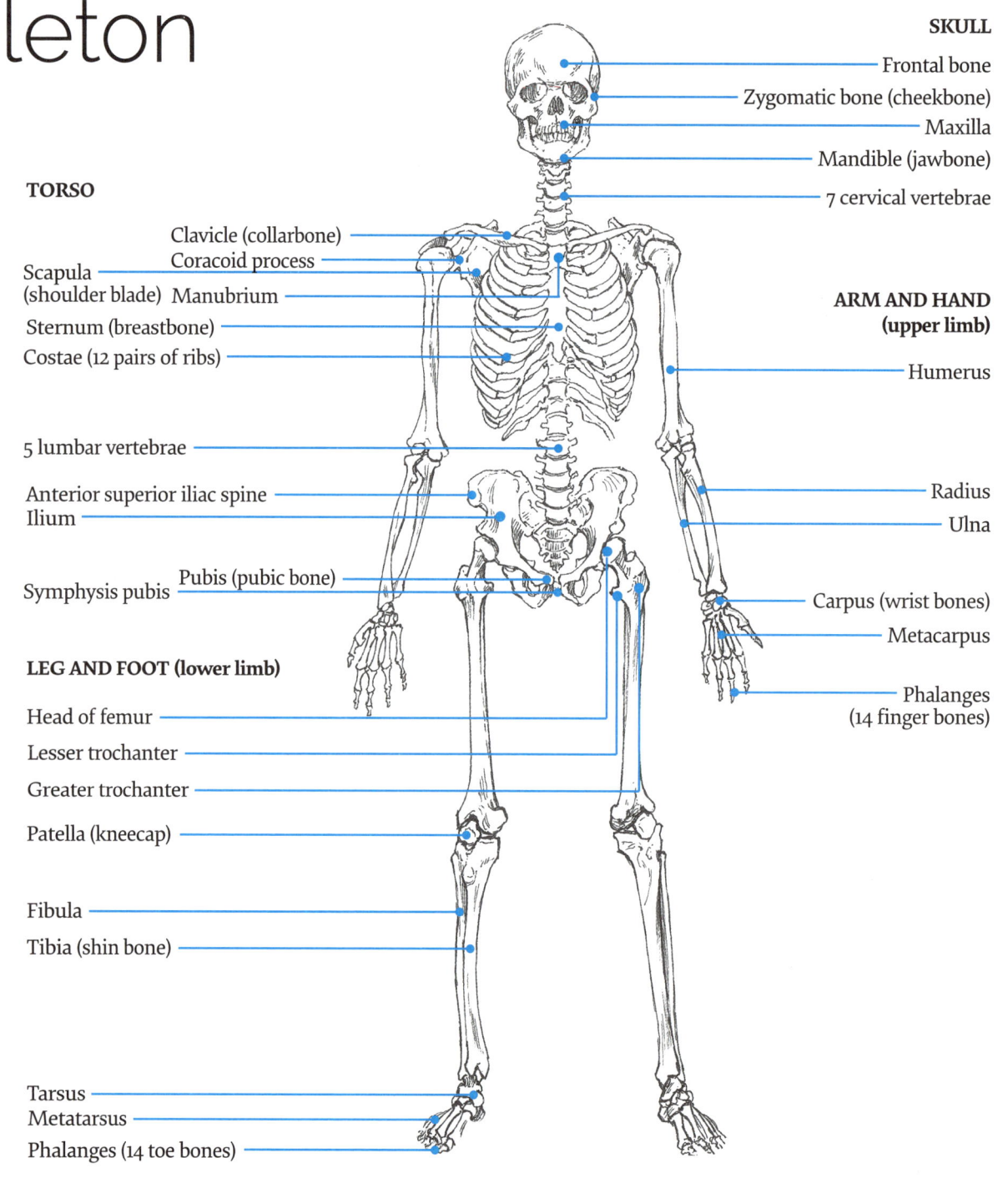

TORSO

- Clavicle (collarbone)
- Coracoid process
- Scapula (shoulder blade)
- Manubrium
- Sternum (breastbone)
- Costae (12 pairs of ribs)
- 5 lumbar vertebrae
- Anterior superior iliac spine
- Ilium
- Symphysis pubis
- Pubis (pubic bone)

LEG AND FOOT (lower limb)

- Head of femur
- Lesser trochanter
- Greater trochanter
- Patella (kneecap)
- Fibula
- Tibia (shin bone)
- Tarsus
- Metatarsus
- Phalanges (14 toe bones)

SKULL

- Frontal bone
- Zygomatic bone (cheekbone)
- Maxilla
- Mandible (jawbone)
- 7 cervical vertebrae

ARM AND HAND (upper limb)

- Humerus
- Radius
- Ulna
- Carpus (wrist bones)
- Metacarpus
- Phalanges (14 finger bones)

STRUCTURE AND PROPORTIONS OF THE BODY

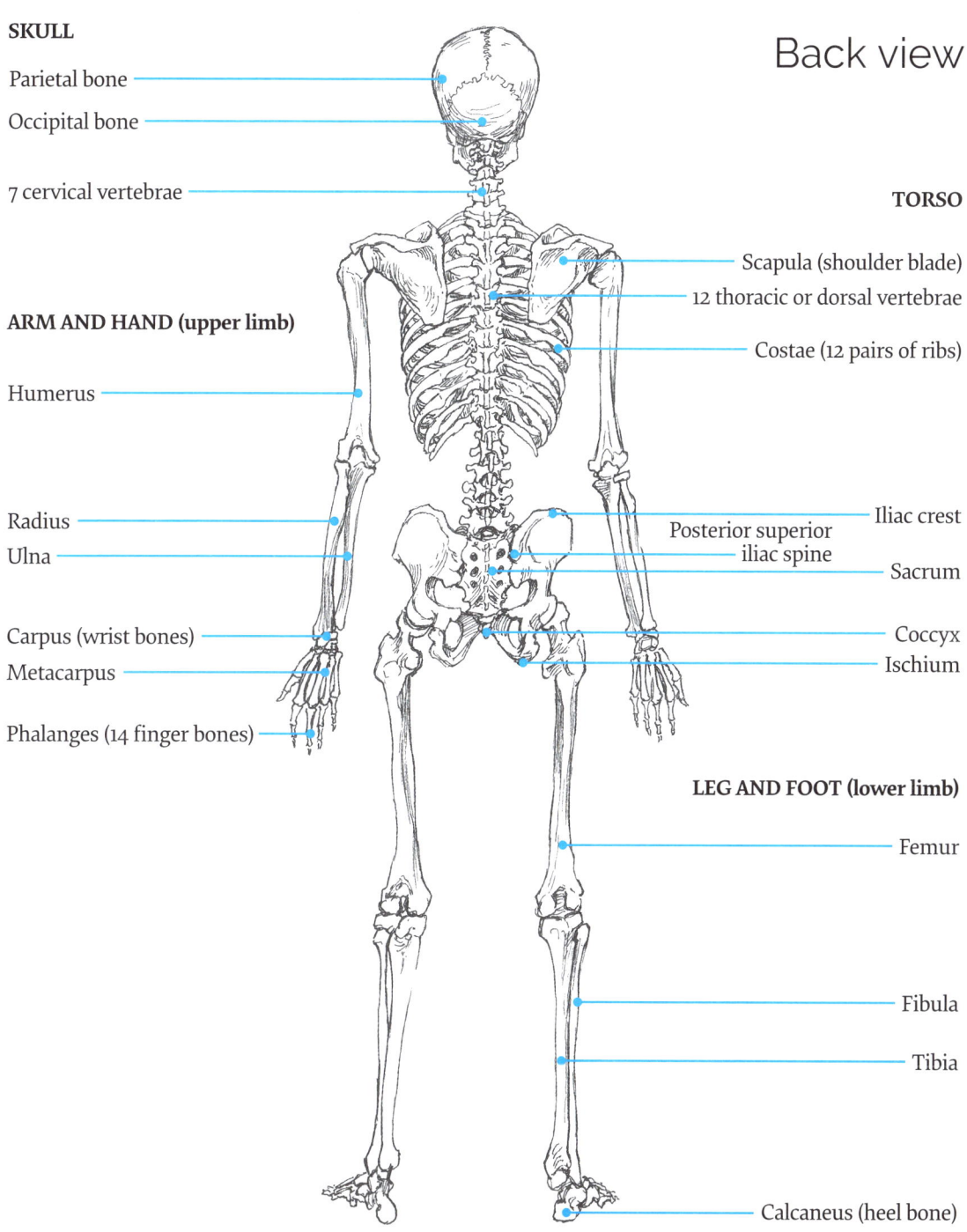

STRUCTURE AND PROPORTIONS OF THE BODY | 21

Side view

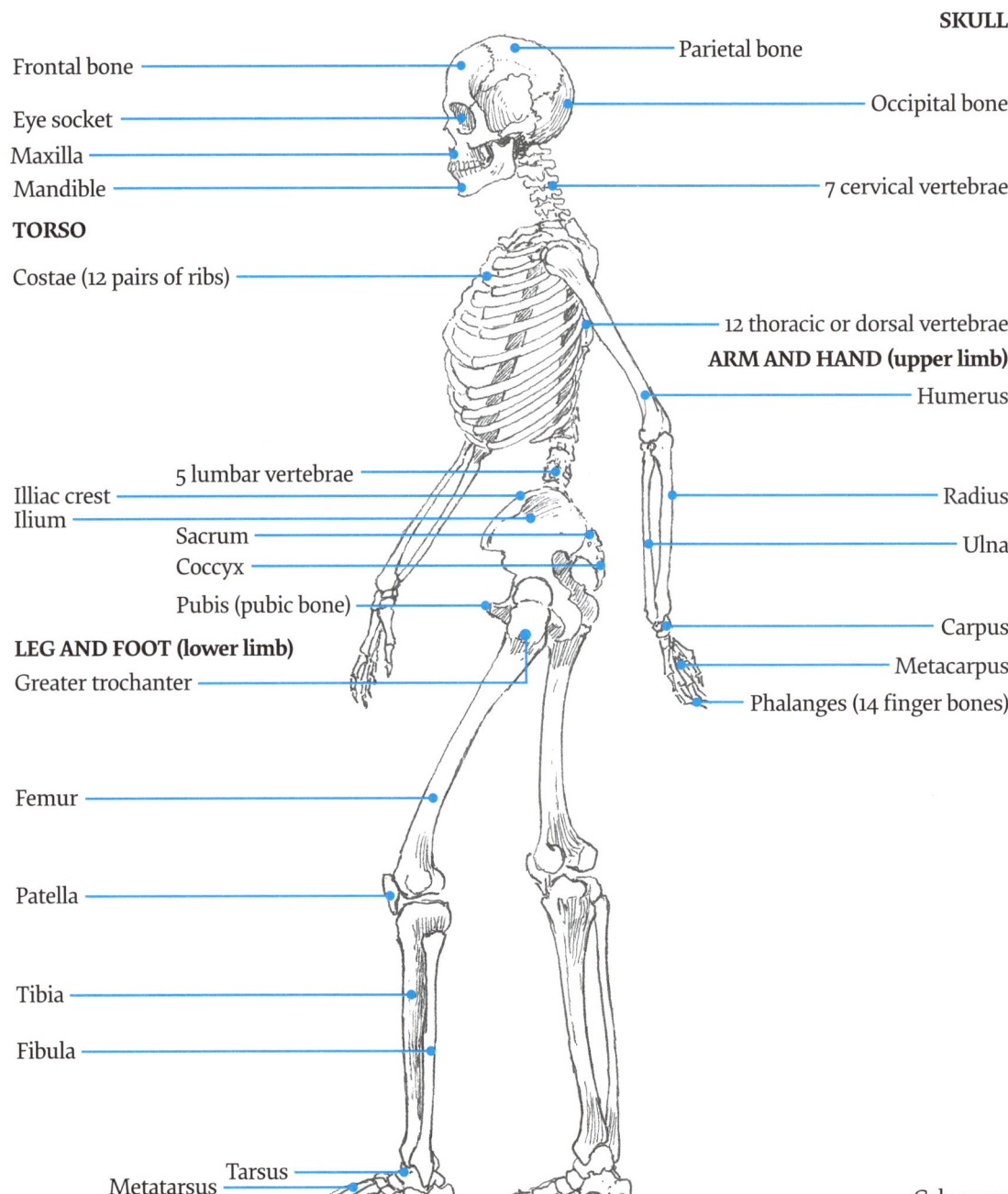

SKULL
- Parietal bone
- Frontal bone
- Occipital bone
- Eye socket
- Maxilla
- Mandible
- 7 cervical vertebrae

TORSO
- Costae (12 pairs of ribs)
- 12 thoracic or dorsal vertebrae

ARM AND HAND (upper limb)
- Humerus
- 5 lumbar vertebrae
- Illiac crest
- Ilium
- Radius
- Sacrum
- Ulna
- Coccyx
- Pubis (pubic bone)
- Carpus
- Metacarpus
- Phalanges (14 finger bones)

LEG AND FOOT (lower limb)
- Greater trochanter
- Femur
- Patella
- Tibia
- Fibula
- Tarsus
- Metatarsus
- Calcaneus
- Phalanges (14 toe bones)

STRUCTURE AND PROPORTIONS OF THE BODY

The muscles
Front view

We show here the musculature of the whole body, so as to give some idea of the complexity of the sheaths of muscles over the bone structure. Later in the book, we shall also be looking at some of the deeper muscles in the body, but here only the more superficial muscles are on show.

The drawings that follow are based on a male body. Of course there are slight differences between the male and female musculature, but not much in the underlying structure. The main differences are in the chest area and the pubic area. There are also slight proportional differences and we will look at these later in the chapter. But this complete figure of the muscles of a human being will give you a good idea as to how the muscles are placed over the body.

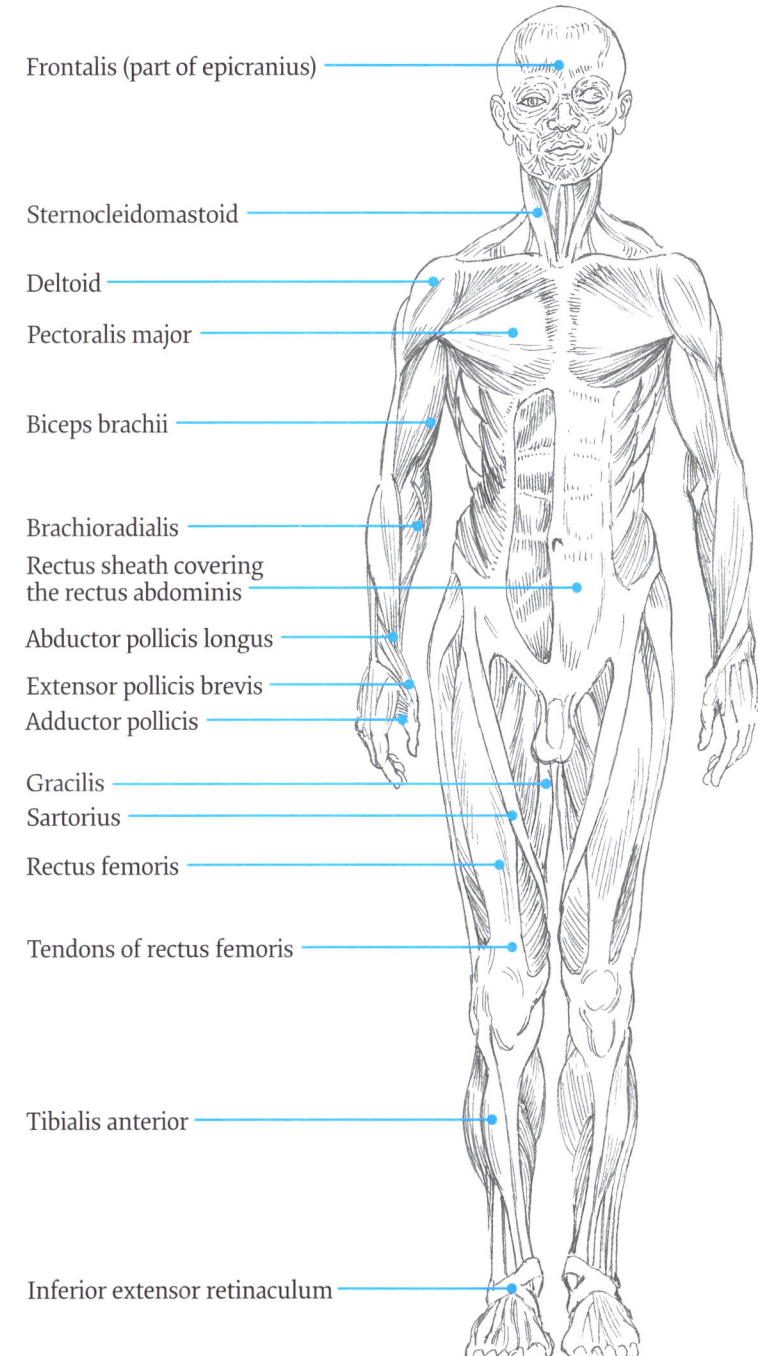

Frontalis (part of epicranius)
Sternocleidomastoid
Deltoid
Pectoralis major
Biceps brachii
Brachioradialis
Rectus sheath covering the rectus abdominis
Abductor pollicis longus
Extensor pollicis brevis
Adductor pollicis
Gracilis
Sartorius
Rectus femoris
Tendons of rectus femoris
Tibialis anterior
Inferior extensor retinaculum

STRUCTURE AND PROPORTIONS OF THE BODY

Back view

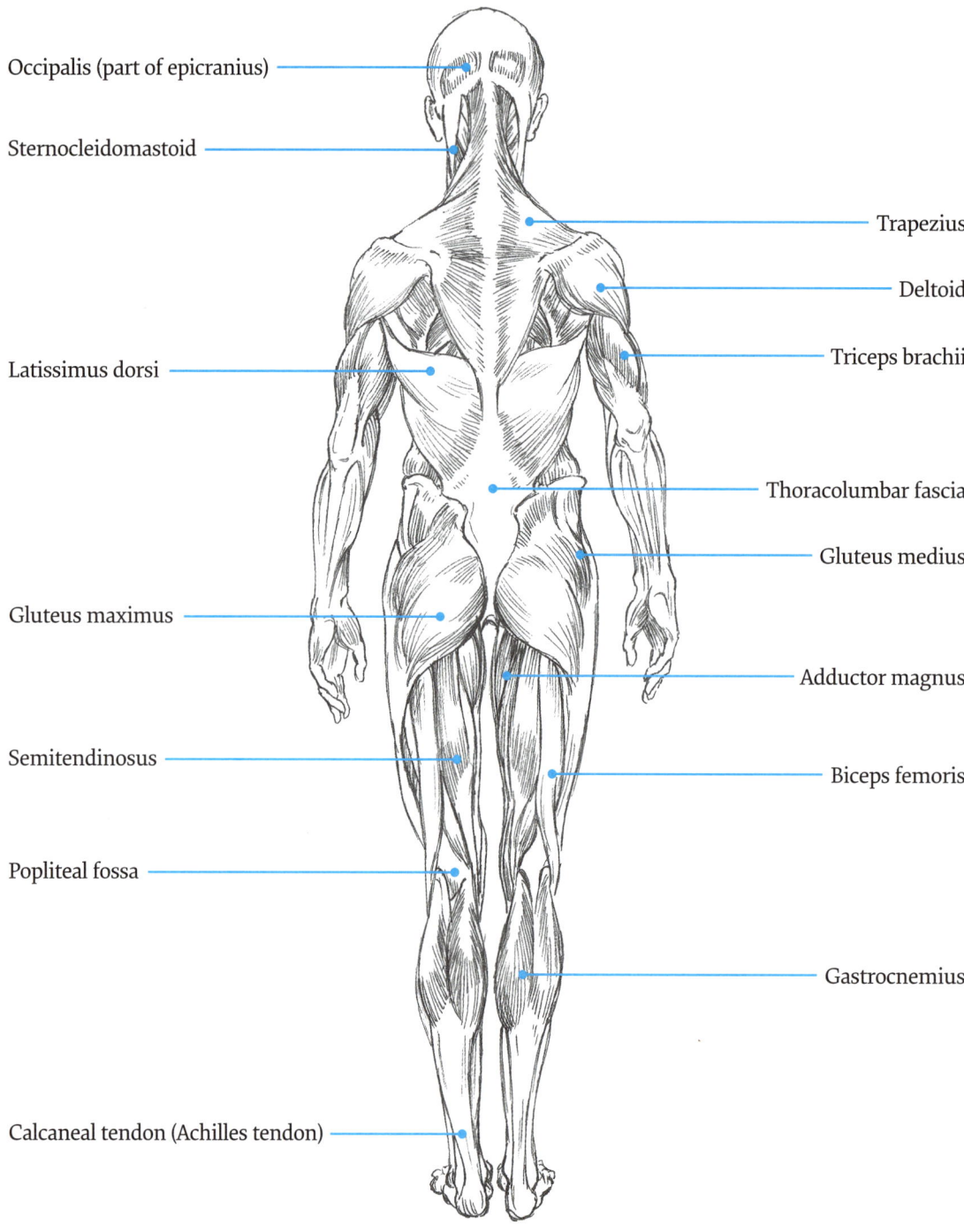

- Occipalis (part of epicranius)
- Sternocleidomastoid
- Latissimus dorsi
- Gluteus maximus
- Semitendinosus
- Popliteal fossa
- Calcaneal tendon (Achilles tendon)
- Trapezius
- Deltoid
- Triceps brachii
- Thoracolumbar fascia
- Gluteus medius
- Adductor magnus
- Biceps femoris
- Gastrocnemius

STRUCTURE AND PROPORTIONS OF THE BODY

Side view

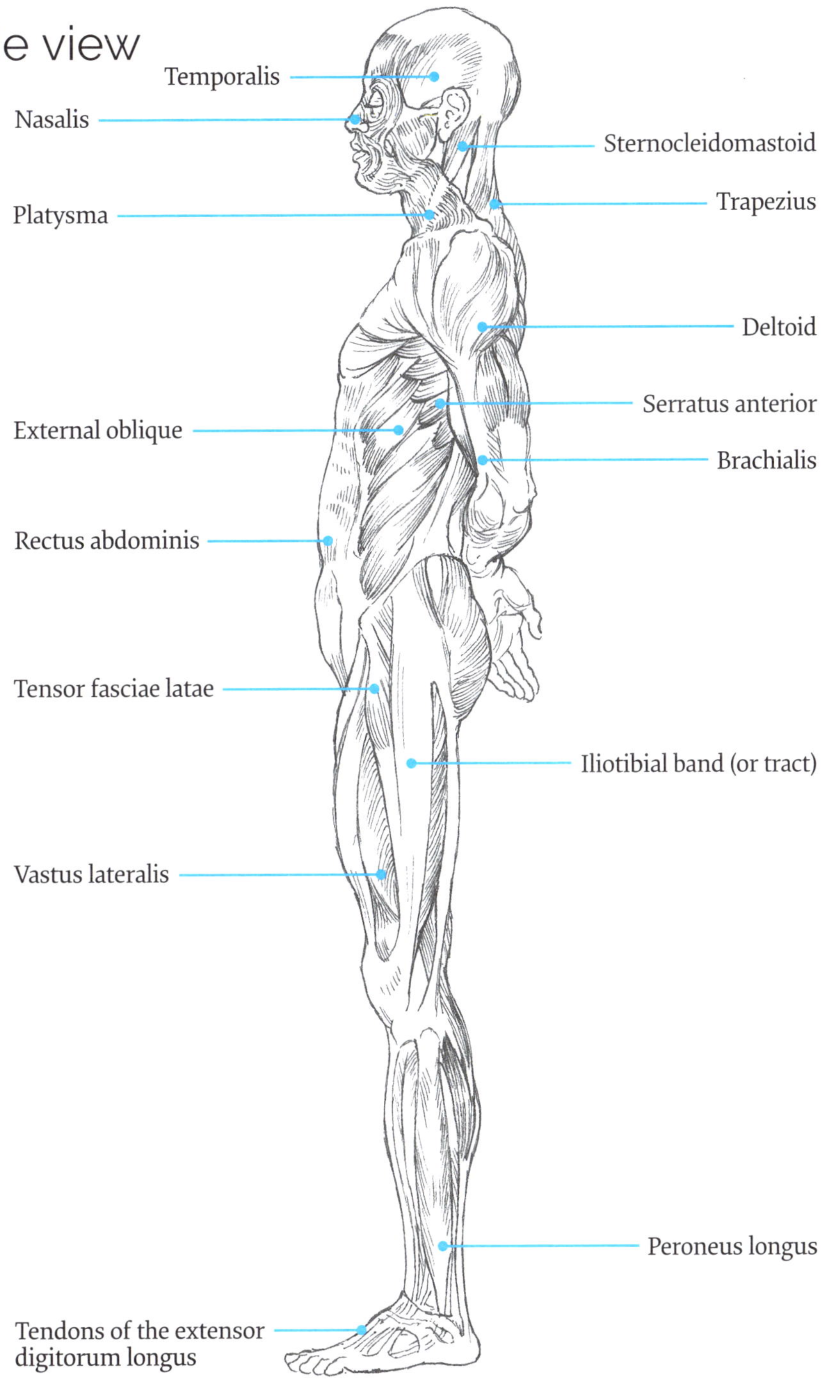

- Temporalis
- Nasalis
- Platysma
- Sternocleidomastoid
- Trapezius
- Deltoid
- External oblique
- Serratus anterior
- Brachialis
- Rectus abdominis
- Tensor fasciae latae
- Iliotibial band (or tract)
- Vastus lateralis
- Peroneus longus
- Tendons of the extensor digitorum longus

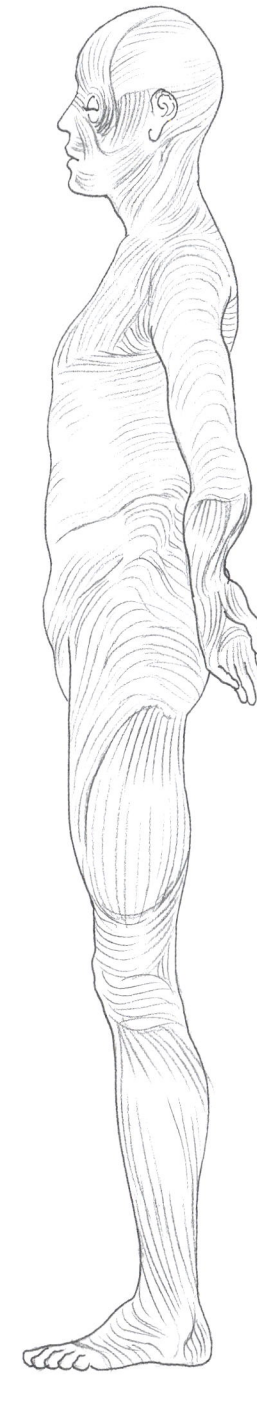

The skin surface tensions are the cleavage lines of the human skin, or the direction in which the skin will crease. Muscle fibres tense along banded patterns, in order to accommodate bodily movement. An incision along these lines will heal well, because the skin's tension pulls the cut together. A cut across them will pucker and scar.

STRUCTURE AND PROPORTIONS OF THE BODY

Differences between the male and female skeleton

There are differences in structure between the male and female skeleton. Generally speaking, the bones of a female skeleton are smaller and more slender. Also the surface of the bone is usually rougher in the male and smoother in the female.

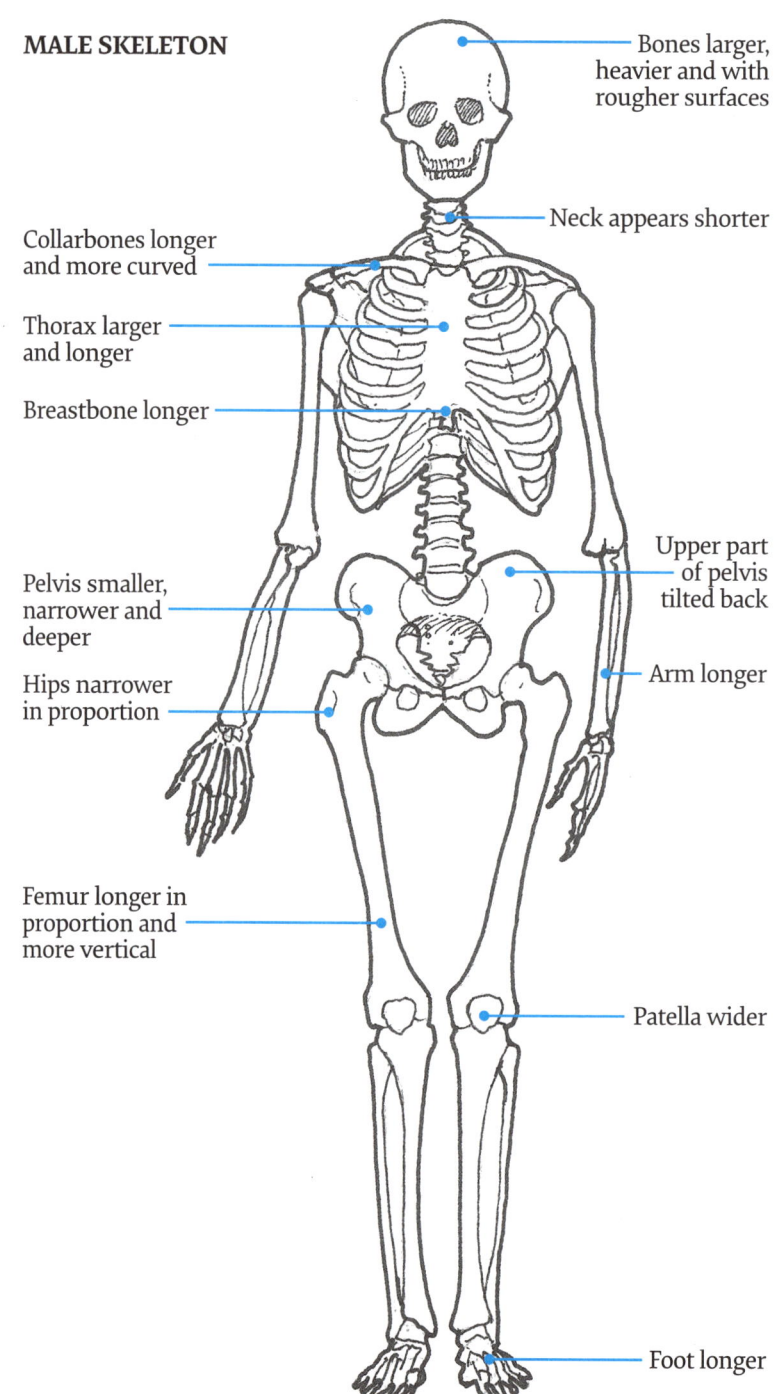

MALE SKELETON

- Bones larger, heavier and with rougher surfaces
- Neck appears shorter
- Collarbones longer and more curved
- Thorax larger and longer
- Breastbone longer
- Upper part of pelvis tilted back
- Pelvis smaller, narrower and deeper
- Hips narrower in proportion
- Arm longer
- Femur longer in proportion and more vertical
- Patella wider
- Foot longer

STRUCTURE AND PROPORTIONS OF THE BODY

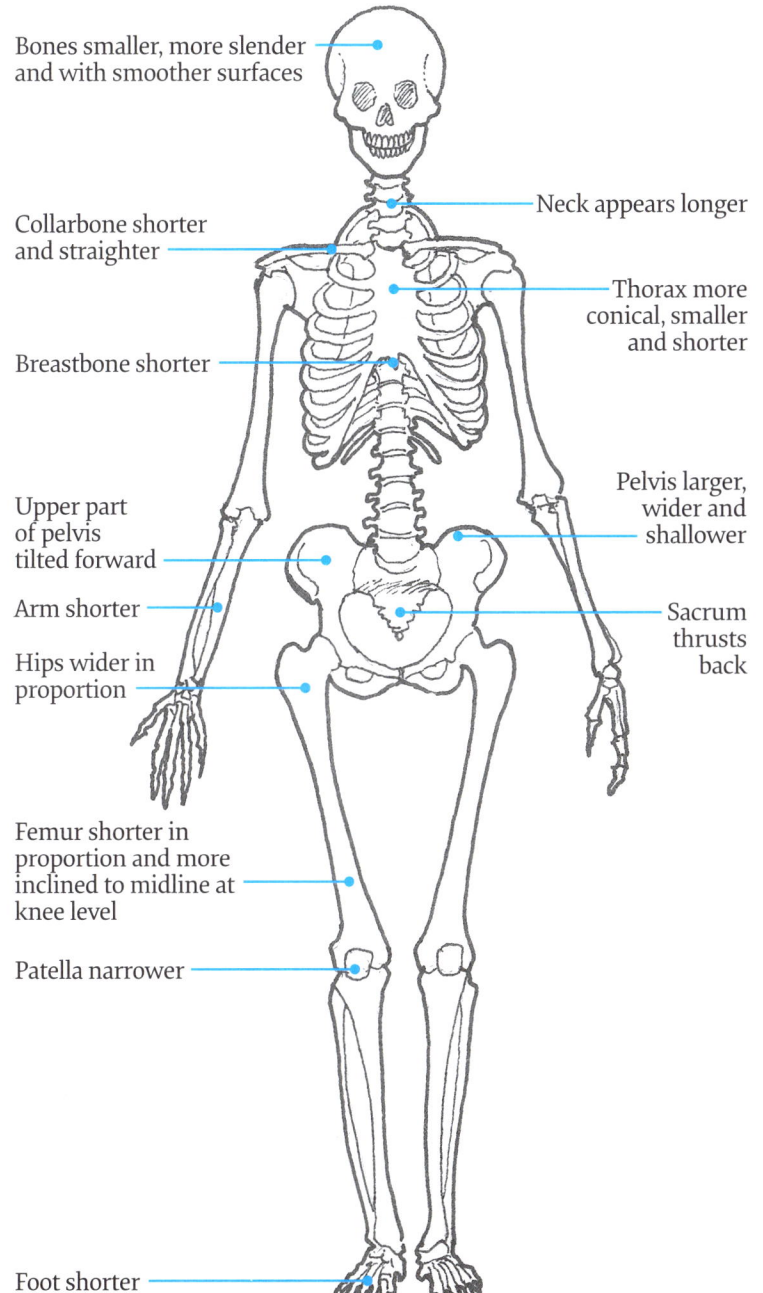

FEMALE SKELETON

- Bones smaller, more slender and with smoother surfaces
- Neck appears longer
- Collarbone shorter and straighter
- Thorax more conical, smaller and shorter
- Breastbone shorter
- Pelvis larger, wider and shallower
- Upper part of pelvis tilted forward
- Sacrum thrusts back
- Arm shorter
- Hips wider in proportion
- Femur shorter in proportion and more inclined to midline at knee level
- Patella narrower
- Foot shorter

Then, taking the other more obvious differences, the female ribcage is more conical in shape and the breastbone is shorter than the male; this gives an appearance to female shoulders of sloping more than the male. In the male skeleton, the thorax is longer and larger, and the breastbone longer; this makes the shoulders look more square and the neck shorter.

Another clear difference between the two sexes is in the disposition of the pelvis. In the female it is broader and shallower than in the male structure. The pubic arch is wider and the sacrum thrusts backwards while the upper part of the pelvis is tilted forwards to accommodate pregnancy and provide the birth canal. In conjunction with this, the female thigh bone (the femur) is generally shorter and inclined more towards the midline at knee level than the male thigh. The effect of this is to make the hips of the female look wider in relation to their height.

Other differences are that the patella, or knee bone, is narrower in the female, and the feet shorter. This is all in proportion to the height of the full figure. Just as the leg is slightly shorter in the female skeleton, so also is the arm in relation to the rest of the skeleton. This all becomes more obvious when you see the skeleton covered with muscles and fat and skin, while in the skeleton itself it is not quite so noticeable. In some cases it is quite difficult to tell the difference between a male and a female skeleton.

STRUCTURE AND PROPORTIONS OF THE BODY

Proportions of the figure

Take some time to study the proportions of the human figure. The drawings shown here are not the precise proportions of every individual but represent an average.

In these diagrams, the basic unit of measurement is the length of the head, from the highest point on the top of the skull to the bottom of the chin. The length of the body – from the top of the head to the soles of the feet – is subdivided by the length of the head.

Viewed from the front, the height of the average adult – male or female – is approximately seven-and-a-half to eight times the length of their own head, measured from top to bottom. As we saw on the previous pages, women are generally smaller-boned than men but the ratio of head to overall height remains the same.

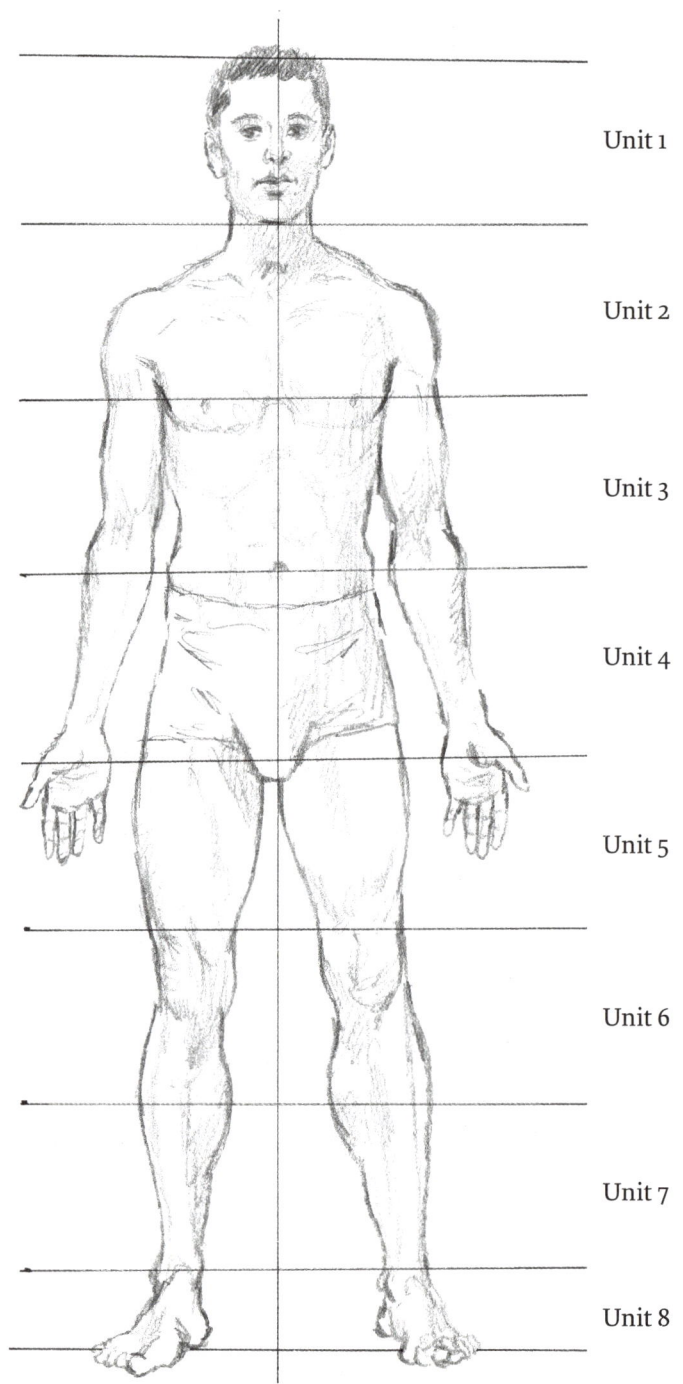

Unit 1

Unit 2

Unit 3

Unit 4

Unit 5

Unit 6

Unit 7

Unit 8

STRUCTURE AND PROPORTIONS OF THE BODY

Notice how the halfway mark of the human figure is the lower end of the torso and the top of the legs. The second unit down is the level of the nipples on the chest, and the navel is three units down.

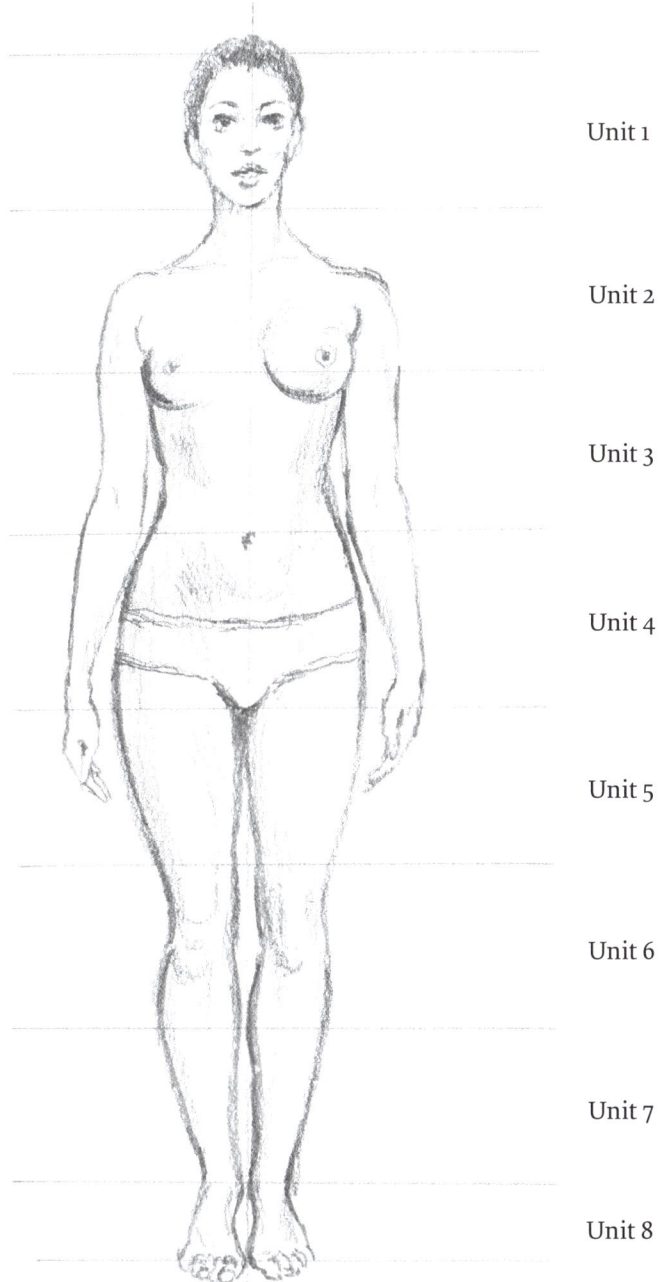

Unit 1

Unit 2

Unit 3

Unit 4

Unit 5

Unit 6

Unit 7

Unit 8

STRUCTURE AND PROPORTIONS OF THE BODY

Individual proportions

The greatest difference between adult bodies tends to be in the amount of flesh spread over the skeletal frame. While the proportion of head to height may be the same, the relative width of the body can be vastly different. This may be a result of lifestyle choices such as diet and exercise or of the individual's metabolism.

A broad appearance may be caused by muscle rather than fat, but the distribution and appearance of the bulk will be very different.

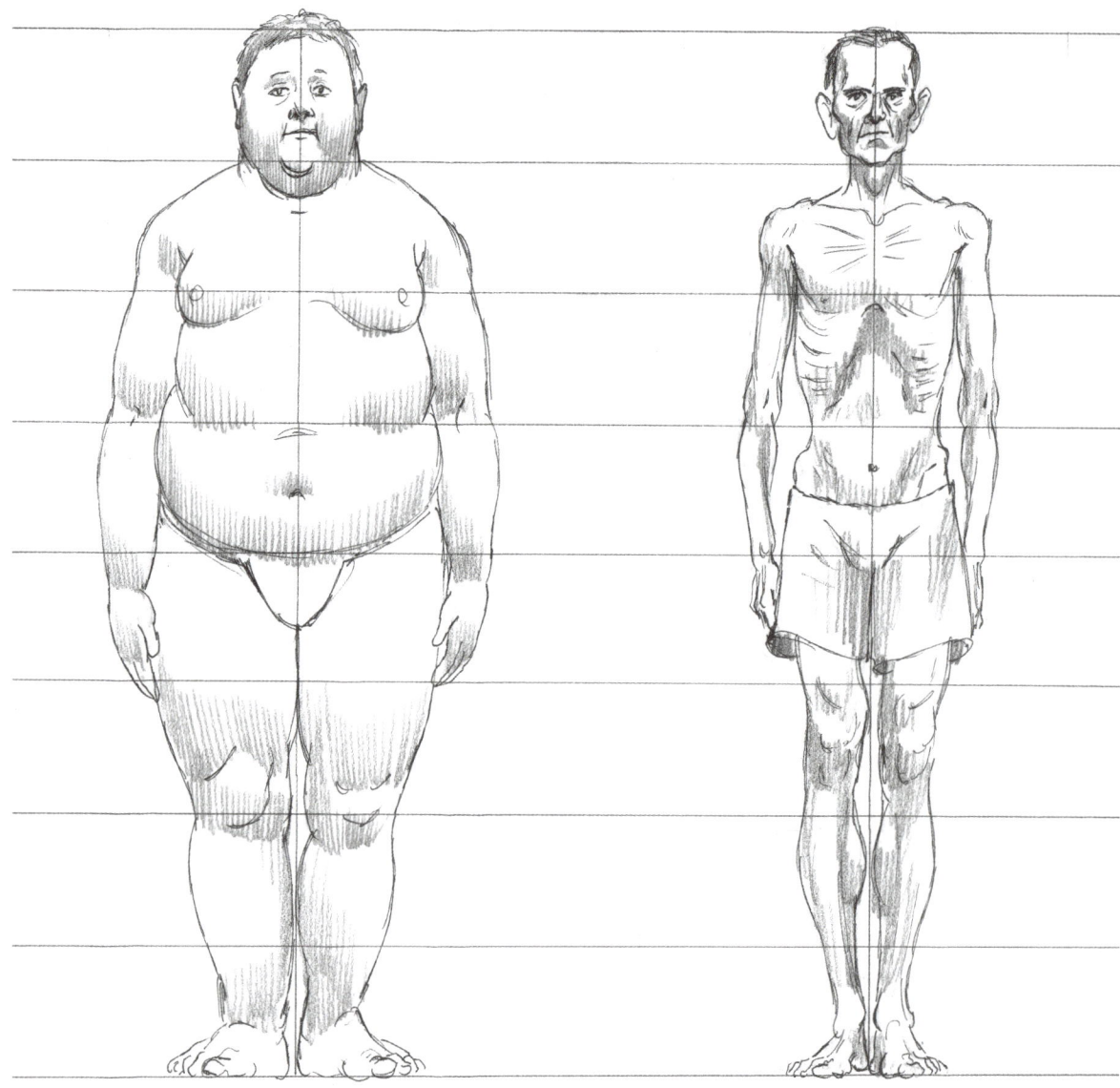

Most extra fat gathers around the central area of the body, and the first area to increase in width is usually the waist. The upper parts of the legs and arms are often thicker and there tends to be extra bulk around the neck and chest.

At the other extreme, when someone is below normal weight, the human frame is reduced to a very meagre stringy-looking shape. The width of the torso and limbs is dictated only by the bone structure.

Proportions of children

The proportions of children's bodies change very rapidly and because children grow at very different speeds what is true of one child at a certain age may not always be so true of another. Consequently, the drawings here can only give an average guide to children's changes in proportion as they get older.

The thickness of children's limbs varies enormously but often the most obvious difference between a child, an adolescent and an adult is that the limbs and body become more slender as part of the growing process. In some types of figure there is a tendency towards puppy fat which makes a youngster look softer and rounder.

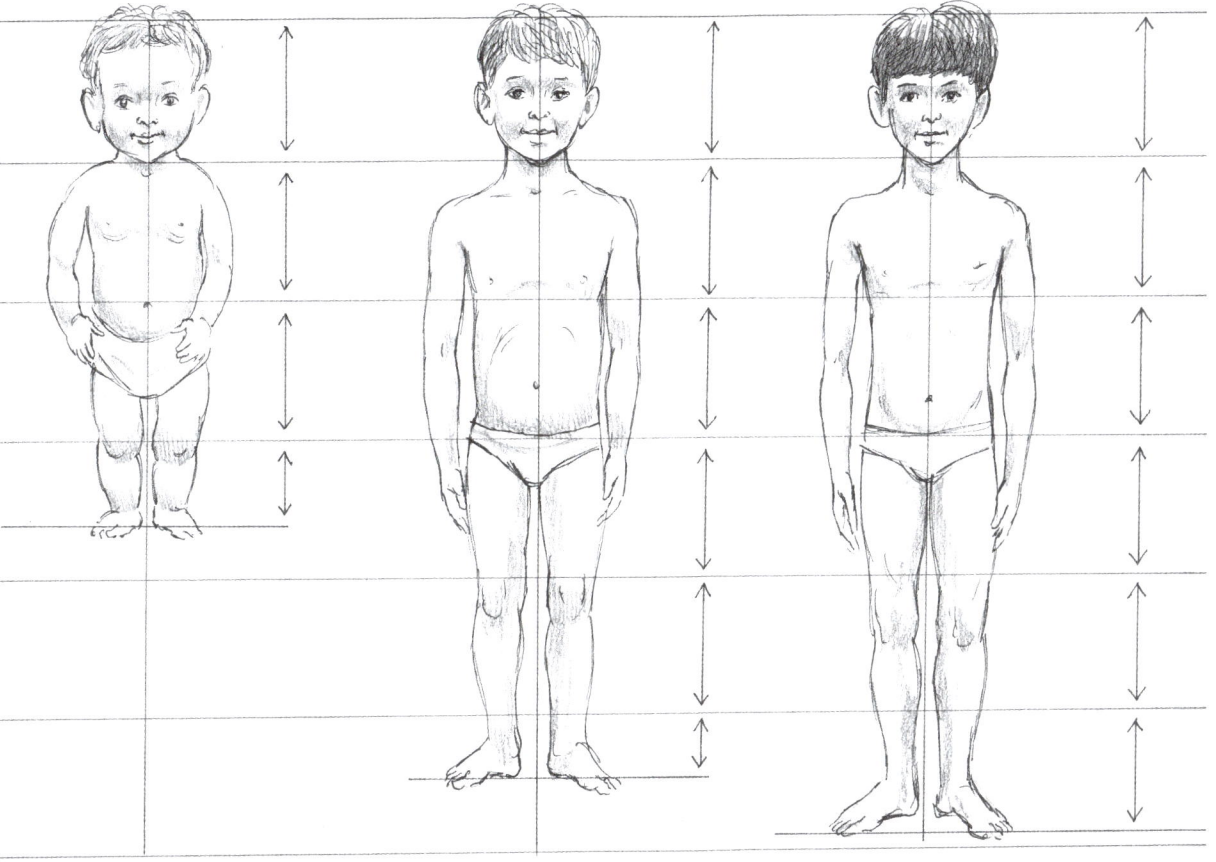

At the beginning of life the head is much larger in proportion to the rest of the body than it will be later. On the left I have drawn a child of about 18 months old, giving the sort of proportion you might find in a child of average growth. The height is only three and a half times the length of the head, which means that the proportions of the arms and legs are much smaller in comparison to those of an adult.

At the age of about six or seven, a child's height is a little over five times the length of the head, though again this is a bit variable. At about 12 years, the proportion is about six times the head size. Notice how in the younger children the halfway point in the height of the body is much closer to the navel, but this gradually lowers until it reaches the adult proportion at the pubic edge of the pelvis where the legs divide.

STRUCTURE AND PROPORTIONS OF THE BODY

Proportions in perspective

Unless your model is standing straight in front of you and on the same level, the body will often appear to be foreshortened, or in perspective. This has the effect of changing the usual proportions somewhat.

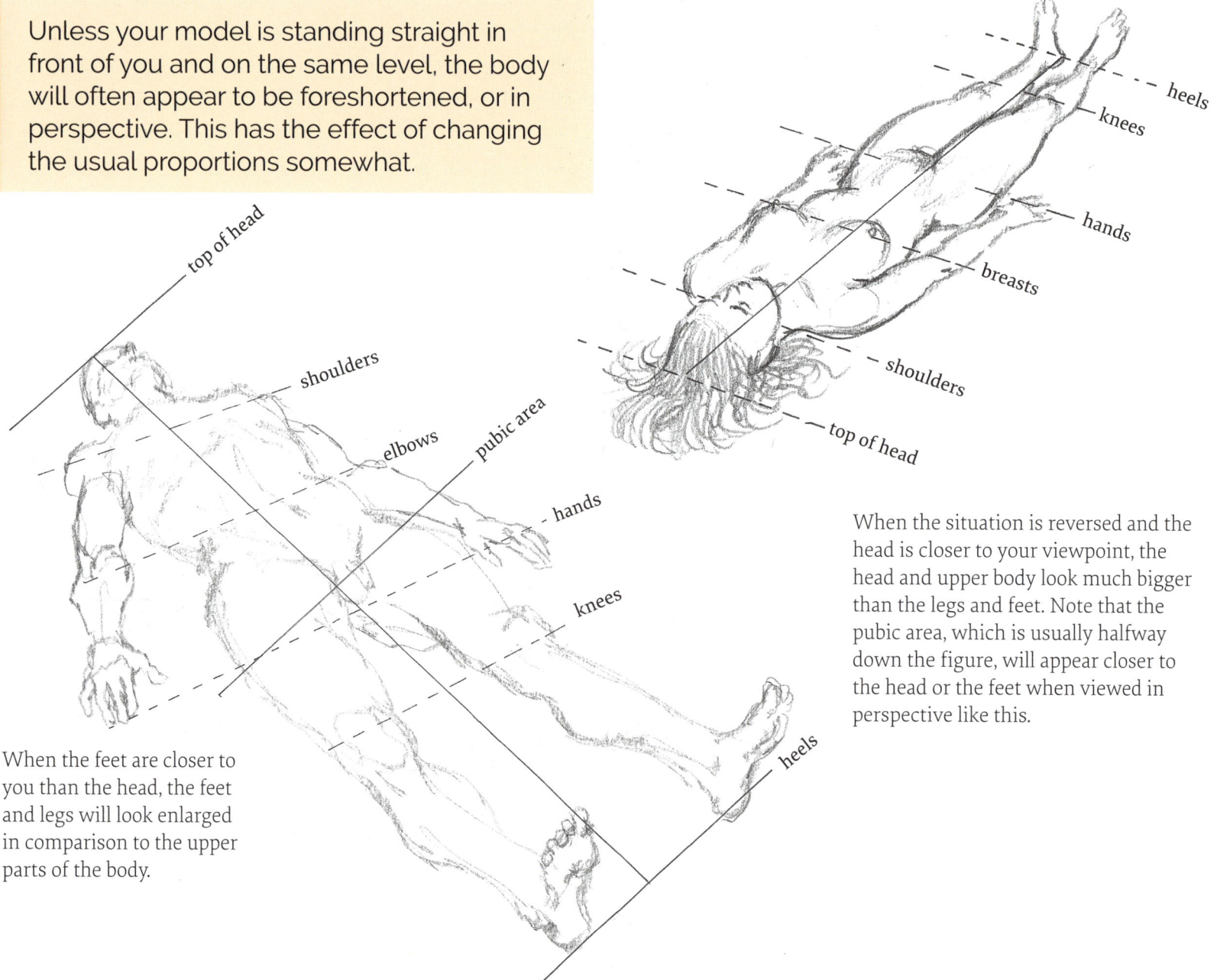

When the feet are closer to you than the head, the feet and legs will look enlarged in comparison to the upper parts of the body.

When the situation is reversed and the head is closer to your viewpoint, the head and upper body look much bigger than the legs and feet. Note that the pubic area, which is usually halfway down the figure, will appear closer to the head or the feet when viewed in perspective like this.

Extreme foreshortening

Looking at the figure from the feet end, the feet and legs look enormous and the chest and head almost disappear in relation to them. The arms, with the hands towards you, look like a series of rounded bulges, with the large hands and fingers looking much wider than they are long.

Sometimes the shoulders can't be seen and the head is just a jutting jaw with the merest suggestion of a mouth, an upwardly pointing nose and the eyes, brows and hair reduced to almost nothing.

Standing at the head end, you will find that everything has to be reassessed. The head is very large but you can mostly see just the top of it and the shoulders and chest or shoulder blades, which bulk large.

Try measuring the difference between the legs and the torso and you will find that although you know the legs are really half the length of the whole figure, from this angle they are more like a quarter of the full length.

STRUCTURE AND PROPORTIONS OF THE BODY

Chapter Two
THE HEAD IN DETAIL

The skull, or cranium, is made up of several bones, although by the time an individual reaches puberty many of them have fused together in a process called ossification; in doing so they provide a solid case for the delicate instruments inside. The joins of these bones are called sutures.

Although the muscles of the head are not very large in comparison with the rest of the body, they are significant because so many of them work to change our facial expressions. We will be looking in detail at the muscles involved in expressing a whole range of emotions, from anger to contentment.

When it comes to drawing portraits, observing the shape of the whole head – not just the face – is key to getting a good result. We will consider the proportions of the head and how it appears from different angles. Close study of all the facial features will further inform your drawing. The shape and location of the eyes is very important; and the length and shape of the nose and the disposition of the mouth give us the rest of the expressive face. Finally, we will explore the various aspects of making a portrait, from observing the age and appearance of your sitter, to the angle of the head, lighting and adding colour.

Proportions of the head

The head proportions shown here are broadly true of adult humans of any race or culture. If this is the first time you have studied these measurements you may find some of them a little surprising; for example the eyes are not situated in the top half of the face, but exactly halfway down the head.

Profile view

This view of the head can be seen proportionately as a square which encompasses the whole head. When this square is divided across the diagonal, it can be seen immediately that the mass of the hair area is in the top part of the diagonal and takes up almost all the space, except for the ears.

When the square is divided in half horizontally it's also clear that the eyes are halfway down the length of the head. Where the horizontal halfway line meets the diagonal halfway line is the centre of the square. The ears appear to be at this centre point, but just behind the vertical centre line.

A line level with the eyebrow also marks the top edge of the ear. The bottom edge of the ear is level with the end of the nose, which is halfway between the eyebrow and the chin. The bottom edge of the lower lip is about halfway between the end of the nose and the chin.

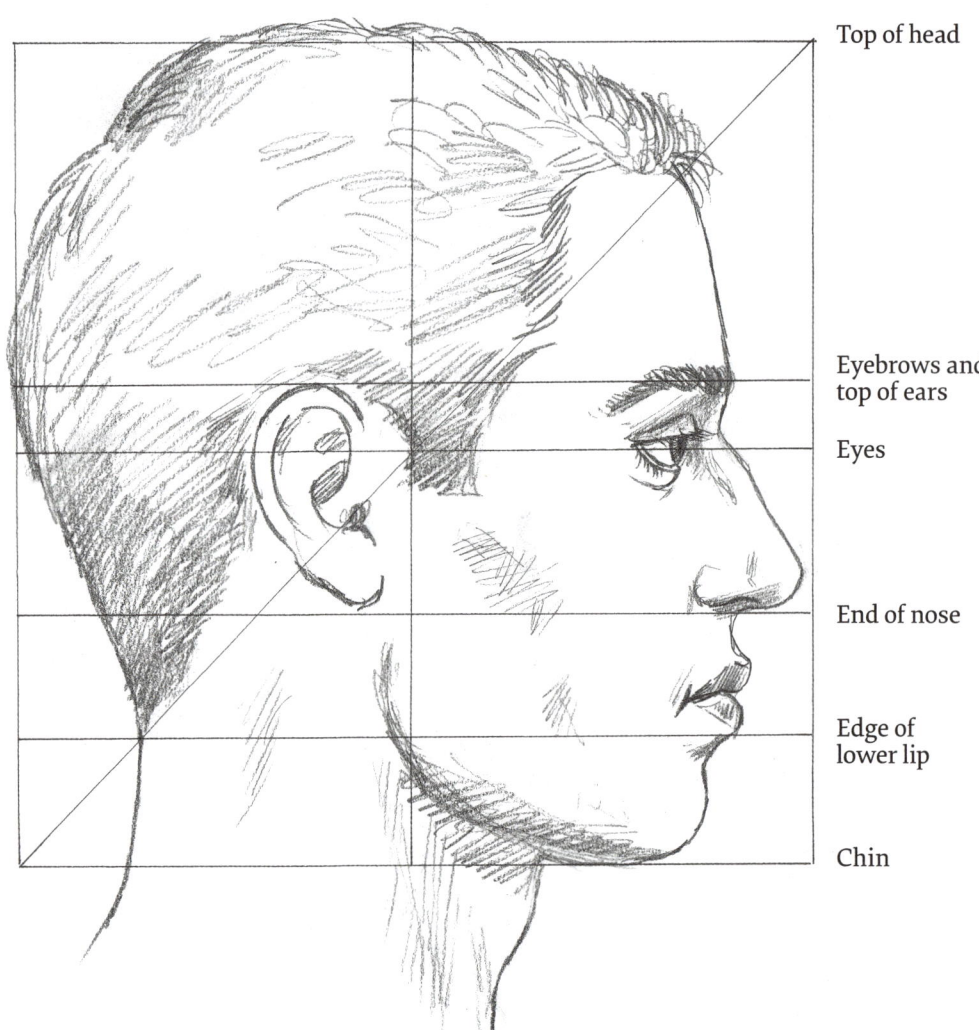

36 THE HEAD IN DETAIL

Front view

From the front, as long as the head isn't tilted, it is about one and a half times as long as it is wide. The widest part is just above the ears.

As in the side view, the eyes are halfway down the length of the head and the end of the nose is halfway between the eyebrows and the chin; the bottom edge of the lip is about halfway between the end of the nose and the chin.

The space between the eyes is the same as the length of the eye. The width of the mouth is such that the corners appear to be the same distance apart as the pupils of the eyes, when looking straight ahead.

These are very simple measurements and might not be quite accurate on some heads, but as a rule you can rely on them – artists have been doing so for many centuries.

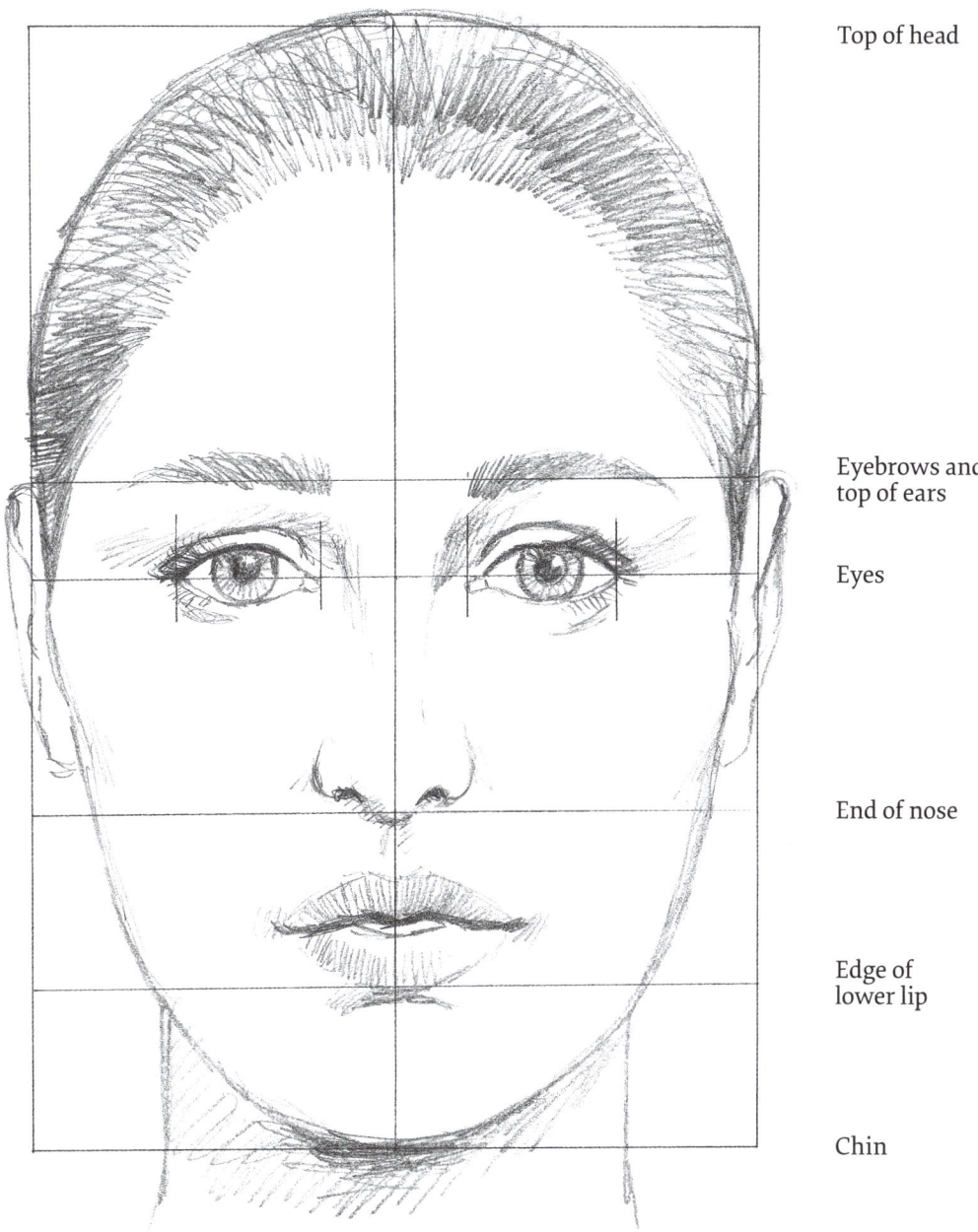

THE HEAD IN DETAIL

Children's heads

There are significant proportional differences between the heads of children and adults which the artist has to bear in mind; I have the listed the main ones below. The features, too, change with growth. In adults the eyes are closer together and are set halfway down the head. Nose, cheekbones and jaw become more clearly defined and more angular as we mature.

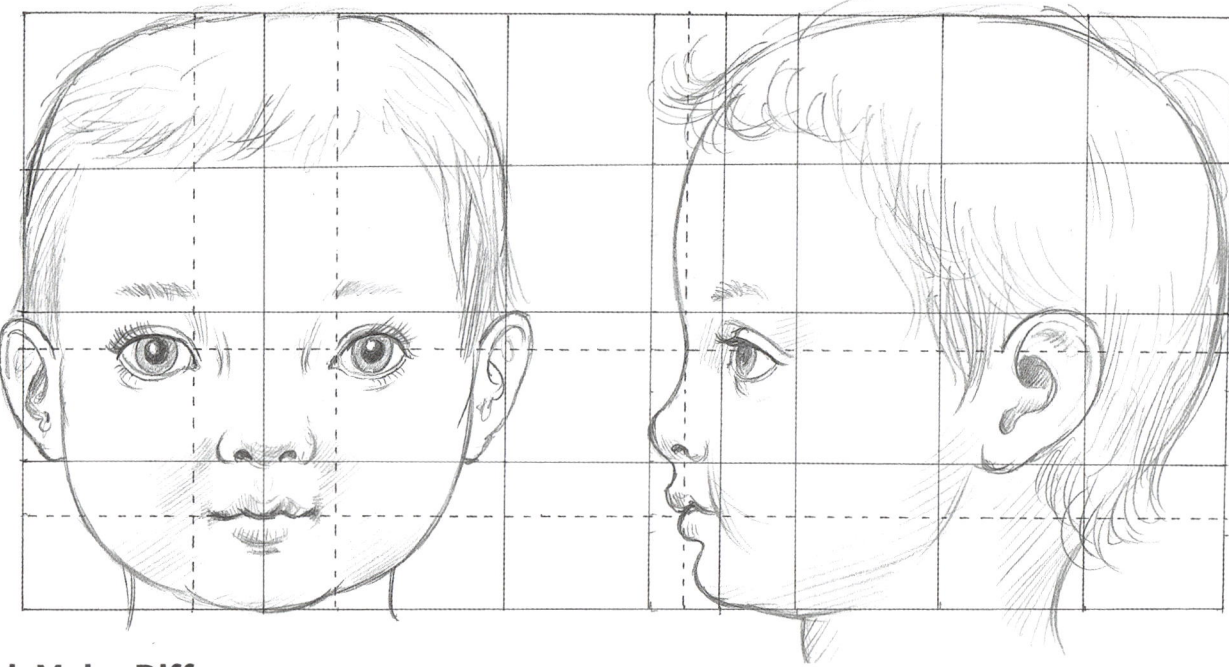

The Head: Major Differences

- In relation to its body, a child's head is much larger; this will be evident even if you can only see the head and shoulders. A child's head is much smaller than an adult's, but the proportion of head to body is such that the head appears larger.
- The cranium or upper part of the child's skull is much larger in proportion to the rest of the face. This gradually alters as the child grows and reaches adult proportions.
- The child's eyes appear much larger in the head than an adult's, whereas the mouth and nose often appear smaller. The eyes also appear to be wider apart. The nose is usually short with nostrils facing outward so that it appears upturned.

- The jawbones and teeth are much smaller in proportion to the rest of the head, again because they are still not fully developed. The rule with the adult – that places the eyes halfway down the head – does not work with a child, where the eyes appear much lower down.
- With very young children, the forehead is high and wide, the ears and eyes very large, the nose small and upturned, the cheeks full and round and the mouth and jaw very small. Also there are no lines to speak of on the face.
- The hair is finer, even if luxuriant, and so tends to show the head shape much more clearly.

The head from different angles

Studying the overall structure of the head from various angles gives us a thorough understanding of the appearance of our subject and is key to getting a good likeness. Notice how, as the head turns, the look of each feature changes, sometimes quite dramatically.

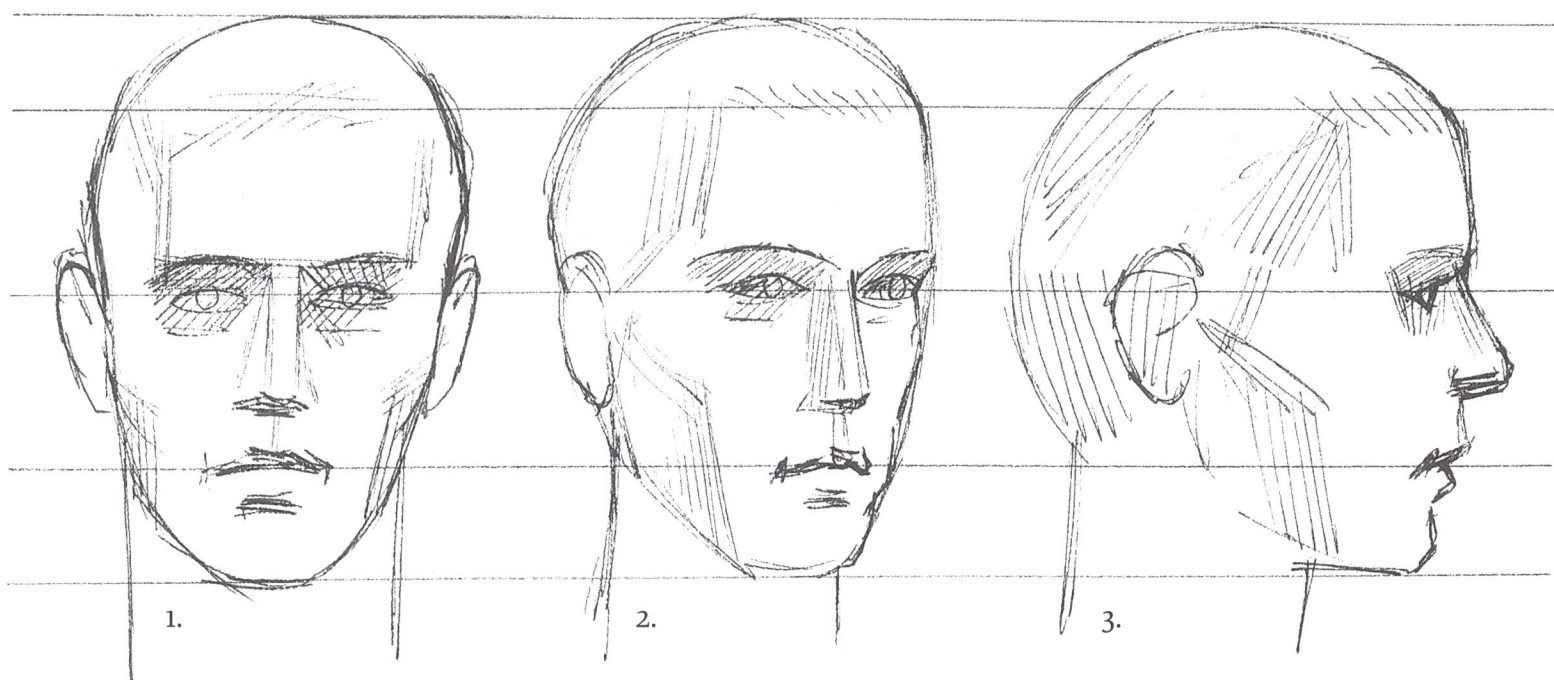

The head is often observed turning from full face towards a profile view. Looking at the full face (1), both eyes are the same shape, the mouth is fully displayed, and the nose is indicated chiefly by the nostrils. As shown in our diagram, when the head turns, the features remain the same distance apart and stay in the same relationship horizontally.

However, as the head rotates away to a three-quarter view (2), we begin to see the shape of the nose becoming more evident, while the far side of the mouth compresses into a shorter line, and the eye farthest from our view appears smaller than the nearer one.

Continuing towards the profile or side view (3), the nose becomes more and more prominent, while one eye disappears completely. Only half of the mouth can now be seen and – given the perspective – this is quite short in length. Notice how the shape of the head also changes from a rather narrow shape – longer than it is broad – to quite a square one, where width and length are almost the same. We can also see the shape of the ear, which at full face was hardly noticeable.

Next, we shall look at the head in another sequence that opens with the full face, but this time the head will be lifted backwards with the chin tilting up, until very little of the face is seen from below.

Note at the beginning that the front view goes from the top of the head to the tip of the chin, and the facial features are all clearly visible.

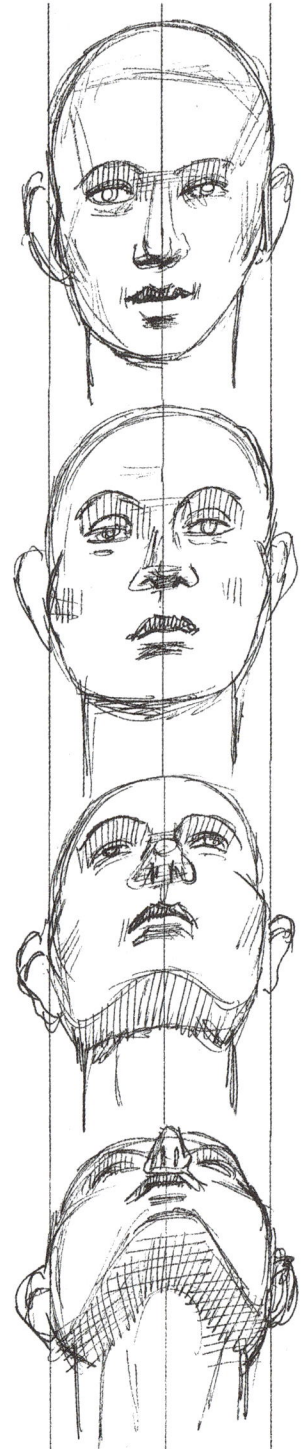

Now, as we tilt the head backwards, we see less of the forehead and start to reveal the underside of the jaw and the nose. The end of the nose now seems to be about halfway down the head instead of three-quarters, as it was in the first diagram. The eyes appear narrower and the top of the head is invisible.

One more tilt of the head shows an even larger area underneath the jaw, and the mouth seems to curve downwards. The underside of the nose, with both nostrils very clearly visible, starts to look as though it is positioned between the eyes, which are even more narrowed now. The forehead is reduced to a small crescent shape and the cheekbones stand out more sharply. The ears, meanwhile, are descending to a position level with the chin, and the neck is very prominent.

One further tilt lifts the chin so high that we can now see its complete shape; and the nose, mouth and eyebrows are all so close together that they can hardly be seen. This angle of the head is unfamiliar to us, and is only usually seen when someone is lying down and we are looking up towards their head.

Note how the head looks vastly different from this angle, appearing as a much shorter, compacted shape.

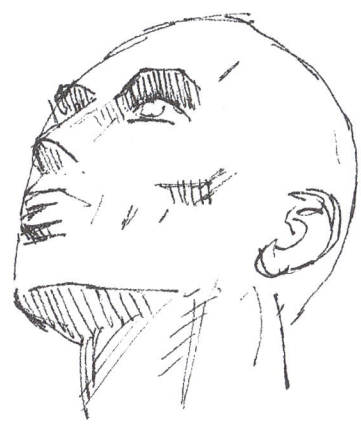

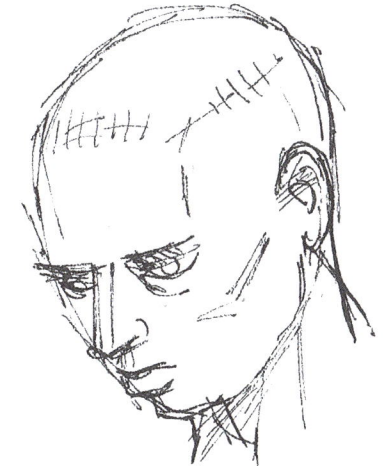

These examples show variations on viewing the head from slightly unusual angles, and you can see how they all suggest different expressions of the body's movement. Although the models for these drawings were not trying to express any particular feelings, the very fact of the movement of the head lends a certain element of drama to the drawings. This is because we don't usually move our heads without meaning something, and the inclination of the head one way or another looks as though something is meant by the action.

Leaning back seen from below

Leaning forward seen from above

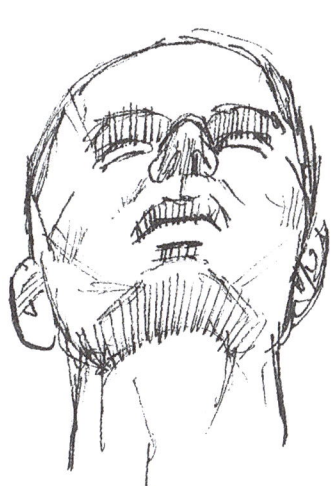

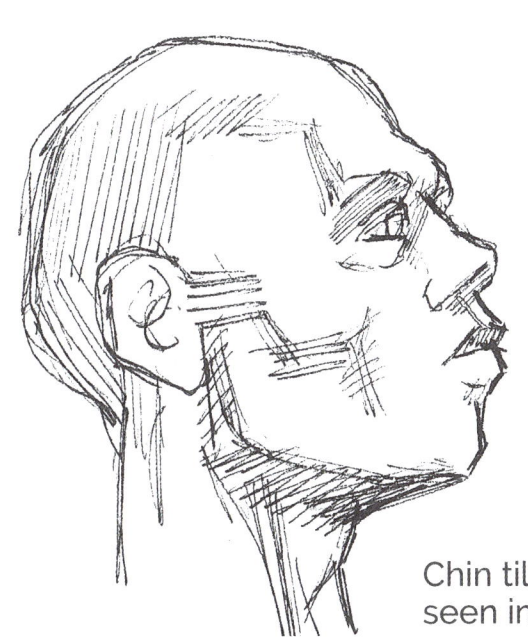

Leaning back seen from below

Chin tilted up seen in profile

Three-quarter view, head tilted towards viewer

THE HEAD IN DETAIL

The skull

The upper part of the skull contains the brain and the organs of sight and hearing. The front and rear parts consist of the thickest bone, where impacts are most likely; the sides of the head are much thinner. There are various openings in the case of the skull such as the nose and ear holes; and the eye sockets, which contain smaller apertures for the passage of the optic nerves to the brain. The lower part of the skull is the mandible, which houses the lower teeth and is hinged at the sides of the upper skull just below the ears. The first (milk) teeth fall out during childhood and are replaced by much larger adult teeth, which fill out the growing jaw.

Front view

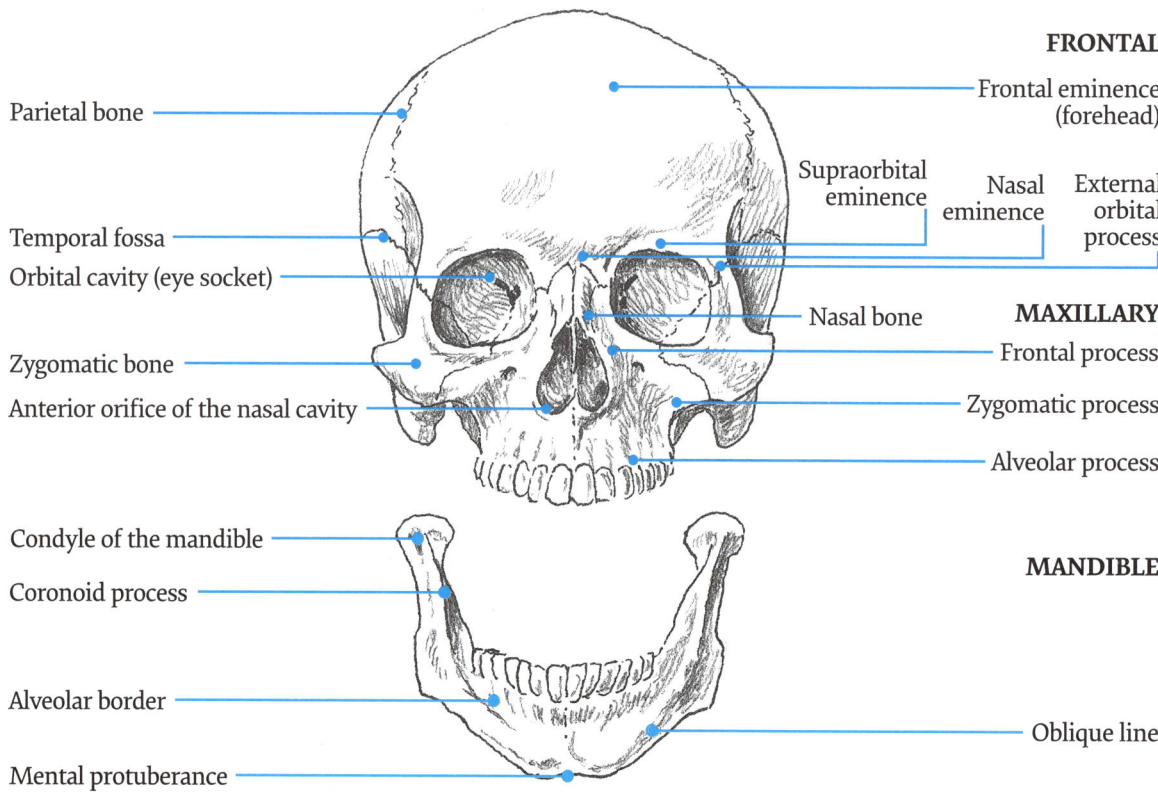

THE HEAD IN DETAIL

Side view

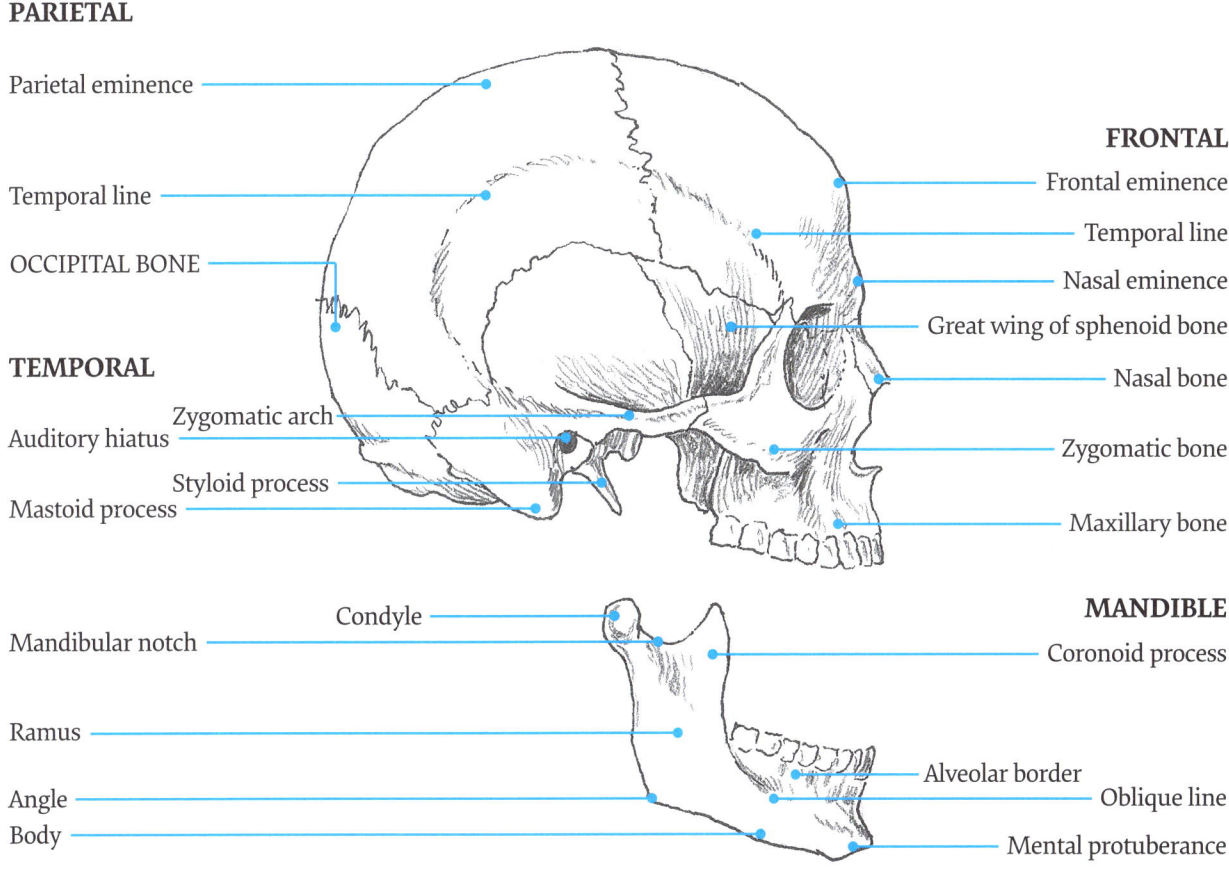

THE HEAD IN DETAIL 43

Top view

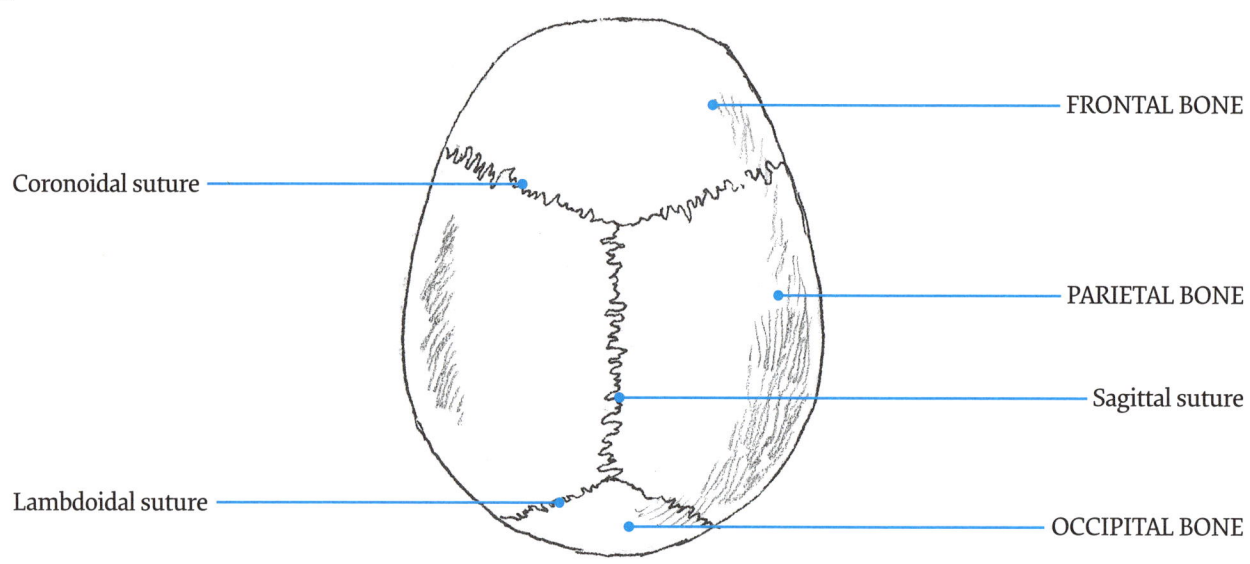

Back view

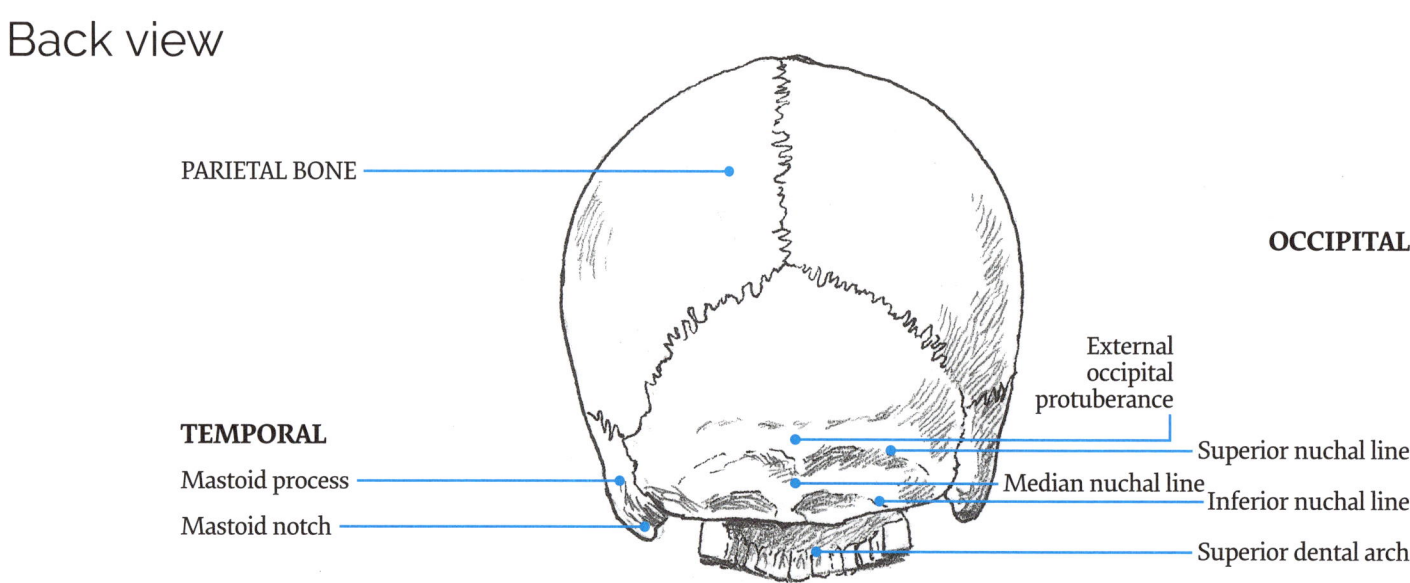

44 THE HEAD IN DETAIL

Differences between the male and female skull

MALE SKULL

Larger and heavier than the female

Contours rougher

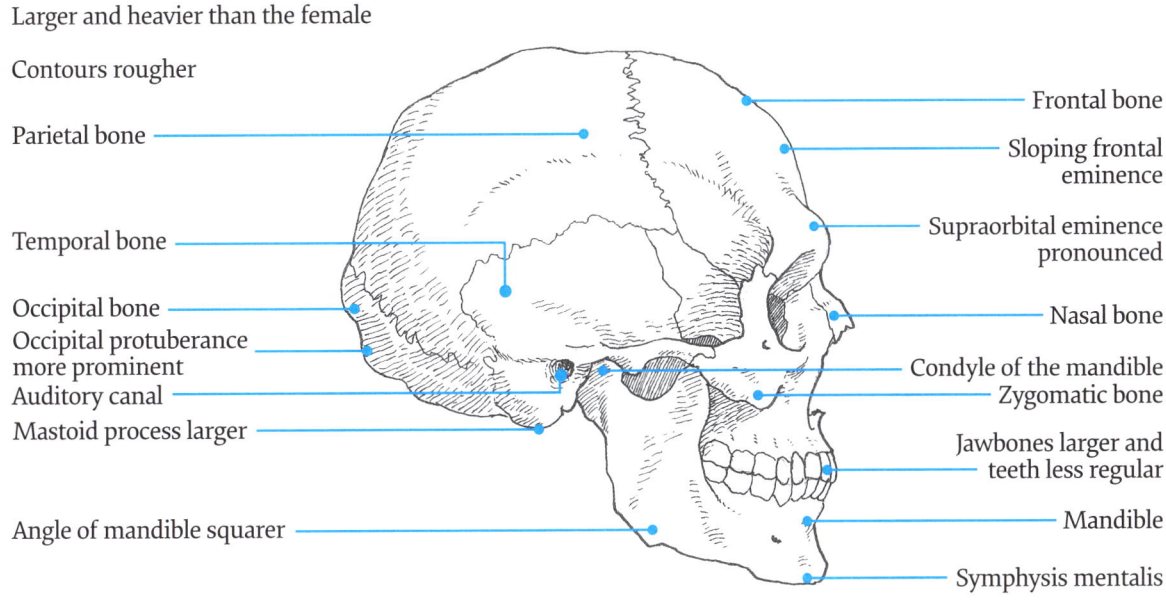

- Parietal bone
- Temporal bone
- Occipital bone
- Occipital protuberance more prominent
- Auditory canal
- Mastoid process larger
- Angle of mandible squarer
- Frontal bone
- Sloping frontal eminence
- Supraorbital eminence pronounced
- Nasal bone
- Condyle of the mandible
- Zygomatic bone
- Jawbones larger and teeth less regular
- Mandible
- Symphysis mentalis

FEMALE SKULL

Smaller, lighter and smoother than the male skull

Contours rounder and smoother

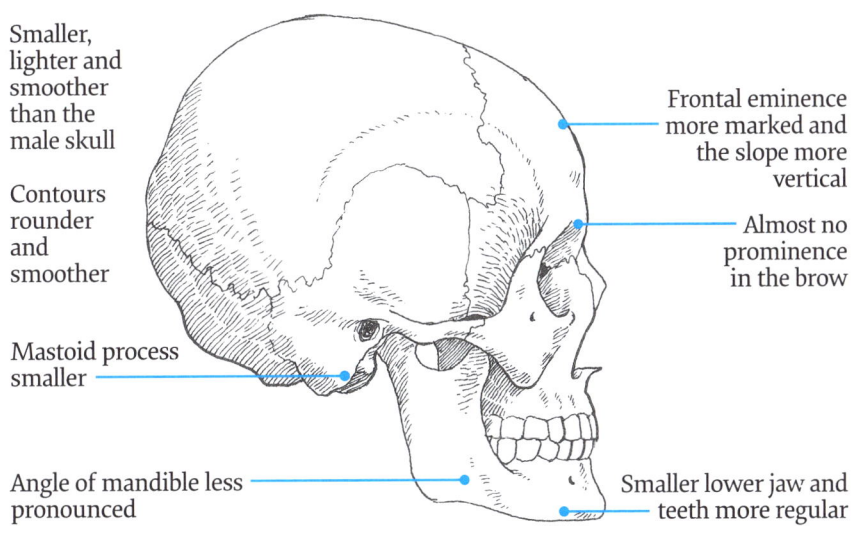

- Mastoid process smaller
- Angle of mandible less pronounced
- Frontal eminence more marked and the slope more vertical
- Almost no prominence in the brow
- Smaller lower jaw and teeth more regular

INFANT SKULL

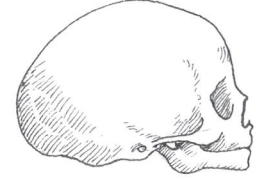

The main difference between the infant skull and the adult one is the smaller size of the face compared with the cranium.

The upper and lower jaws are much smaller due to not having any teeth. As teeth appear, the jaw grows.

THE HEAD IN DETAIL

Muscles of the head

These are the muscles that enable us to eat and drink, and of course they surround our organs of sight, sound, smell and taste. Although they don't have the physical power of the larger muscles of the limbs and trunk, they do play an important part in our lives.

Front view

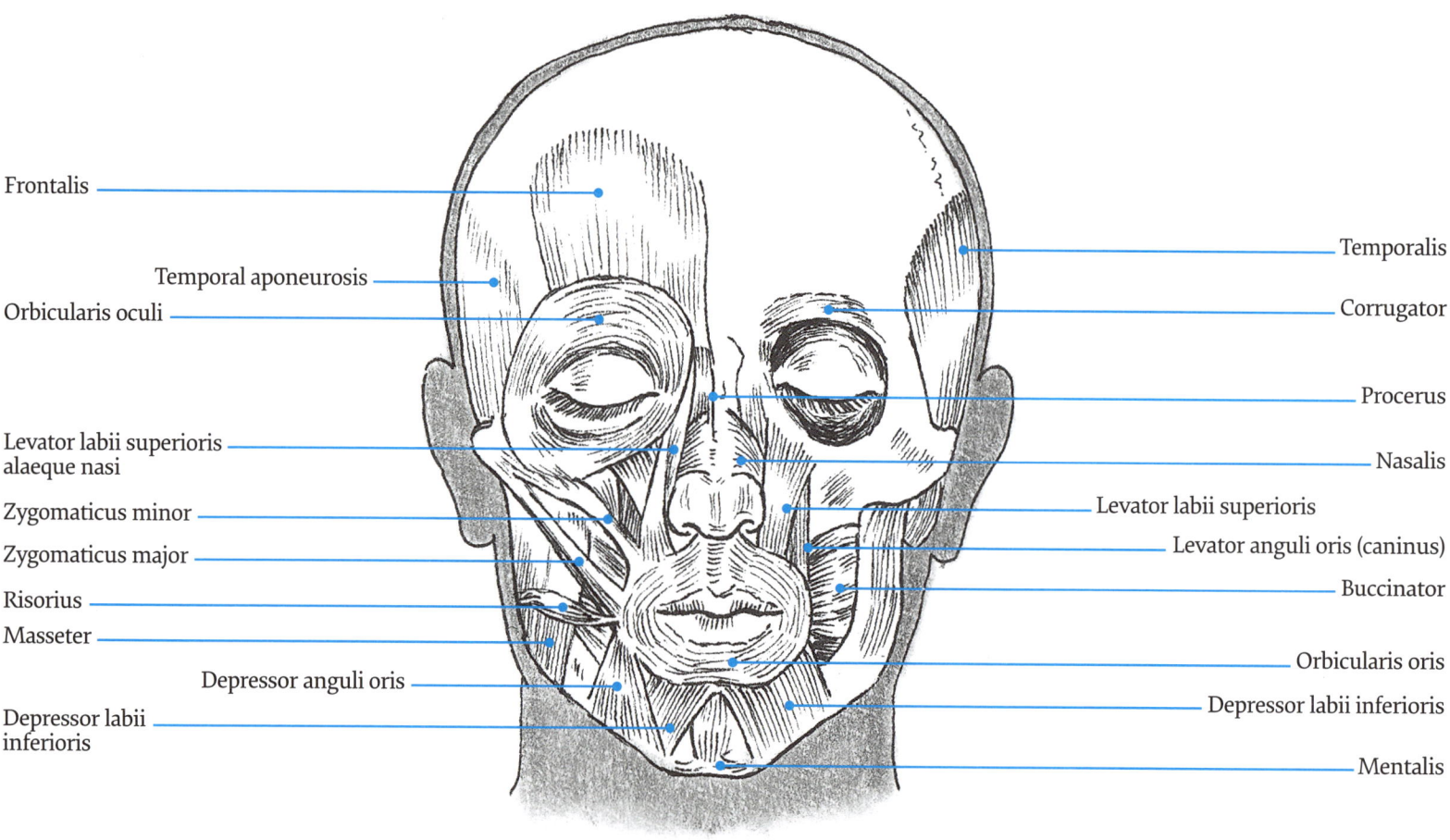

- Frontalis
- Temporal aponeurosis
- Orbicularis oculi
- Levator labii superioris alaeque nasi
- Zygomaticus minor
- Zygomaticus major
- Risorius
- Masseter
- Depressor anguli oris
- Depressor labii inferioris
- Temporalis
- Corrugator
- Procerus
- Nasalis
- Levator labii superioris
- Levator anguli oris (caninus)
- Buccinator
- Orbicularis oris
- Depressor labii inferioris
- Mentalis

THE HEAD IN DETAIL

Side view, deep layer

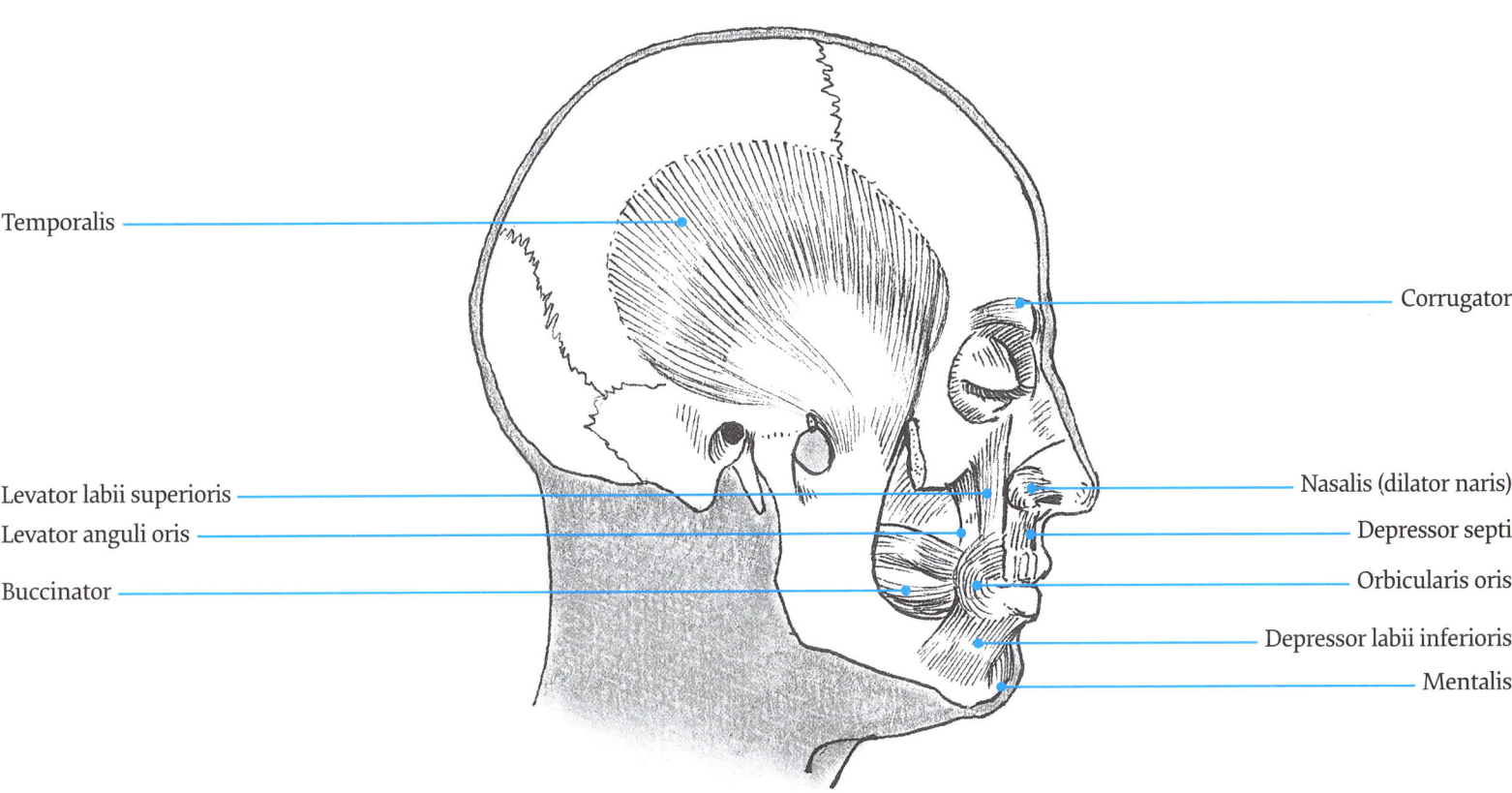

THE HEAD IN DETAIL

Side view, superficial layer

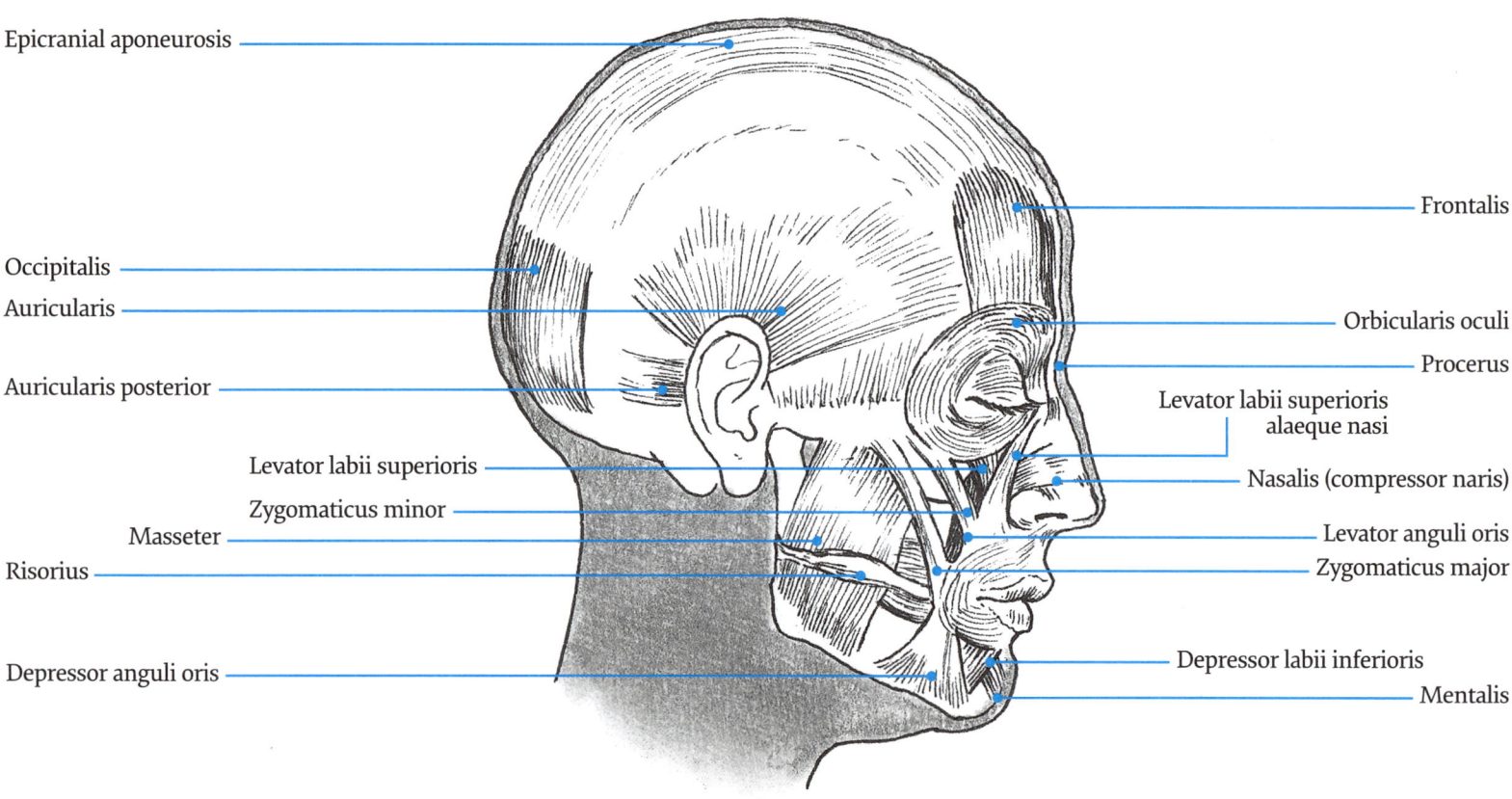

Muscles of the neck

I have included the muscles of the neck with the head because, in most respects, their effect can be closely aligned with the head structure.

Front view

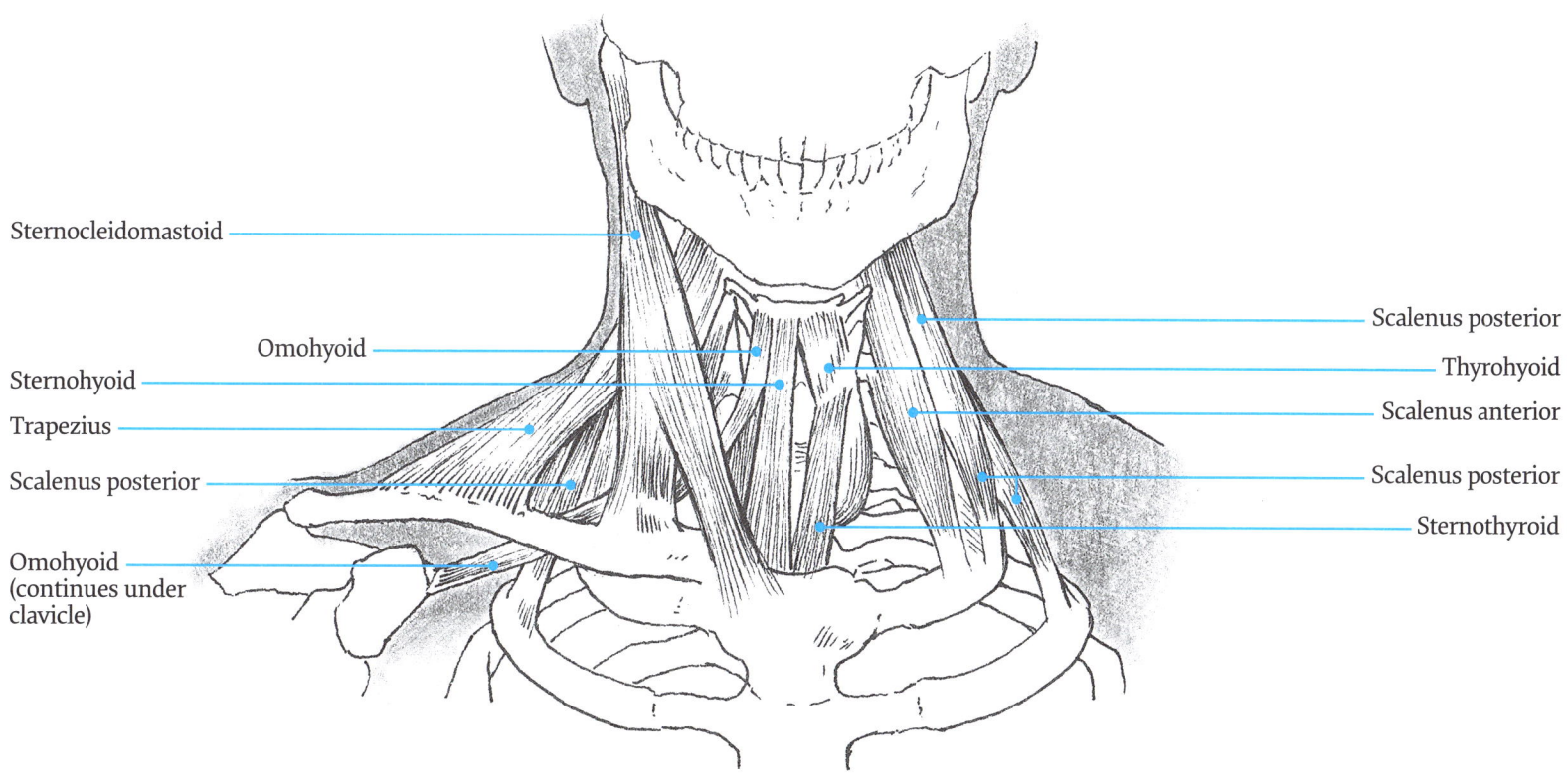

- Sternocleidomastoid
- Omohyoid
- Sternohyoid
- Trapezius
- Scalenus posterior
- Omohyoid (continues under clavicle)
- Scalenus posterior
- Thyrohyoid
- Scalenus anterior
- Scalenus posterior
- Sternothyroid

THE HEAD IN DETAIL

Side view

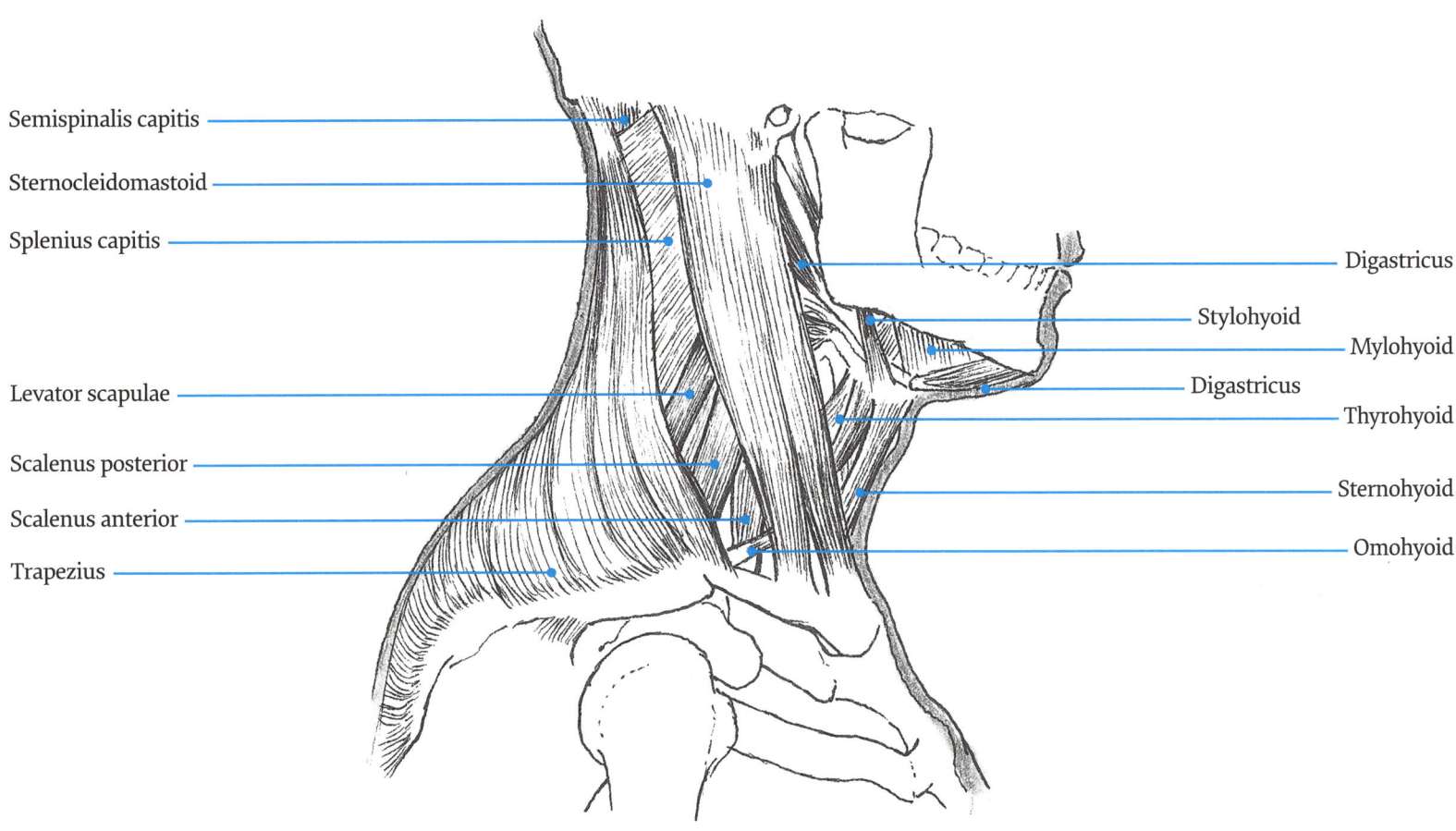

THE HEAD IN DETAIL

Surface of the head showing the muscles

This drawing, made from a very clear and detailed photograph, shows the muscles that can be seen on the surface of a mature man's face.

The temporal line shows clearly at the temple of the forehead, and the temporalis and frontalis muscles, although these don't stand out strongly, are being pulled tightly across the bone structure of the skull.

Around the eye the orbicularis oculi and the procerus muscles are visible.

Around the mouth and nose can be discerned the levator labii superioris alaeque nasi, the compressor naris and the dilator naris (both part of the nasalis), the depressor labii inferioris, the levator anguli oris and the depressor anguli oris.

Further back near the ear is the edge of the zygomatic bone called the zygomatic arch, with the zygomaticus major, which is the muscle that stretches across from the arch to the corner of the mouth. Also on the jaw can be seen the bulge of the masseter muscle.

On the neck is shown the trapezius, the sternocleidomastoid and the sternothyroid.

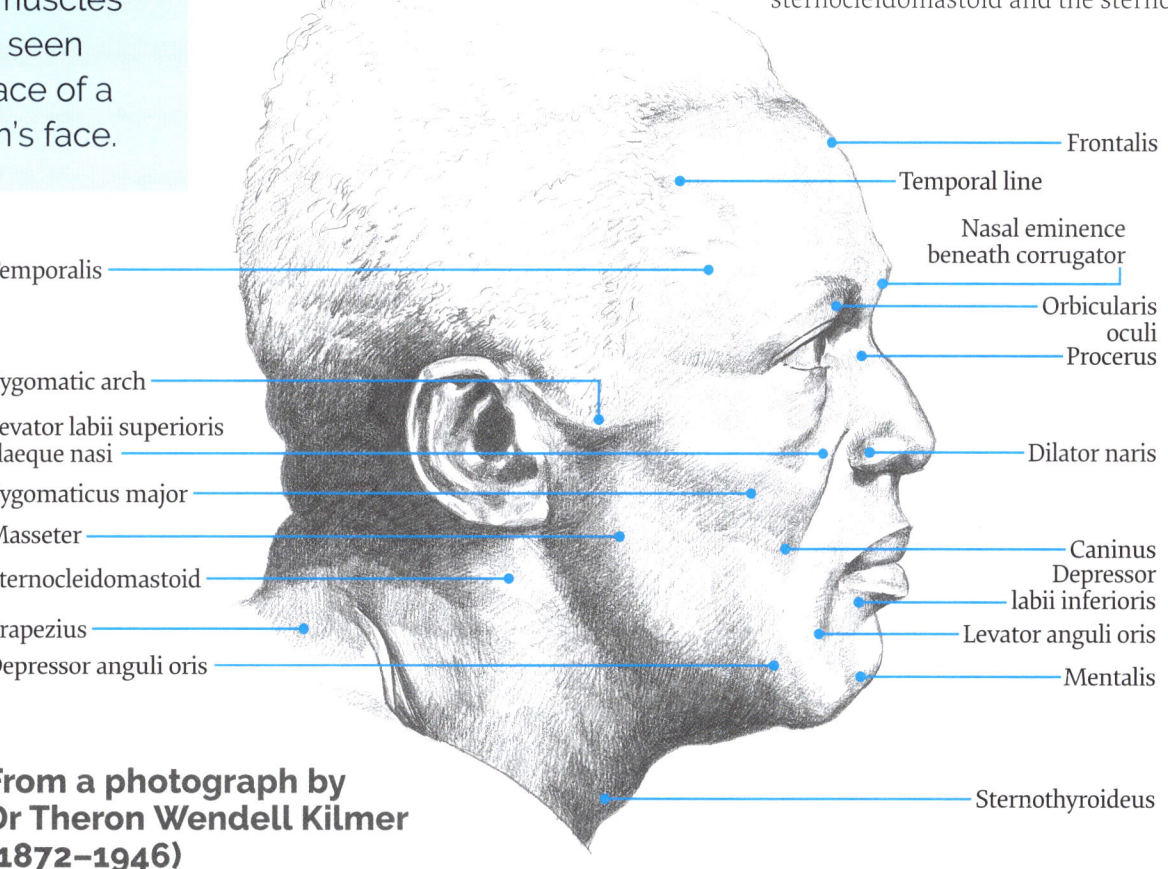

From a photograph by Dr Theron Wendell Kilmer (1872–1946)

THE HEAD IN DETAIL

The head drawn by master artists

The same groups of muscles can be seen on a drawing by Peter Paul Rubens. It is interesting to note that as soon as you start to look for these muscles of the face, they become clearer and it is easier to draw them correctly.

After Peter Paul Rubens (1577–1640)

In this drawing, *Self-portrait* from 1913 after the Irish artist William Orpen, we see the main muscles of the face again quite clearly. It is probably easier to see them on a more mature face and one that does not have too much flesh on it, because younger or more rounded faces don't show the muscles so clearly.

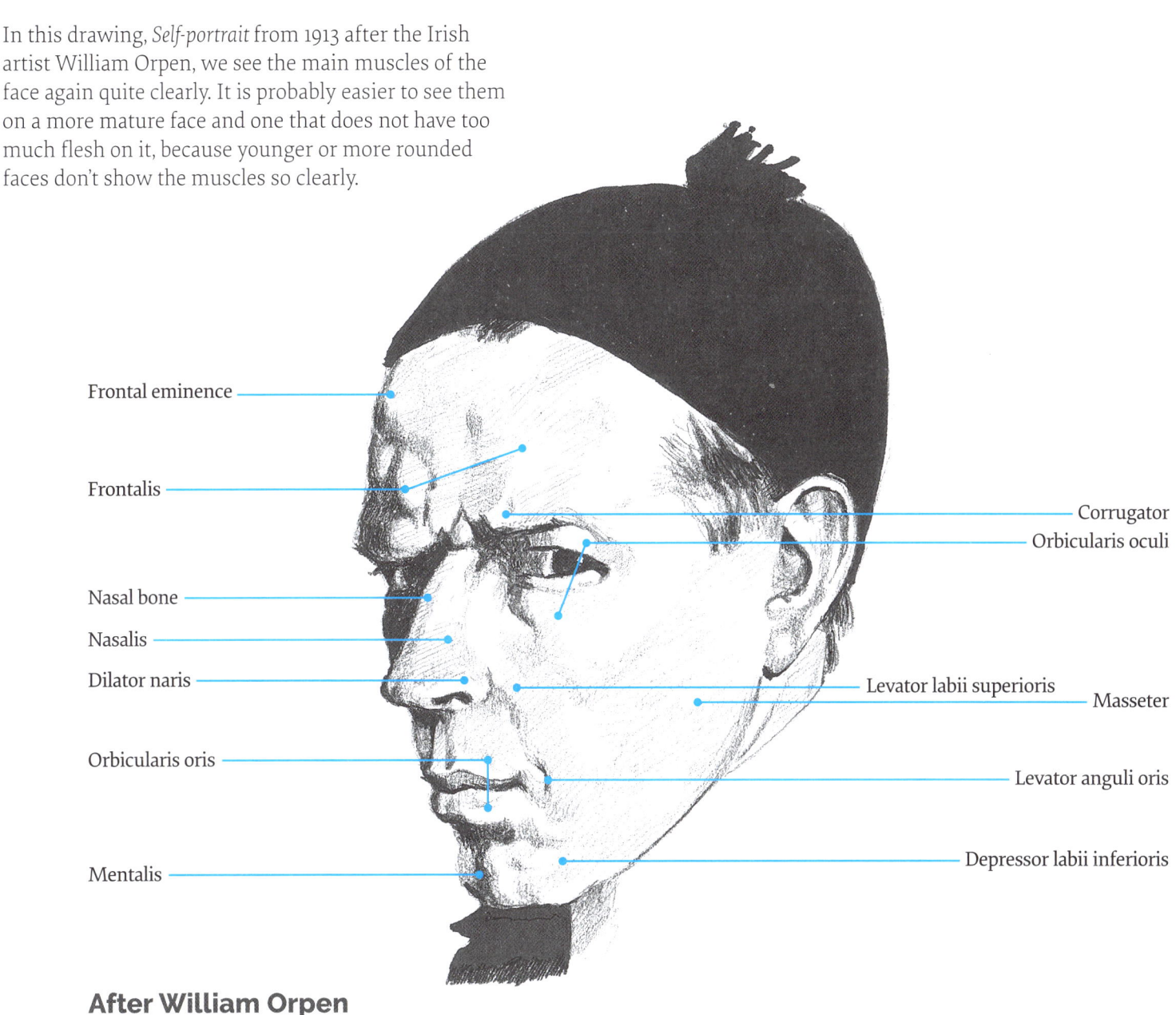

After William Orpen (1878–1931)

Facial expressions

Here we look in detail at the muscles involved in expressing a whole range of emotions, from anger to contentment. Familiarity with the muscle structure underlying the face is very useful for capturing the character of a human subject accurately.

Muscles used when smiling, grinning and laughing

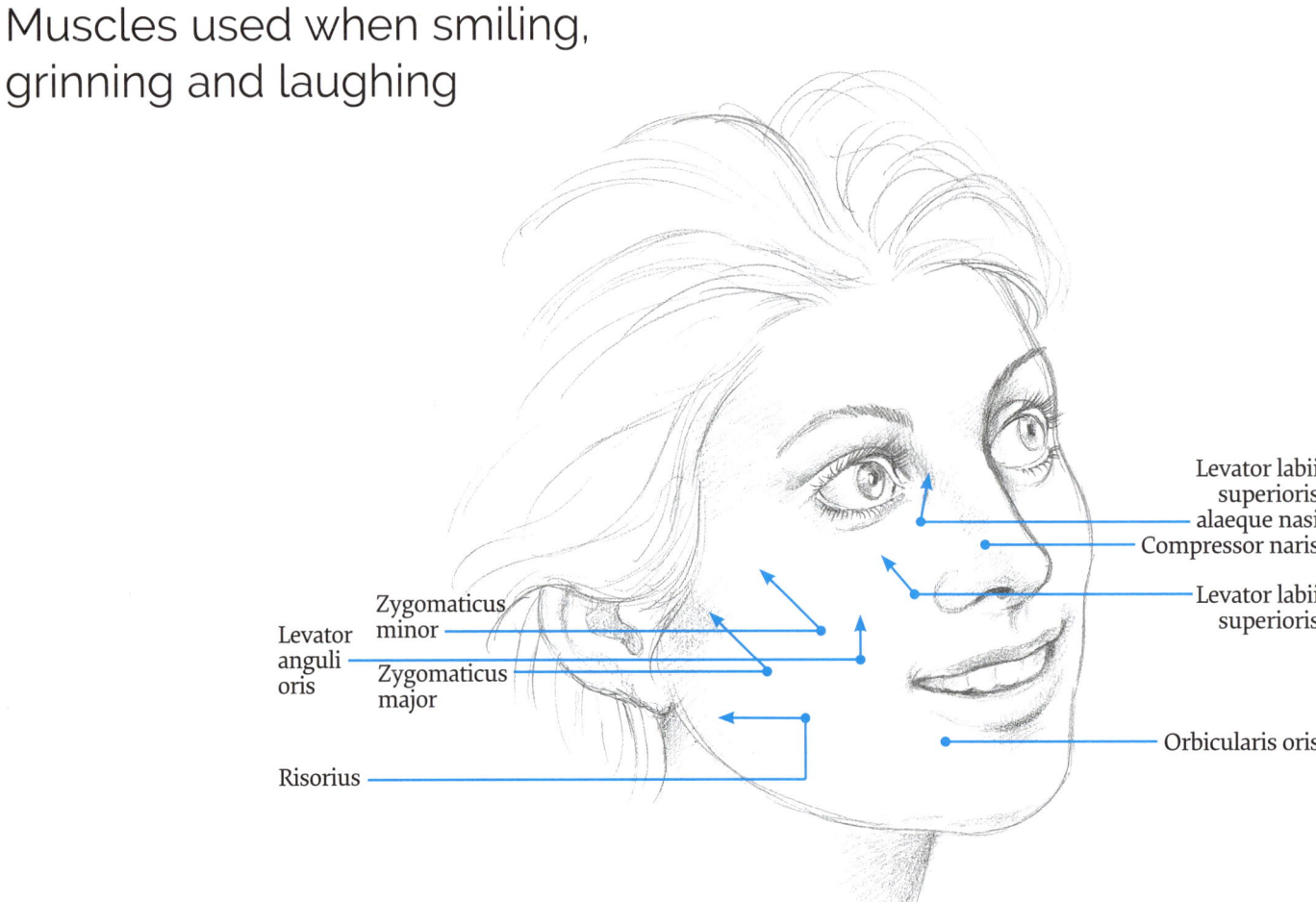

- Levator labii superioris alaeque nasi
- Compressor naris
- Levator labii superioris
- Zygomaticus minor
- Levator anguli oris
- Zygomaticus major
- Orbicularis oris
- Risorius

THE HEAD IN DETAIL

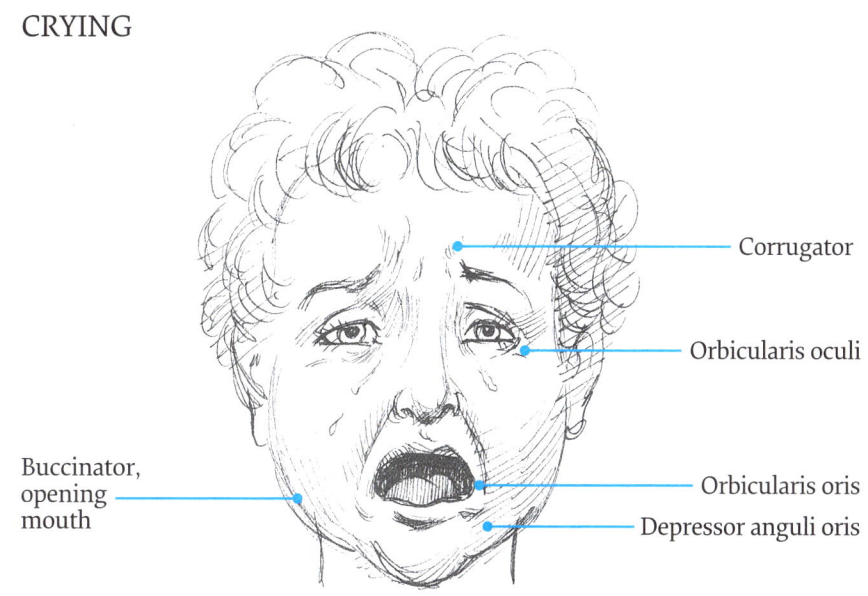

THE HEAD IN DETAIL 55

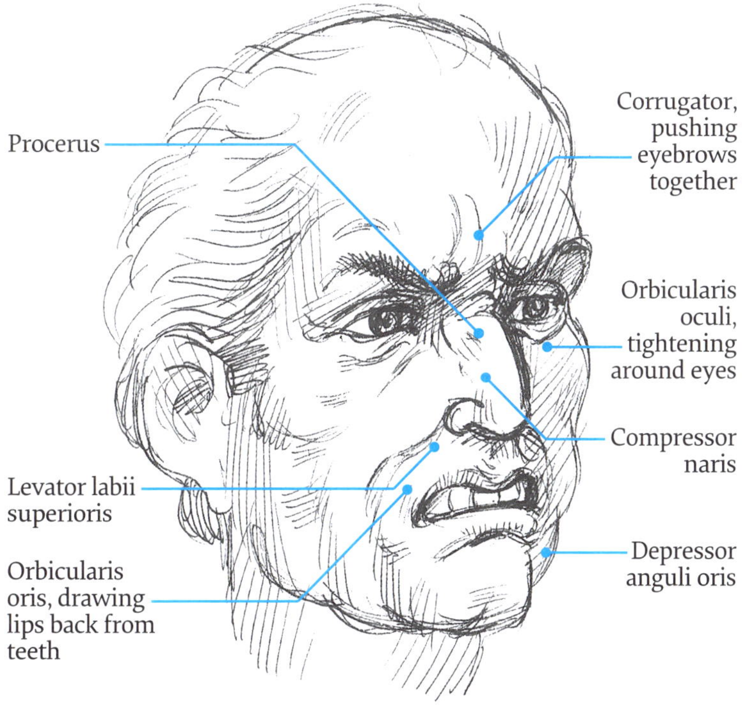

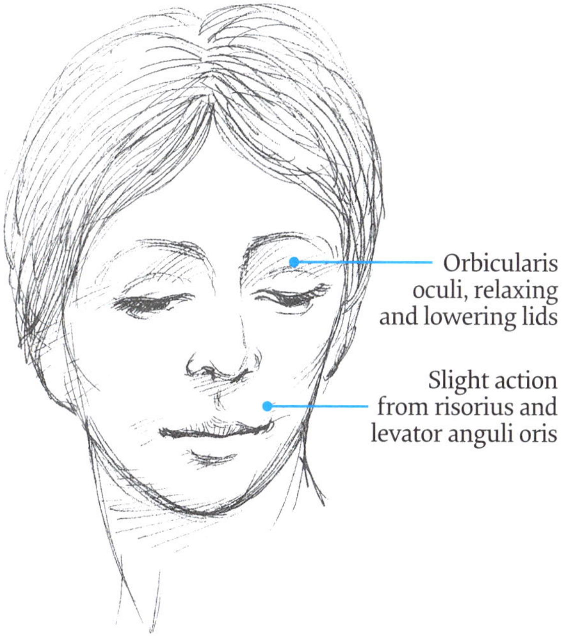

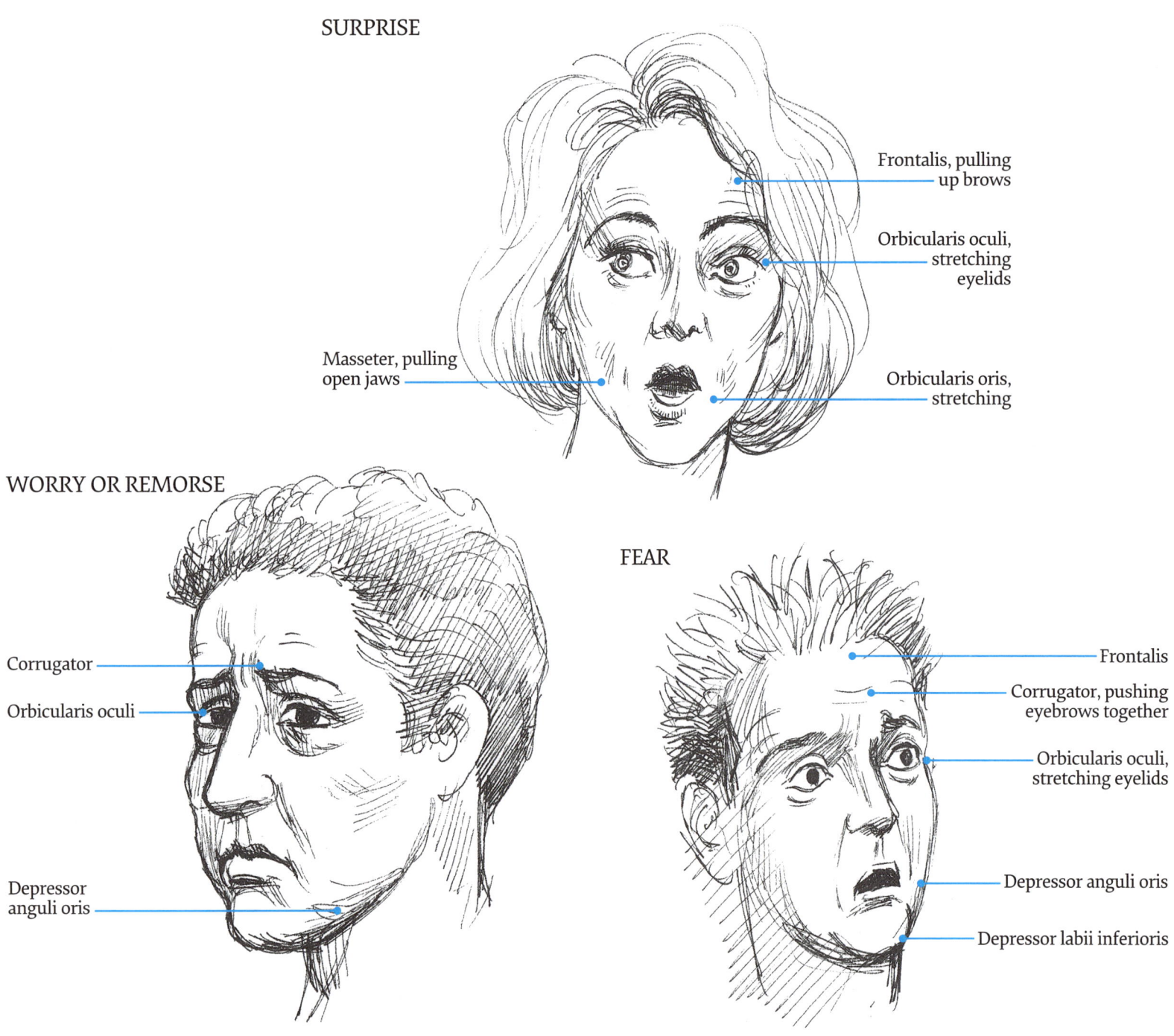

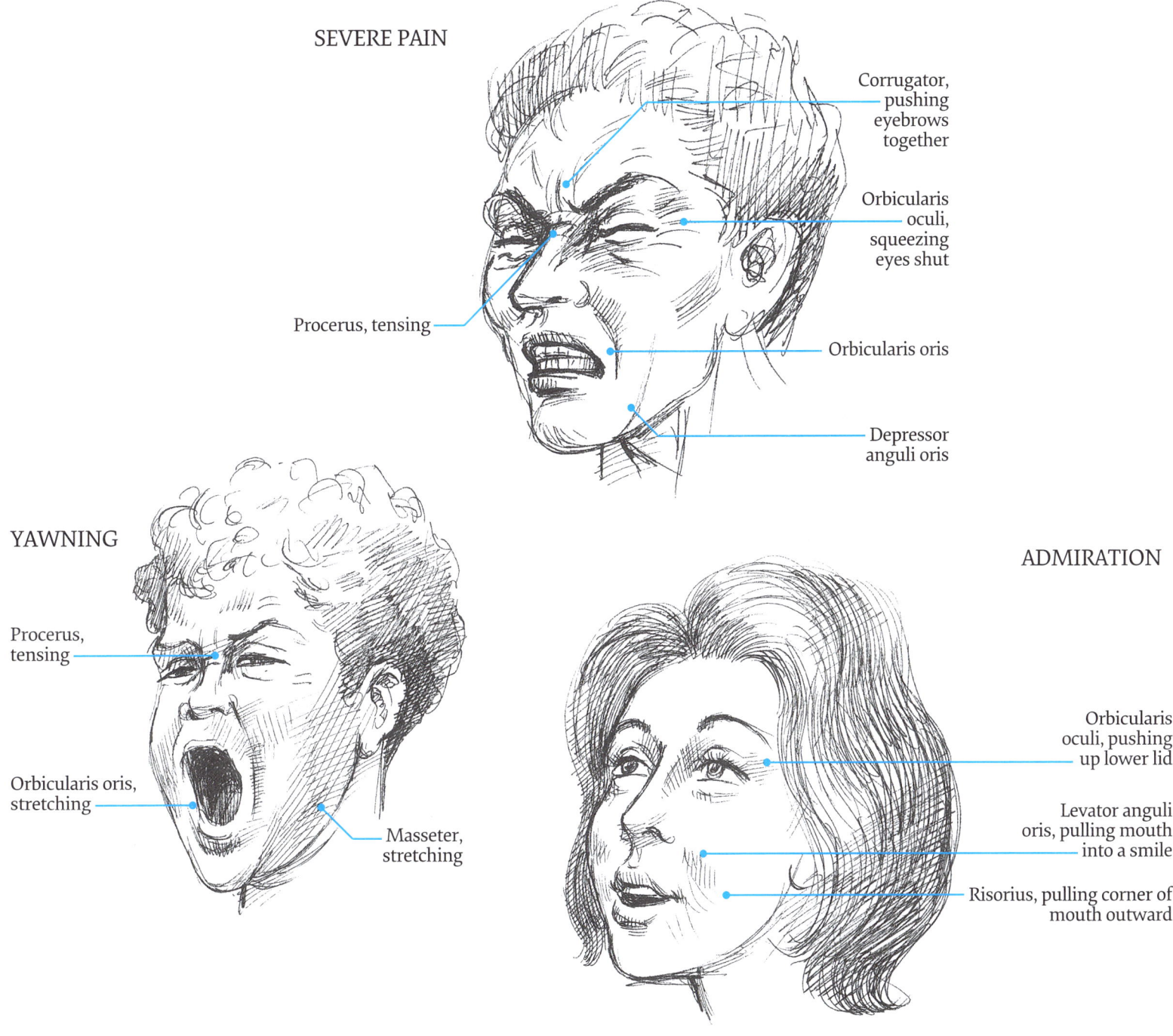

Features of the face

Here we look at the individual features of the face: the eye, the mouth, the nose and the ear, giving some information about the normal formation of these features. What we will show is the basic structure of these features and their most obvious shape, but bear in mind that the features of individuals do vary quite dramatically sometimes.

Eyes

First note that the normal position of the eye, when open and looking straight ahead, has part of the iris hidden under the upper eyelid, and the lower edge of the iris just touching the lower lid.

FRONT VIEW

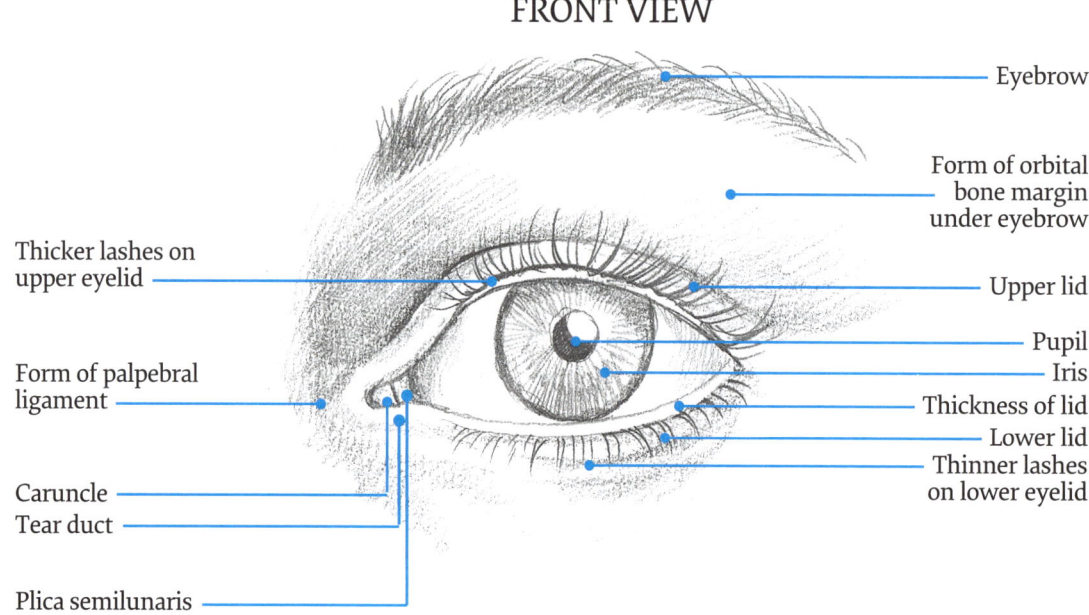

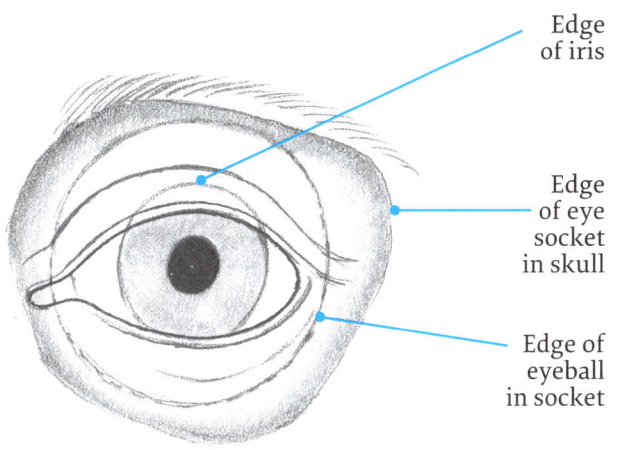
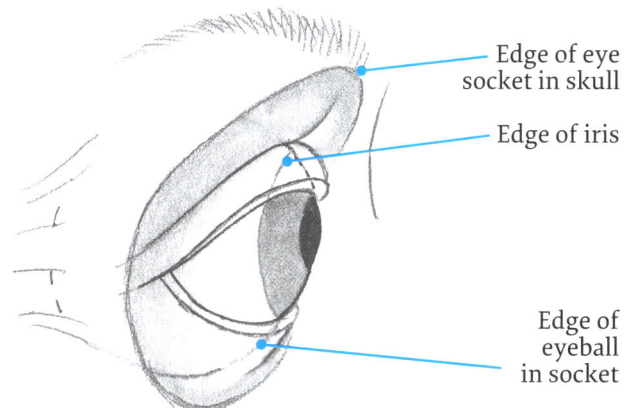

VARIOUS EYE SHAPES

Narrow eyes

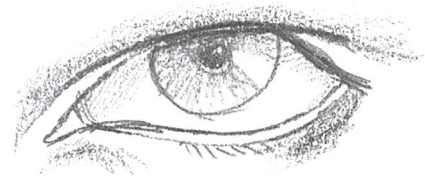

Round eyes

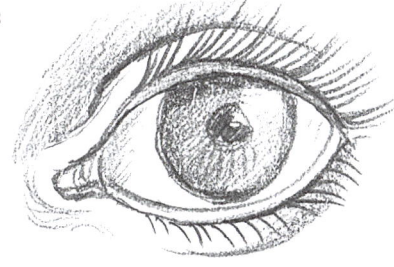

Heavy-lidded eyes

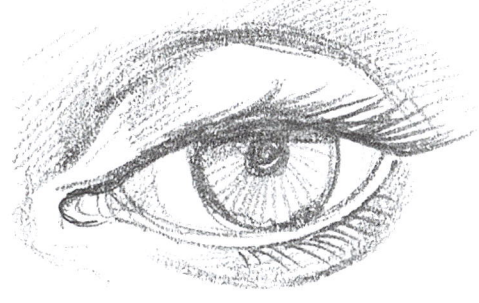

Eyes with uncreased lids

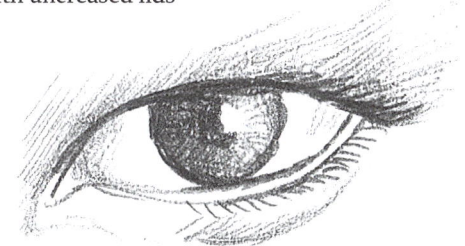

THE HEAD IN DETAIL

EXPRESSIVE EYES

Study this selection of eyes: male and female, old, young, front view, looking down and up. Detailed studies like these are worth doing whenever you can.

THE HEAD IN DETAIL

Noses

The nose is the most prominent of the features on the head, and although not all that complex, needs some study to be able to draw it convincingly. Types of noses are more easily identified in profile than from a front view, as can be seen in the examples below.

NOSES: SIDE VIEWS

Long nose | Short straight nose | Aquiline nose | Hook nose | Broken nose | Retroussé or snub nose

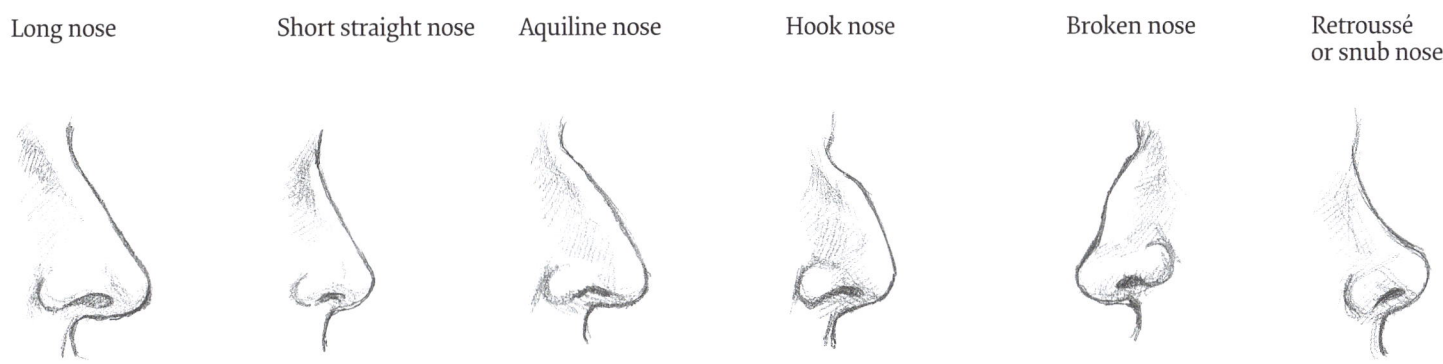

FRONT VIEWS

Normal, strong nose | Retroussé or snub nose | Aquiline nose

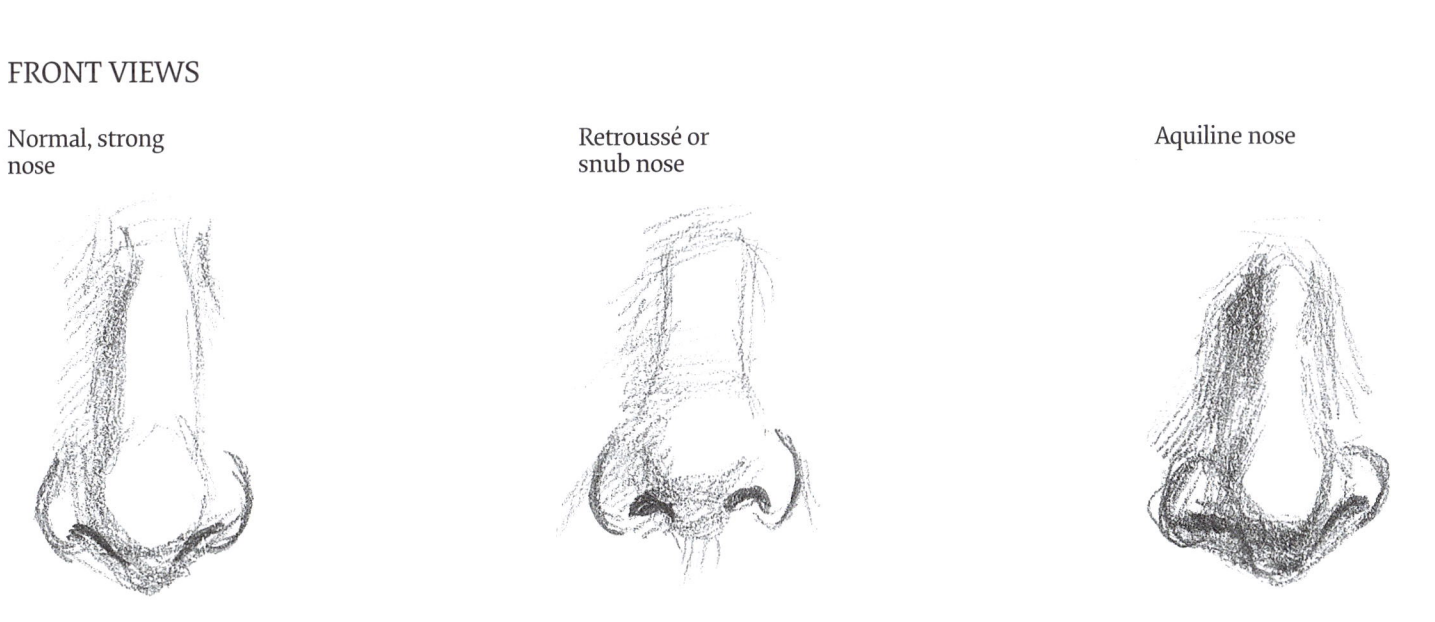

THE HEAD IN DETAIL

Mouths

Drawing the mouth does not pose many problems as long as you remember that the most significant and strongest line of the mouth is the part where the lips meet – not the outline of the lips, which is often incorrectly supposed to be more important.

FRONT VIEWS

Full lips

Thin lips

Average 'Cupid's bow' lips

SIDE VIEWS

Full lips

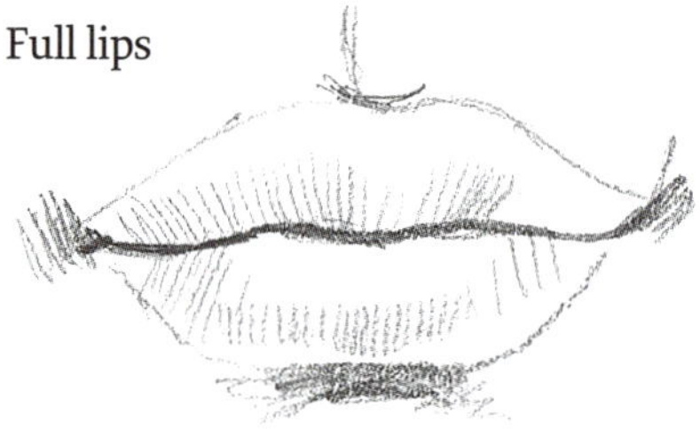

Thin lips

Average lips

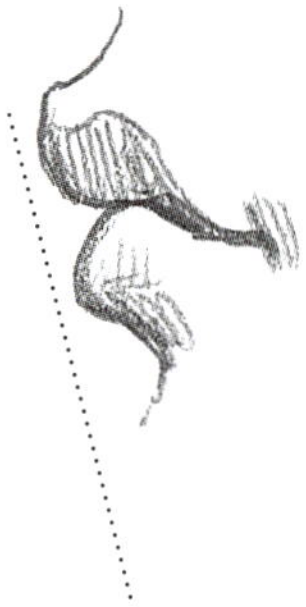

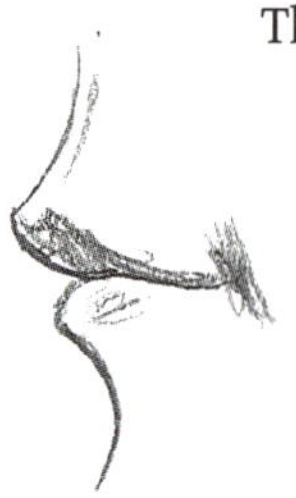

Angled: lower lip behind upper lip

Lower and upper lips protrude the same amount (pouting)

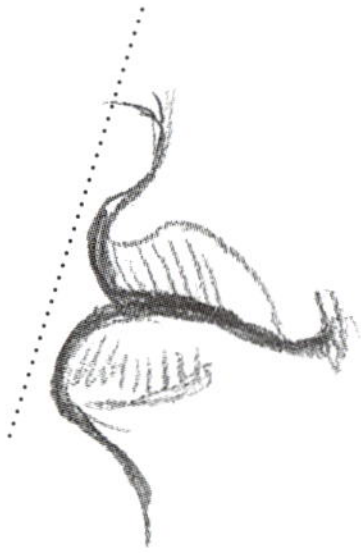

Angled: lower lip projecting beyond upper lip

THE HEAD IN DETAIL

EXPRESSIVE MOUTHS

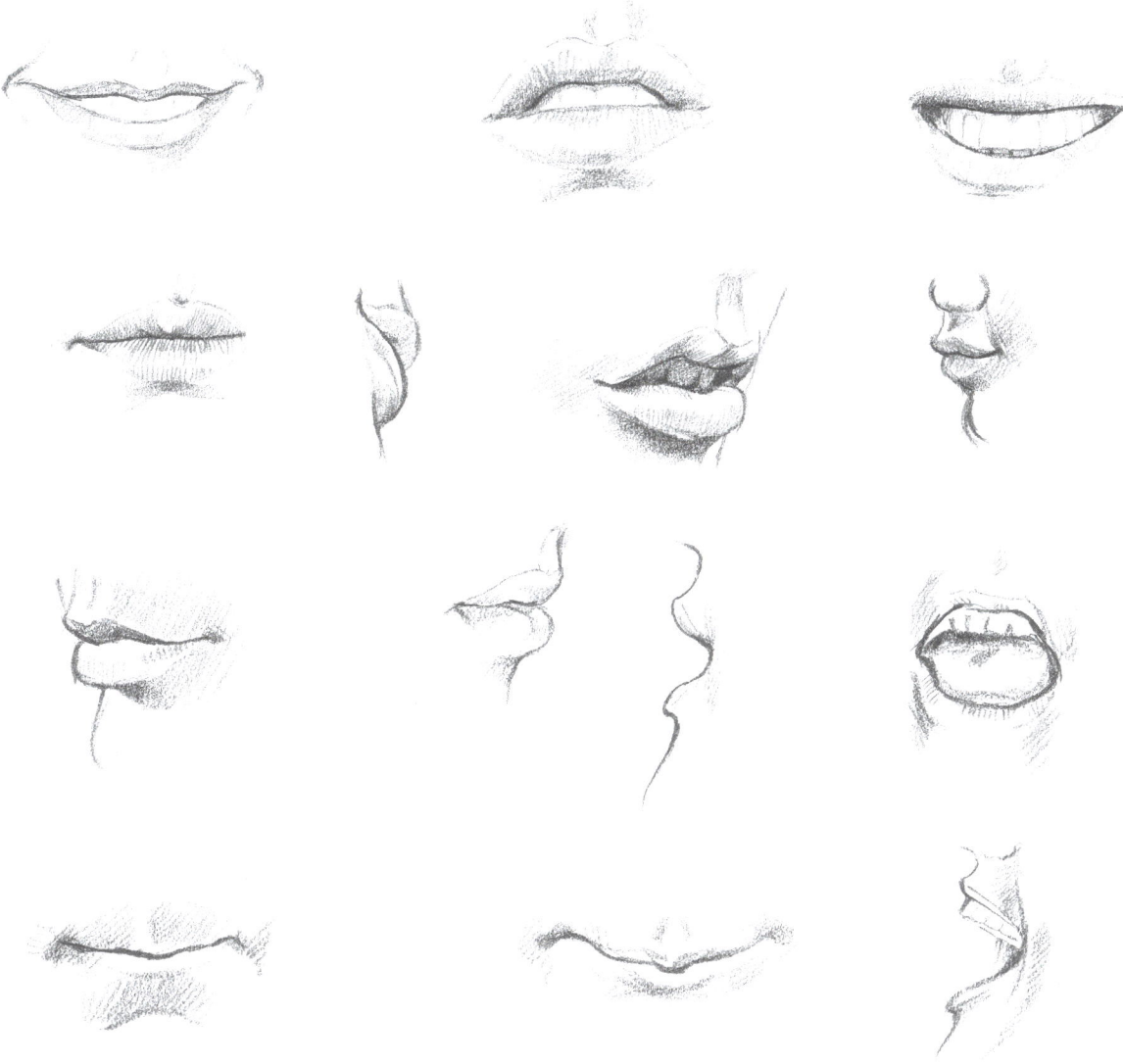

These illustrations show a range of mouths, open, closed, smiling and shouting, seen from above, below and the side. When the mouth is seen partly from one side, the farther side will look much shorter and more curved than the side closest to you. In a smile the lips become stretched and so appear slightly thinner. When the mouth is closed it can be full and soft-looking or pressed together and thinner, depending partly on age and disposition. Very young children's mouths are extremely rounded and soft and usually fuller in shape.

Ears

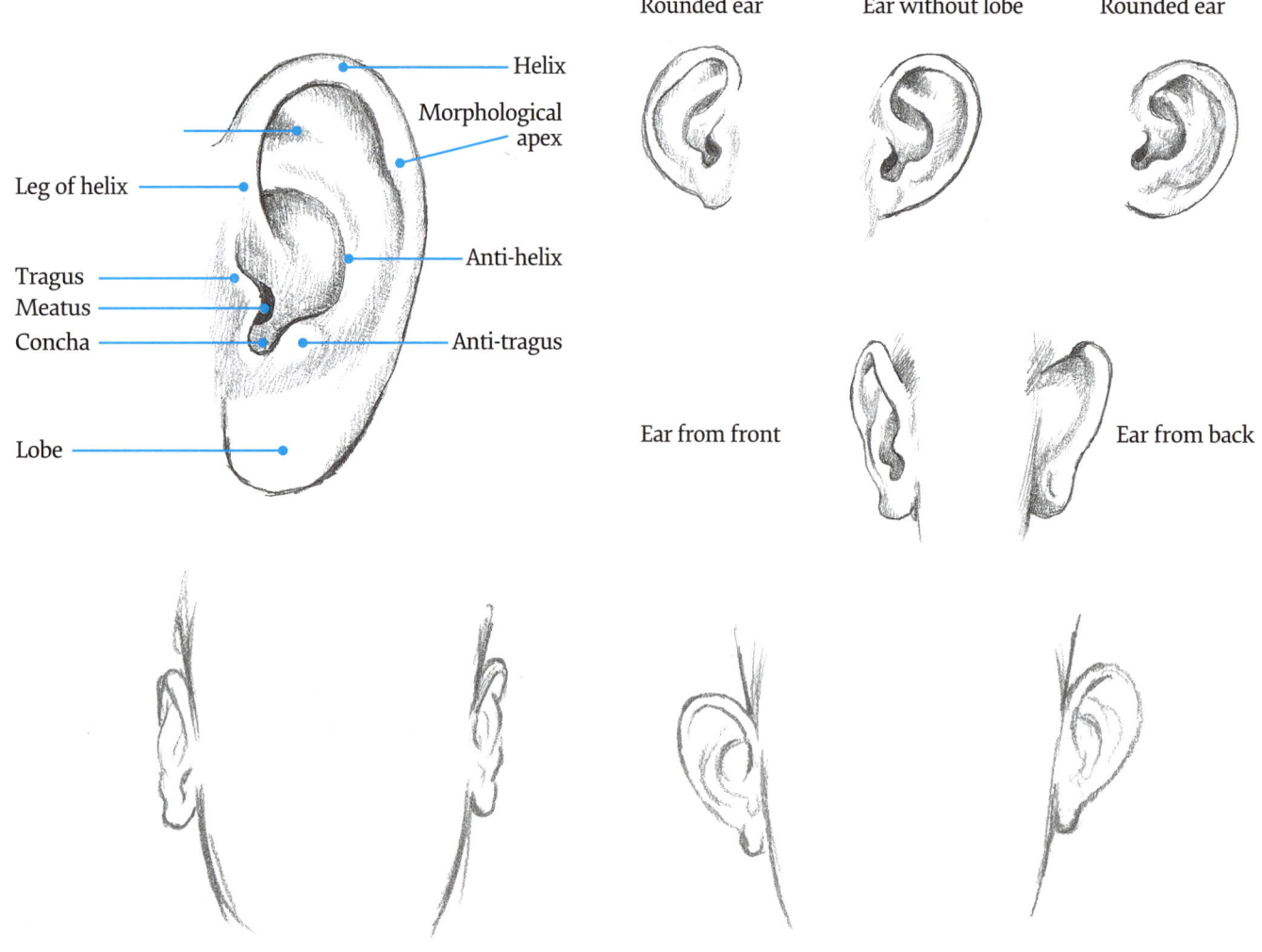

Ears are only difficult because we rarely look at them. The diagram above shows an ear of average shape and although there are many variations the basic structure remains the same. Some ears are much flatter against the side of the head and are not noticeable from the front; others stick out like jug handles and can be quite a strong feature on a head with short hair. Apart from their size and the amount they protrude, they are not an instantly recognizable feature in the human face.

Hair

When it comes to hair, the most obvious differences are in length and whether the hair is curly or straight. There tends to be less range in style among men, though facial hair can radically change the look of someone's face, as can the advent of thinning hair with age. Shown here are examples of how to tackle various types of hair and hair styling, including the vigorous growth of beard and moustache in the drawing below right, after Vincent Van Gogh.

THE HEAD IN DETAIL

The effects of age

When you have studied the shape and proportions of the head and the facial features, you can consider how you might apply your knowledge to drawing real people. The next part of this chapter focuses on portraiture.

The age of your sitter is perhaps the most fundamental thing that you need to convey in your drawing. In youth, the face has a clarity and charm that are surprisingly difficult to capture. With age, experience of the world begins to tell and the character of your sitter becomes evident in the habitual lines on their face.

As we saw on page 38, children's heads don't match the proportions of an adult head. The greatest difference is the size of the cranium in relation to the lower jaw, but also the eyes are more widely spaced than in an adult and the cheeks are usually rounder. All the features fit into a much smaller space, and of course there are hardly any lines on the face.

The little boy is a bit older but doesn't have a fully grown jaw yet, and his eyes and ears look much larger in relation to his nose and mouth than they would in an adult.

THE HEAD IN DETAIL

Here are drawings of a young woman at her peak and one of an old man – my youngest daughter and myself. See the difference in the quality of the hair, on the one soft and shiny, the other white and sparse. Then look at the surface of the skin. Although my daughter is grinning widely she has very few lines on her face and her eyes are very clear. My own skin is furrowed with lines of all kinds, especially around the eyes and on the forehead. The cheeks look more hollow and the mouth is defined only by its edge. I appear to be staring intently; that's because I am of course drawing myself in a mirror.

Artist's Note

Be careful not to overdo the characterful lines of your sitter's face as you risk making them look older than they would like. Making people look younger is not normally a problem because most of us have an image of ourselves as younger than we are in reality.

THE HEAD IN DETAIL

Draw a head in proportion

This exercise is an opportunity to apply your anatomical knowledge of the head to create a realistic looking portrait, step by step. You may experiment with using some color as I have, or stick to graphite pencil for your shading.

STEP 1

This method of measuring the head uses the proportions shown on pages 36–7. It is very helpful if you are not too sure about judging proportions.

- Remember that when the head is level, the eyes are halfway down its length. Mark in the top of the head and the bottom of the chin, and make a mark halfway between them. Then sketch in the shape of the eyes, remembering that the space between each eye is the same length as the eye itself.
- Then mark in the nose end about halfway between the eye line and the chin line.
- The bottom of the ear is roughly level with the nostril and the top of the ear is level with the eyebrow just above the eye.
- Now mark in the mouth line which is slightly closer to the end of the nose than the chin.
- The hairline is roughly halfway between the top of the head and the eyeline (though hairlines can vary considerably).

STEP 2

With all these marks made you can now attempt a simple line drawing of the main shape of the head and position of the neck. Try to get the shapes of the eyes, the nose and the mouth as accurate as possible, because this is how we all recognize a face. The position, shape and thickness of the eyebrows are also very characteristic. The ears and hairline, while not quite so fundamental, can help to achieve a likeness.

STEP 3

Now you can erase your guidelines and start to shade the face and the hair carefully but still in a very light tone. Apart from the darker area of the hair, there is more shading in the lower part of the face, especially around the jawline. Note the upper lip looks darker than the lower lip, but there is a shadow under the lower lip. Add a bit of tone under the eyebrows, particularly in the inside corner between the eye and the nose. Darken the pupils and iris of the eyes but leave a little bit of paper showing for the highlight near the pupil.

STEP 4

Now, if you are following my color scheme, add some warm pinkish or orange color to the whole face, but very lightly. It must not be very noticeable. Then darken all the shaded parts of the head. Half close your eyes as you look at the person and it will be more obvious where the darker parts are. The hair can be worked on with even, darker tones and so can the pupils of the eyes, the eyebrows, the nostrils, the line where the mouth opens and around the edges of the jawline, neck and forehead.

Draw a tilted head

It is important to draw the shape of the head and the position of the features from different angles, as the appearance can differ radically (see also pages 39–41). Before attempting the exercise on the facing page, study the angled heads below. Compare the finished versions with the structural drawings and note how the proportions and appearance of the features change.

THE HEAD IN DETAIL

In this exercise you are faced with a very unusual position of the head. The degree of difficulty accentuates the necessity of correctly drawing the outline of the head. If you don't spend time getting this stage right, the result will be unsatisfactory, no matter how beautiful your detailed drawing. Generally, the first few minutes of a drawing determine how good or bad it will be.

Because of the unusual angle don't expect the shapes to be conventional or even what you know. Observation here is the real key, and if you observe keenly there is more chance of a powerful drawing resulting from your efforts.

STEP 1

The key to this drawing is understanding the construction of the shapes. When you are ready, draw the outline and lightly sketch in the features, as precisely as you can.

STEP 2

Pay special attention to the shape under the jaw and how it combines with the neck to make a large, open shape. The features – eyes, nose and mouth – are all pushed together in a smaller space than is usual, because of the angle.

STEP 3

Add all the embellishments of light, shade and detail, using emphasis accurately to create both a good line and a convincing portrait.

THE HEAD IN DETAIL

Portraits: different approaches

While a portrait should resemble the sitter in some way, that doesn't mean it must be time-consuming and full of detail. On these pages we shall consider several examples of portraits that approach the subject in different ways before embarking on a short portrait project.

The first one is of a woman who was busy drawing in one of the classes I used to teach. There wasn't enough time to get much in, so I concentrated on the eyes, nose, and mouth and merely sketched in the chin, forehead, and hair.

The next subject was unable to sit for long, so once again I drew the main features of the face and just indicated the rest of the head. Notice how the background tone that shows up the profile clearly is just as important as the face itself.

These two drawings are also of people who were engaged in some other activity but sufficiently motionless for me to sketch in the face and head and, in the case of the woman on the left, the hands too. I included these because they gave a completely different feel to the final drawing.

You've probably noticed that so far none of these subjects are looking at the artist while they're being drawn. It's often easier for people not to face the artist because it can be rather disconcerting to be stared at so directly and for quite some while, too.

The next drawing is of a woman looking upwards, which tilts the head slightly back and makes the main shape different. There is much indirect light, which creates an interesting reflected edge to the darker side of the face.

This portrait is a complete profile view of a man's head, with a strong dark background behind the face and a lighter one behind the back of the head. Profile views were very popular in the early Renaissance period in Italy, and you might find it quite a good way to start drawing, as it seems easier to catch the exact shape of the face and head. However, it won't be the view that most people like to see in a portrait.

THE HEAD IN DETAIL

This time the model is looking downwards, and the significant thing here is the spectacles. These are often omitted from portraits as they can act as a sort of disguise to the face. Of course, if your model always wears spectacles, removing them will result in a portrait that looks less like the person that everyone is familiar with. Notice how much shadow there is on the lower half of the face, because the model's head is inclined.

The next two drawings are both of people looking directly towards the artist, and of course this is often the best way to draw someone because it's how they are most recognizable. This man is looking almost challengingly towards the artist, and you can see that he isn't afraid to meet someone's eye.

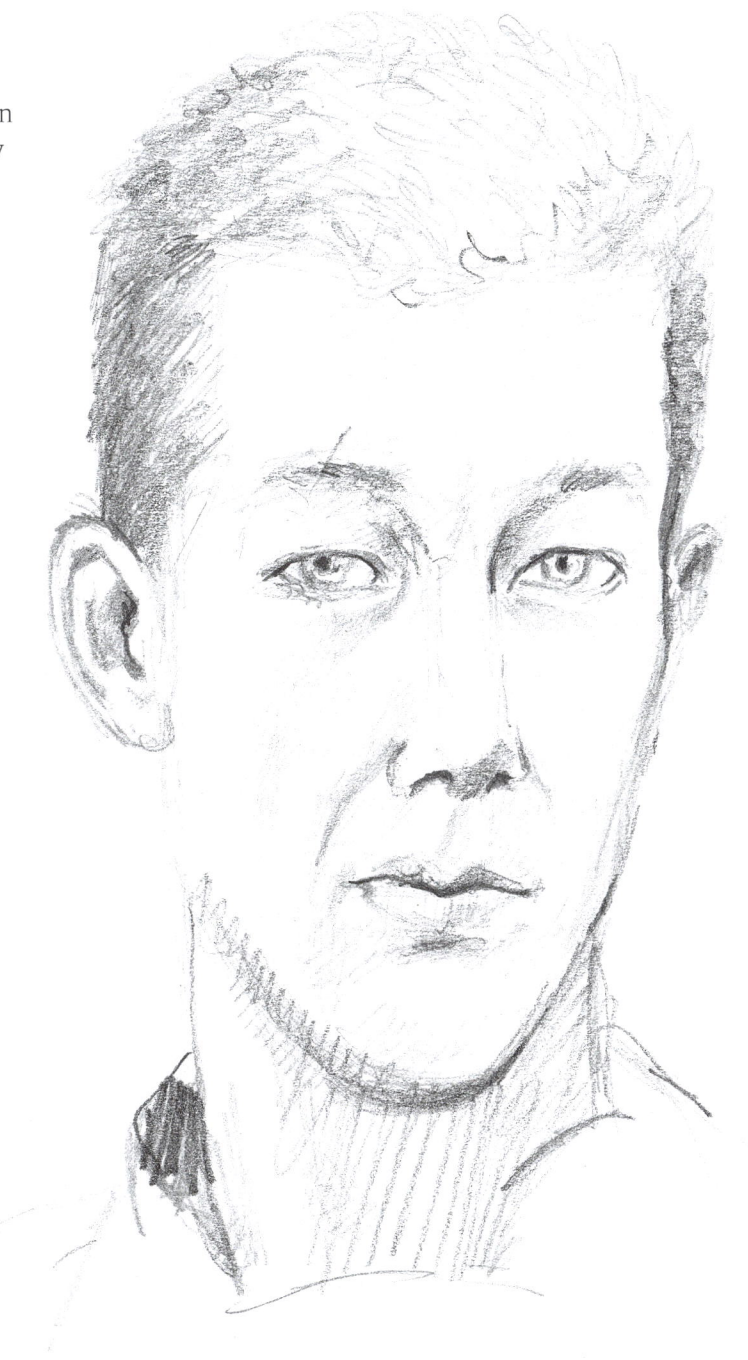

This young boy is my eldest son, drawn when he was quite young. He found it difficult to keep still long enough for me to draw much detail, but we just about managed it. It's noticeable that he didn't look directly at me as I was drawing his eyes.

THE HEAD IN DETAIL

Lighting the head

Before you start to draw a portrait, consider the lighting around your subject as it can alter their appearance quite substantially. Look at these examples which show what happens when you light a face deliberately in order to draw it.

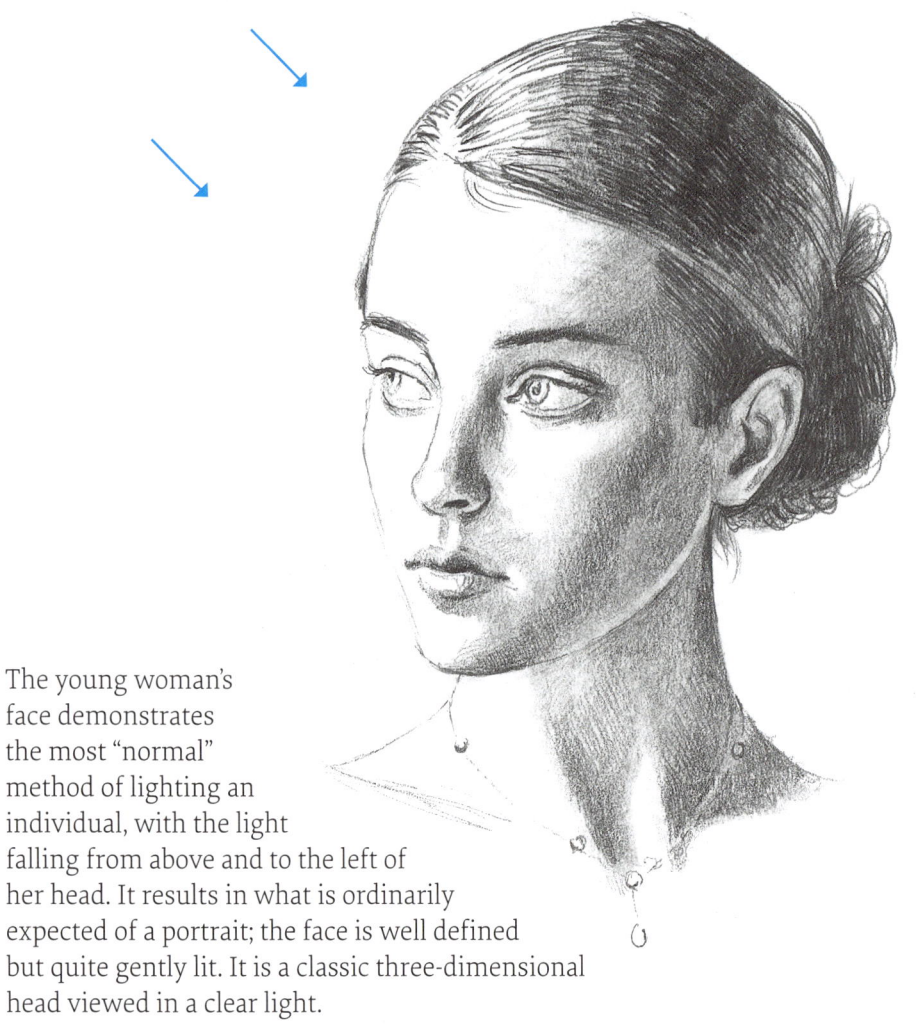

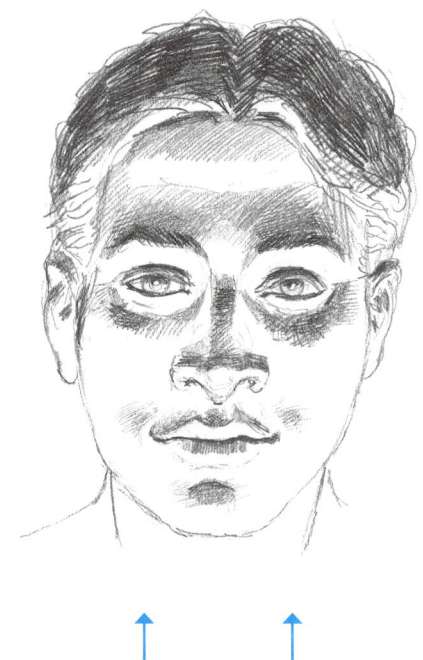

The young woman's face demonstrates the most "normal" method of lighting an individual, with the light falling from above and to the left of her head. It results in what is ordinarily expected of a portrait; the face is well defined but quite gently lit. It is a classic three-dimensional head viewed in a clear light.

The second head shows what happens if you reverse everything. "Uplighting" is the familiar method of showing a "sinister" face, with which everyone is familiar from horror films. The light emphasizes the cheekbones below the eyes, the nose is shown with the bridge and upper nostrils darkened, the top of the head is in shadow and the lower jaw is lit up. It looks scary because it subverts all our expectations of a normal, friendly human face.

The next two pictures show the difference between the effects of daylight and of artificial light.

The daylight example comes from a picture taken outside in the sunshine. The sunlight in this case is very diffuse and gives a fairly even distribution of light, with subtle shadows on the side of the head that is facing away from the sun.

The second example shows a strong directional light that could only come from an artificial source, delivering some strongly illuminated portions and deeper shadows on the other side. However, there is a certain amount of reflected light on the shadowy side, which is probably due to the light bouncing off other surfaces in the room. The dark background is a useful device for making the head more prominent.

And so, as you can see, the lighting in a picture can be chosen just as much as any other part of the drawing.

A portrait in steps

For this portrait, the aim is to get closer to your subject and to focus on how to use color in your drawing. My sitter was looking directly at me, resting her chin on her hand, which lends a relaxed and intimate feel to the portrait. Drawing her hand also allowed me to show her collection of large rings, which add interest and hint at her individuality.

STEP 1

As usual, start with a careful but simplified drawing of the main shapes of the face, hair, and hand. Try to gauge the size and distance between the features accurately, using the measuring methods shown on page 52 if necessary.

80   THE HEAD IN DETAIL

STEP 2

The next stage is to draw all the features in detail, correcting any mistakes as you go. This stage is the most challenging and may take the longest, as it is when you will get your likeness down on paper. Look carefully at the shapes of the eyes, noting how the farther eye differs in shape from the nearer one and the eyelids cover the tops of the irises. The far nostril is hidden, and a slight upward curve of the mouth can be seen on the near side. The shapes of the wrist and hand are also important in this composition, so take time to get them right.

STEP 3

In this step the color becomes significant. First of all make sure all the tonal areas are put in with colored strokes, not too heavily, in order to build up the main areas of color. I used brown and black for the hair, pink, red, and pale brown for the skin areas, plus a touch of background color (burnt sienna), and some blue for the eyes. Keep the color light and general at this stage.

> ### Artist's Note
>
> When it comes to tonal values in a portrait, you may well find that the color of the human face is not always uniform. If a person has quite dramatic changes of color in their facial features, you could be tempted to put them in very strongly. However, this would reduce the structural composition, turning it into a caricature of the real person. In order to avoid this, grade your color gradually from one part of the face to the next and the result will look more natural.

STEP 4

In this last step you will need to really increase the strength and solidity of the colors. The hair demands a lot of dark areas, sometimes solid black. A little touch of this black tone will strengthen the eyebrows, lashes, and pupils of the eyes, as well as the darker shadows around the edges of the nostrils, mouth, wrist, hand, and fingers. The warm pink and brown colors can add more depth to the face, mouth, hand, and arm. Also increase the background color strength. Once the depth and strength of color is established, carefully touch in any small marks to increase the intensity of the eyes, features, and hand. When you are satisfied with the look of your portrait, stop and enjoy your efforts.

THE HEAD IN DETAIL

Chapter Three

THE TORSO IN DETAIL

The torso and head are two sections of the human body that most artists are interested in drawing, chiefly because of their subtlety and the challenge of rendering them convincingly. Of the two, the torso is less familiar, because we don't usually see it totally unclothed.

The main skeleton is in three parts: the spinal vertebrae; the ribcage with the shoulder girdle, from which the arms depend; and the pelvis from which the legs depend. The numerous muscles stretched across the skeleton are extremely difficult to draw, owing to the way that layers of muscle and fat overlie one another and disguise a good deal of the bone structure. This chapter will feature diagrams of the deeper muscles, but only to show how they affect the appearance of the more superficial ones.

The significant thing about the torso from an artist's point of view is that although it looks like a pretty solid piece of work, it is actually highly mobile. It can bend forwards, backwards and sideways, and stretch out and contract to some extent. It can also twist around, enabling the shoulders to face sideways from the hips. Because the large muscles in the back and the front of the torso are so prominent, it is usually easy to see them working. However there are not so many seen on the surface and some of these are affected by muscles underneath them.

Look out for the differences between the male and female torso: whereas the muscles are very pronounced on an athletic male figure, the female shape is smoother and large muscles like the pectoralis major are not so visible under the mammary glands.

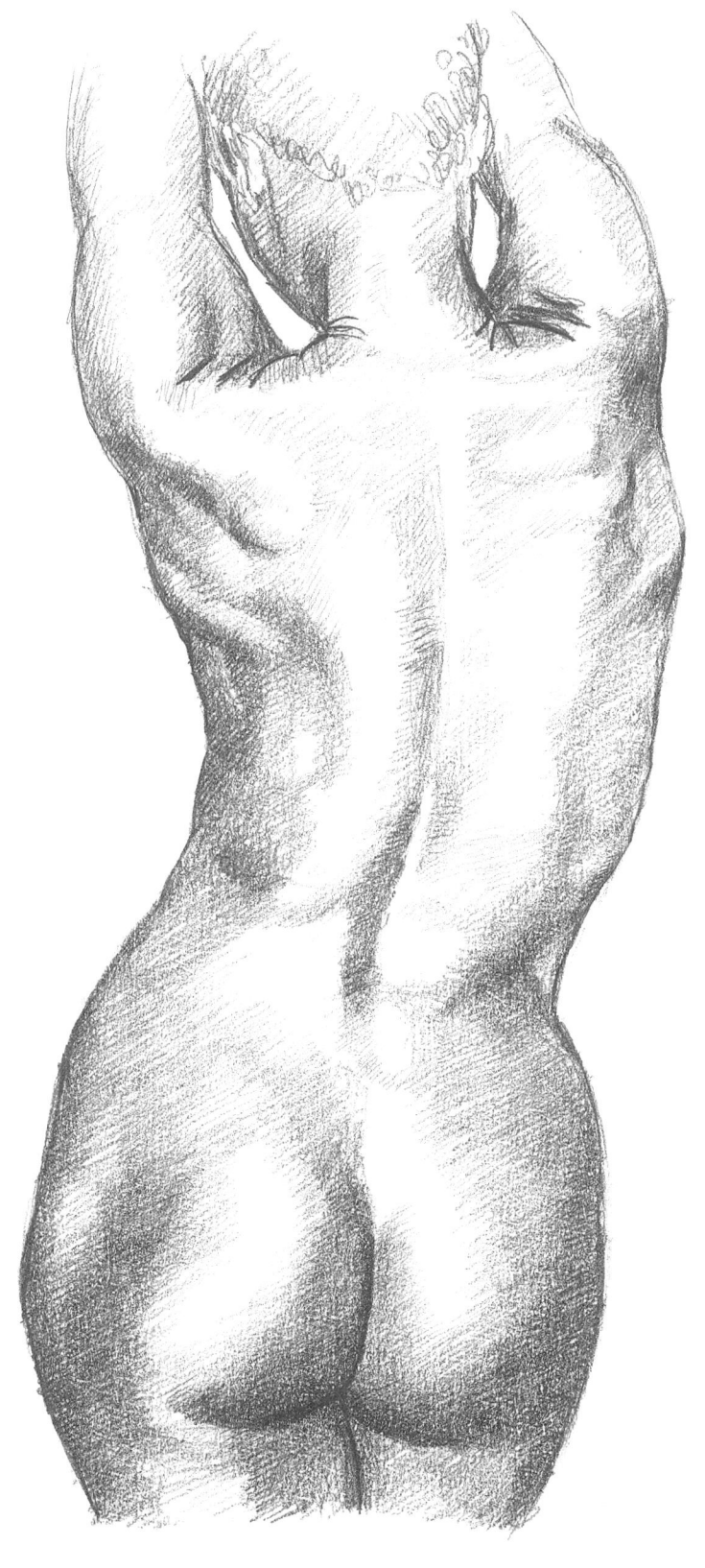

Skeleton of the head and torso

Front view

The thorax is the area of the trunk between the neck and the abdomen, including the sternum or breast bone, the 12 ribs or costae, and the 12 thoracic vertebrae. These make up the thoracic cage (the ribcage) which protects the heart, lungs, and viscera. Below the thorax, the abdomen is made up of the lumbar vertebrae or column, and the pelvic bones.

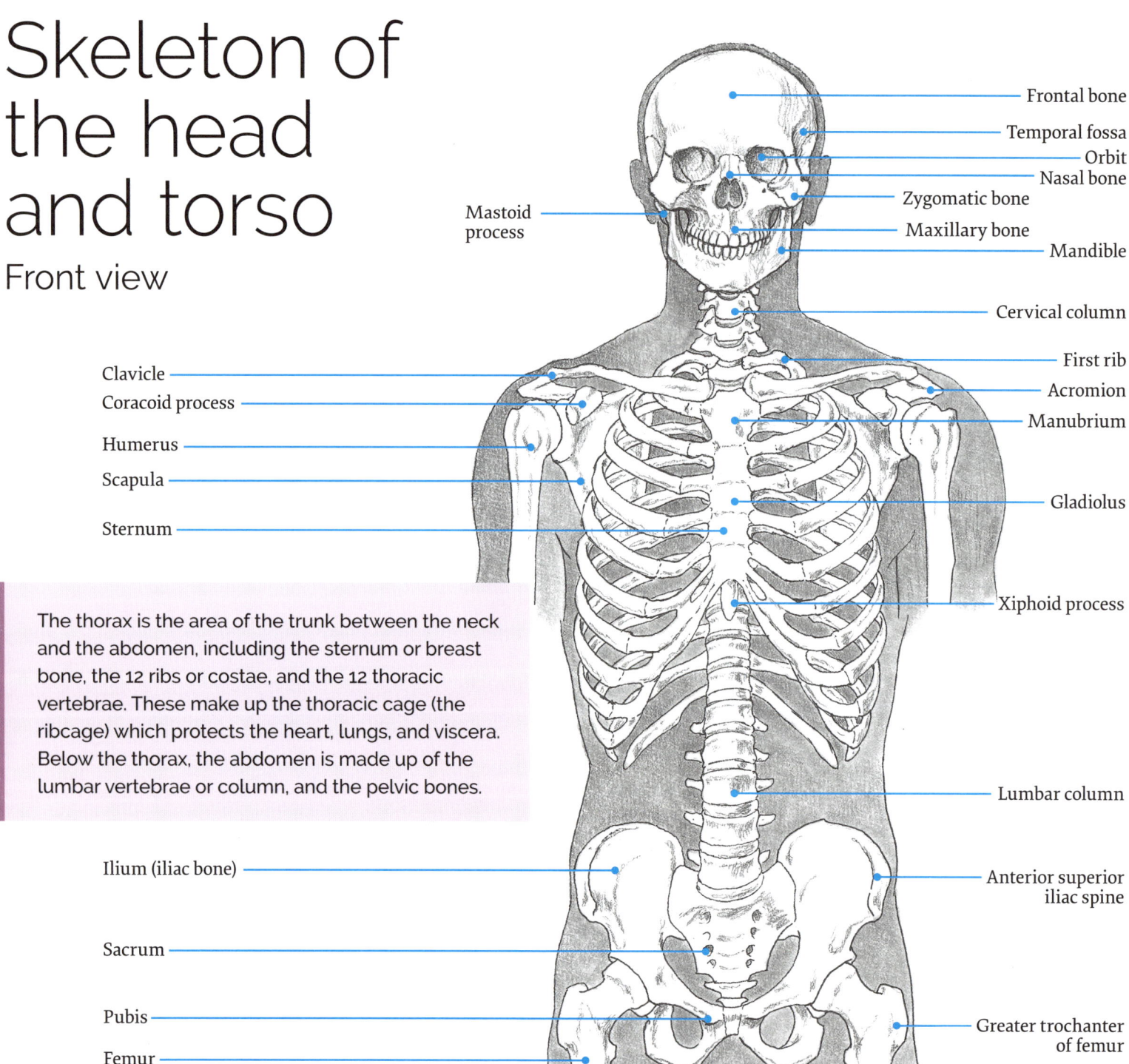

THE TORSO IN DETAIL

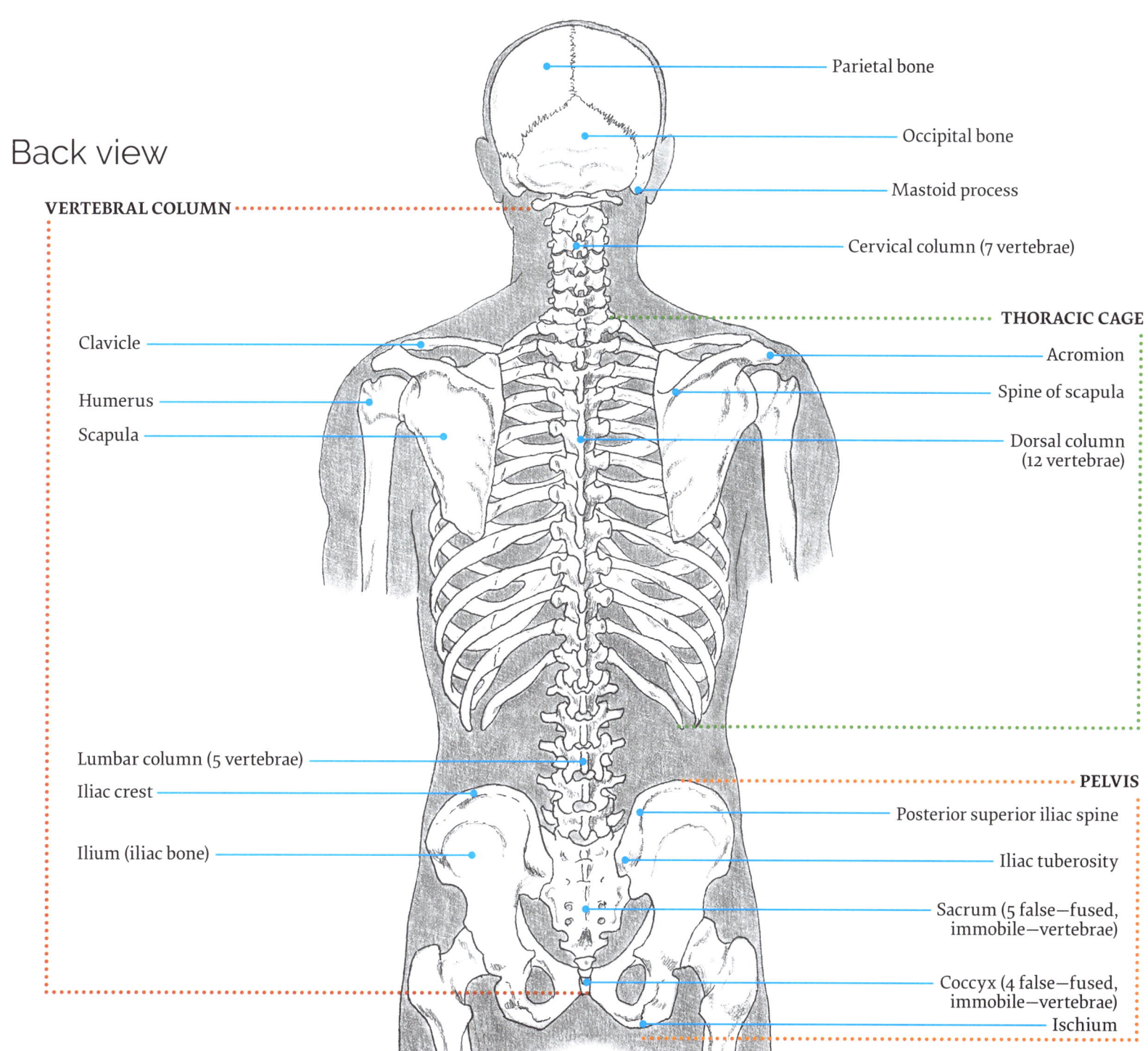

THE TORSO IN DETAIL

Side view

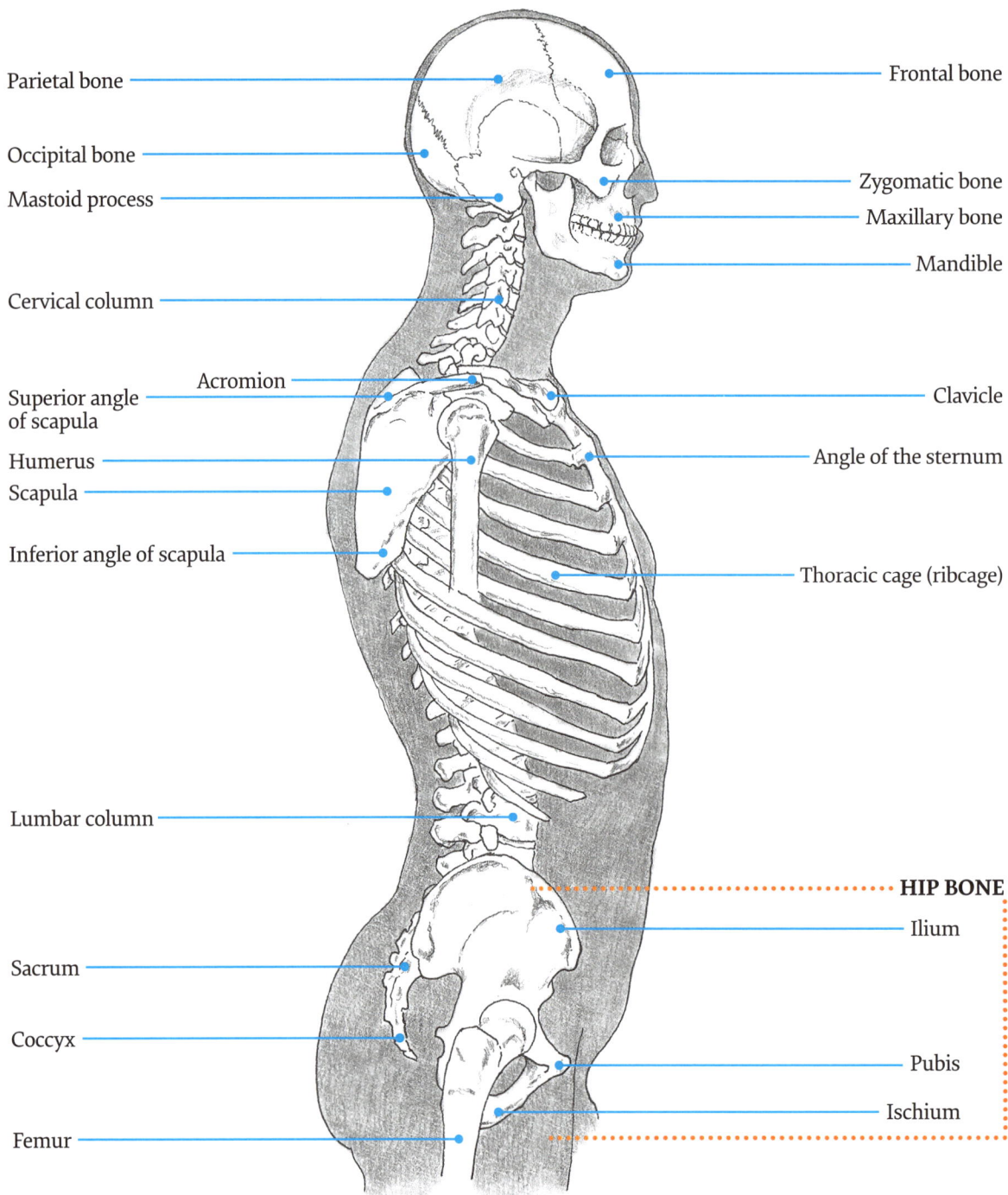

The vertebral column
Side view

We examine the vertebral column by itself here, because it is such an important part of the whole skeleton that it needs to be seen separately, without the distractions of the ribs and the pelvis. Note the curved form, and the way the parts are larger at the lower end and smaller at the higher end – a brilliant piece of natural architecture.

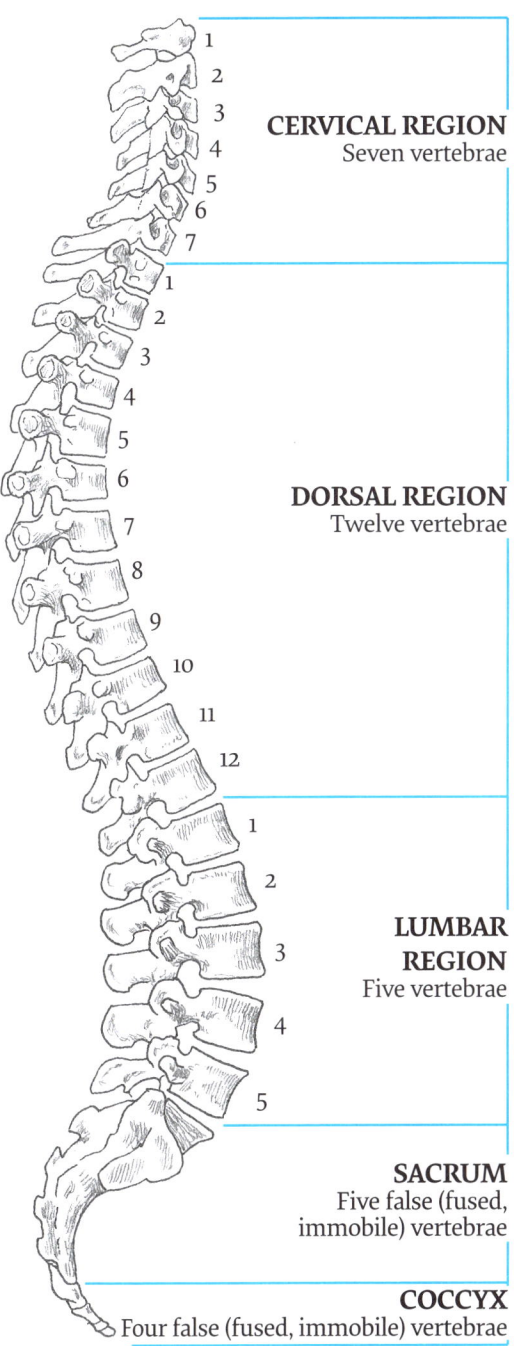

CERVICAL REGION
Seven vertebrae

DORSAL REGION
Twelve vertebrae

LUMBAR REGION
Five vertebrae

SACRUM
Five false (fused, immobile) vertebrae

COCCYX
Four false (fused, immobile) vertebrae

The pelvis

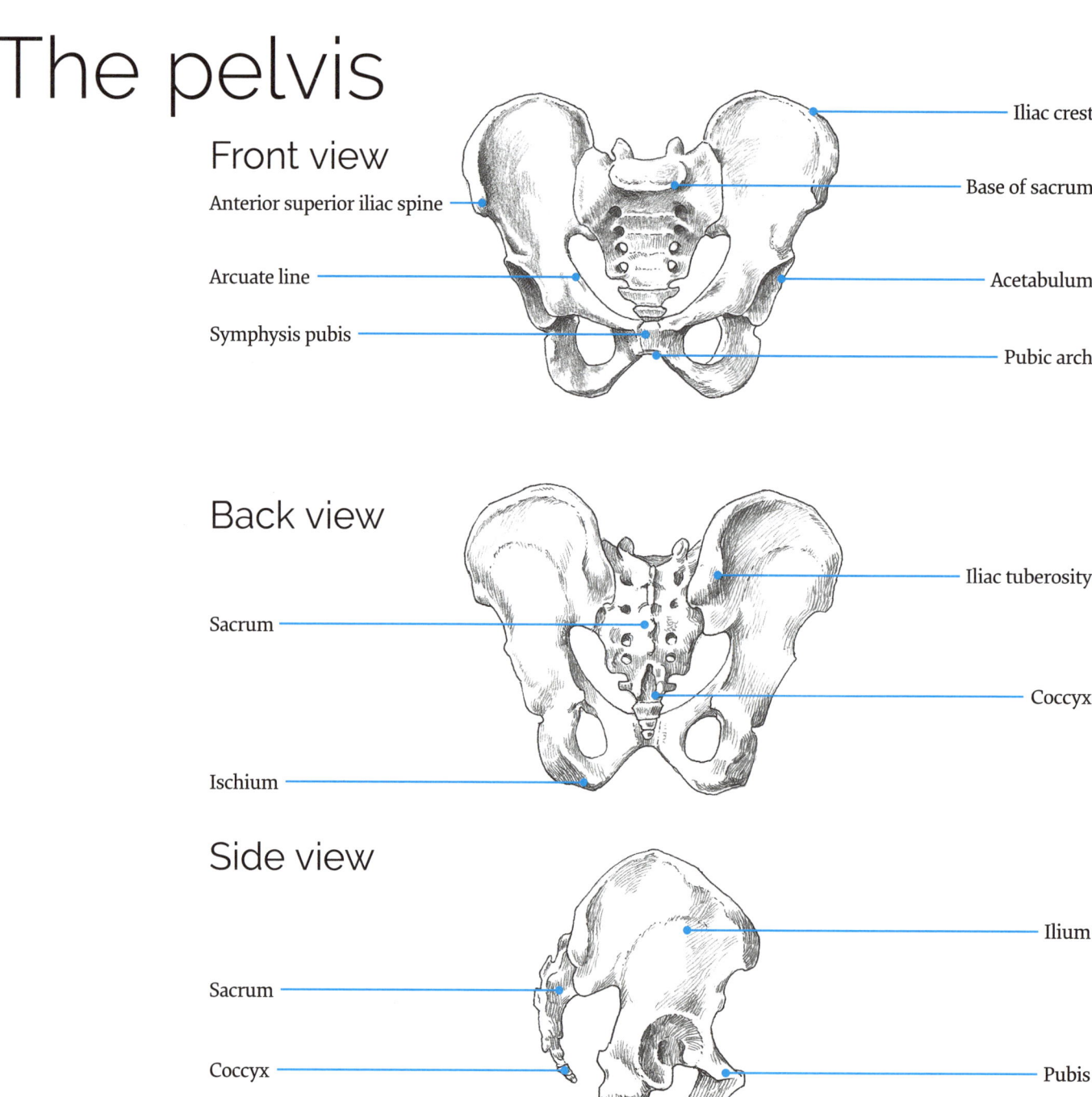

Muscles of the trunk and neck

Front view

The muscles of the trunk are in the main quite large and fairly flat in shape. They are layered over the ribcage and pelvis and cover the big joints of the hips and shoulders. There are deeper layers of muscle in the back that sometimes help shape the more superficial muscles and we'll look at these later in the chapter (see pages 98–100).

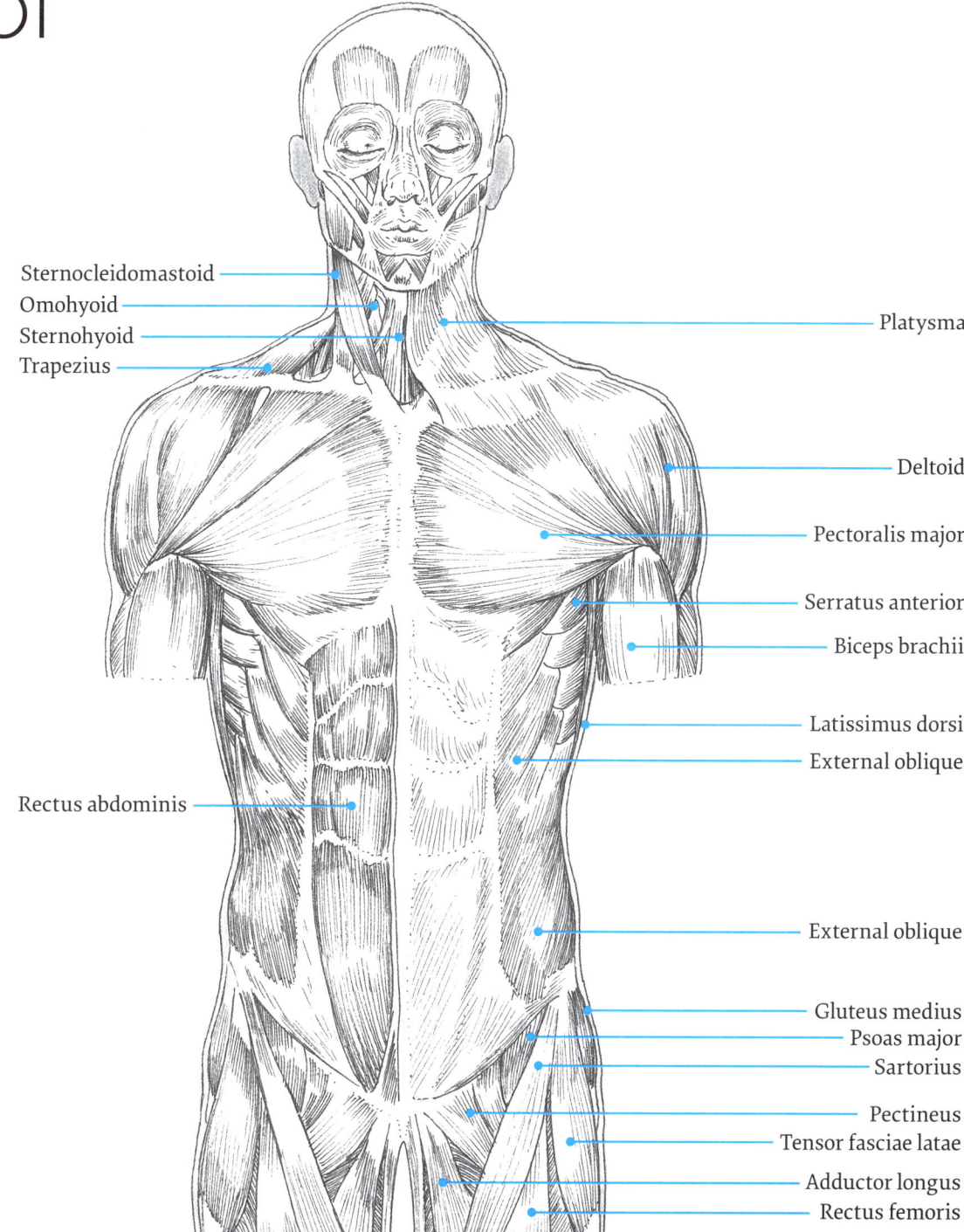

THE TORSO IN DETAIL

Back view

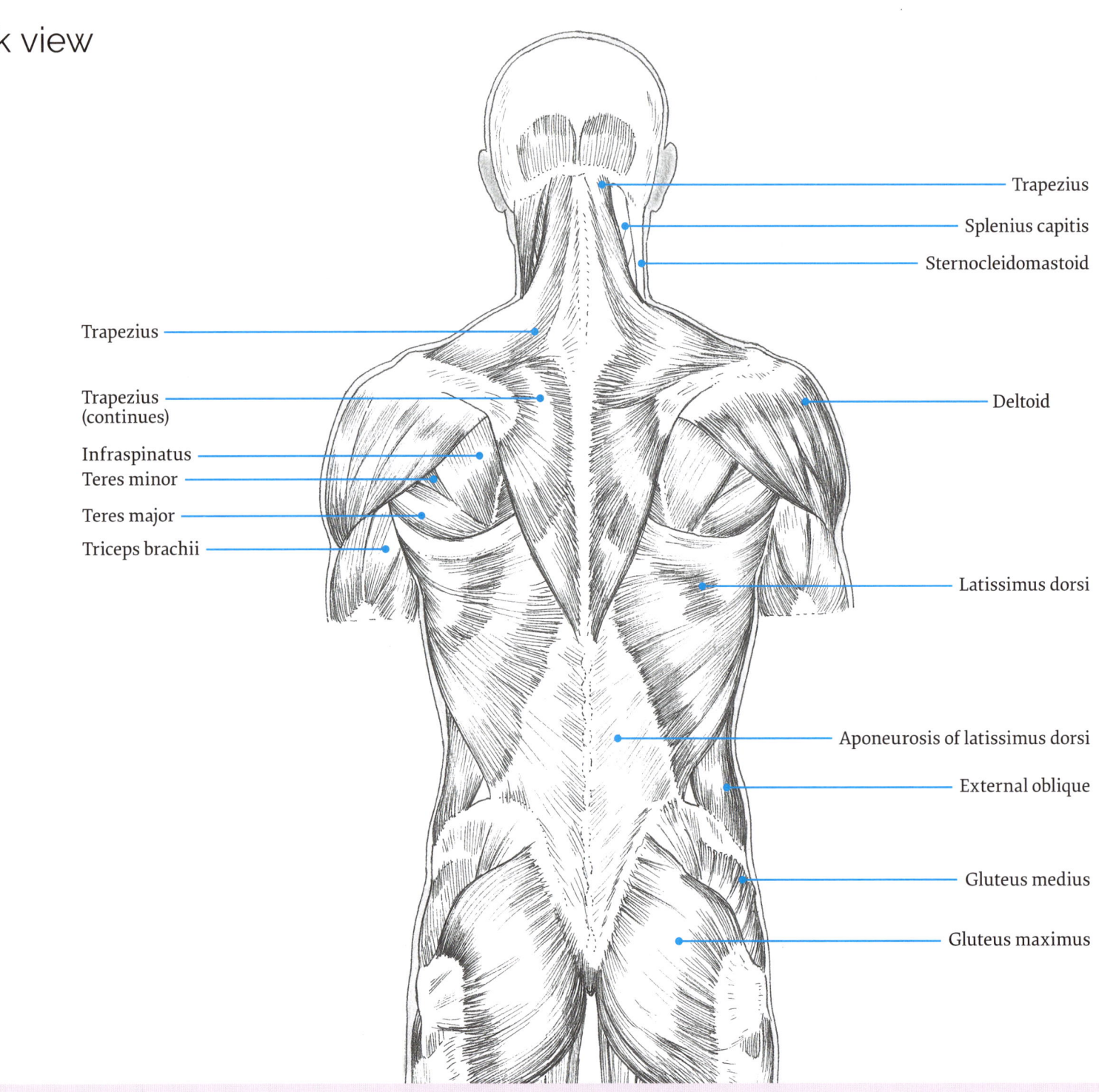

92 THE TORSO IN DETAIL

Side view

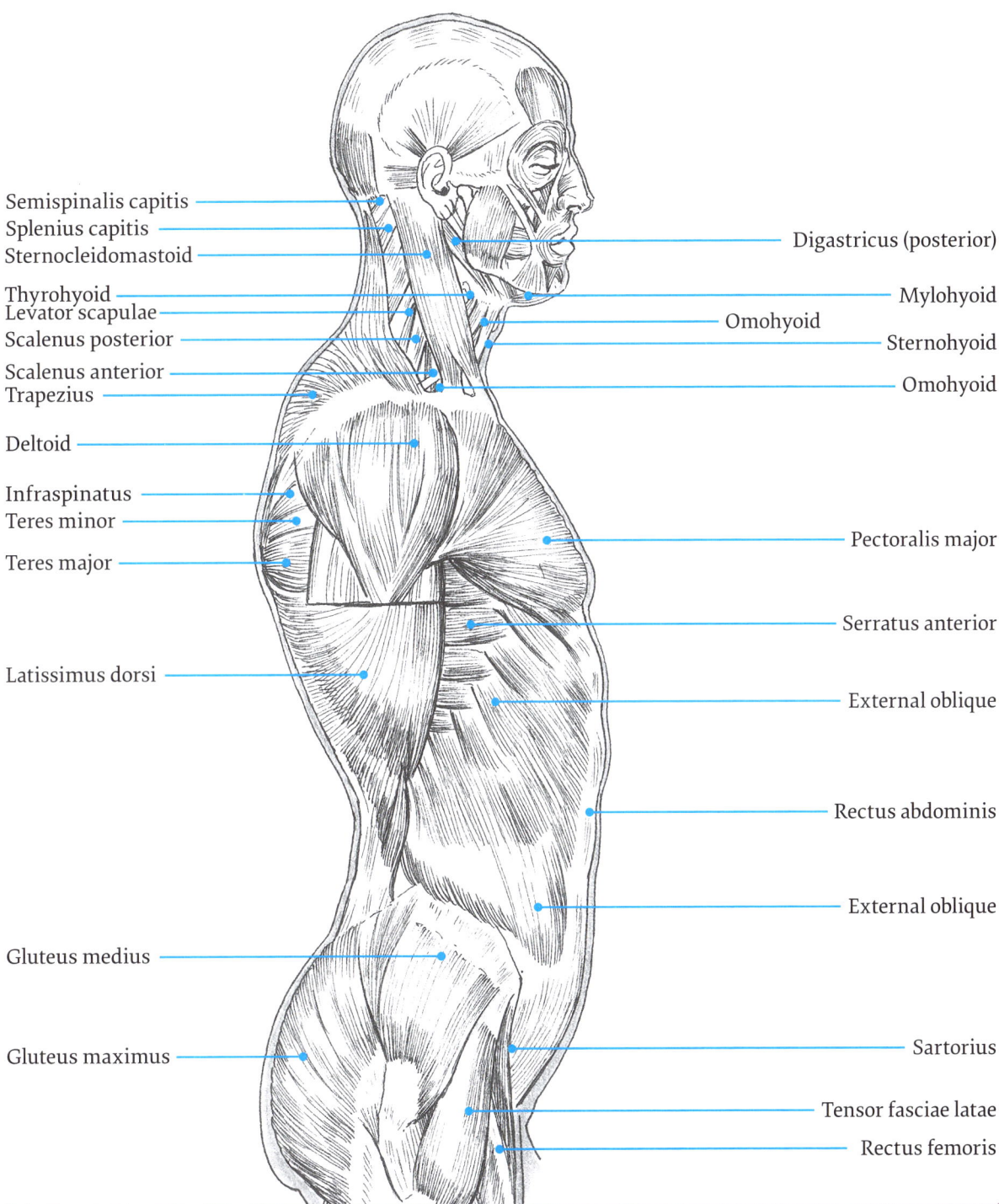

THE TORSO IN DETAIL

Muscles and bones of the torso

Because so much of the skeleton is hidden, it may be difficult to differentiate between muscle and bone. However, listed below are the bones that are visible on most bodies of average build. There may be some people with more developed areas of fatty deposit that disguise the less obvious ones, but usually the following bones can be seen:

- Clavicle
- Sternum
- Parts of the scapula
- Seven cervical vertebrae
- First and twelfth thoracic vertebrae, in certain positions
- First and twelfth ribs
- Pubis
- Iliac crest
- Iliac tuberosity
- Anterior superior iliac spine

For an artist, recognizing these bony points on the surface of the body is very useful, since they make good measuring points. Unlike the muscles and fatty parts, they do not move.

ABDOMINAL MUSCLES flex torso forwards into curled position, straightening arch of lumbar vertebrae. Compress viscera to force expiration, or strain in childbirth and defecation. The three layers create strong walls on either side of the abdomen.

DELTOID contraction of entire muscle will raise arm to horizontal plane. Partial contraction will result in pulling the arm backward or forward.

ERECTOR SPINAE GROUP made up of the LONGISSIMUS, the SPINALIS and the ILIO-COSTALIS. Lift torso when rising from stooped position. Straighten spine, extend spine backwards or to either side. Draw pelvis backwards and upwards. Help support the weight of the head. Sometimes referred to as the Sacrospinalis.

INFRASPINATUS rotates arm outwards and backwards.

INTERNAL and EXTERNAL OBLIQUE flex trunk. Isolated action of one side turns anterior surface of trunk to that side. Bends spinal column laterally. Co-operates with the other abdominal muscles. Simultaneous contraction of muscles of both sides, results in forward bending of trunk. If chest is fixed, pelvis is brought into flexion. Constricts abdominal cavity, ribs are compressed and pulled downwards.

LATISSIMUS DORSI throws back shoulders. Draws arm backwards and towards the centre line. Rotates it inwards and lowers it. If shoulders are fixed, it raises trunk and suspends it.

LEVATOR SCAPULAE steadies scapula during movements of the arms.

PECTORALIS MAJOR draws arm forward, rotates it inwards and lowers arm.

QUADRATUS LUMBORUM holds firm the twelfth rib and pulls lumbar region of the spine to its own side and helps straighten or raise pelvis.

RECTUS ABDOMINIS flexes trunk.

RHOMBOIDS MAJOR and MINOR elevate, rotate scapula. Draw it towards the median line.

SEMISPINALIS CAPITIS two deep neck muscles beneath trapezius, where they help to draw head backwards or rotate it to either side.

SERRATUS ANTERIOR draws scapula forwards and laterally. Helps trapezius in raising the arm above the horizontal plane.

SERRATUS POSTERIOR MUSCLES steady the erector spinae group. Superior pair elevate upper ribs, helping us to breathe in. Inferior pair are expiratory, depressing lower ribs as we breathe out.

SPLENIUS CAPITIS pulls head backwards and sideways, rotates head.

SPLENIUS CERVICIS pulls neck backwards and sideways, rotates atlas (top vertebra) along with head.

SUBCLAVIUS fixes and pulls clavicle downwards and forwards.

SUBSCAPULARIS (beneath scapula) rotates arm inward.

SUPRASPINATUS raises and rotates arm outwards.

TERES MAJOR raises arm forwards or sideways from trunk. Rotates arm inwards.

TERES MINOR rotates arm outwards.

TRAPEZIUS extends head, inclines it to one side and turns head in opposite direction. Middle part lifts scapula. Inferior part lowers scapula.

Look out too for the suprasternal notch: this is the space between the two clavicles where they meet the manubrium or the upper part of the sternum (breast bone). It is a useful marker for measuring the head and shoulders because it remains at a fixed point at the base of the neck. The notch is visible on the vast majority of humans.

There are more than a hundred muscles in the torso, and they tend to be paired on either side of the body's medial line, and layered in groups. A series of divided muscles support and articulate the spine. There are broad, thin sheets of muscle enfolding the abdomen and the pelvis. Thick, heavy muscles give strength to the shoulders and hips. The diagonally arranged muscles of the ribcage help with breathing and the flexibility of the upper torso.

In the box on the opposite page, I have detailed the major muscles of the torso and some of the movements they produce by contracting or flexing. Try performing some of these movements and feeling your own muscles at work.

Front view

First we show the relaxed torso, in order to relate the muscles to the bone structure.

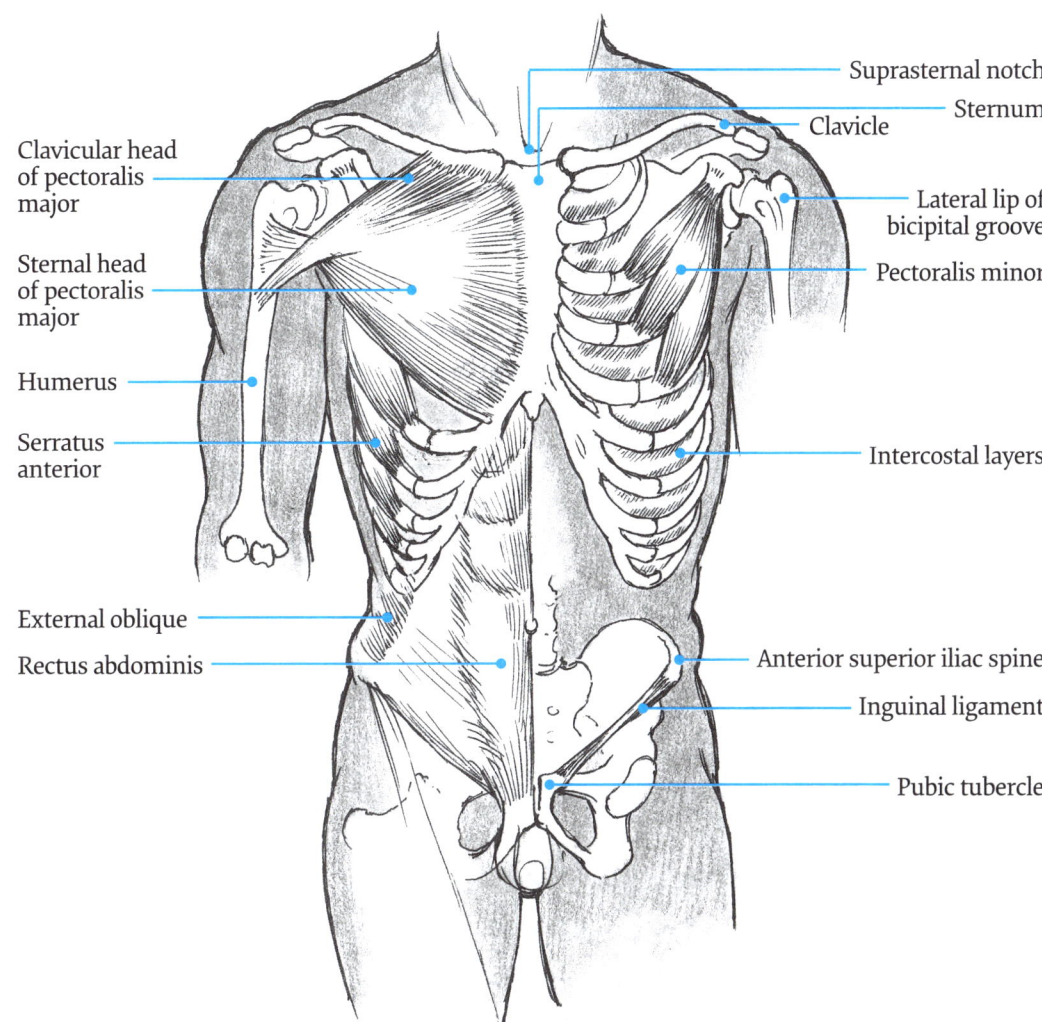

THE TORSO IN DETAIL

Side view
Showing the internal oblique

Side view
Showing the external oblique

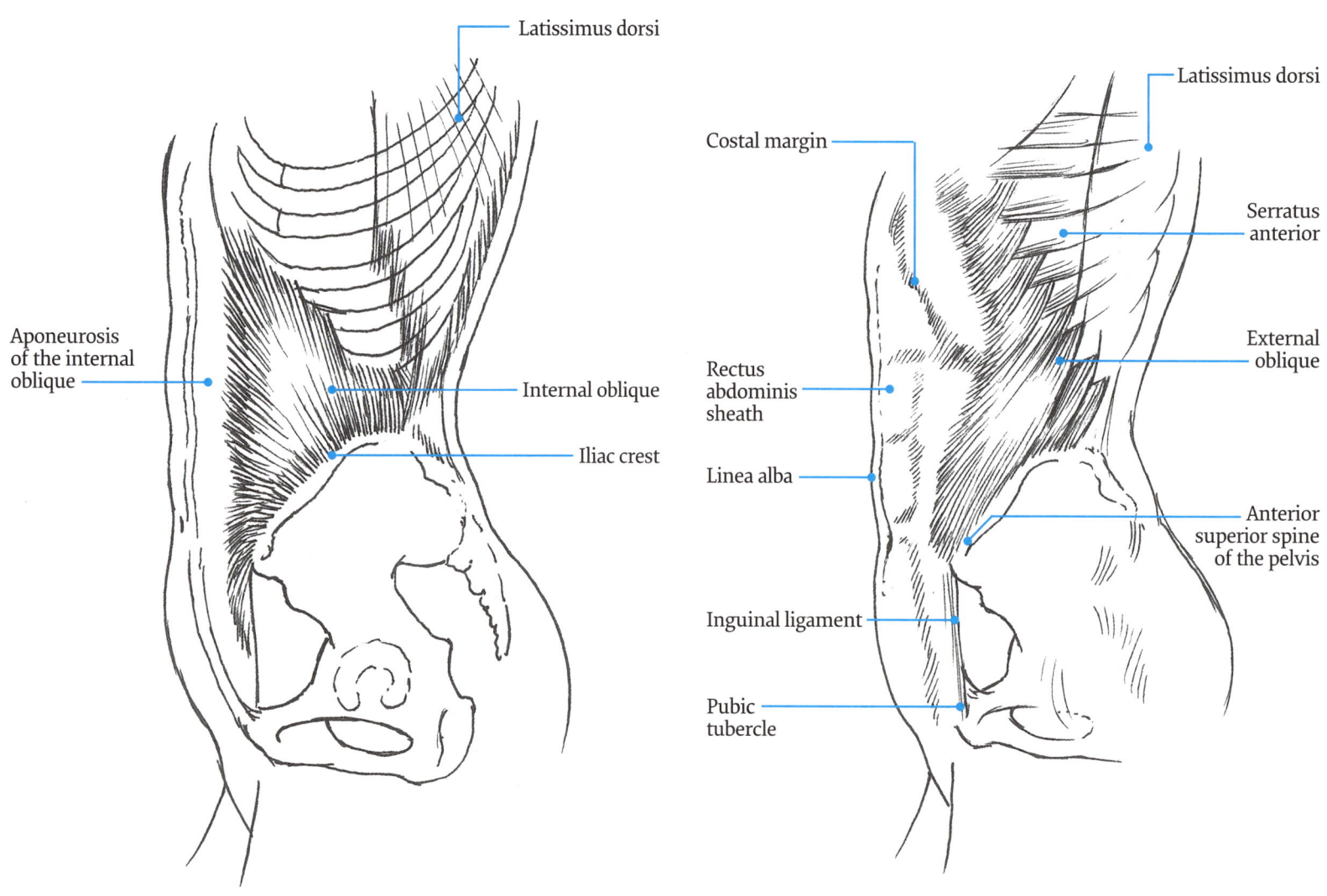

96 THE TORSO IN DETAIL

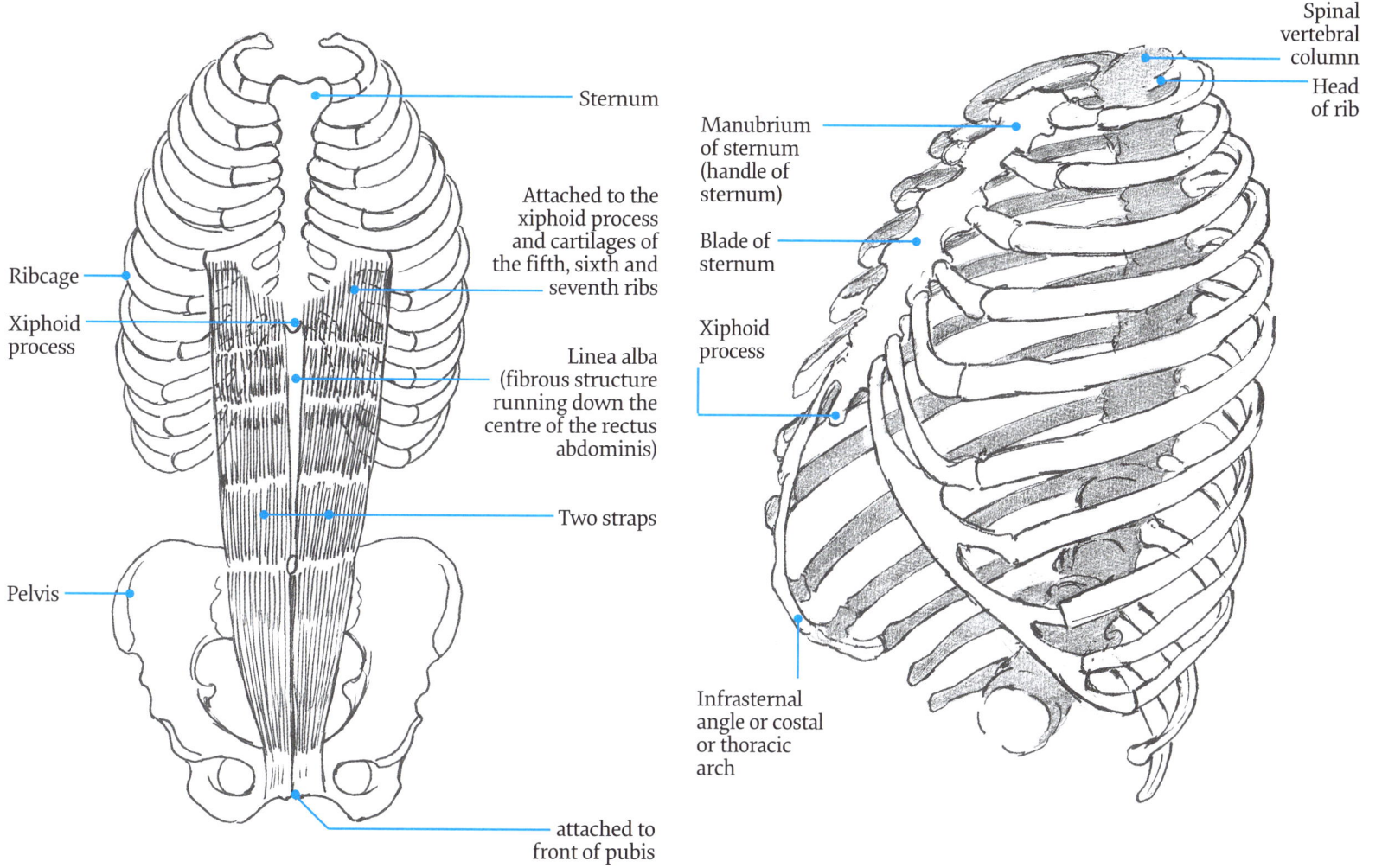

Deep muscles of the spine

This diagram helps to clarify the muscles along the spinal vertebrae, shown in three columns overlaying each other. The three muscles of the erector spinae group are shown on the right.

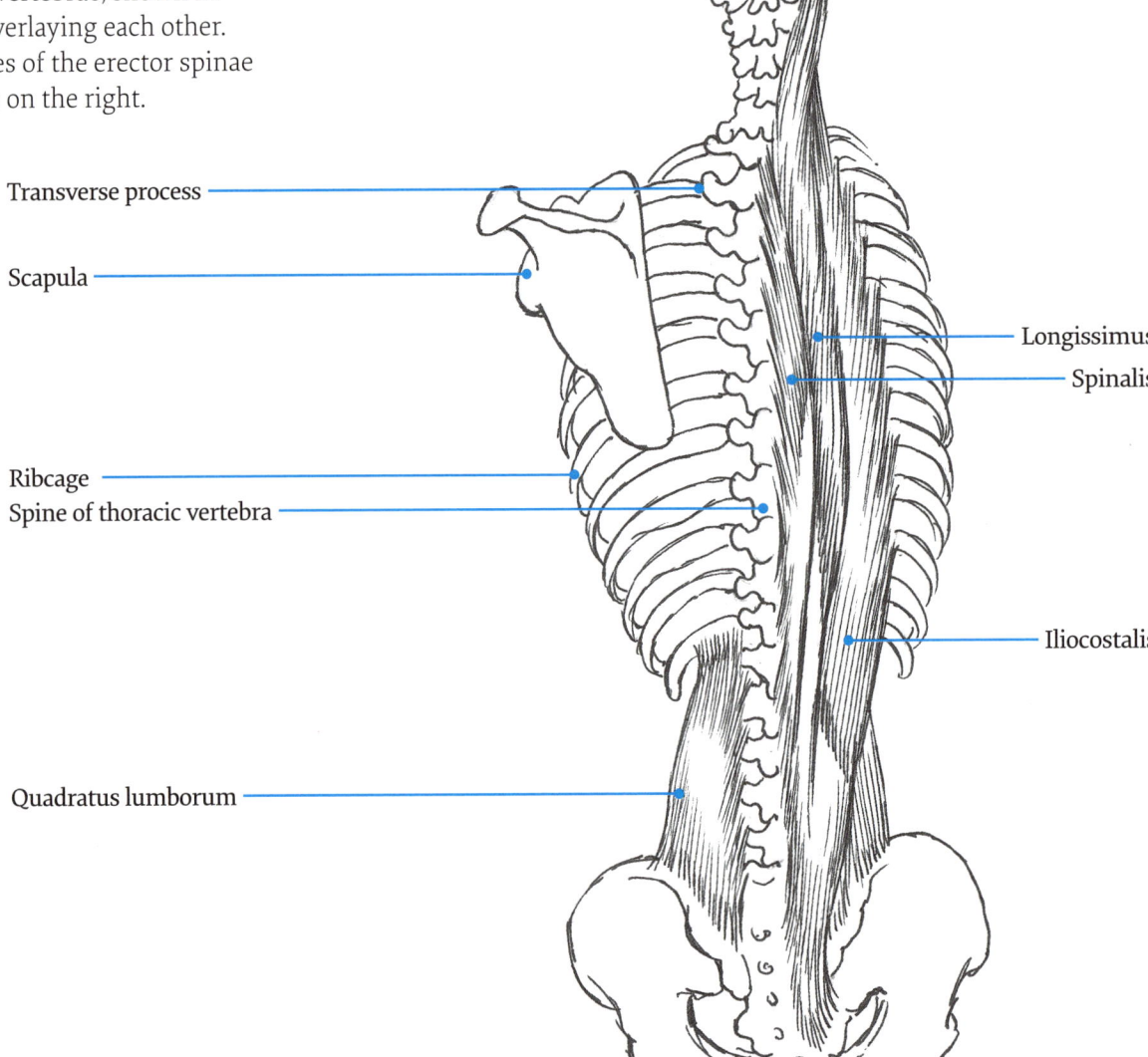

- Mastoid process
- Transverse process
- Scapula
- Longissimus
- Spinalis
- Ribcage
- Spine of thoracic vertebra
- Iliocostalis
- Quadratus lumborum

THE TORSO IN DETAIL

Mid-depth muscles of the back

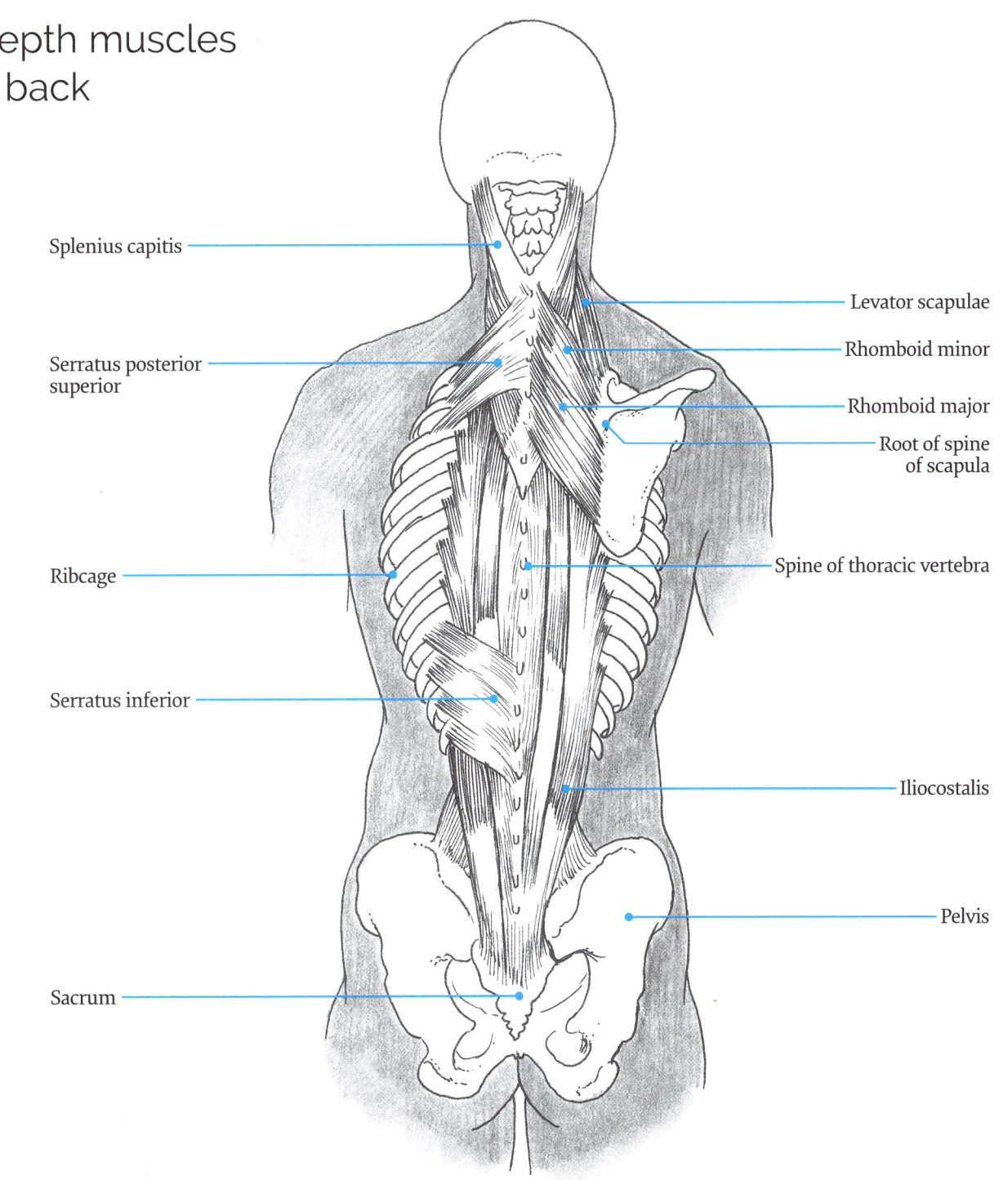

THE TORSO IN DETAIL

Superficial muscles of the back

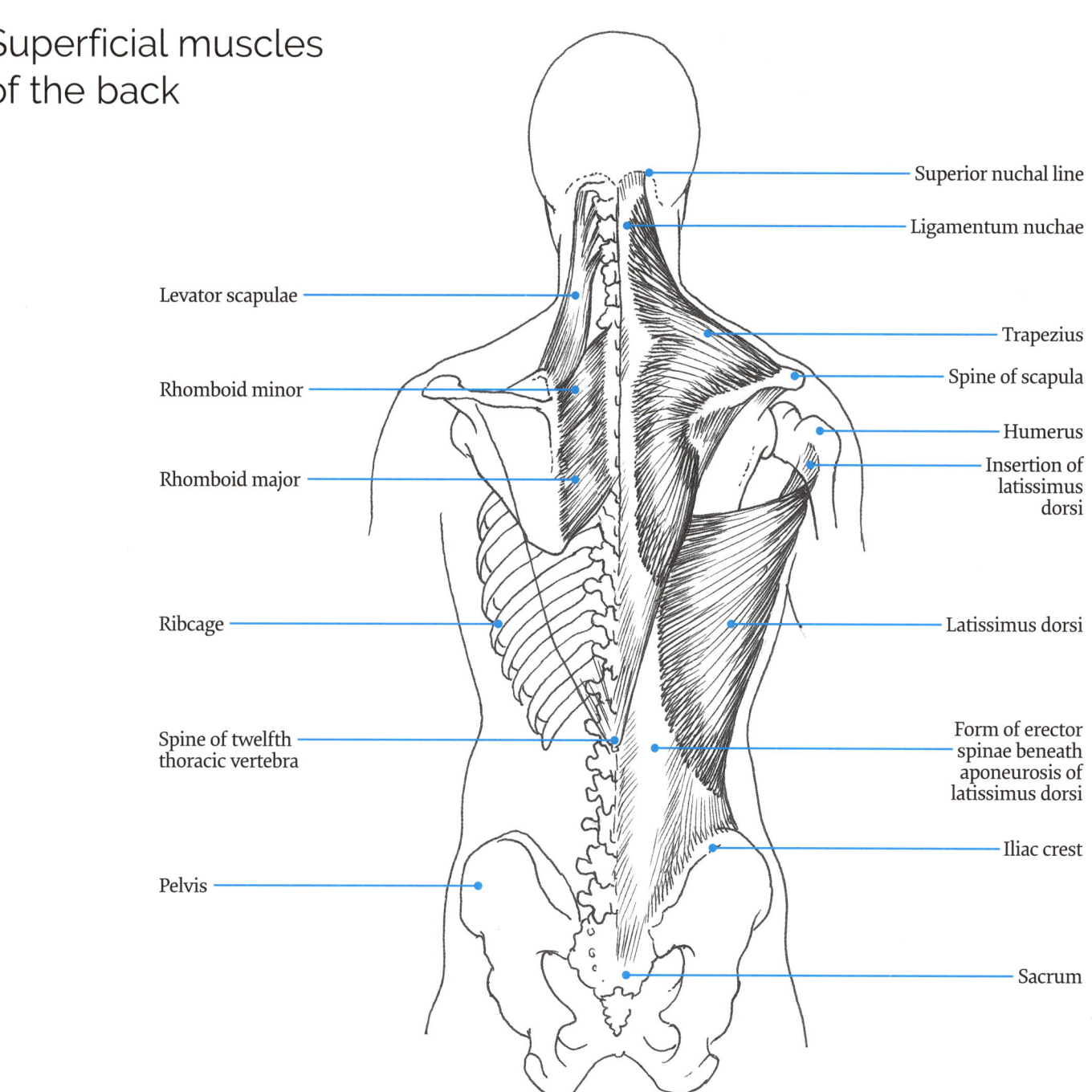

Views of the torso
Front view of the male torso with arms raised

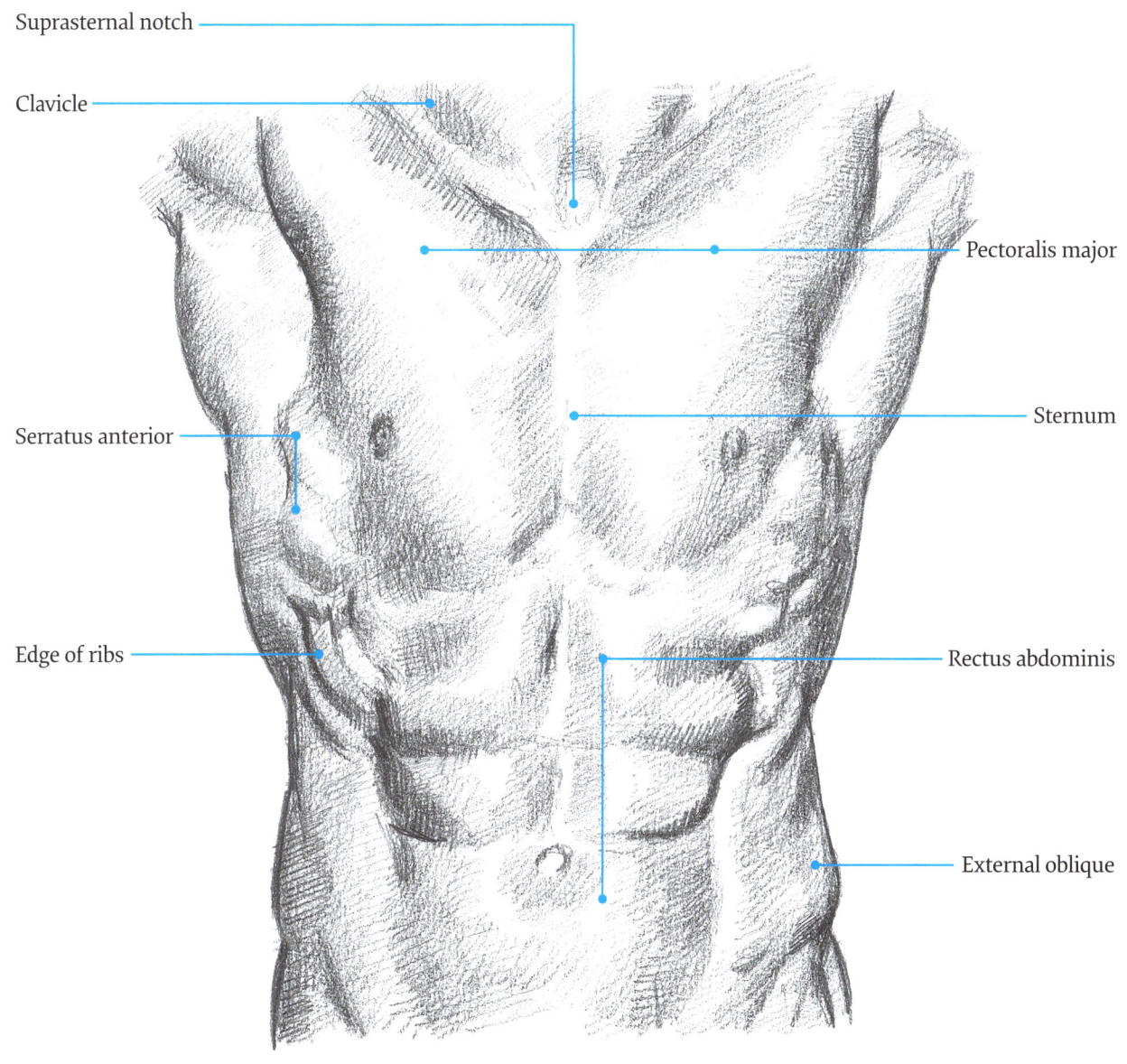

- Suprasternal notch
- Clavicle
- Pectoralis major
- Serratus anterior
- Sternum
- Edge of ribs
- Rectus abdominis
- External oblique

THE TORSO IN DETAIL

Side view of the male torso with arms raised

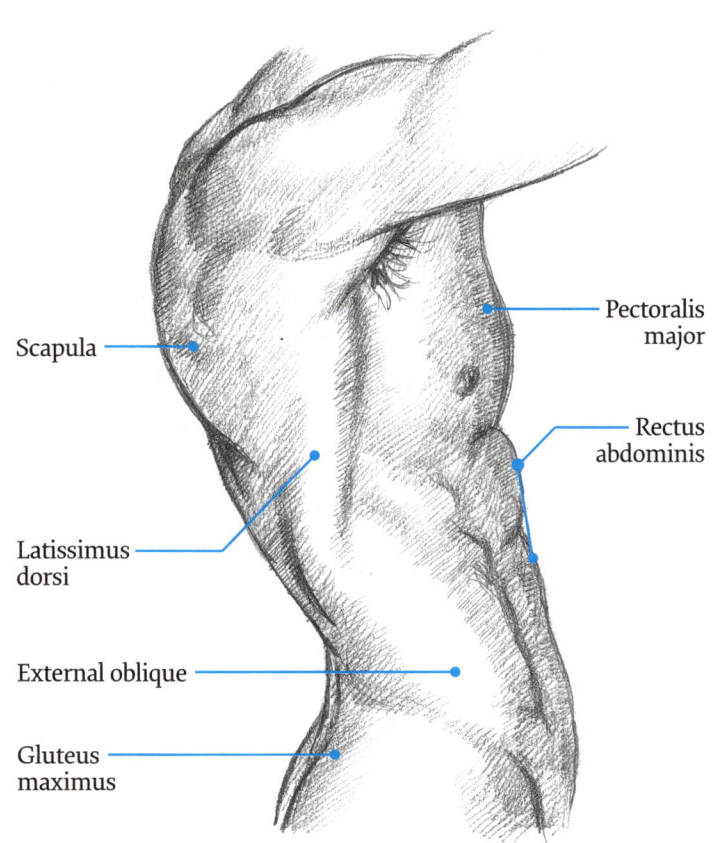

- Scapula
- Latissimus dorsi
- External oblique
- Gluteus maximus
- Pectoralis major
- Rectus abdominis

Back view of the male torso with arms raised

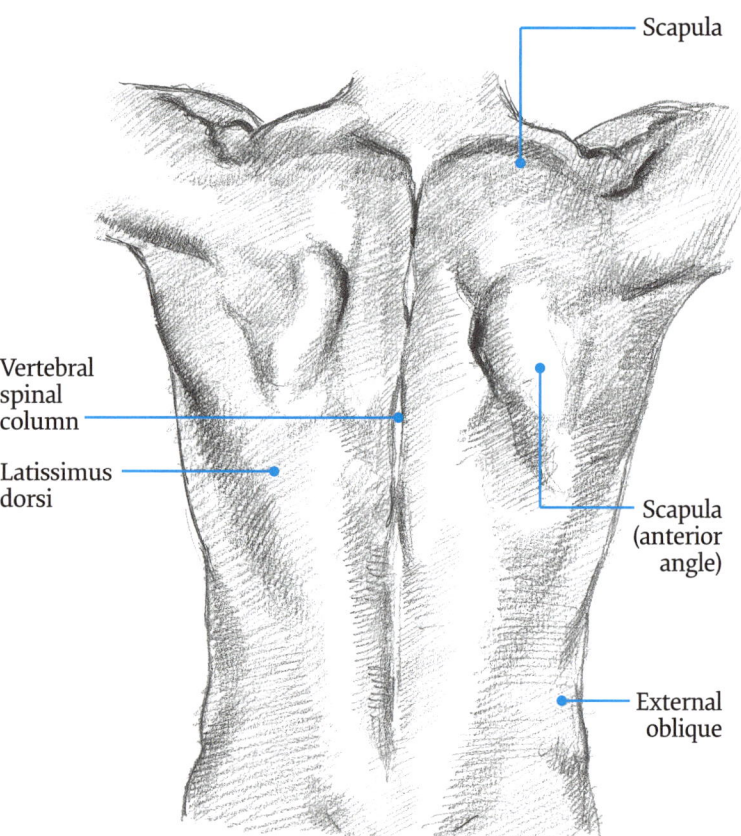

- Vertebral spinal column
- Latissimus dorsi
- Scapula
- Scapula (anterior angle)
- External oblique

THE TORSO IN DETAIL

Back view of the female torso with arms raised and spine curved

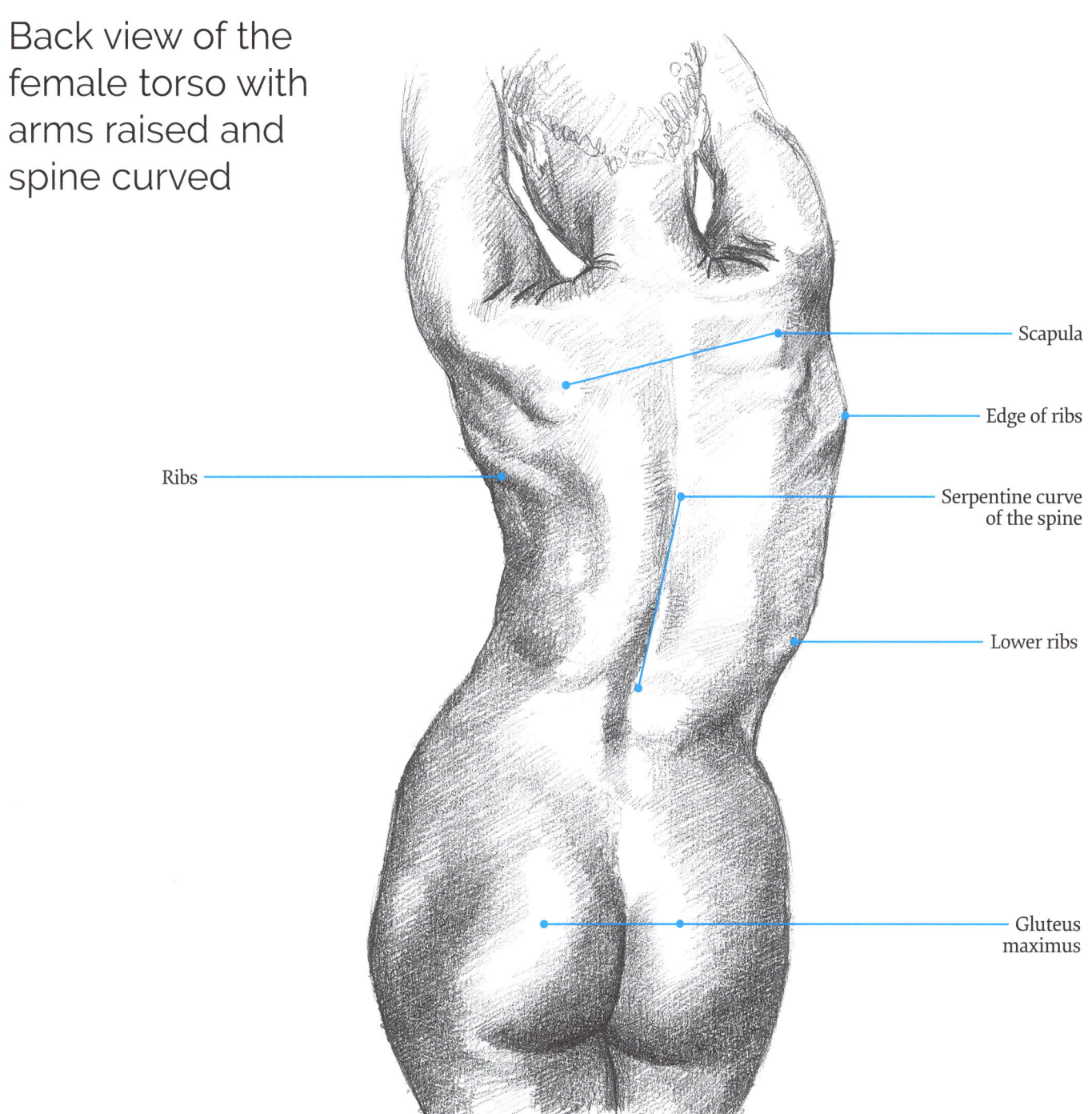

- Scapula
- Edge of ribs
- Ribs
- Serpentine curve of the spine
- Lower ribs
- Gluteus maximus

THE TORSO IN DETAIL

Supine view of the female torso, stretched

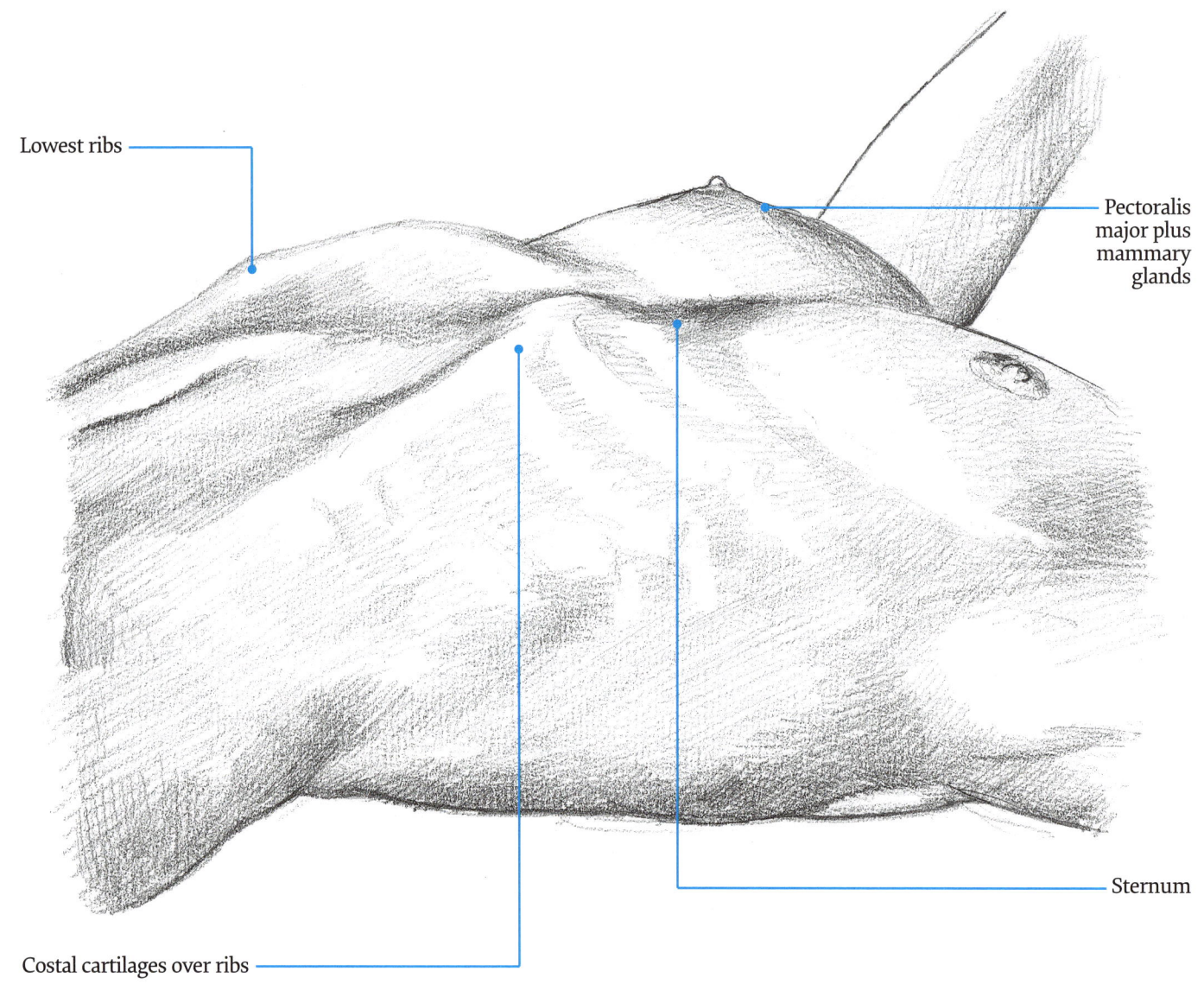

- Lowest ribs
- Pectoralis major plus mammary glands
- Sternum
- Costal cartilages over ribs

THE TORSO IN DETAIL

Side view of the male torso bending to the ground

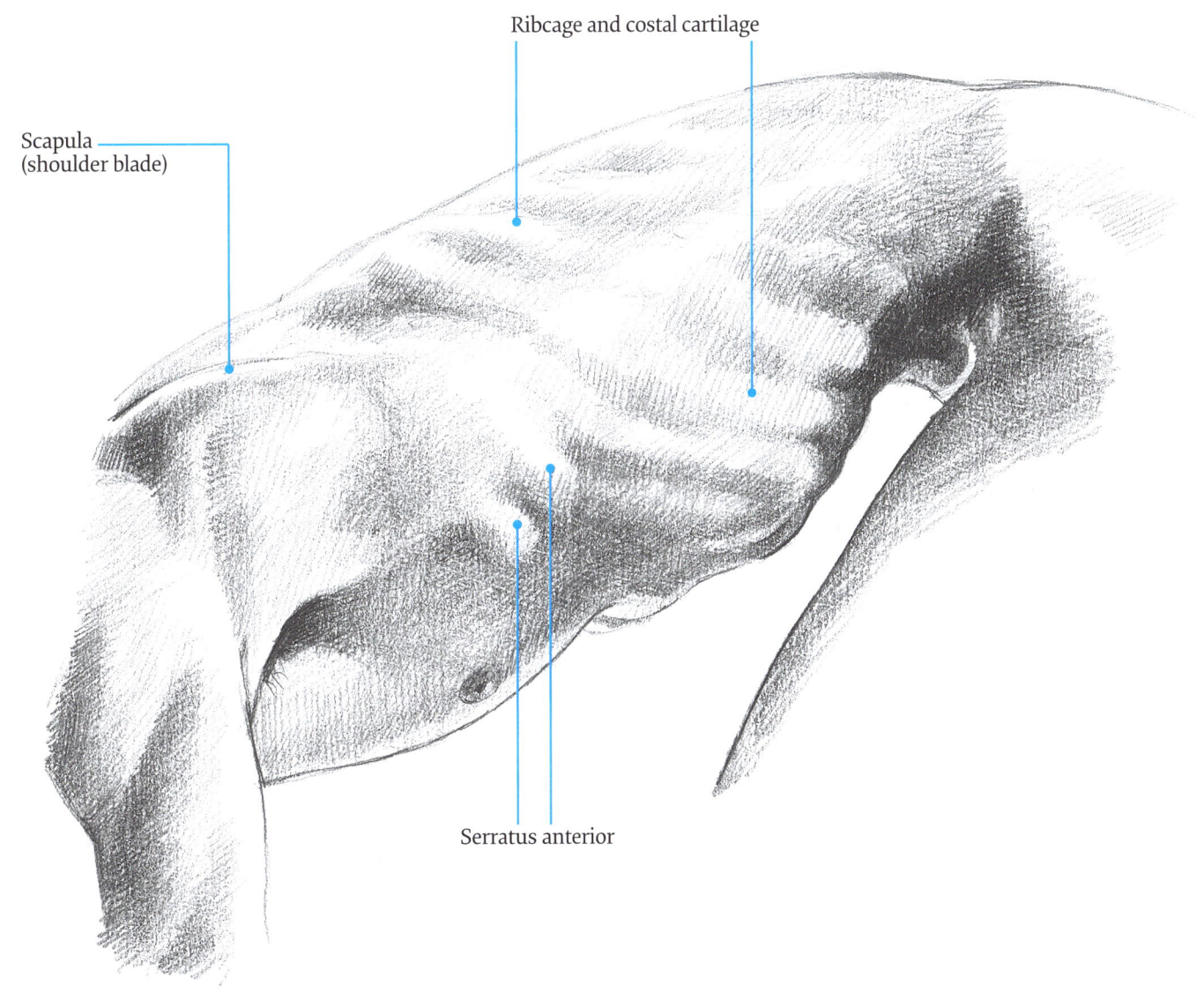

Scapula (shoulder blade)

Ribcage and costal cartilage

Serratus anterior

THE TORSO IN DETAIL

The male torso stretched backwards with arms raised

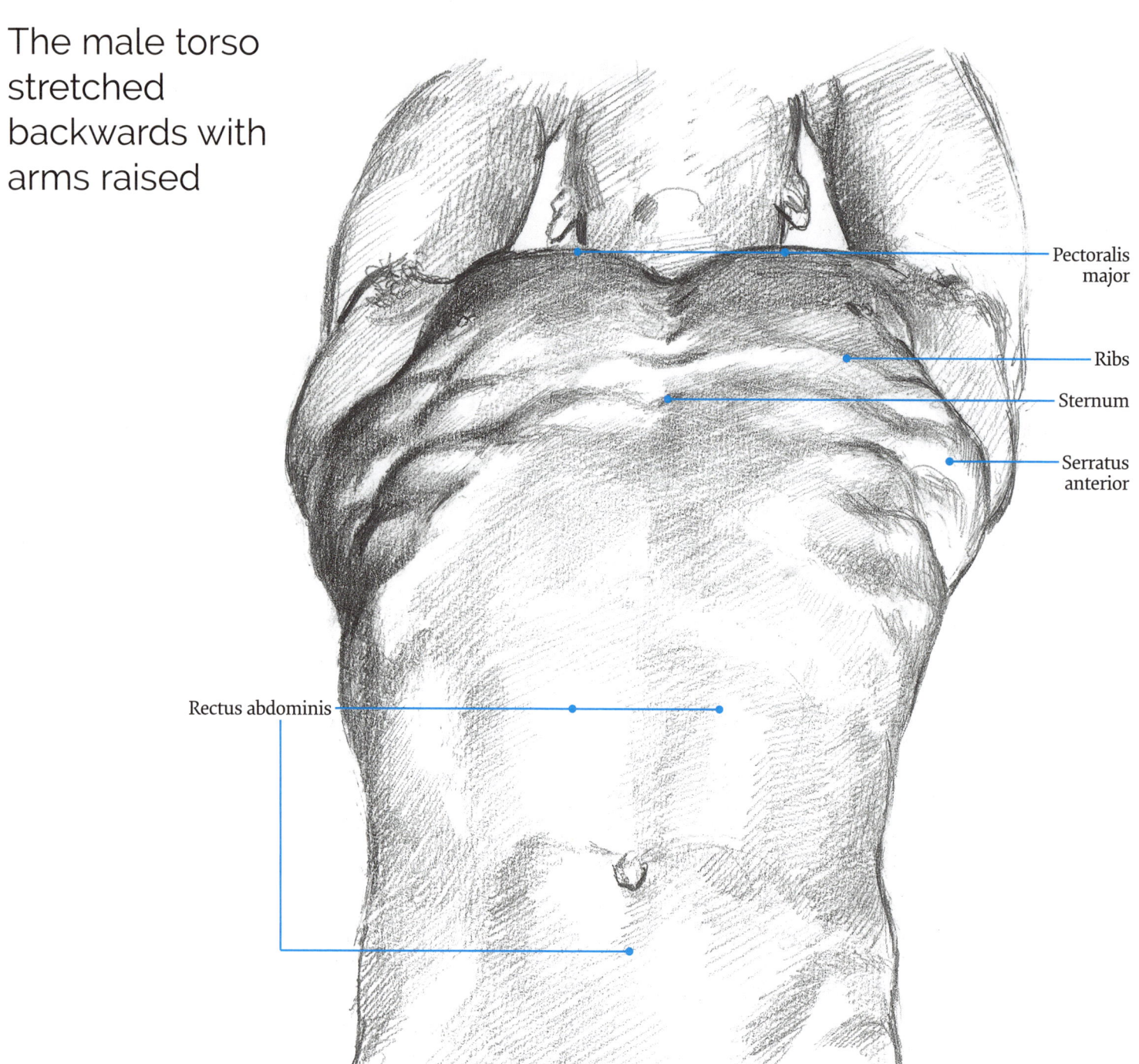

- Pectoralis major
- Ribs
- Sternum
- Serratus anterior
- Rectus abdominis

Back view of the female torso, reclining

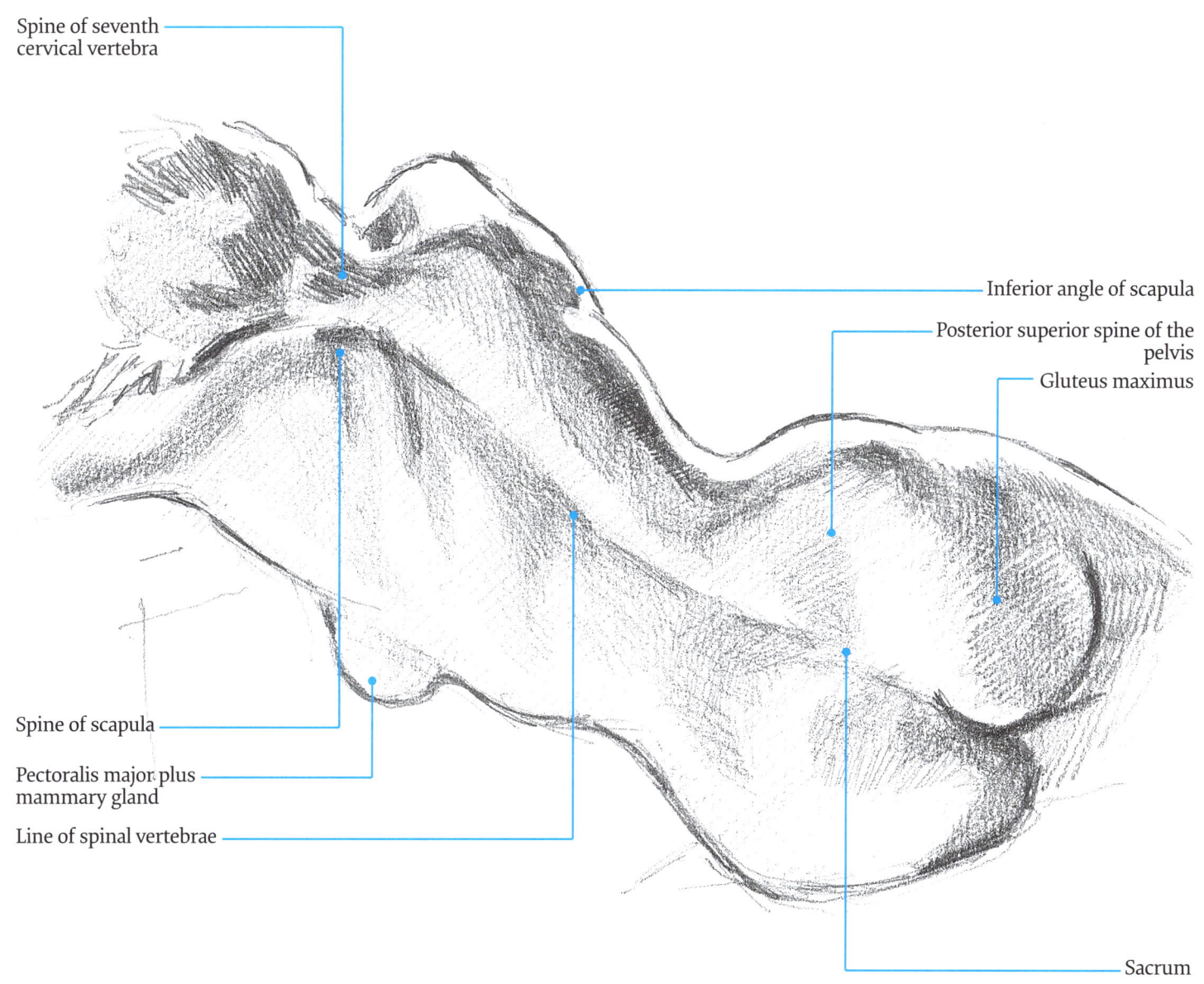

- Spine of seventh cervical vertebra
- Inferior angle of scapula
- Posterior superior spine of the pelvis
- Gluteus maximus
- Spine of scapula
- Pectoralis major plus mammary gland
- Line of spinal vertebrae
- Sacrum

THE TORSO IN DETAIL 107

Views of the torso after master artists

AFTER RAPHAEL (1483–1520)

The selection of master drawings on the next few pages shows how well these artists knew their anatomy despite the lack of medical knowledge at the time. The definition of the muscles and bone structure under the skin is beautifully rendered in these works, and they are worth studying in order to see how carefully the shapes under the skin were reproduced.

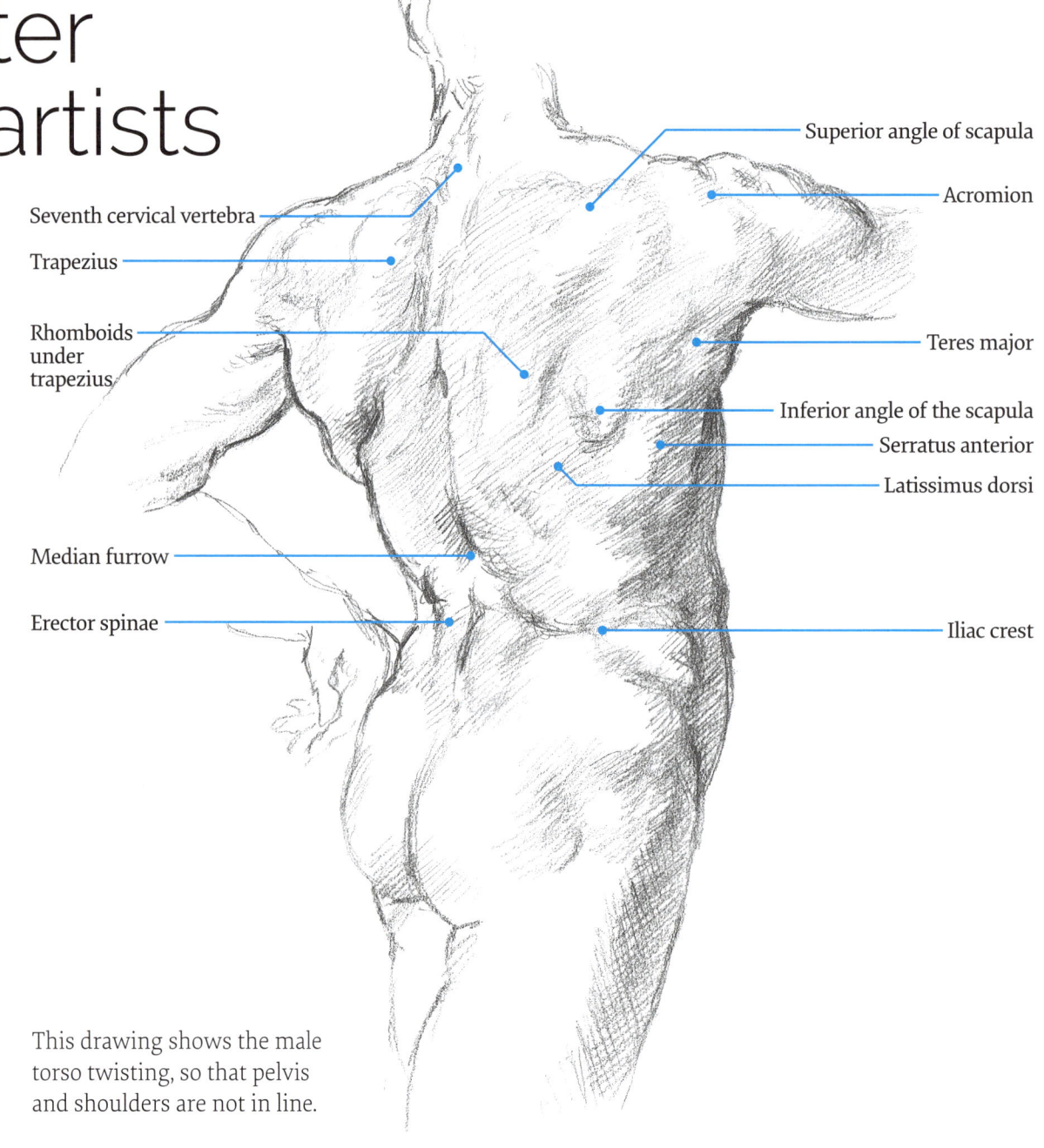

This drawing shows the male torso twisting, so that pelvis and shoulders are not in line.

108 THE TORSO IN DETAIL

AFTER SEBASTIANO DEL PIOMBO (c.1485–1547)

The front view of the torso also has a statuesque quality, partly due to the effect of the musculature.

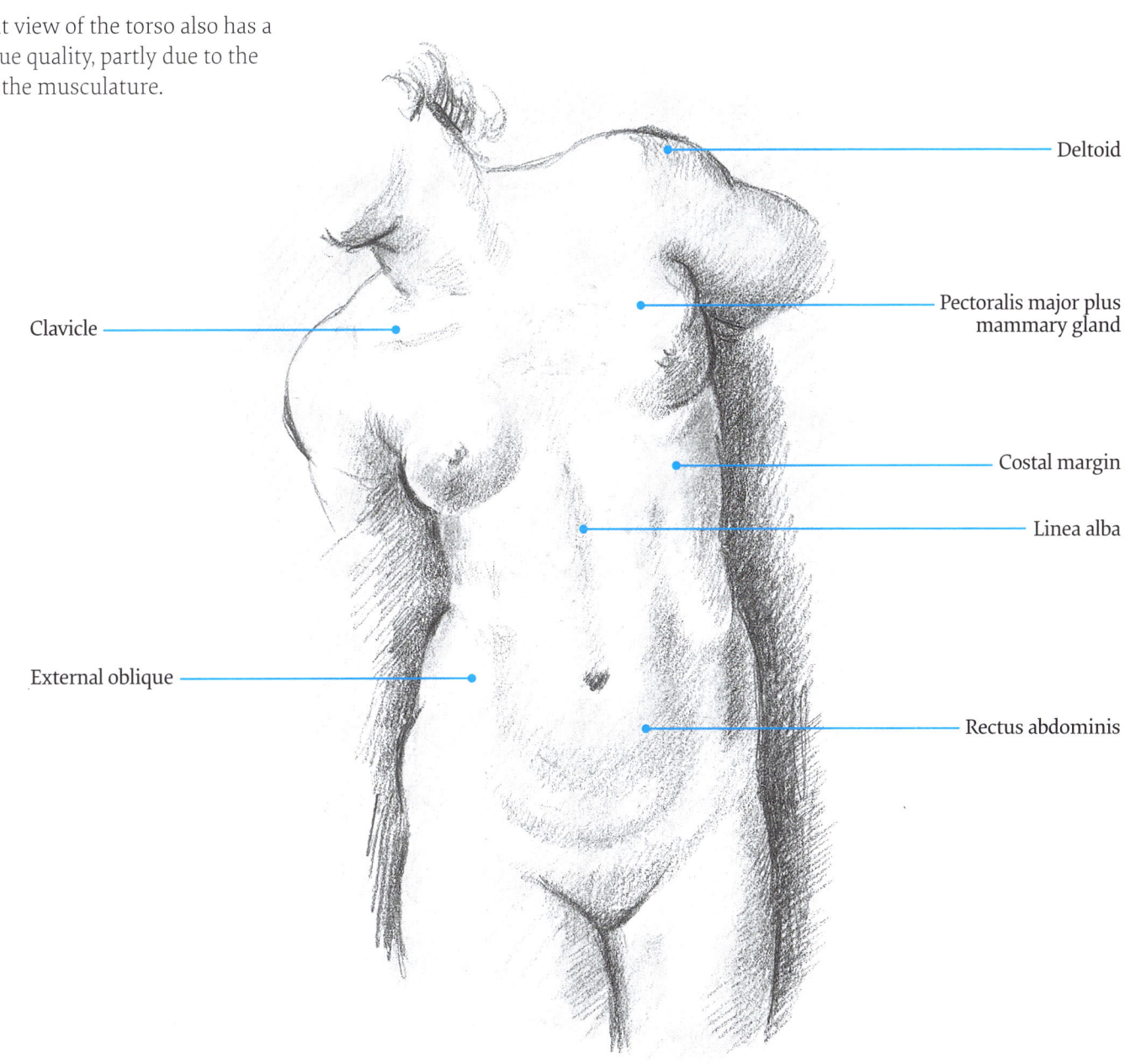

- Deltoid
- Pectoralis major plus mammary gland
- Clavicle
- Costal margin
- Linea alba
- External oblique
- Rectus abdominis

THE TORSO IN DETAIL

AFTER RAPHAEL

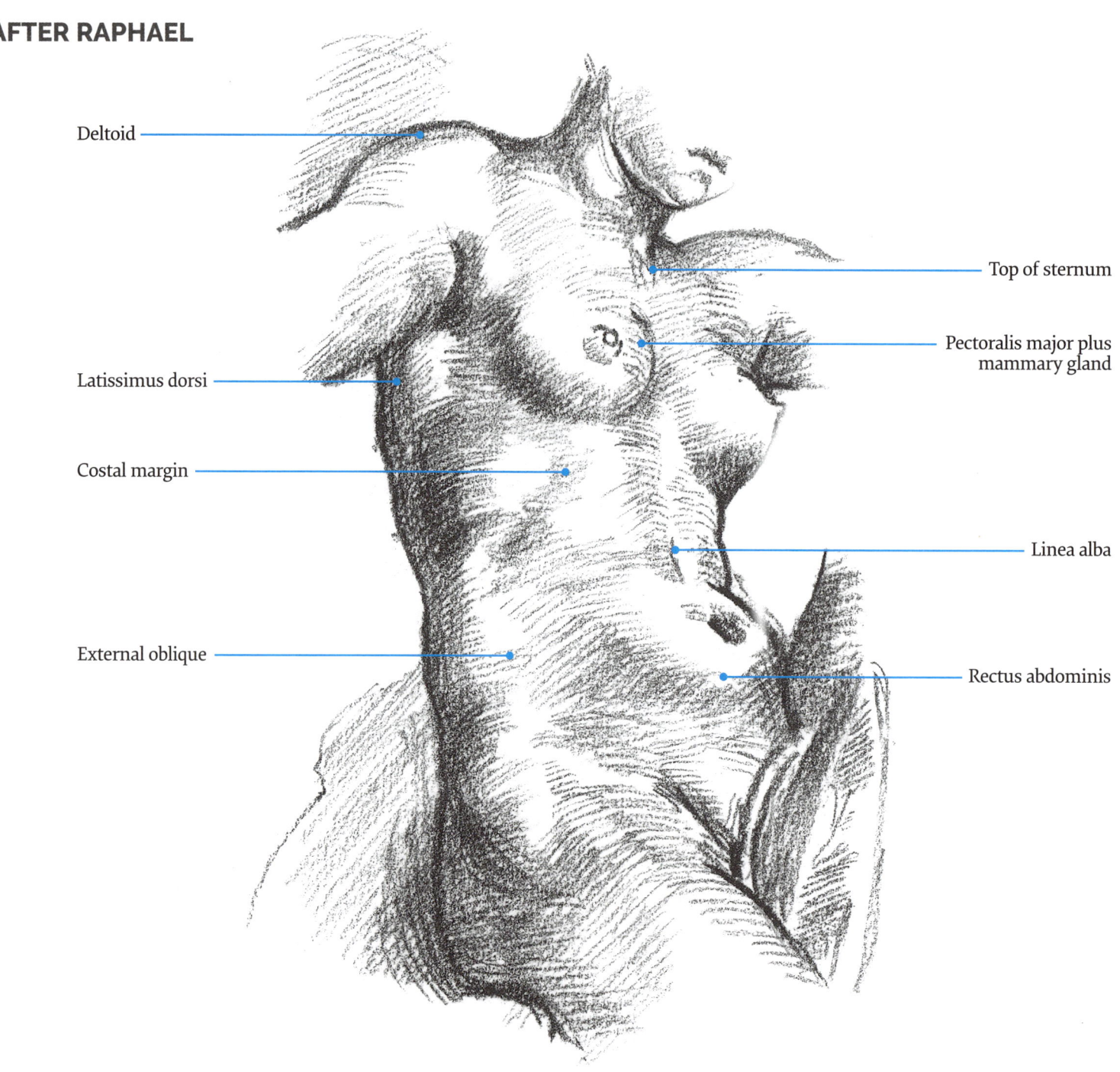

- Deltoid
- Latissimus dorsi
- Costal margin
- External oblique
- Top of sternum
- Pectoralis major plus mammary gland
- Linea alba
- Rectus abdominis

AFTER PIERRE PAUL PRUD'HON
(1758–1823)

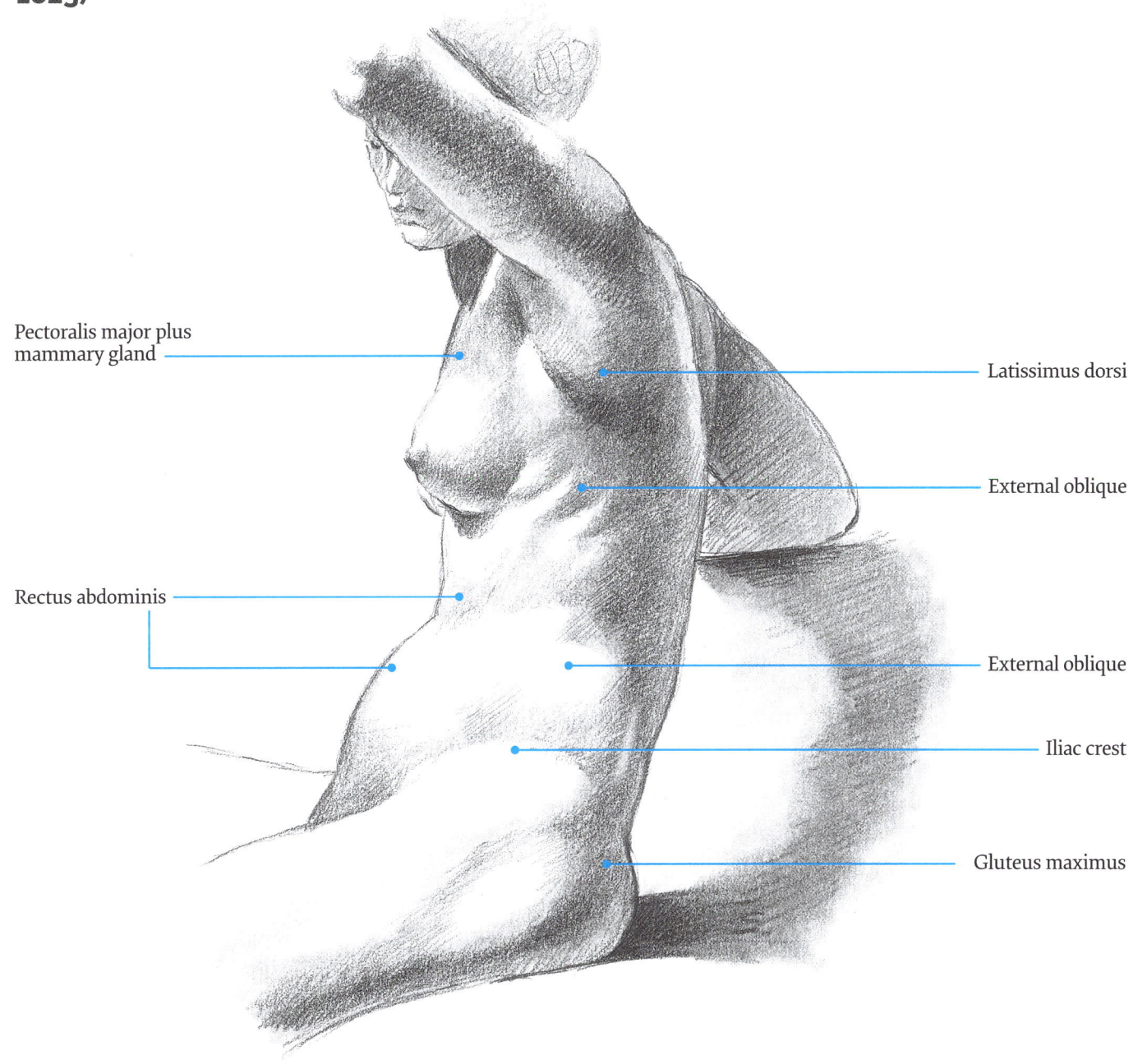

THE TORSO IN DETAIL

AFTER JAN GOSSAERT [MABUSE] (c.1478–1541)

The following three drawings of the male torso demonstrate the flexibility and strength of the section between the ribcage and the pelvis.

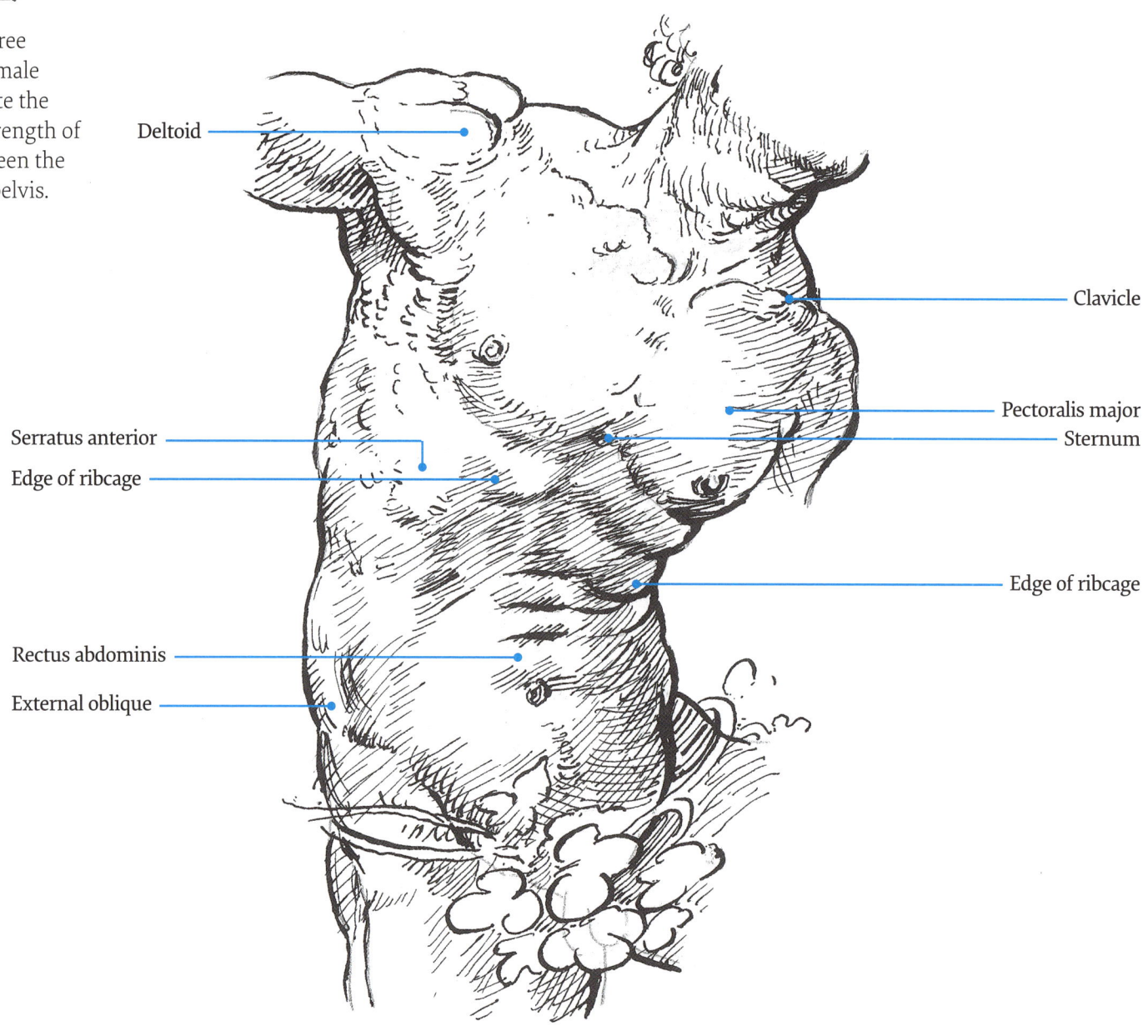

AFTER MICHELANGELO BUONARROTI
(1475–1564)

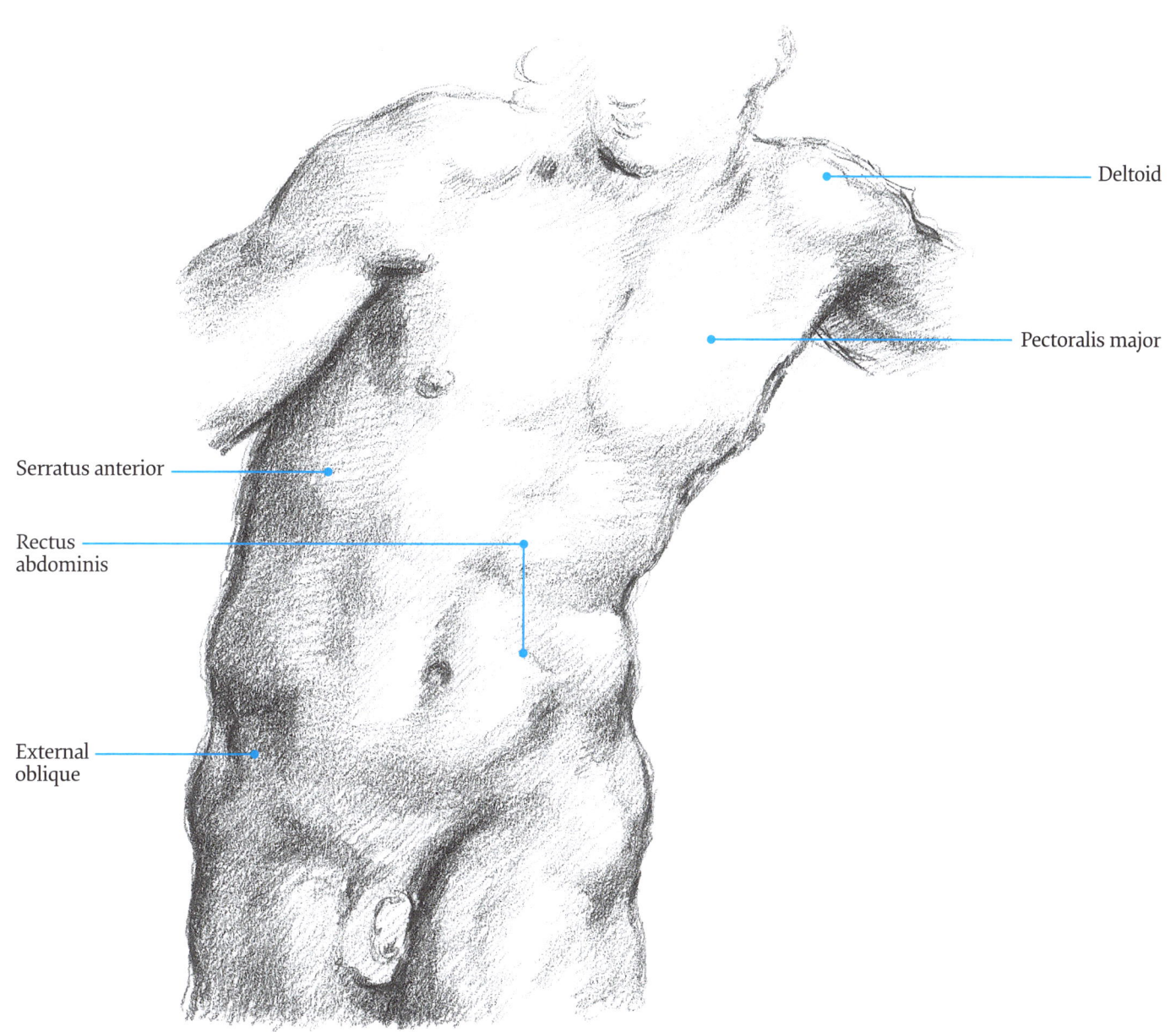

THE TORSO IN DETAIL

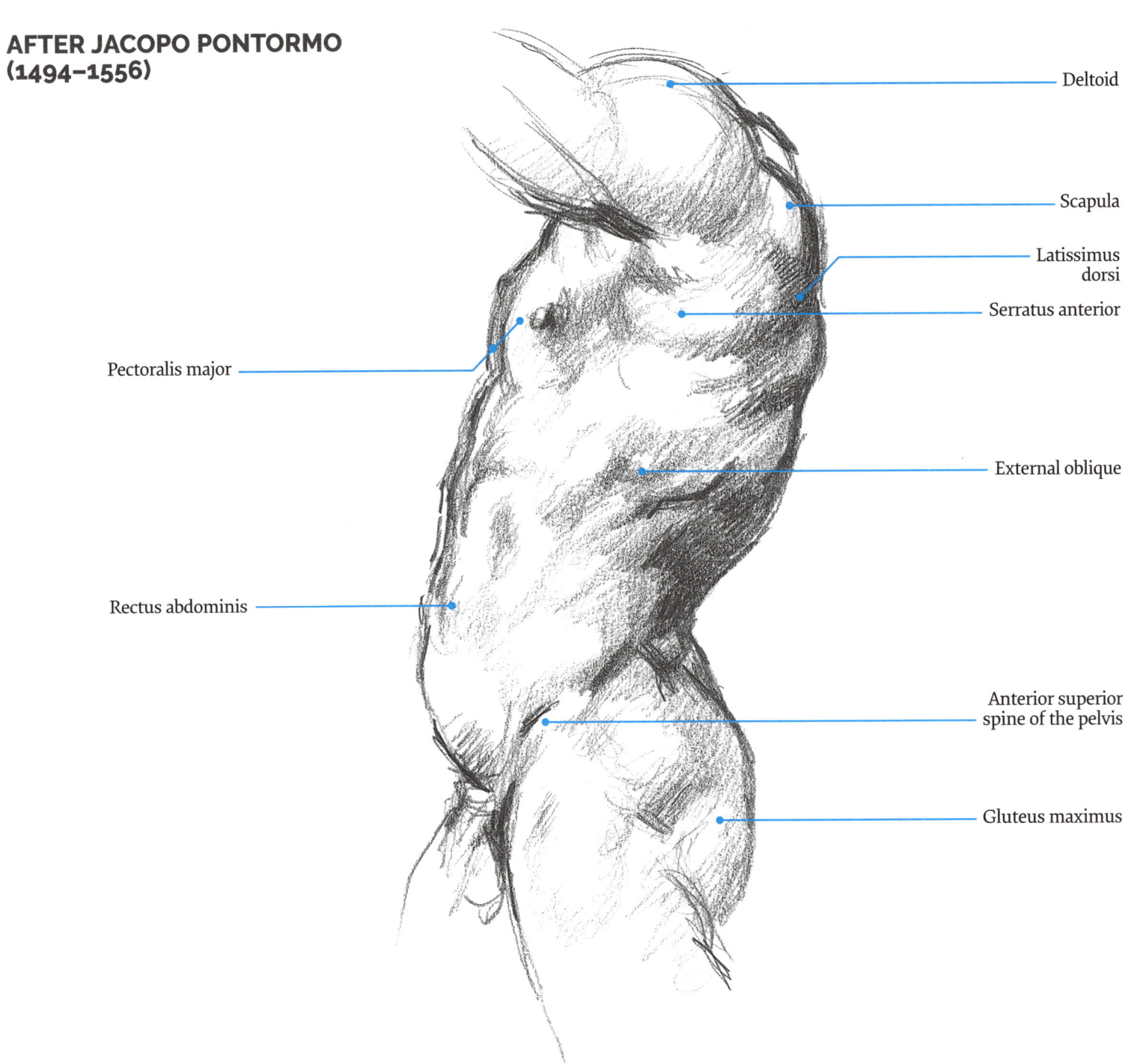

AFTER PIERRE MIGNARD (1612–1695)

Over the next pages I have shown more torso shapes after master artists, giving dynamic effects through the twisting and turning of the shoulders and hips.

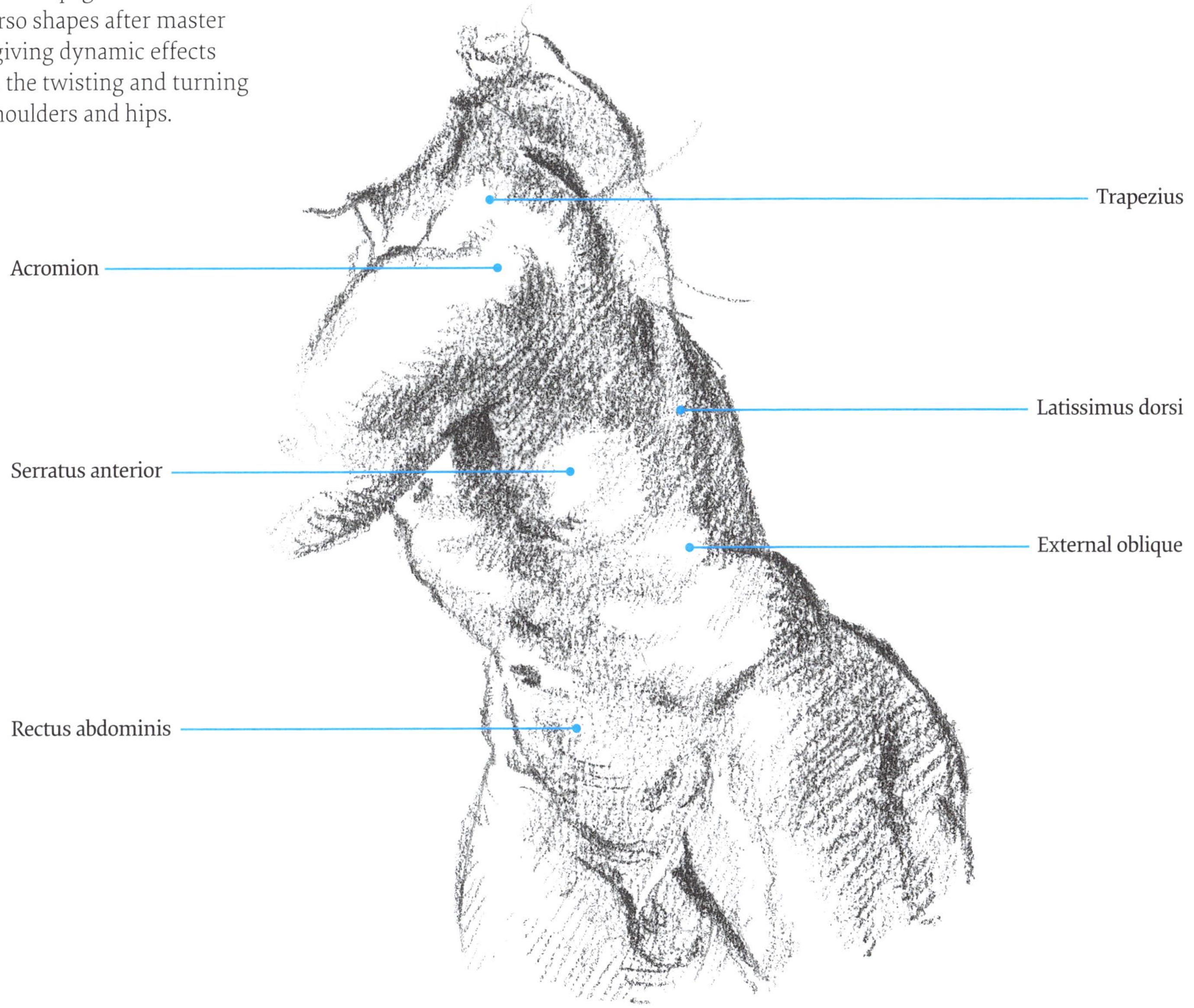

- Trapezius
- Acromion
- Latissimus dorsi
- Serratus anterior
- External oblique
- Rectus abdominis

THE TORSO IN DETAIL

AFTER BARTOLOMMEO PASSAROTTI (1529–1592)

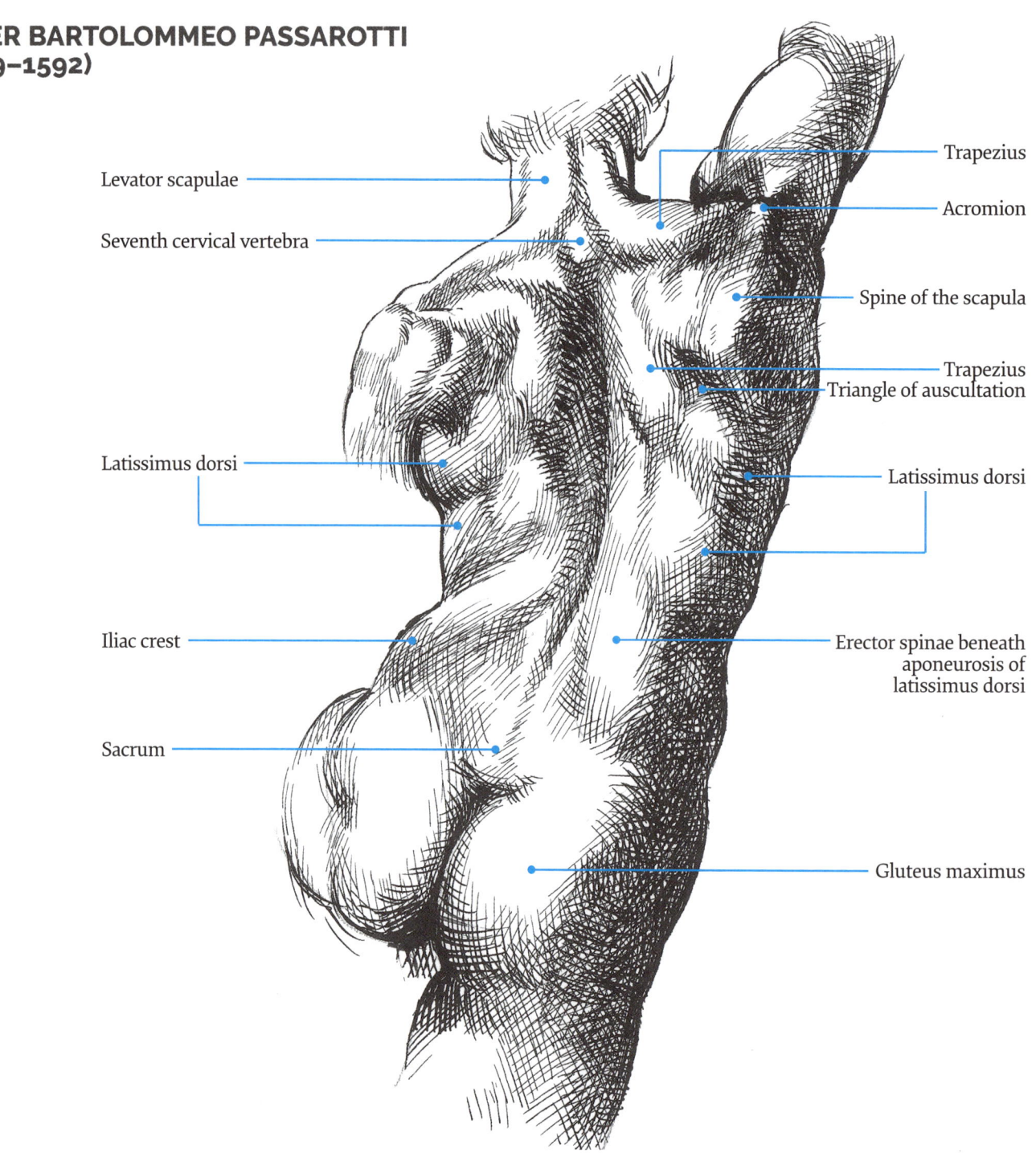

116 THE TORSO IN DETAIL

AFTER FRANZ VON STUCK (1863–1928)

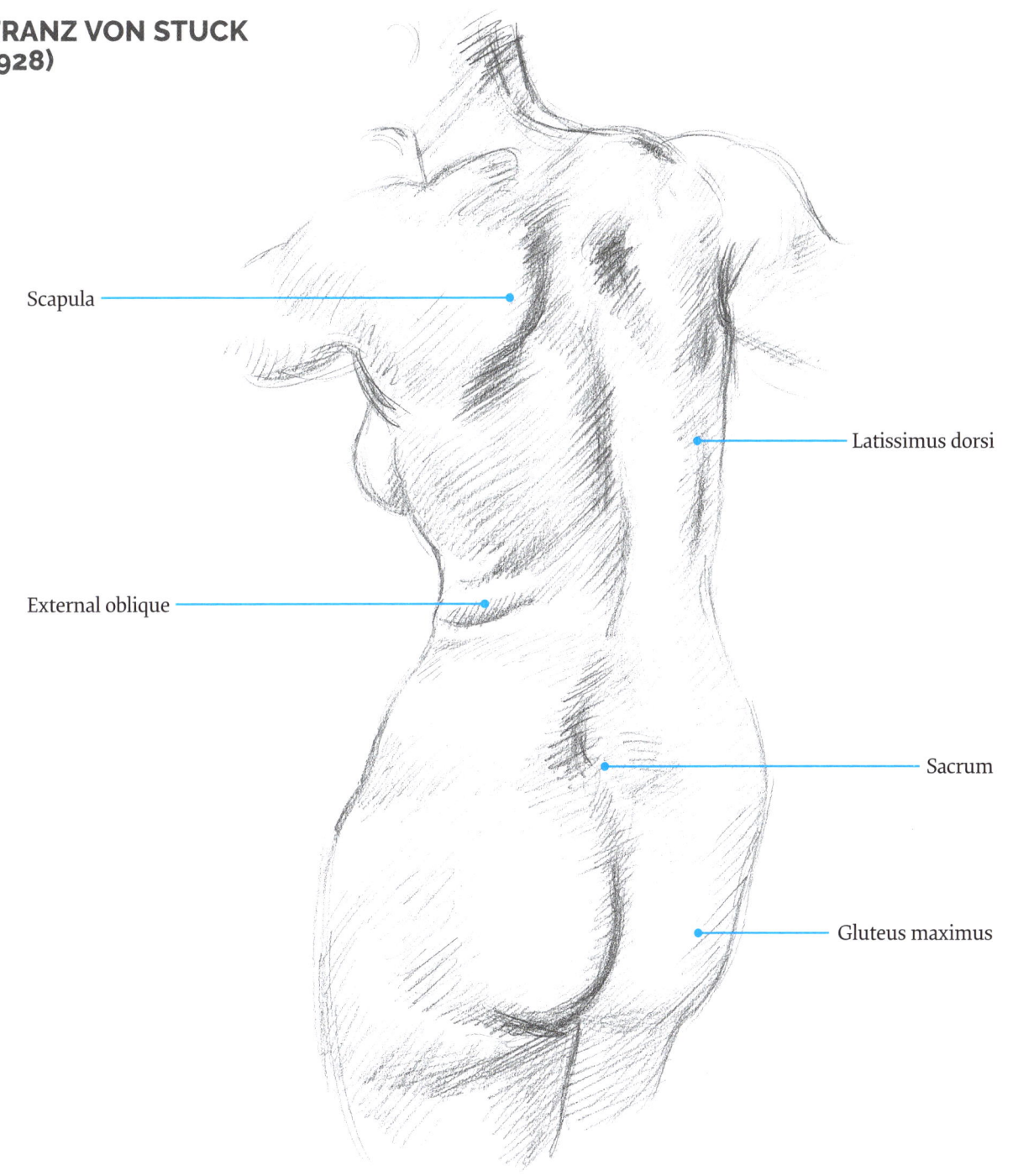

- Scapula
- Latissimus dorsi
- External oblique
- Sacrum
- Gluteus maximus

THE TORSO IN DETAIL

AFTER JOHANN ANTON DE PETERS
(1725–1795)

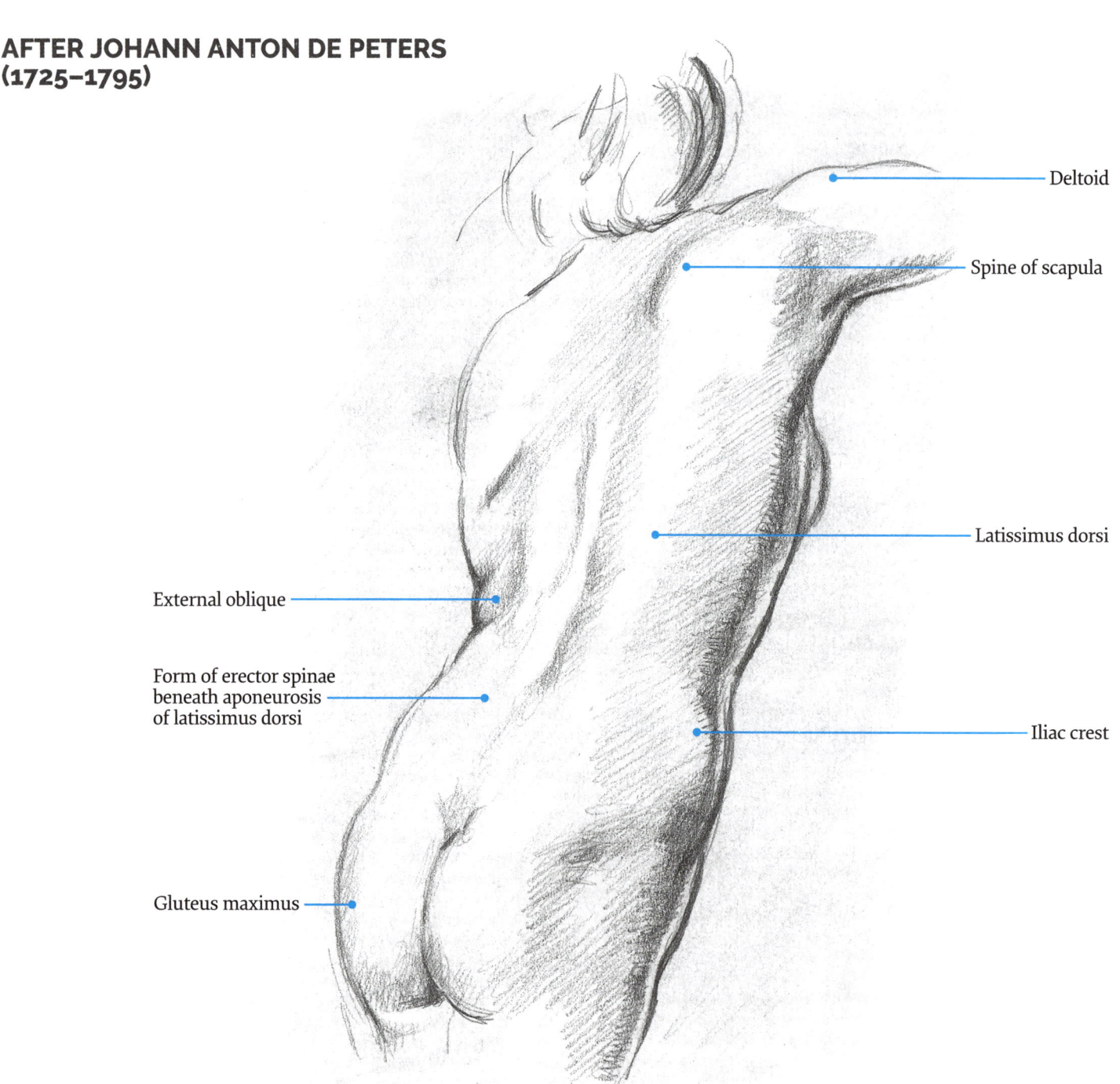

AFTER PETER PAUL RUBENS

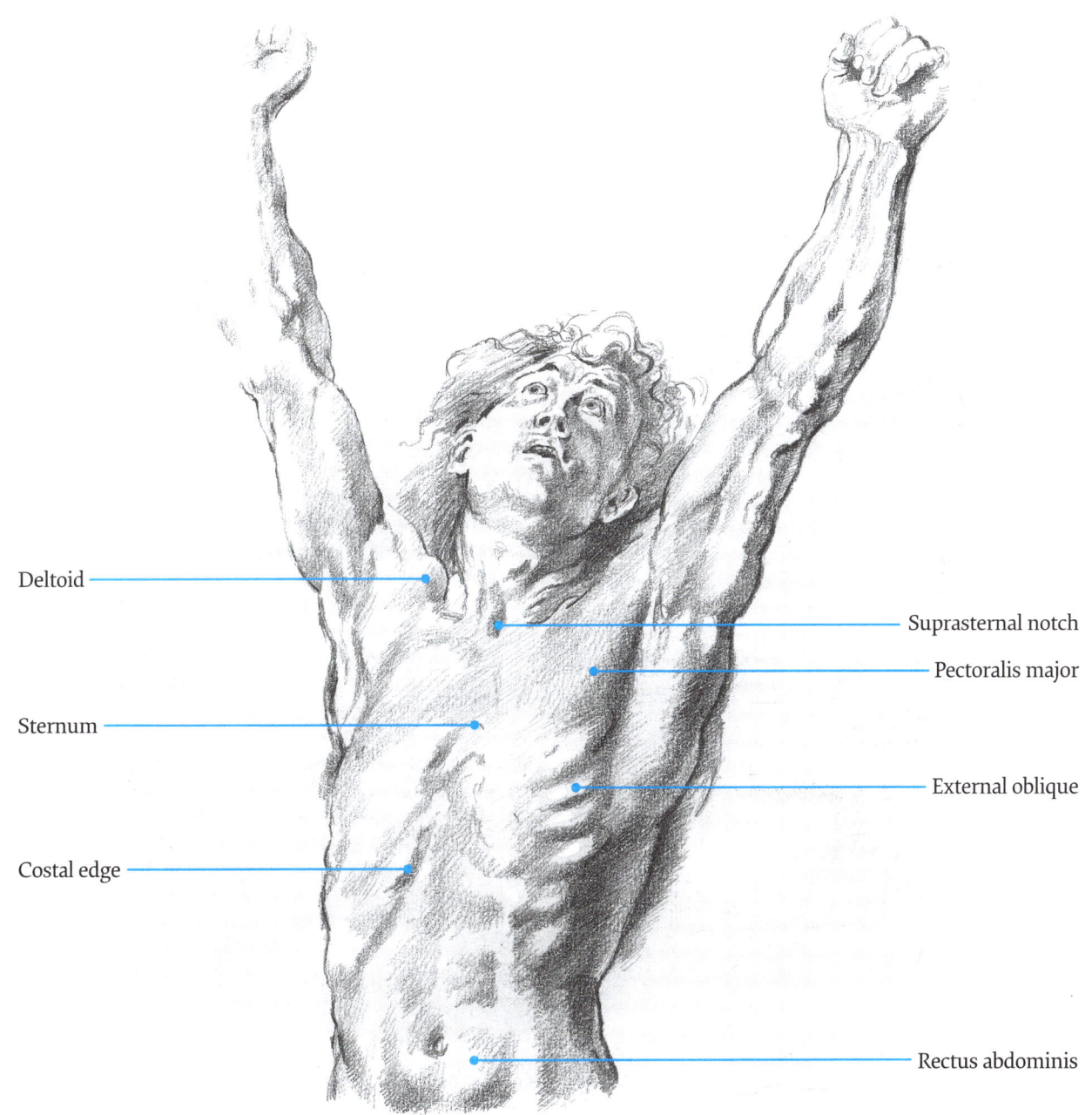

- Deltoid
- Sternum
- Costal edge
- Suprasternal notch
- Pectoralis major
- External oblique
- Rectus abdominis

THE TORSO IN DETAIL

Chapter Four

THE ARMS AND HANDS IN DETAIL

The upper limbs of the body are structured on the basis of the long bones of the humerus, the ulna and the radius, with the additional small bones of the wrist and hand. The design of the arm is very subtle and the hand so flexible and adaptable that almost any movement in any direction is possible. These are the limbs that allow human beings to handle tools, operate machines and do the things that most other animals cannot manage.

The way that the arms work from the shoulders is quite complex and so too is the musculature of the hand; don't be surprised if you find it difficult to retain all the anatomical information. It is worth remembering that the muscles of the upper arm affect the lower arm and even the fingers. As with other parts of the body, the connections are complex and it is difficult to isolate even simple movements to only one set of muscles. Study of these complicated muscle systems is not easy, but worth the effort because of the extra insight it gives us into the workings of the body.

As an artist, your main goal is to gain familiarity with the anatomical structure of the arms and hands, so that when you come to draw them from a surface view, they will be convincing enough to give your drawing some credibility. We will start the chapter with some general views of the arm and hand, and finish it with numerous examples after master artists and a study of your own hand.

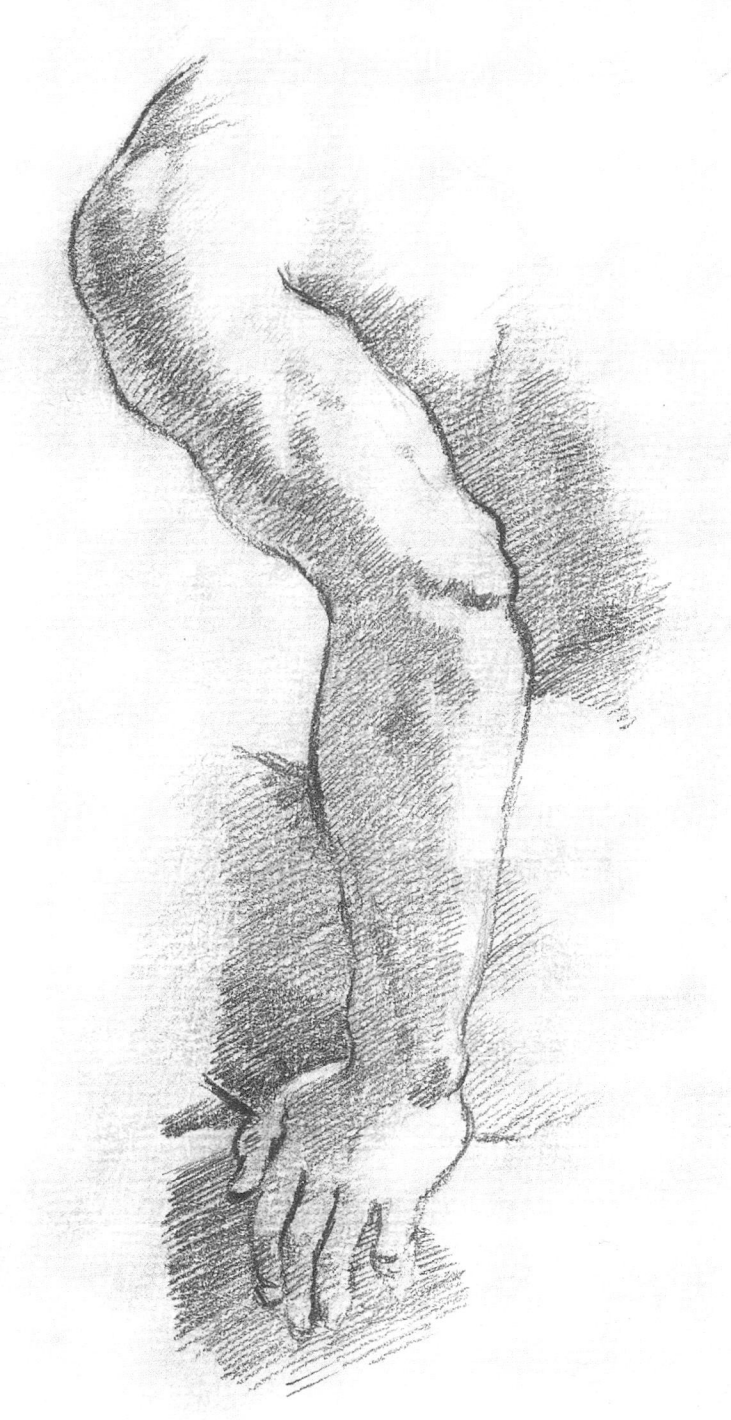

Views of arms and hands

Before we look at the bone and muscle structure of the arm and hand, consider these surface views. The upper limb is a very flexible part of the anatomy, and there will never be enough examples of the different views you will get of the arm. I have tried to show some of the most obvious and characteristic poses.

These drawings show both male and female, seen from different angles. Notice the relationship of the size of the hand with the length of forearm and upper arm. See how flexible the arm is as it moves up and down, bends and stretches. Some of the muscles show clearly, while others disappear. When the arm is pointing towards the viewer, the roundness of each part becomes much larger than the length. Because the arm can twist as well as bend it has a variety of shapes it can make in the air that are well worth studying closely.

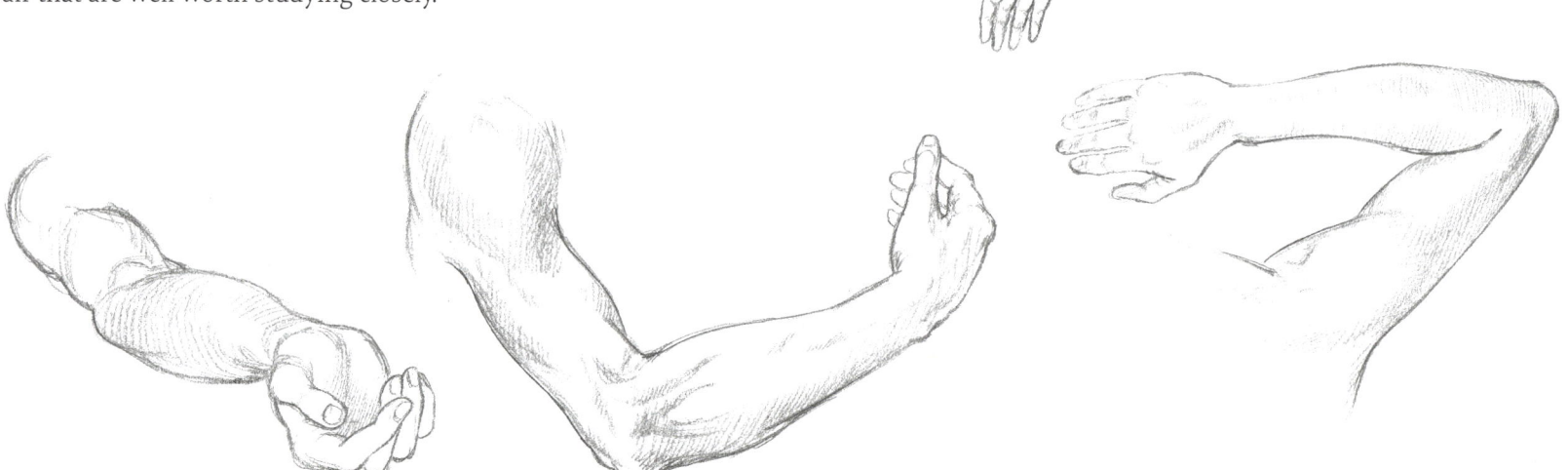

THE ARMS AND HANDS IN DETAIL

Skeleton of the arm and hand
Front view

The bone structure of the arm appears quite straightforward at first glance. However, the areas of the shoulder and the wrist are quite complex and help to allow the many movements of the limb.

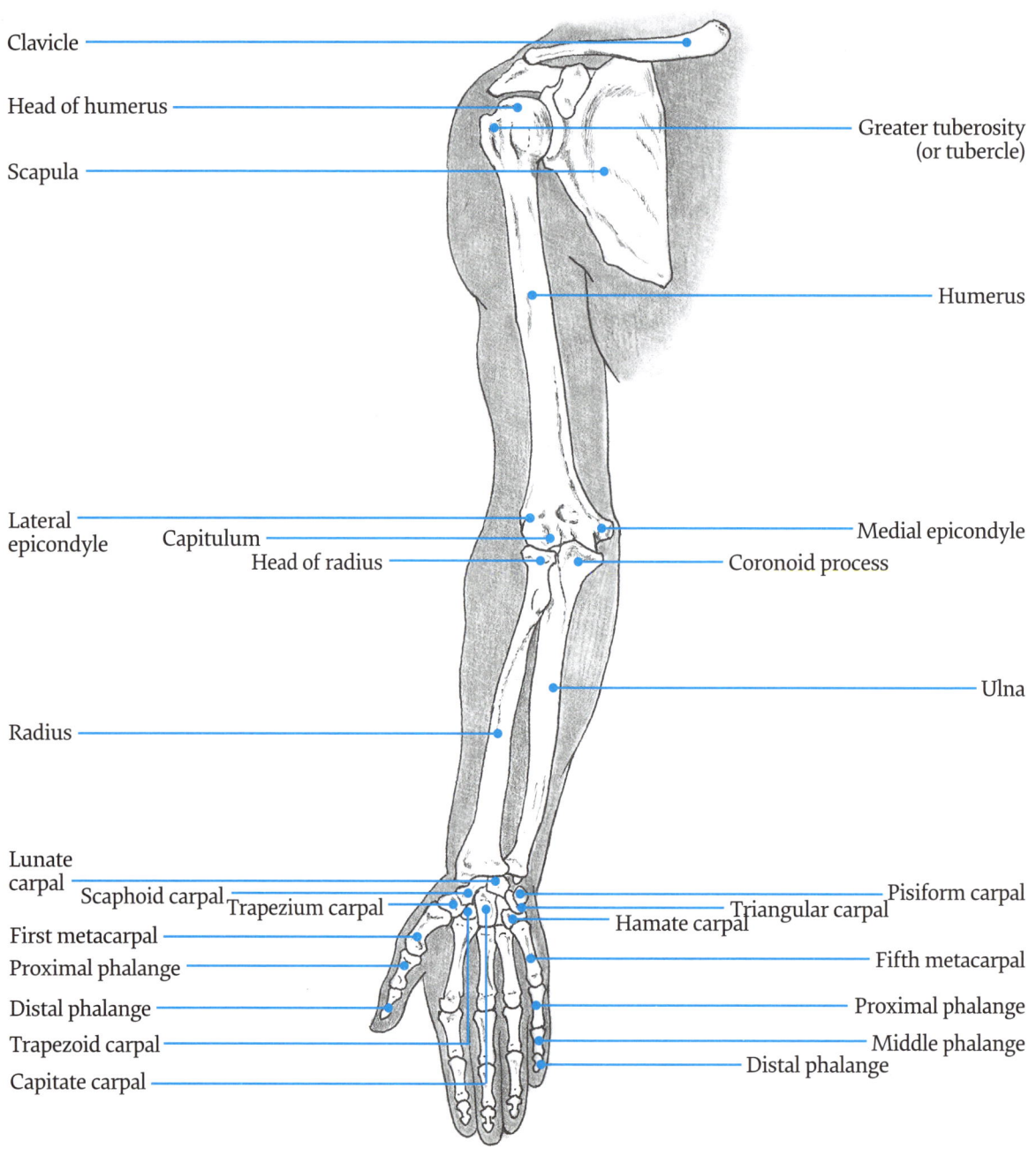

124   THE ARMS AND HANDS IN DETAIL

Back view

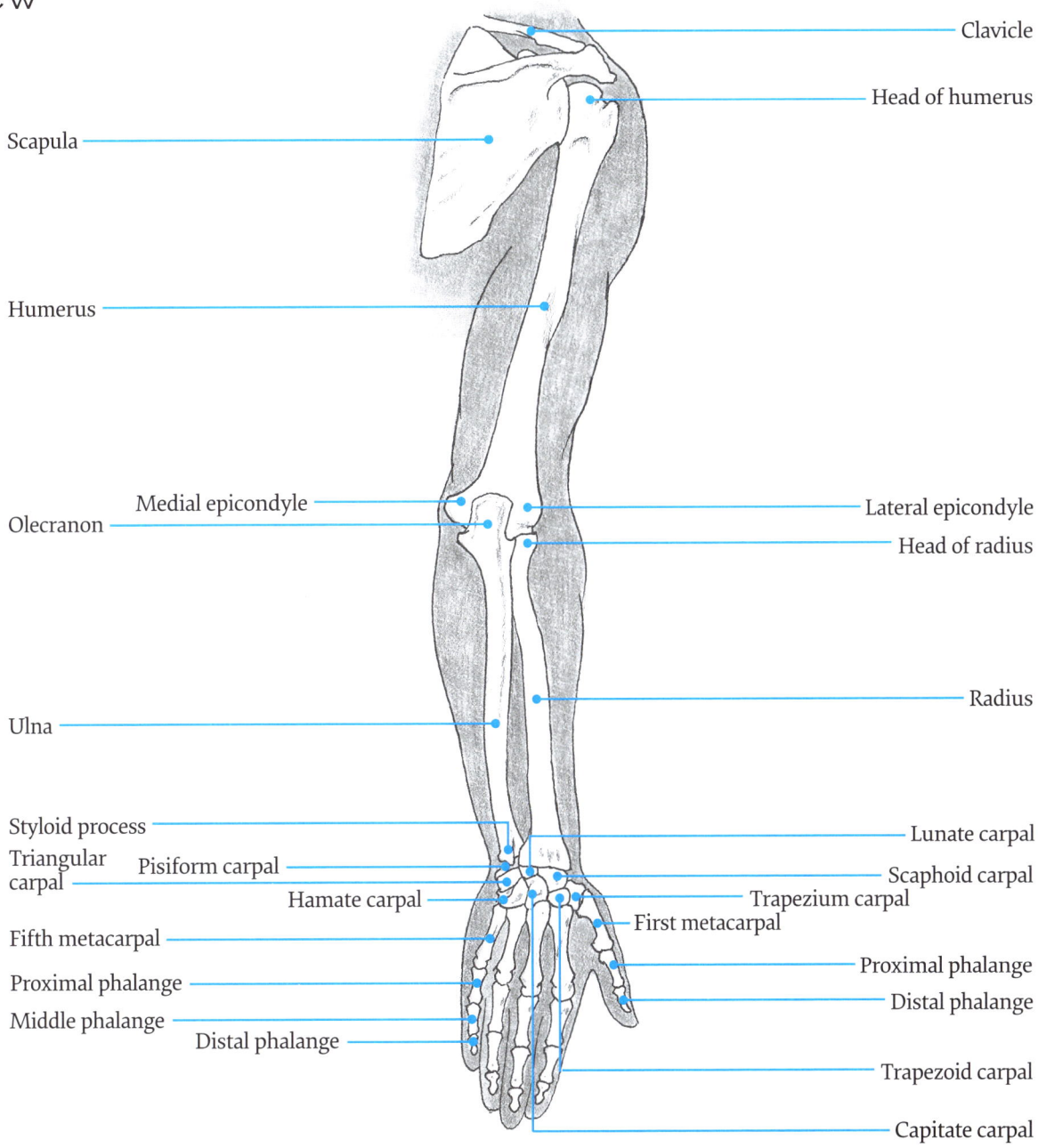

THE ARMS AND HANDS IN DETAIL

Muscles of the arm and hand
Front view

Notice the complexity of the interleaving muscles around the shoulder and elbow, and the long strands of tendons passing through the wrist. The bone structure only appears at the point of the shoulder, the elbow and the wrist, but of course on the hand, the bones of the fingers are more obvious.

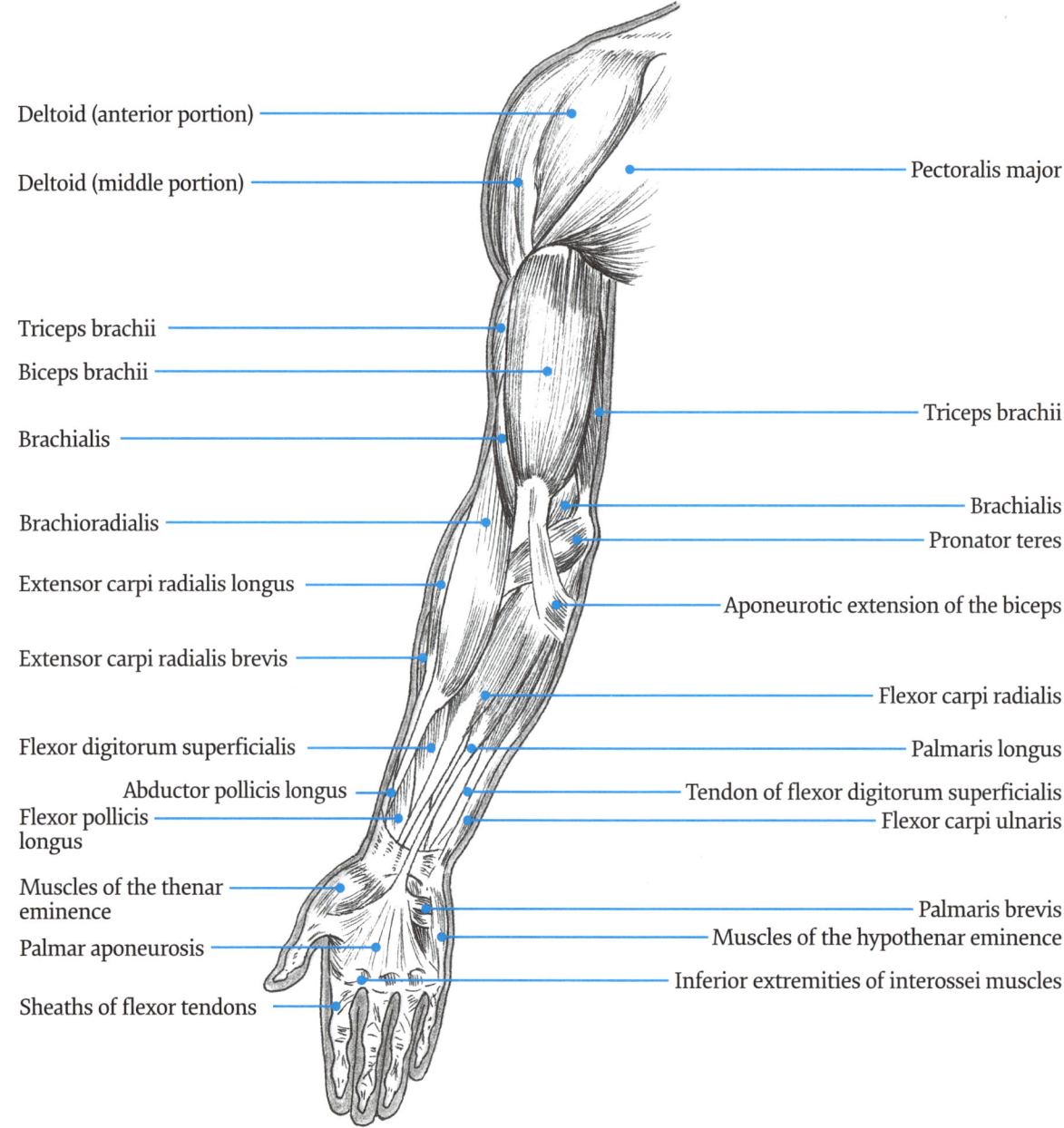

- Deltoid (anterior portion)
- Deltoid (middle portion)
- Triceps brachii
- Biceps brachii
- Brachialis
- Brachioradialis
- Extensor carpi radialis longus
- Extensor carpi radialis brevis
- Flexor digitorum superficialis
- Abductor pollicis longus
- Flexor pollicis longus
- Muscles of the thenar eminence
- Palmar aponeurosis
- Sheaths of flexor tendons
- Pectoralis major
- Triceps brachii
- Brachialis
- Pronator teres
- Aponeurotic extension of the biceps
- Flexor carpi radialis
- Palmaris longus
- Tendon of flexor digitorum superficialis
- Flexor carpi ulnaris
- Palmaris brevis
- Muscles of the hypothenar eminence
- Inferior extremities of interossei muscles

126 THE ARMS AND HANDS IN DETAIL

Back view

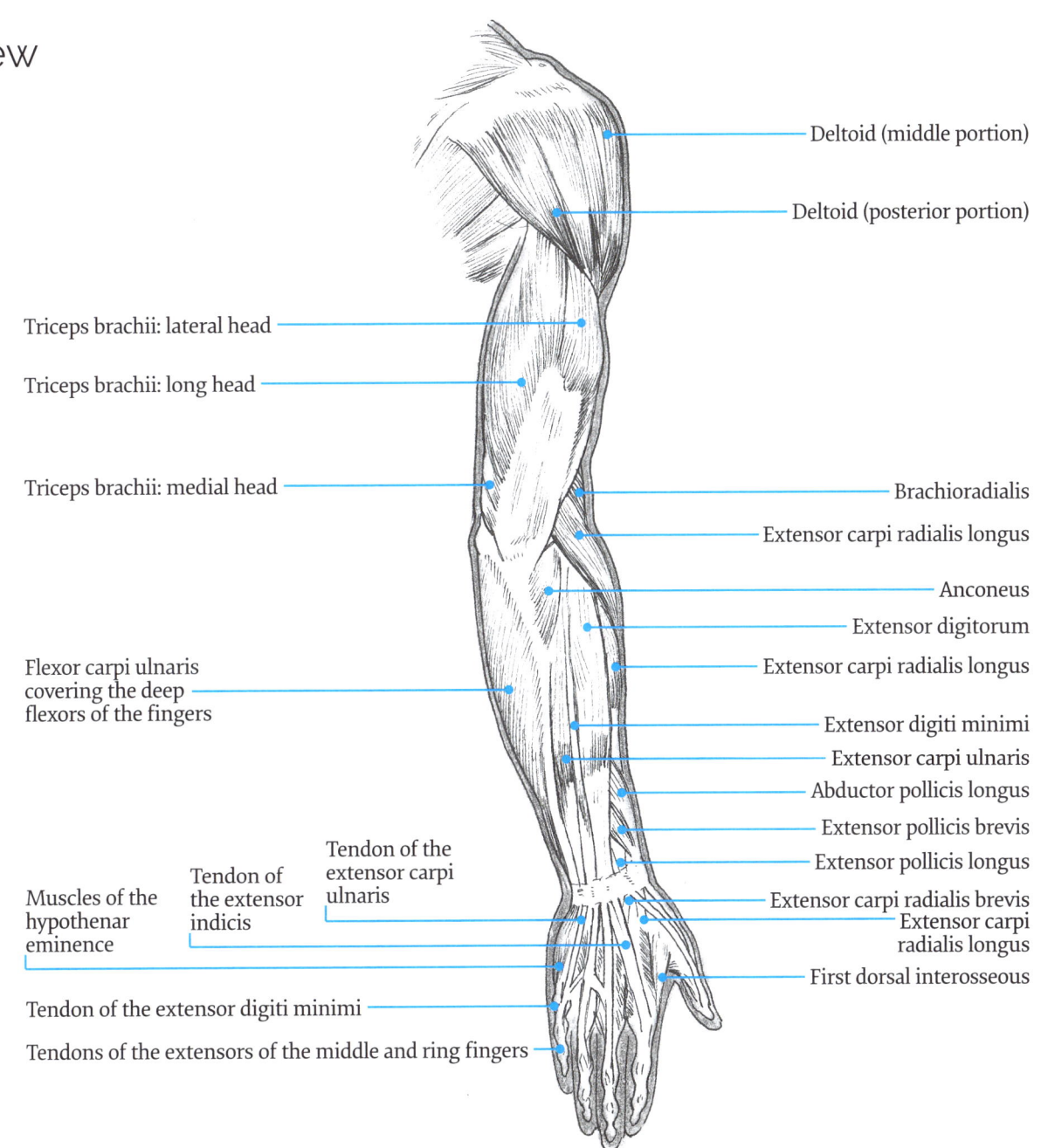

THE ARMS AND HANDS IN DETAIL

Side view, external aspect

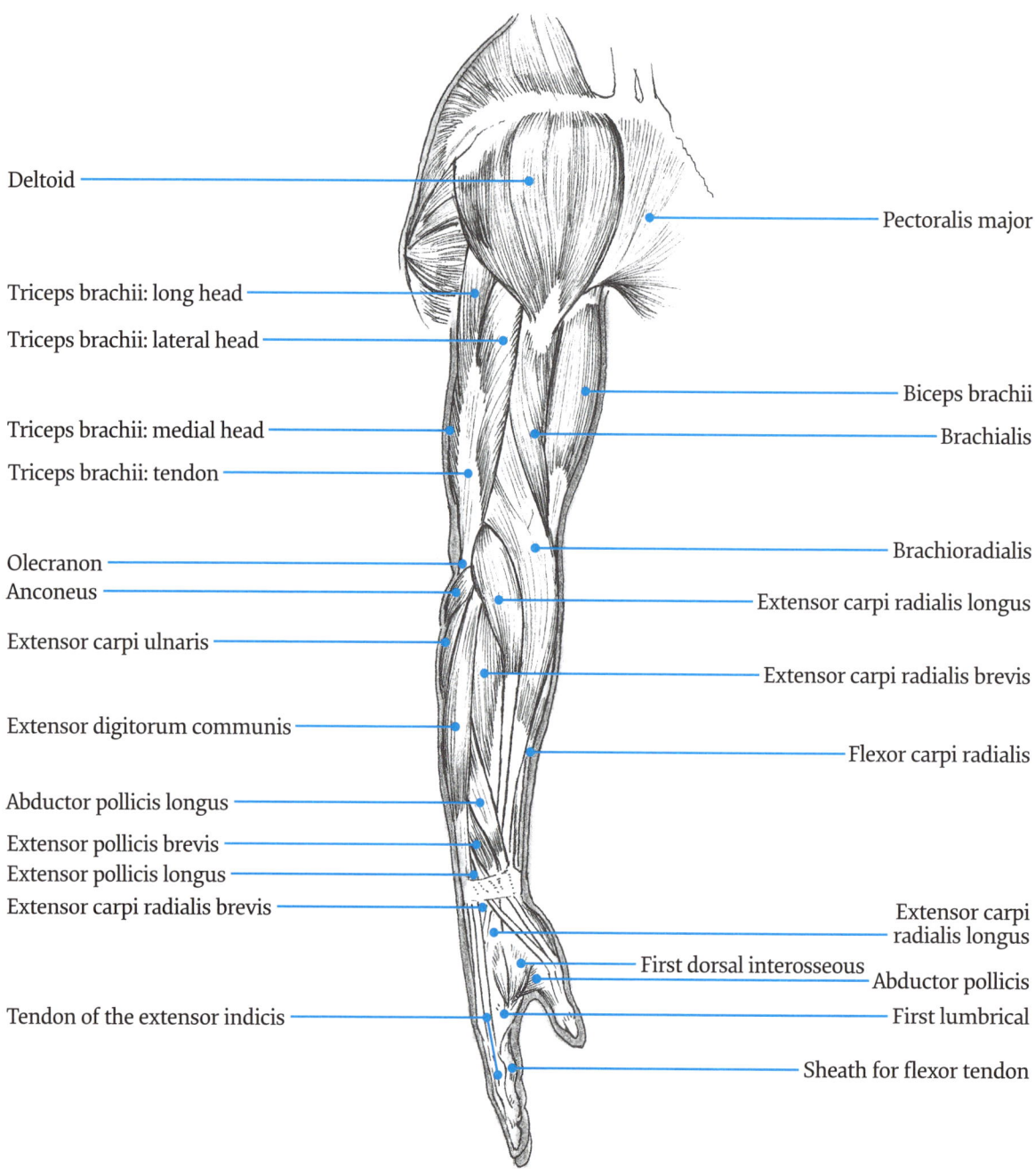

128 THE ARMS AND HANDS IN DETAIL

Side view, internal aspect

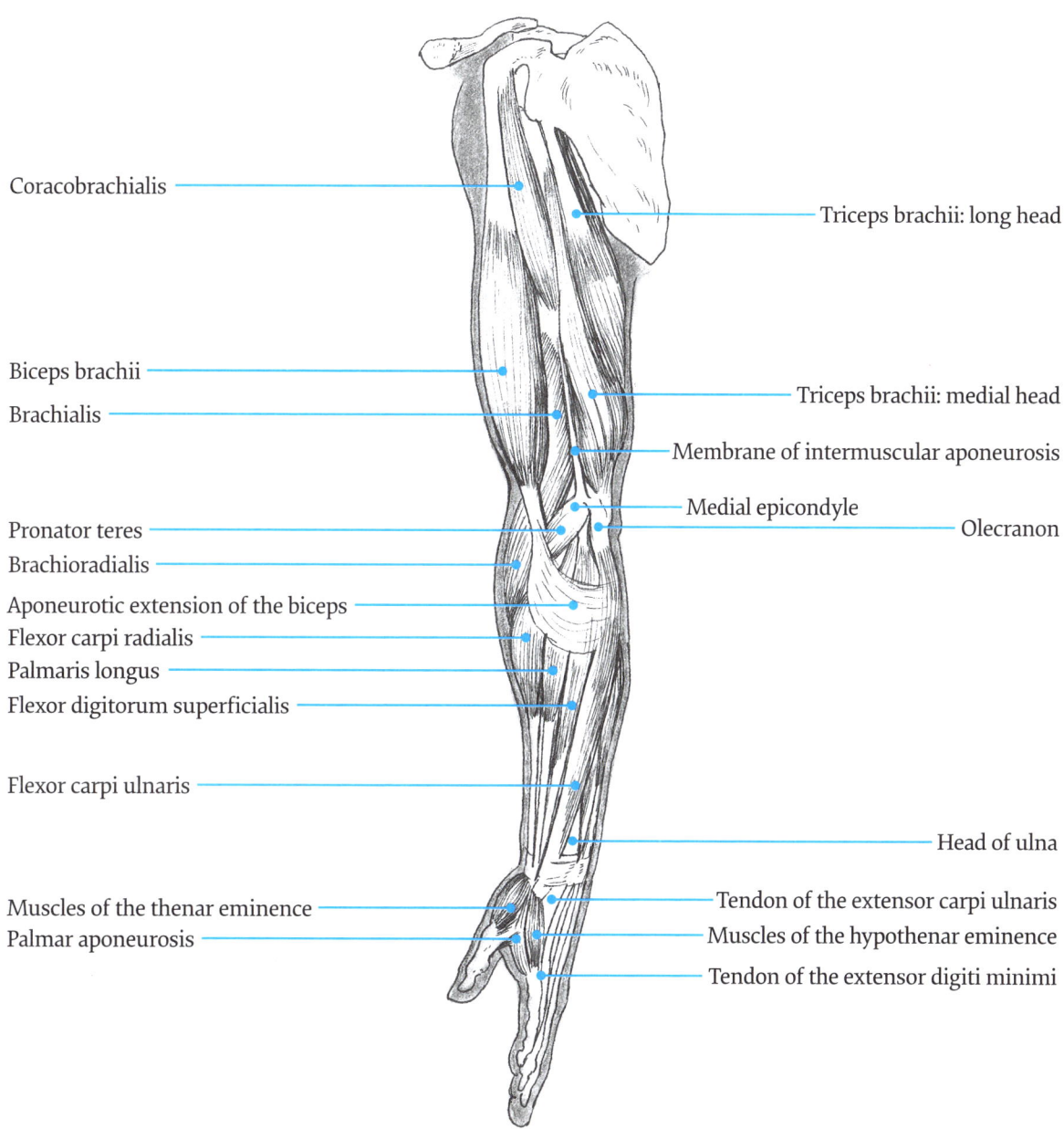

THE ARMS AND HANDS IN DETAIL

Muscle and bone structure of the upper arm and shoulder

Because of the complex attachment of the arm to the torso via the shoulder, we now examine it in some depth. These diagrams show how the muscles are linked to the bone structure and how they all show on the surface of the arm.

BICEPS BRACHII flexes elbow joint and supinates forearm.
BRACHIALIS flexes forearm.
CORACOBRACHIALIS flexes and adducts shoulder.
DELTOID pulls limb forward when arm raised level with shoulder. Raises and holds arm horizontal, and draws limb backwards when horizontal.
INFRASPINATUS and TERES MINOR help to rotate arm backwards.
LATISSIMUS DORSI powerfully draws the arm backwards.
PECTORALIS MAJOR extends arm and draws it across the front of the torso.
PECTORALIS MINOR holds scapula against ribcage and raises ribs during forced breathing. It also pulls shoulder down and forwards.
RHOMBOIDS MAJOR AND MINOR (beneath trapezius) draw scapula towards the median line.
SERRATUS ANTERIOR pulls shoulder forward and gives force to punch. Prevents shoulder blade from swinging to side.
SUBCLAVIUS fixes and pulls clavicle downwards and forwards.
SUBSCAPULARIS (beneath scapula) rotates arm inward.
SUPRASPINATUS raises and rotates arm outwards.
TERES MAJOR with LATISSIMUS DORSI extends, adducts and rotates arm inwards.
TENDON AND APONEUROSIS OF TRICEPS flatten back of arm above elbow.
TRAPEZIUS raises and lowers shoulders and draws head to either side.
TRICEPS BRACHII extends limb.

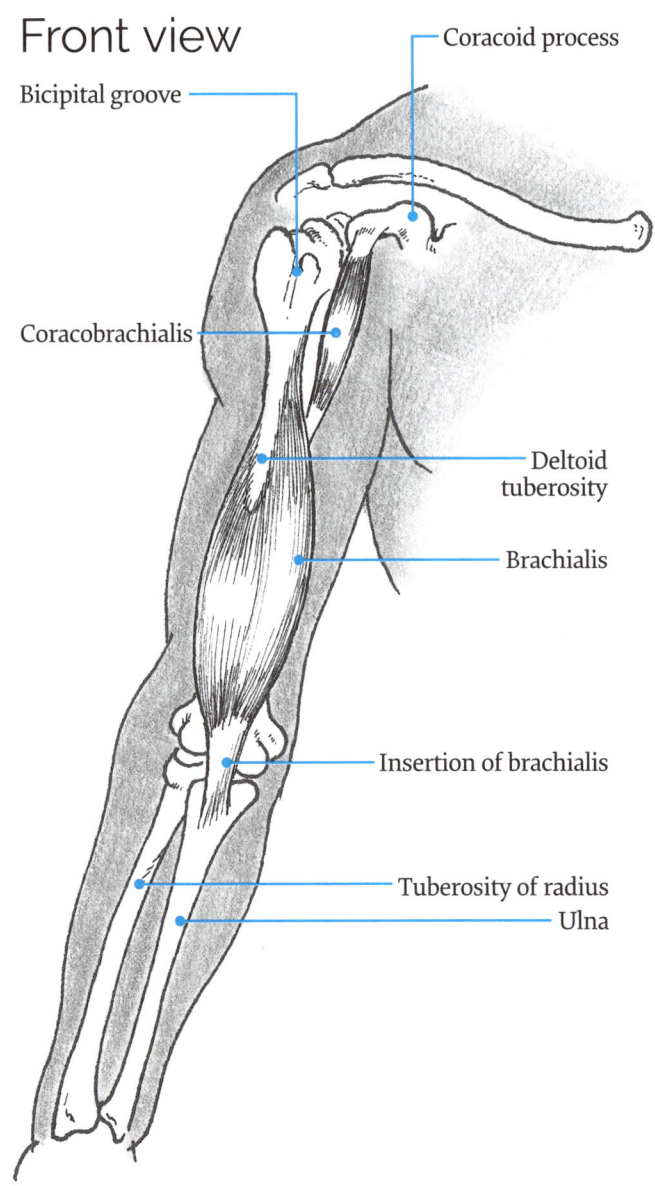

Front view
- Coracoid process
- Bicipital groove
- Coracobrachialis
- Deltoid tuberosity
- Brachialis
- Insertion of brachialis
- Tuberosity of radius
- Ulna

Front view of the shoulder, showing the ribs

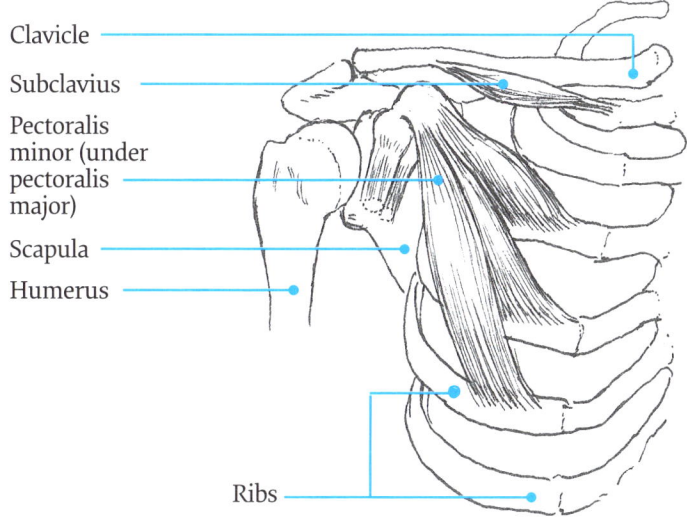

- Clavicle
- Subclavius
- Pectoralis minor (under pectoralis major)
- Scapula
- Humerus
- Ribs

Front view of the shoulder, without the ribs

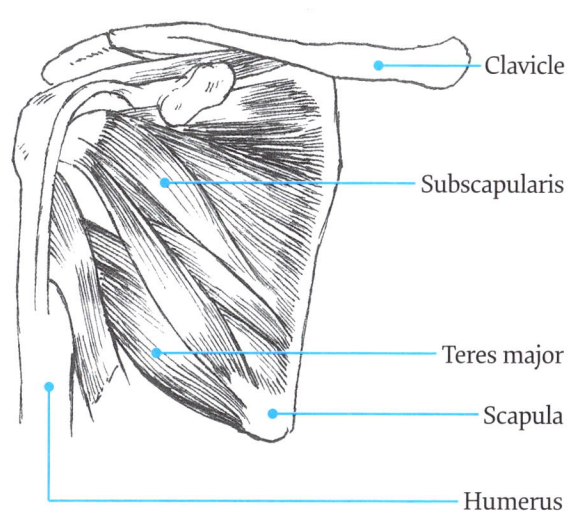

- Clavicle
- Subscapularis
- Teres major
- Scapula
- Humerus

Side view of the shoulder

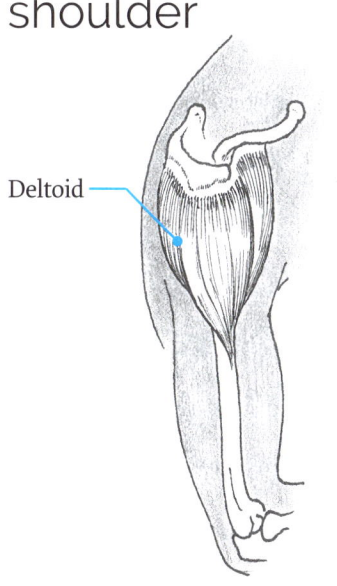

- Deltoid

Surface view of the shoulder from above

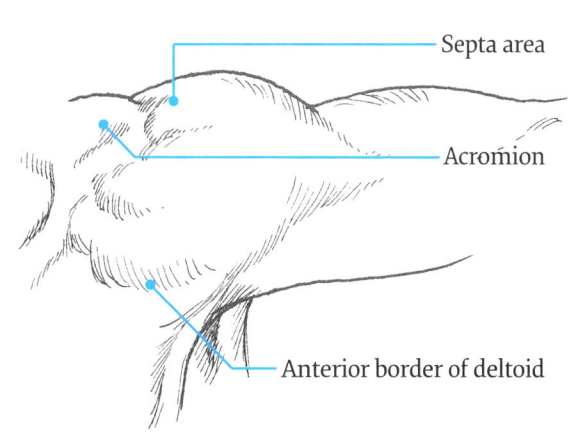

- Septa area
- Acromion
- Anterior border of deltoid

Surface view of the shoulder from the back

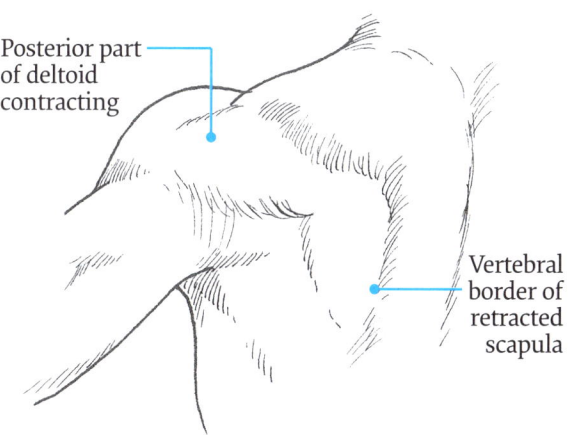

- Posterior part of deltoid contracting
- Vertebral border of retracted scapula

THE ARMS AND HANDS IN DETAIL

Note how these muscles fit underneath and overlay each other, forming a strong mass that enables the arm to move easily in any direction without damage. All the muscles affect each other when flexing or contracting, which translates as a 'rippling' effect on the surface of the arm. This is particularly visible in athletes and weightlifters.

Front view, deep muscles

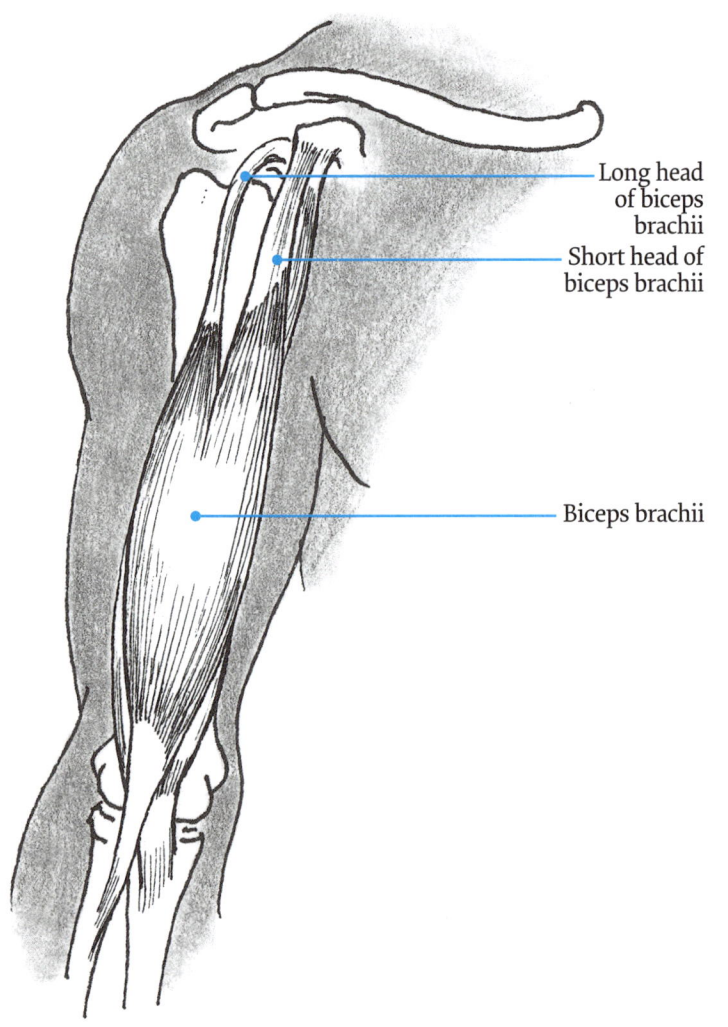

- Long head of biceps brachii
- Short head of biceps brachii
- Biceps brachii

Front view, overlaying muscles

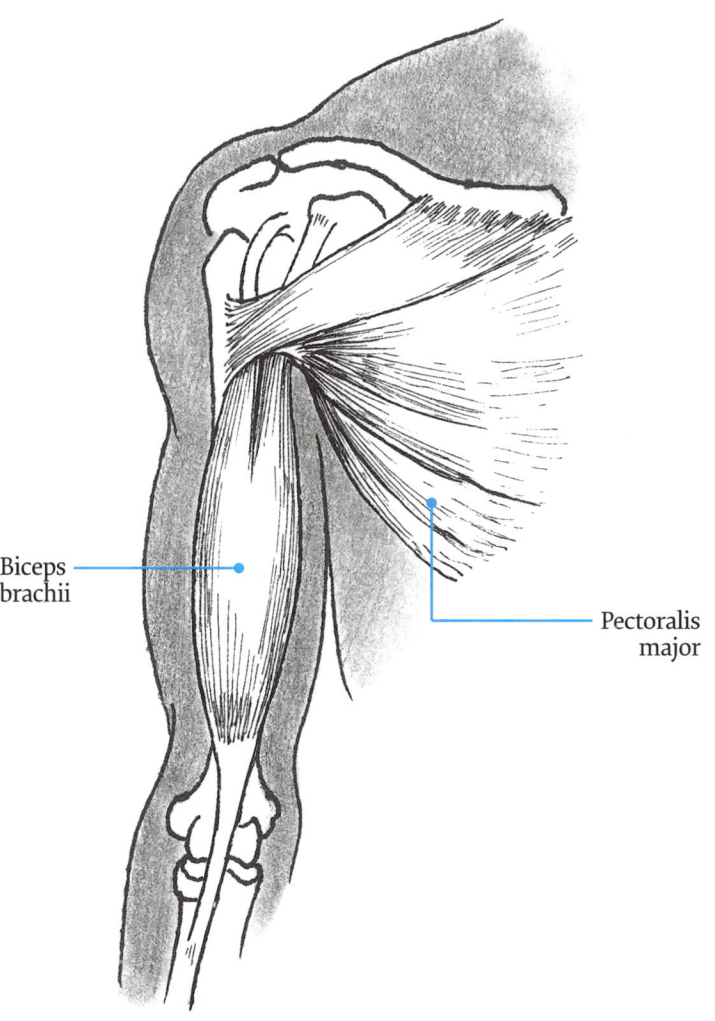

- Biceps brachii
- Pectoralis major

Back view, deep muscles

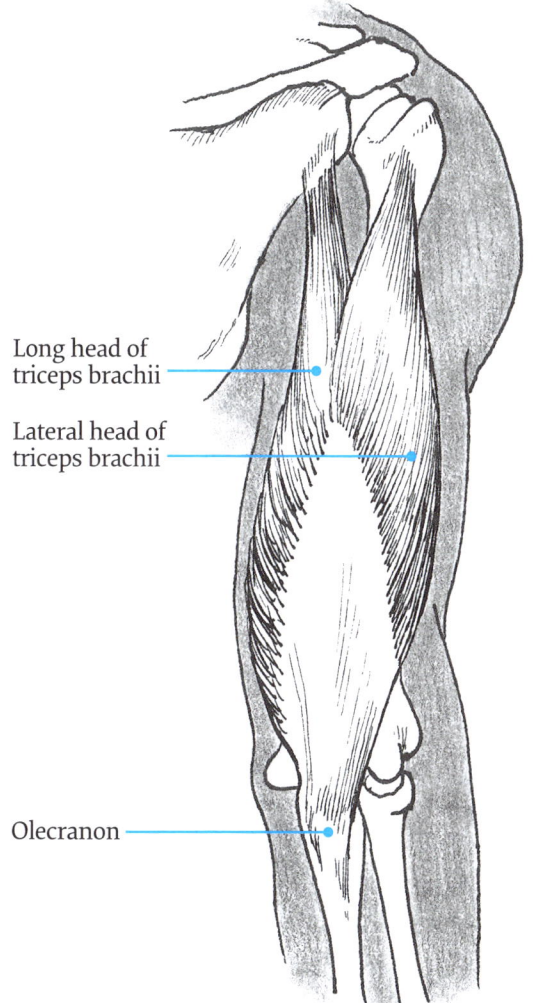

- Long head of triceps brachii
- Lateral head of triceps brachii
- Olecranon

Back view, overlaying muscles

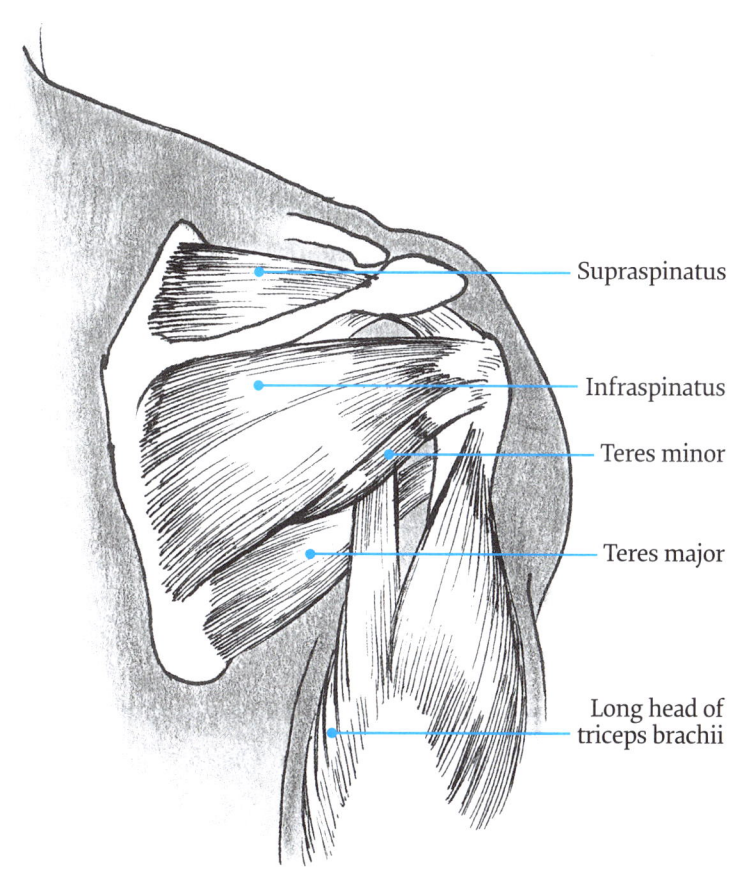

- Supraspinatus
- Infraspinatus
- Teres minor
- Teres major
- Long head of triceps brachii

Upper arm lifting, front view

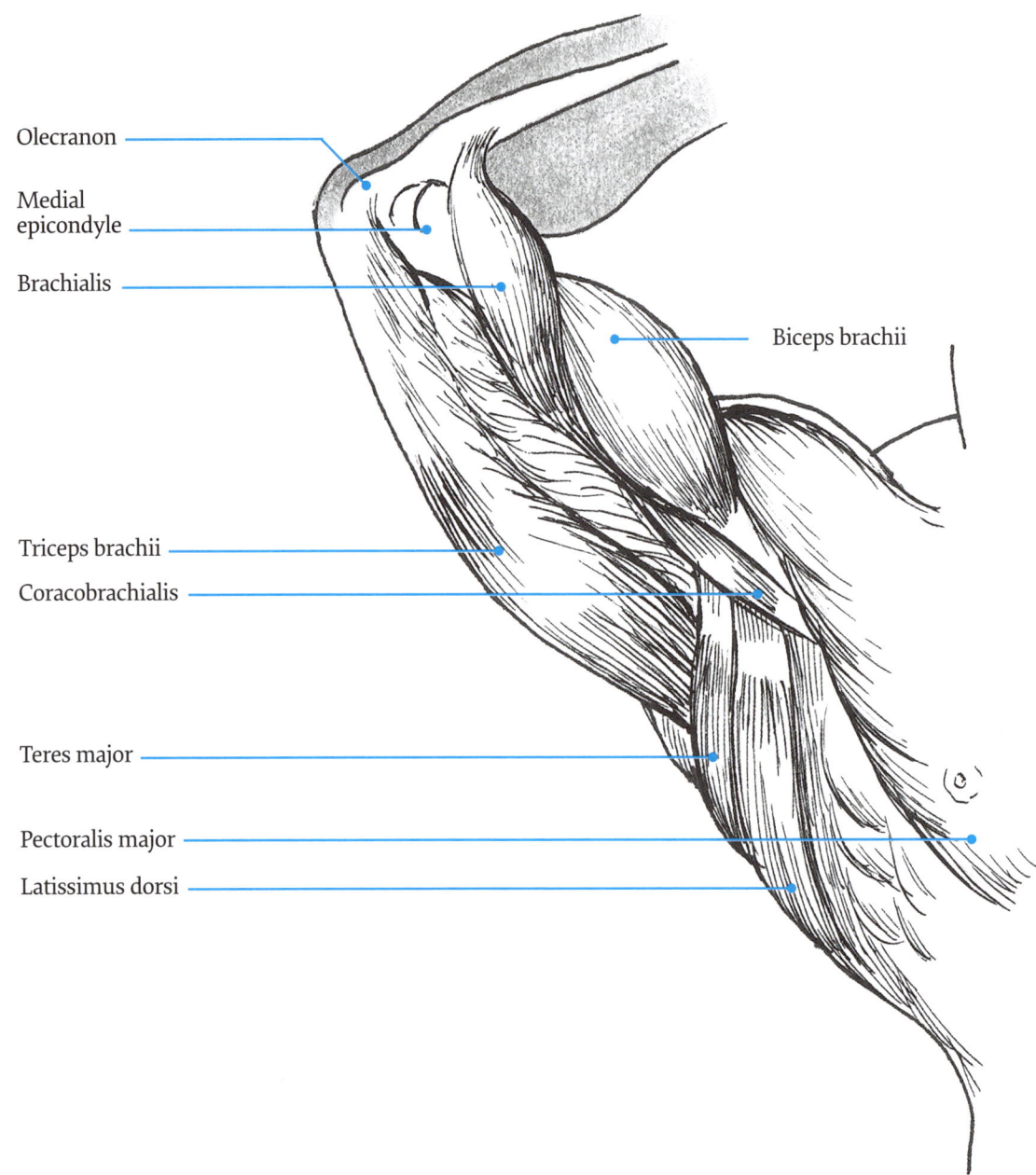

Upper arm flexing, front view

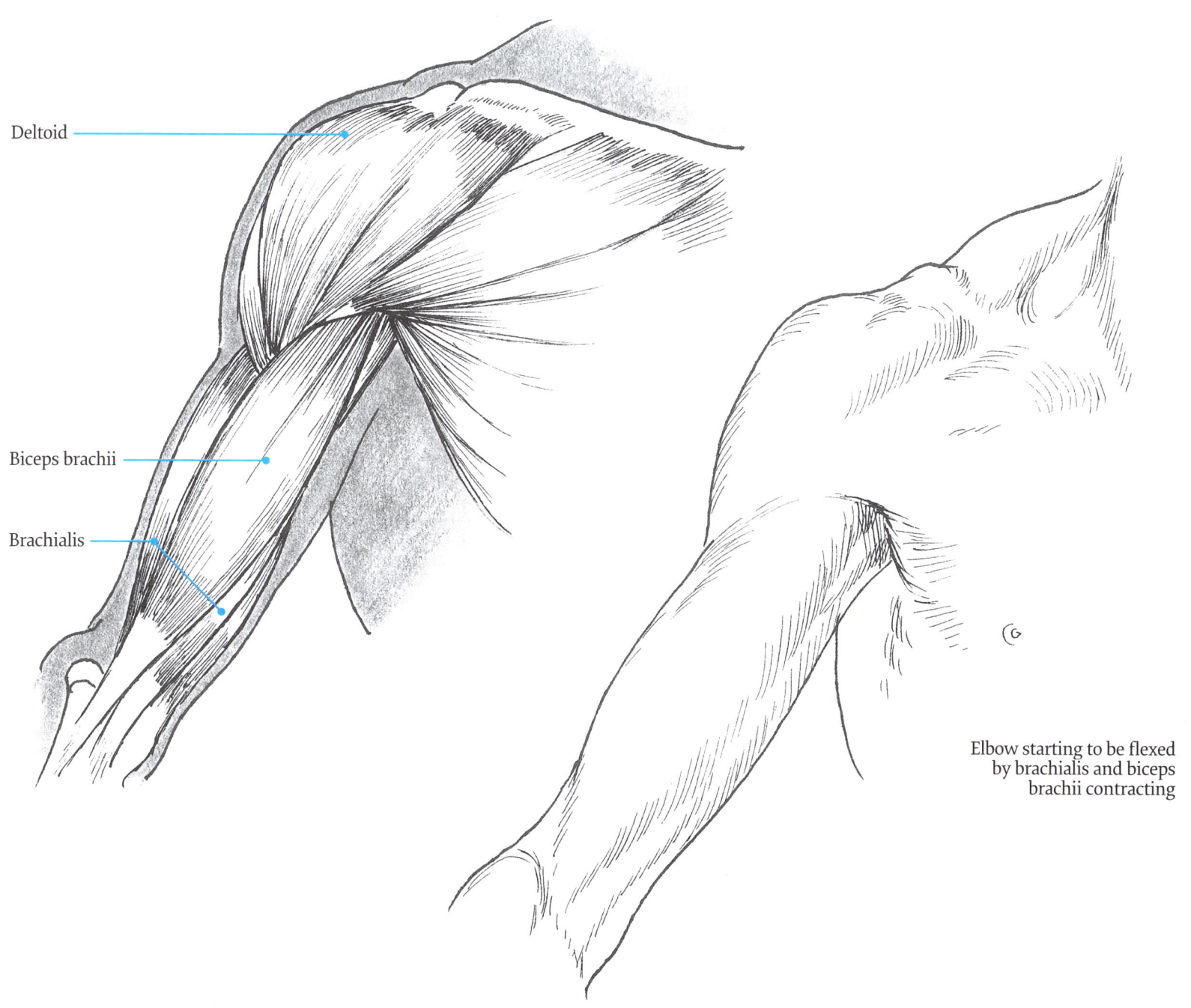

Deltoid

Biceps brachii

Brachialis

Elbow starting to be flexed by brachialis and biceps brachii contracting

THE ARMS AND HANDS IN DETAIL

Turning the arm, back views

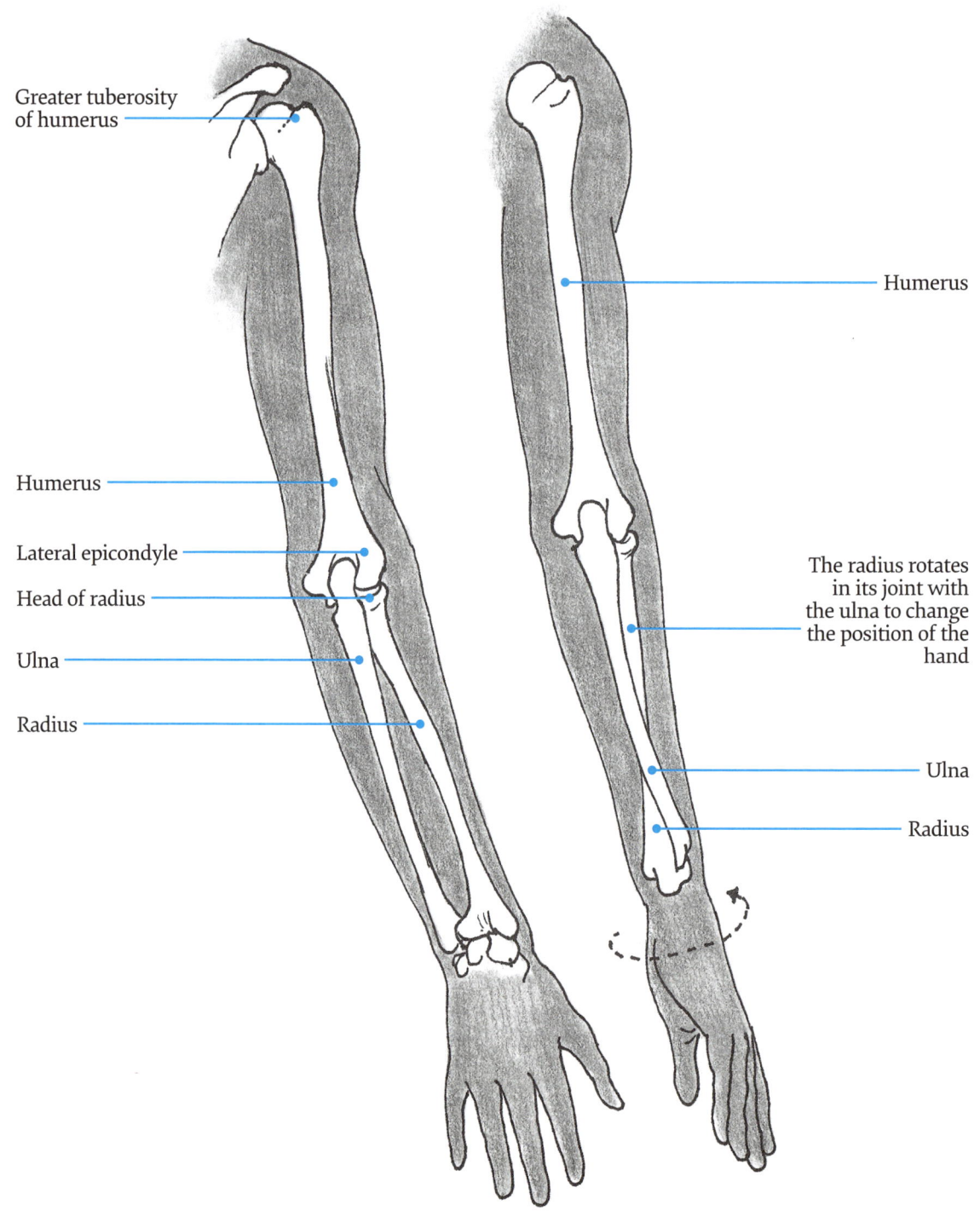

136 THE ARMS AND HANDS IN DETAIL

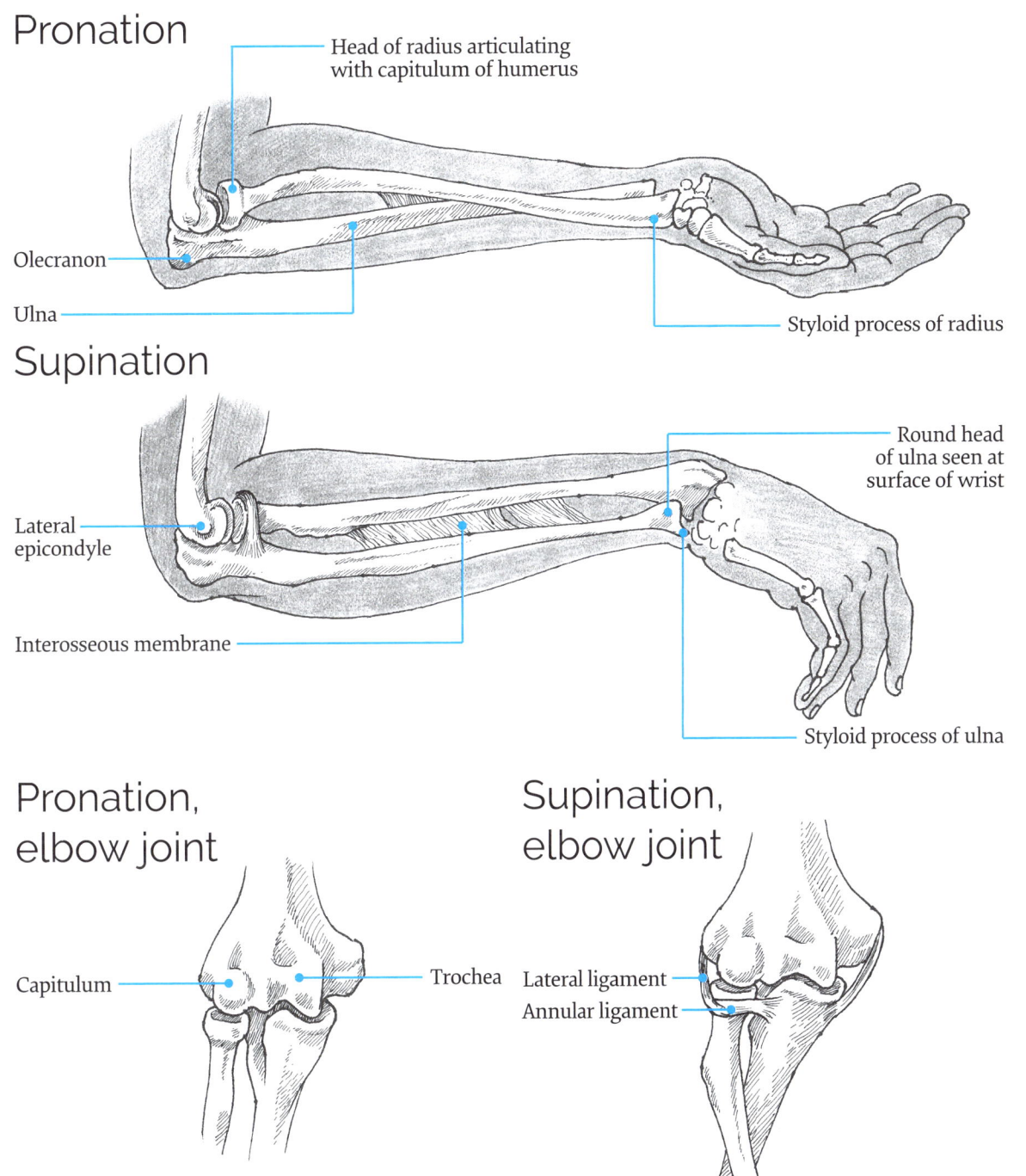

THE ARMS AND HANDS IN DETAIL

Muscles of the lower arm

Palm-up views

ABDUCTOR POLLICIS LONGUS extends and abducts thumb.
ANCONEUS extends forearm.
BRACHIORADIALIS flexes elbow joint.
LONG EXTENSOR MUSCLES on posterior forearm pass into the back of hand.
EXTENSOR DIGITORUM extends fingers (not thumb);
EXTENSOR DIGITI MINIMI extends little finger.
EXTENSOR CARPI ULNARIS extends wrist, adducts hand.
EXTENSOR POLLICIS BREVIS extends proximal phalanx of thumb.
EXTENSOR INDICIS extends forefinger.
EXTENSOR CARPI RADIALIS BREVIS extends the hand at the wrist.
EXTENSOR CARPI RADIALIS LONGUS extends wrist on side of radius.
EXTENSOR POLLICIS LONGUS extends thumb.
FLEXOR CARPI RADIALIS flexes and rotates hand inwards.
FLEXOR CARPI ULNARIS flexes wrist on side of ulna.
FLEXOR DIGITI MINIMI BREVIS flexes little finger.
FLEXOR DIGITORUM PROFUNDUS flexes middle and distal phalanges of fingers (not thumb).
FLEXOR DIGITORUM SUPERFICIALIS flexes middle and distal phalanges of fingers (not thumb) and wrist.
FLEXOR POLLICIS LONGUS flexes distal phalanx.
PALMARIS LONGUS the weakest, least significant muscle, sometimes missing in one forearm, flexes hand.
PRONATOR QUADRATUS causes pronation of radius.
PRONATOR TERES causes pronation of forearm, helps in flexion of forearm.
SUPINATOR the shortest extensor, rotates radius outwards on its own axis.

Here are four views of the lower arm, palm up, showing the layers of muscle from deepest (1) to most superficial (4).

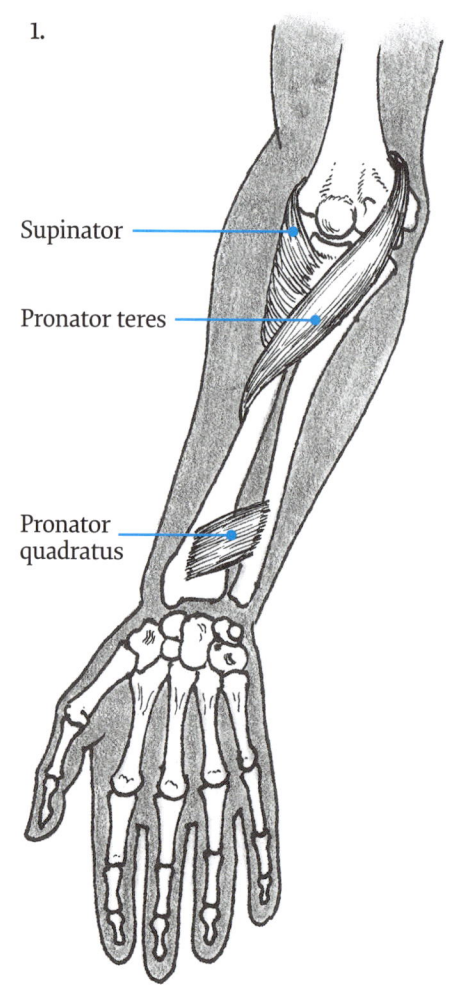

1.

Supinator

Pronator teres

Pronator quadratus

THE ARMS AND HANDS IN DETAIL

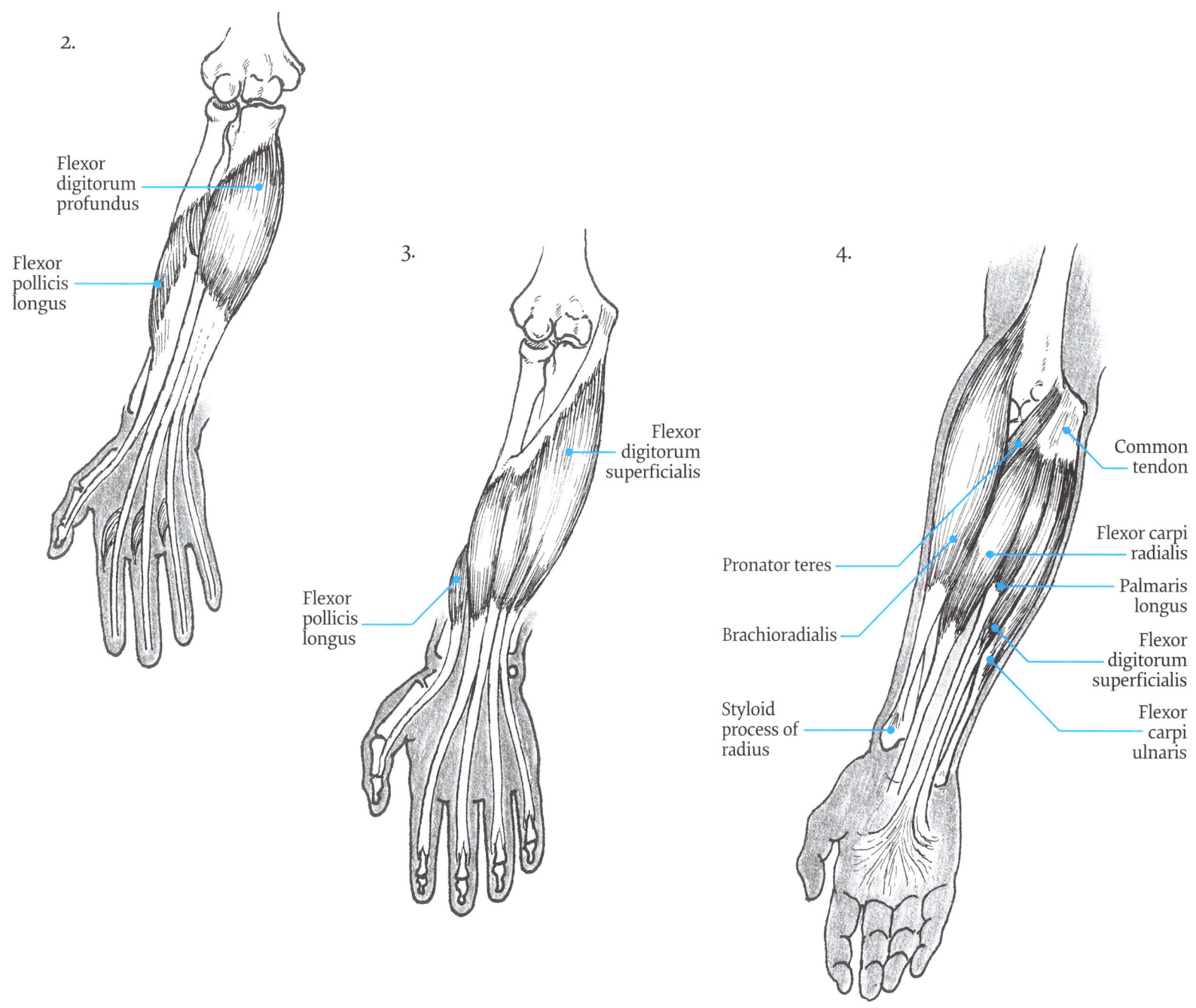

THE ARMS AND HANDS IN DETAIL

Palm-down views

DEEP LEVEL　　　SUPERFICIAL LEVEL

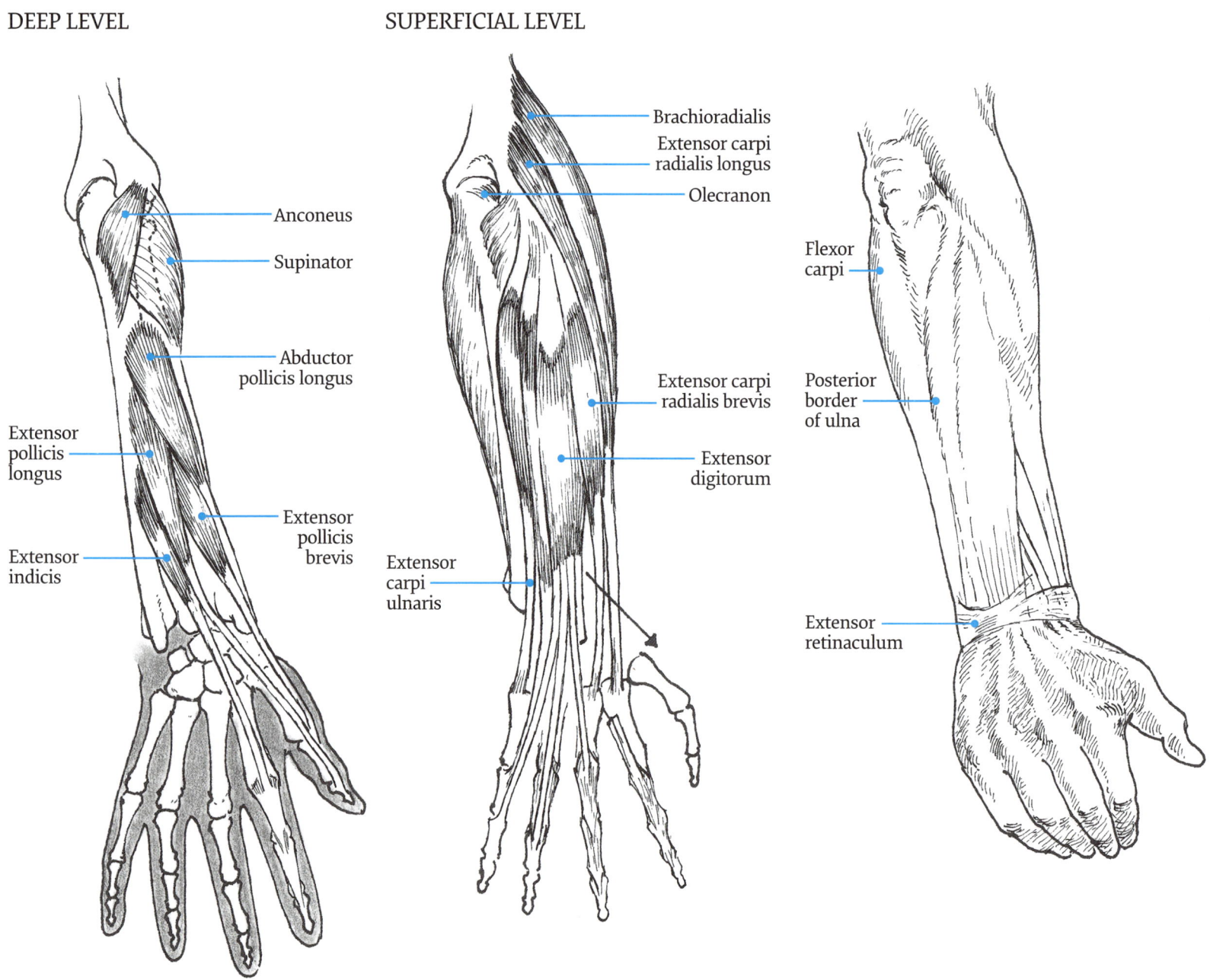

Pivoting forearm

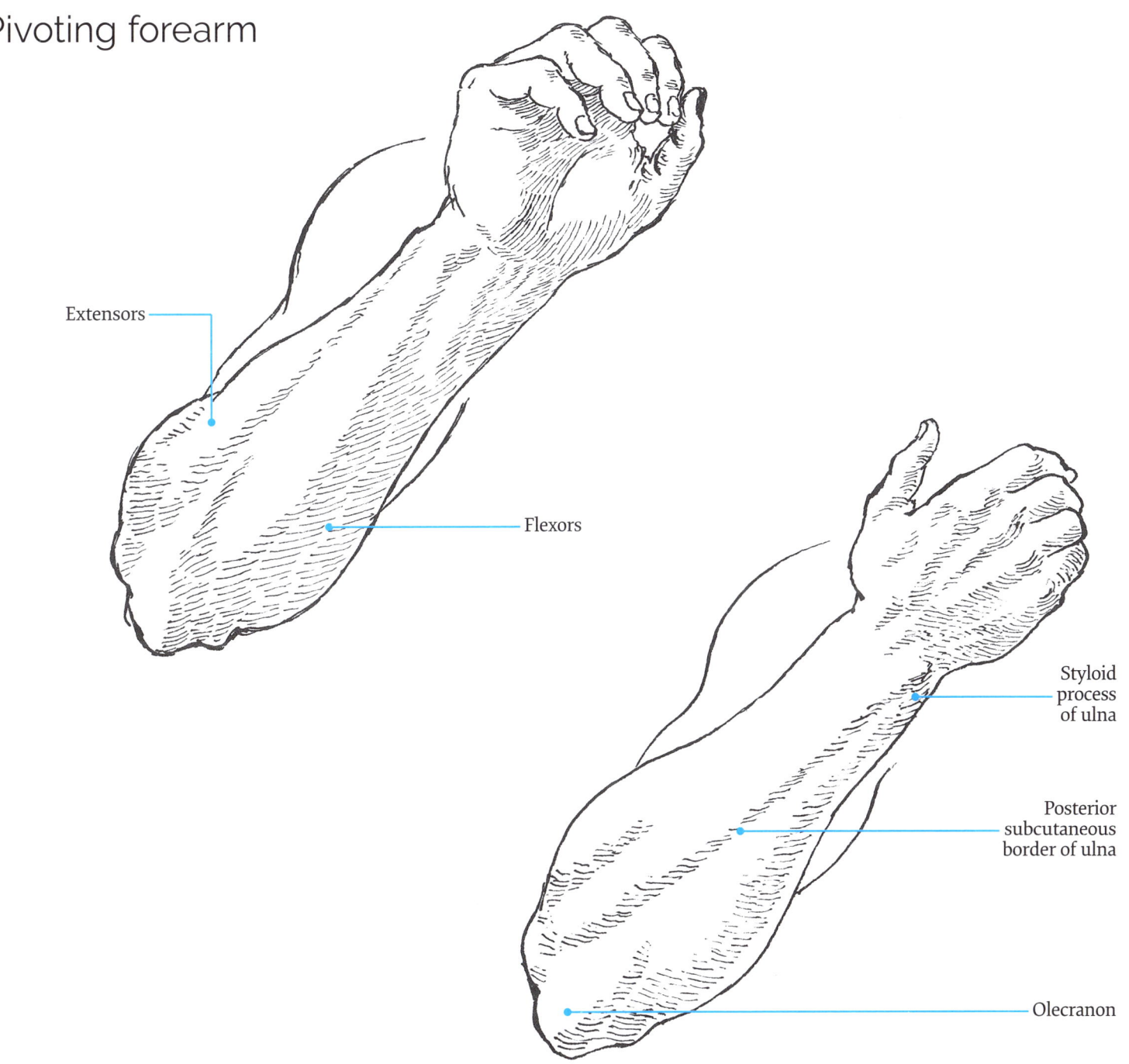

Flexing the whole arm
Flexed arm showing the muscles

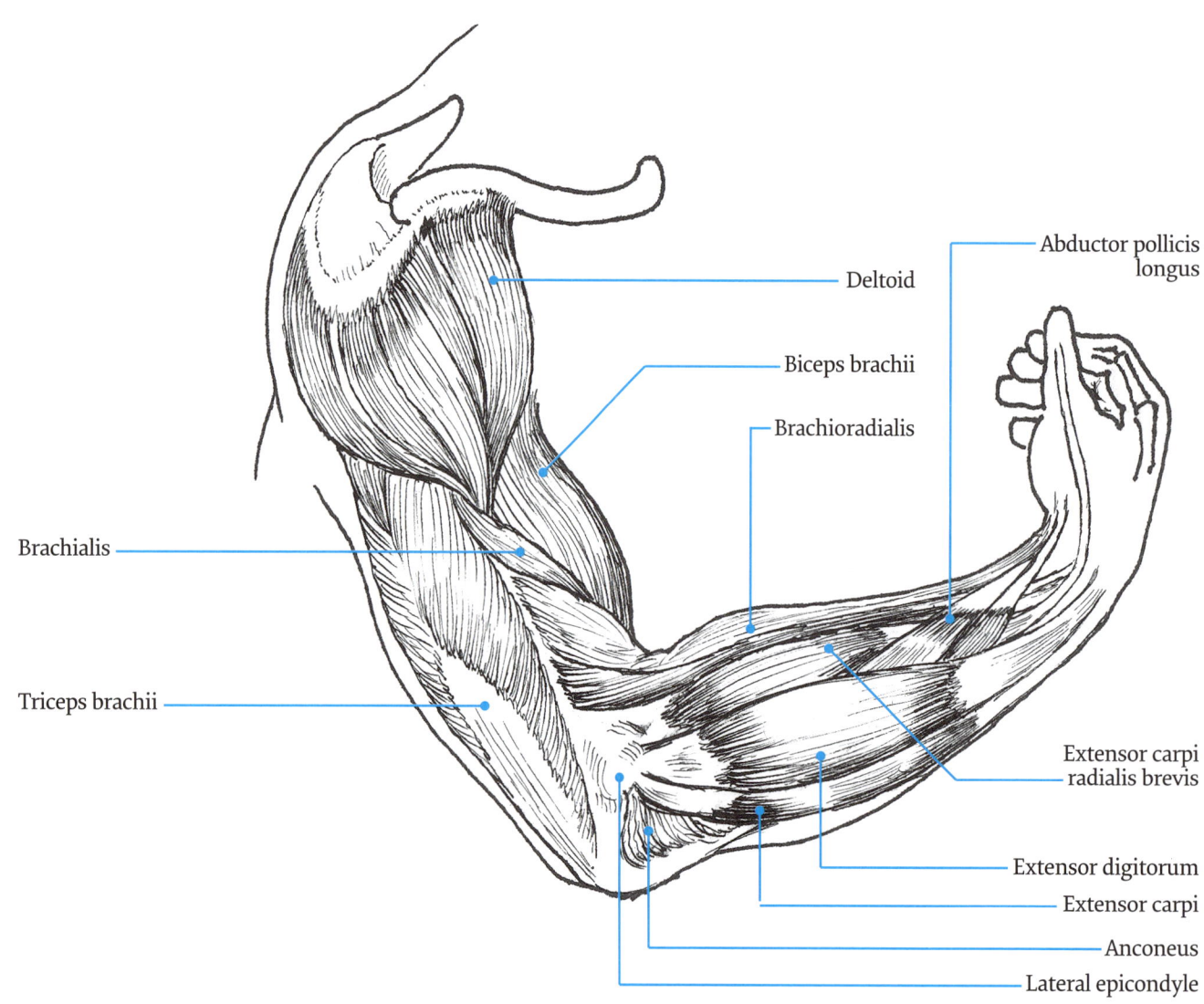

Surface view of the flexed arm

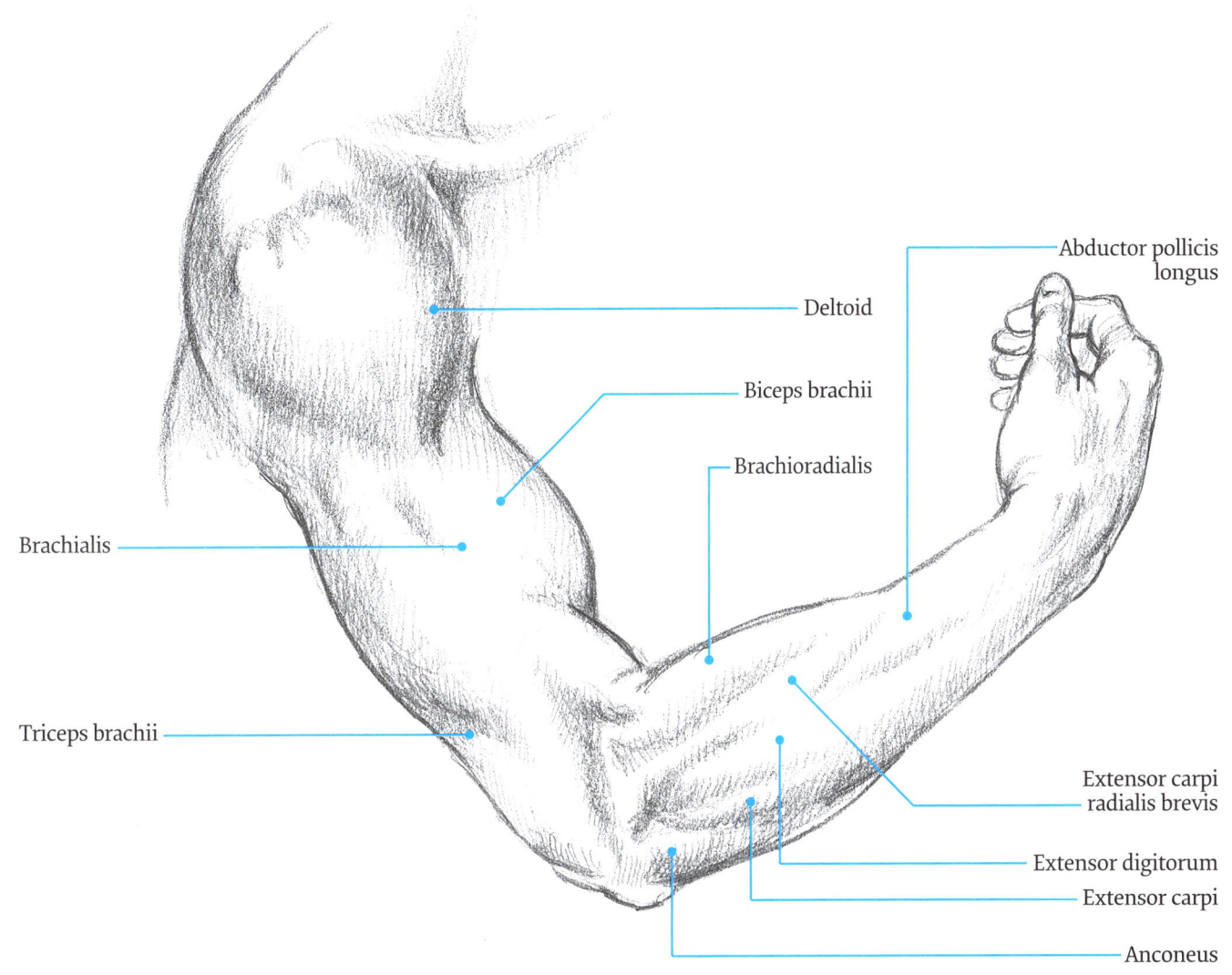

Skeleton of the hand
Palm-down view

As well as combined drawings of the arm and hand, I am also dealing with the hand separately because it is such an intricate part of the upper limb. These diagrams of the bones of the hand seen from different angles are well worth studying, so you will be able to recognize them through the covering of muscle and skin.

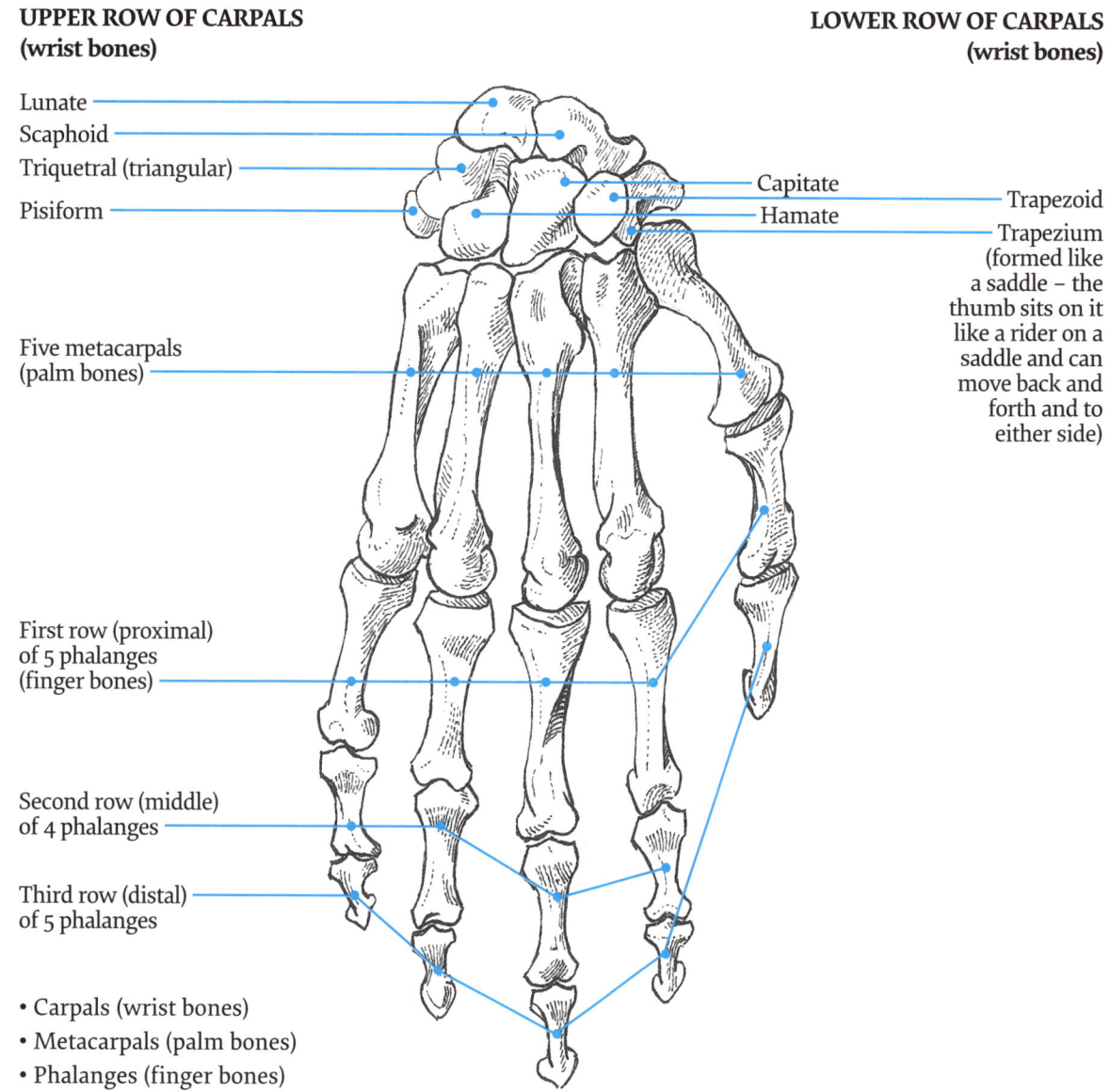

UPPER ROW OF CARPALS (wrist bones)
- Lunate
- Scaphoid
- Triquetral (triangular)
- Pisiform
- Five metacarpals (palm bones)
- First row (proximal) of 5 phalanges (finger bones)
- Second row (middle) of 4 phalanges
- Third row (distal) of 5 phalanges

- Carpals (wrist bones)
- Metacarpals (palm bones)
- Phalanges (finger bones)

LOWER ROW OF CARPALS (wrist bones)
- Capitate
- Hamate
- Trapezoid
- Trapezium (formed like a saddle – the thumb sits on it like a rider on a saddle and can move back and forth and to either side)

144 THE ARMS AND HANDS IN DETAIL

Palm-up view

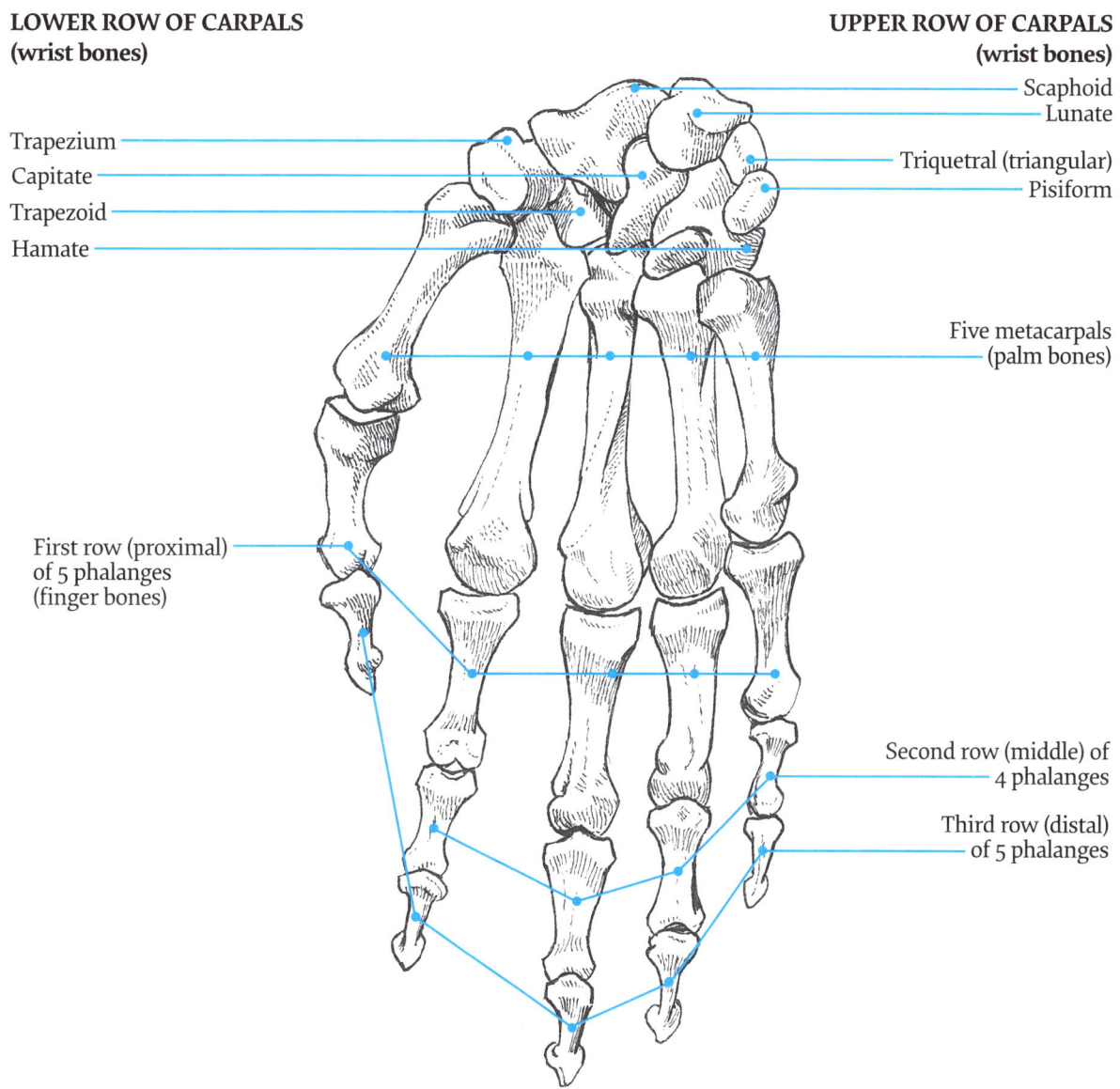

LOWER ROW OF CARPALS
(wrist bones)

Trapezium
Capitate
Trapezoid
Hamate

UPPER ROW OF CARPALS
(wrist bones)

Scaphoid
Lunate
Triquetral (triangular)
Pisiform

Five metacarpals (palm bones)

First row (proximal) of 5 phalanges (finger bones)

Second row (middle) of 4 phalanges

Third row (distal) of 5 phalanges

THE ARMS AND HANDS IN DETAIL

Muscles of the hand
Palm-down view

The hand, being the part of the body which sets human skills apart from all the other animals, is a very complex structure of overlapping muscles and tendons. These allow the fingers and thumb to perform very complicated and subtle motions, enabling humans to construct and handle an enormous number of tools (like the pencil), extending their range of activities far beyond other species.

- Annular ligament of the wrist
- Extensor carpi radialis brevis
- Abductor pollicis longus
- Extensor digitorum (communis)
- Extensor carpi ulnaris
- Extensor pollicis brevis
- Extensor pollicis longus
- Abductor digiti minimi
- Dorsal interossei

The main difficulty in drawing the muscles of the hand is that the most significant ones are situated in the arm and are connected to the hand by long tendons. There are some muscles in the hand itself, but they tend to be hidden under the surface pads of the palm and so are not very evident. The most clearly seen muscles are around the base of the thumb and on the opposite edge of the palm.

Palm-up view

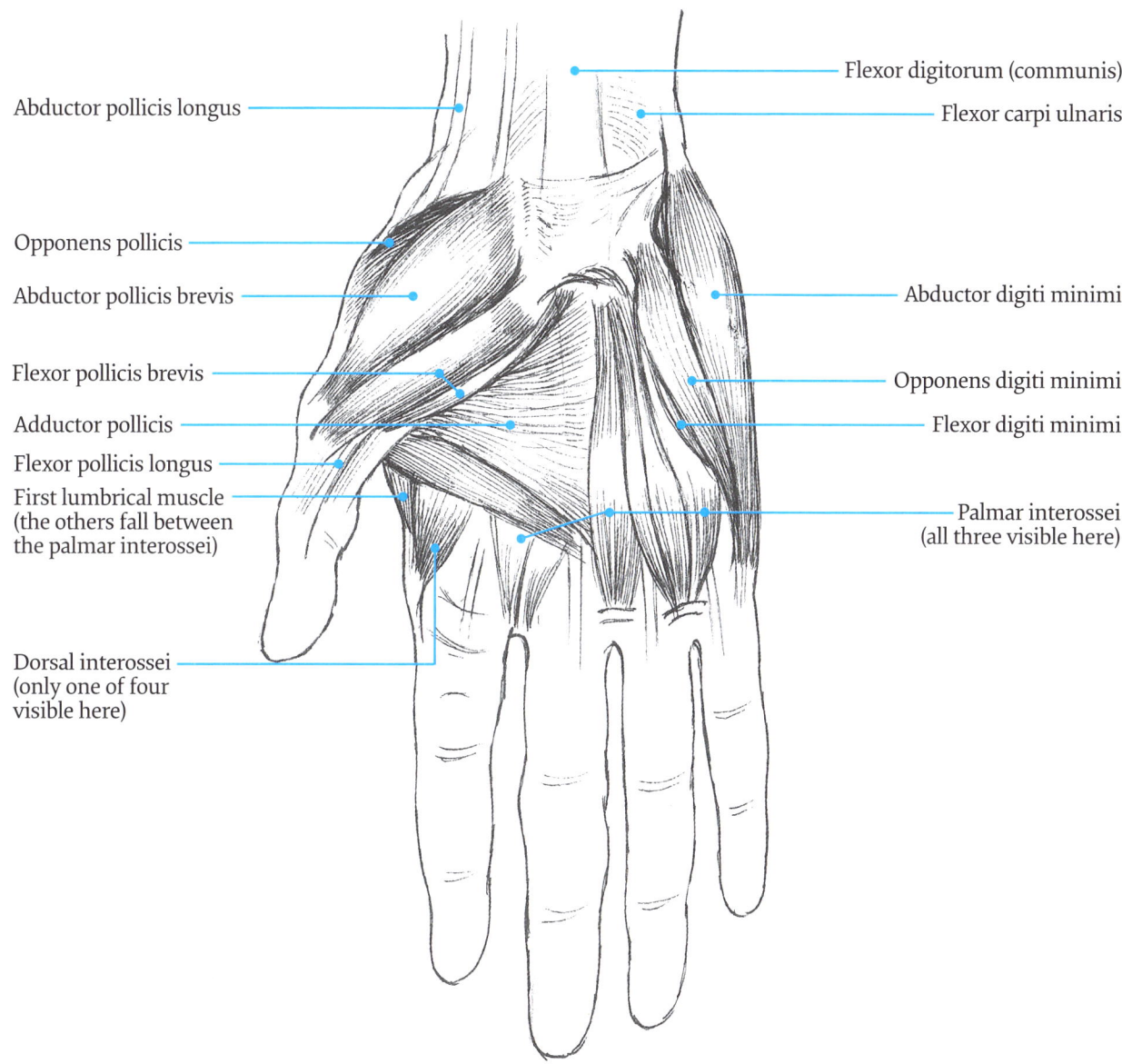

- Abductor pollicis longus
- Opponens pollicis
- Abductor pollicis brevis
- Flexor pollicis brevis
- Adductor pollicis
- Flexor pollicis longus
- First lumbrical muscle (the others fall between the palmar interossei)
- Dorsal interossei (only one of four visible here)
- Flexor digitorum (communis)
- Flexor carpi ulnaris
- Abductor digiti minimi
- Opponens digiti minimi
- Flexor digiti minimi
- Palmar interossei (all three visible here)

THE ARMS AND HANDS IN DETAIL

Muscle and bone structure of the hand

Note that there are no muscles in the fingers, only bones and tendons, tied by fibrous bands. The small fatty pads on the end of fingers carry blood and nerves and cushion flexor tendons.

ABDUCTOR DIGITI MINIMI moves little finger outwards.
ABDUCTOR POLLICIS BREVIS draws thumb forward at a right angle to palm.
ADDUCTOR POLLICIS draws thumb towards palm.
DORSAL INTEROSSEI abduct fingers from midline of hand.
FLEXOR and EXTENSOR RETINACULA enable tendons of hand to change direction at wrist.
FLEXOR POLLICIS BREVIS flexes proximal phalanx of thumb.
LUMBRICALES flex the proximal and extend the middle and distal phalanges.
OPPONENS DIGITI MINIMI draws fifth metacarpal forwards and inwards, to hollow the palm.
OPPONENS POLLICIS allows opposition of thumb.
PALMAR MUSCLES lie beneath palmar aponeurosis (thickened fascia) holding skin to muscles and bones below.
PALMAR INTEROSSEI move fingers inward to midline of hand.

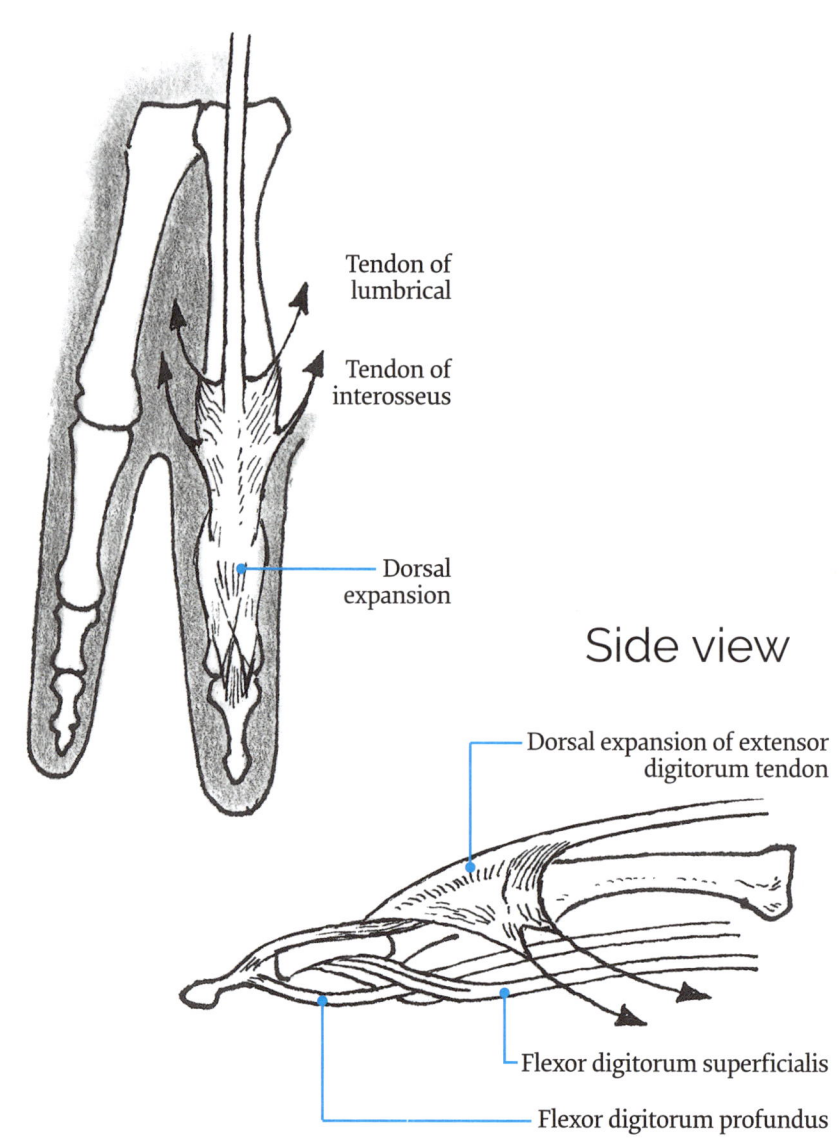

Palm-up view, deep layer

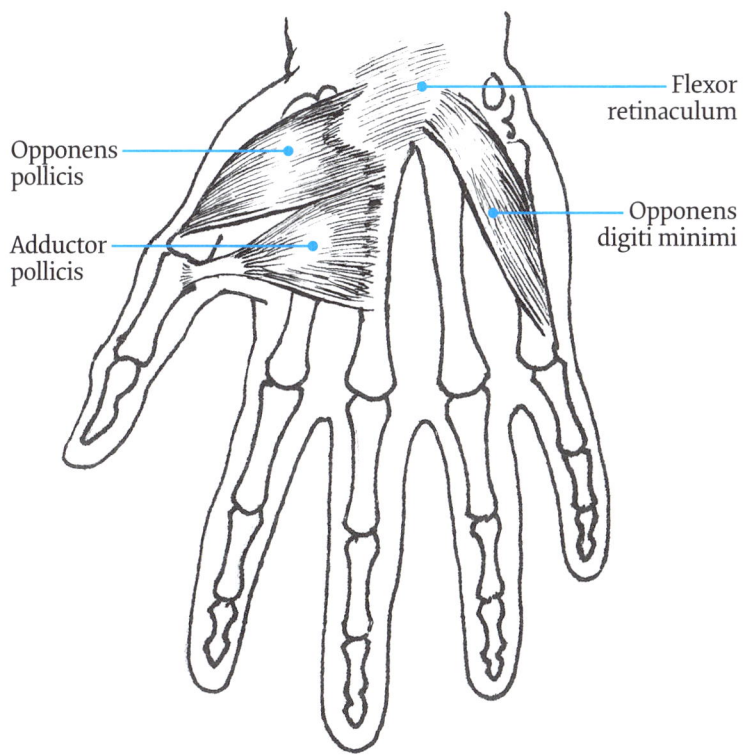

- Opponens pollicis
- Adductor pollicis
- Flexor retinaculum
- Opponens digiti minimi

Palm-up view, next level

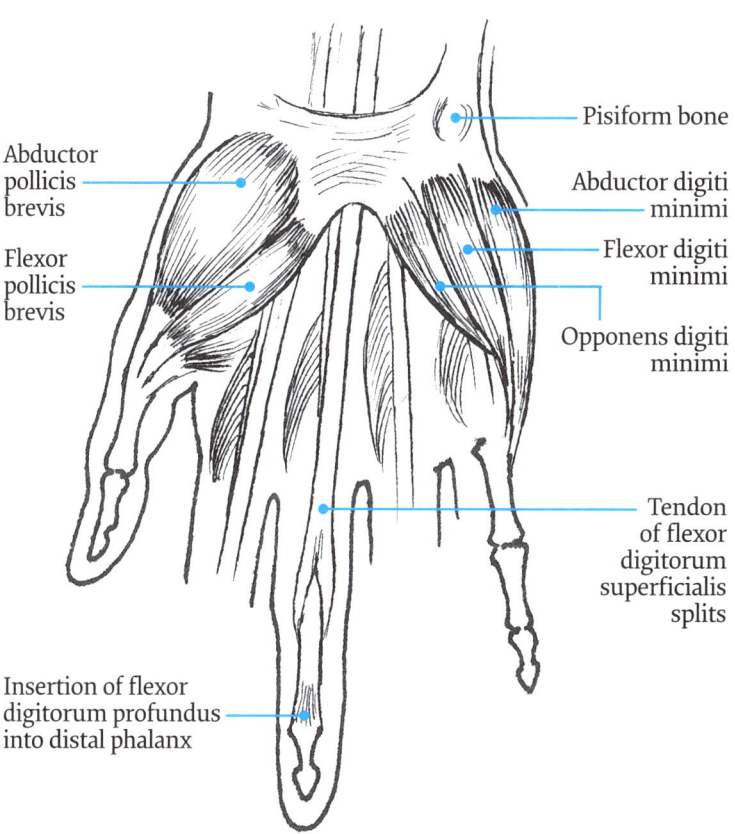

- Abductor pollicis brevis
- Flexor pollicis brevis
- Insertion of flexor digitorum profundus into distal phalanx
- Pisiform bone
- Abductor digiti minimi
- Flexor digiti minimi
- Opponens digiti minimi
- Tendon of flexor digitorum superficialis splits

THE ARMS AND HANDS IN DETAIL

Surface of the hand

Male hand
palm-up view

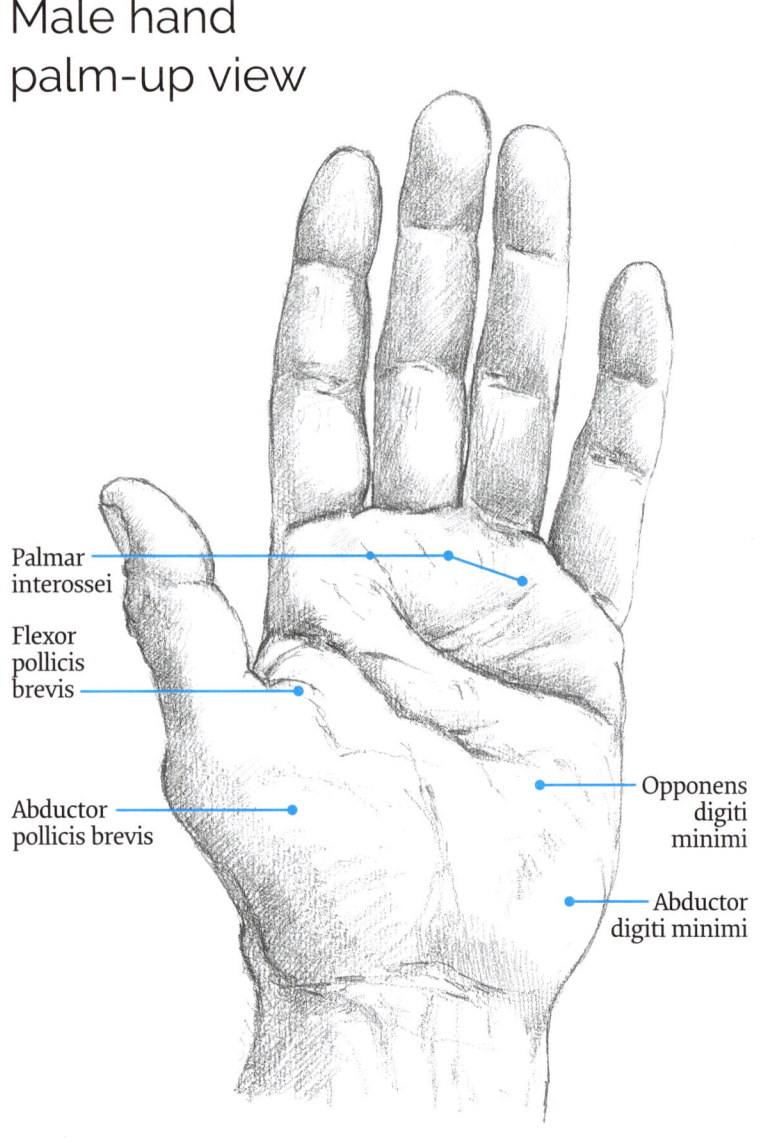

- Palmar interossei
- Flexor pollicis brevis
- Abductor pollicis brevis
- Opponens digiti minimi
- Abductor digiti minimi

Male hand
palm-down view

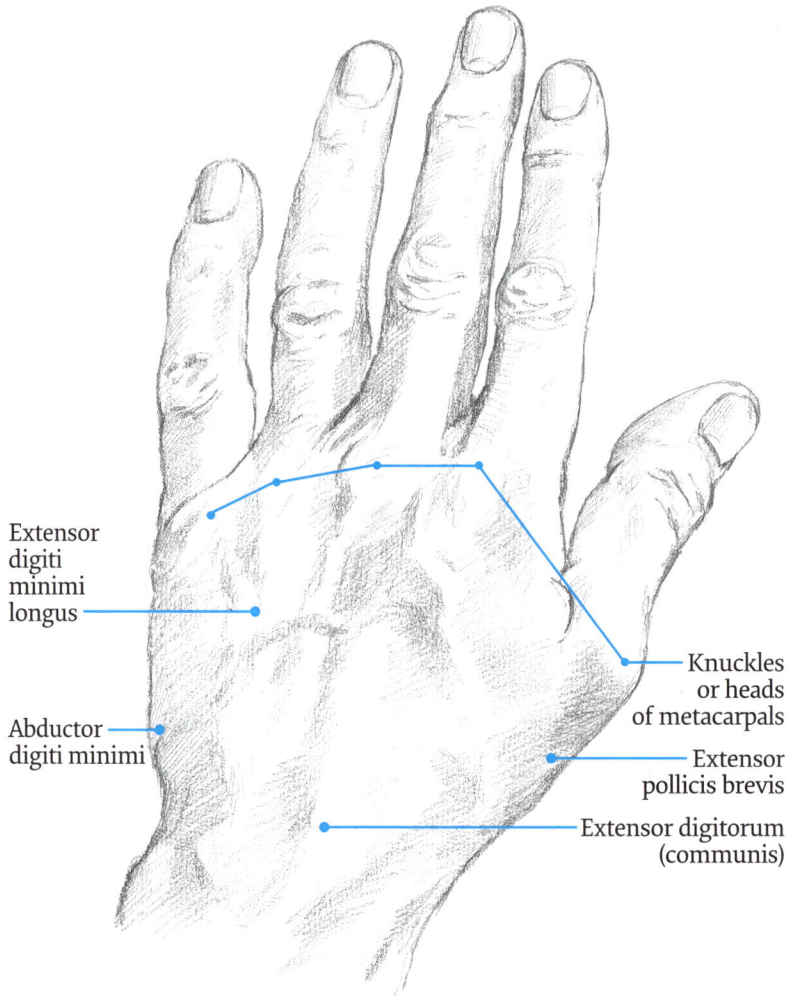

- Extensor digiti minimi longus
- Abductor digiti minimi
- Knuckles or heads of metacarpals
- Extensor pollicis brevis
- Extensor digitorum (communis)

THE ARMS AND HANDS IN DETAIL

The female hand is usually softer-looking and with more tapered fingers than the male. The knuckles of the male hand tend to look more prominent and the fingers are squarer in shape. But don't take this for granted in your drawing: sometimes this typical shape can be reversed.

Female hand palm-down view

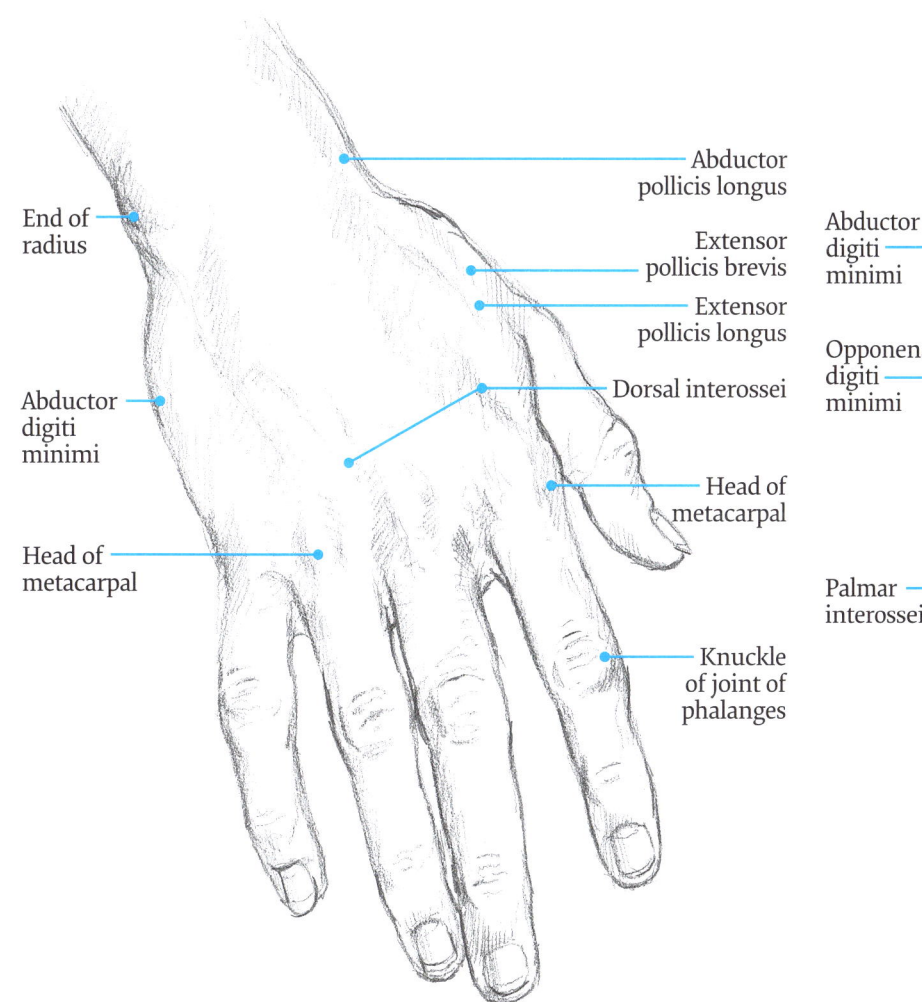

Female hand palm-up view

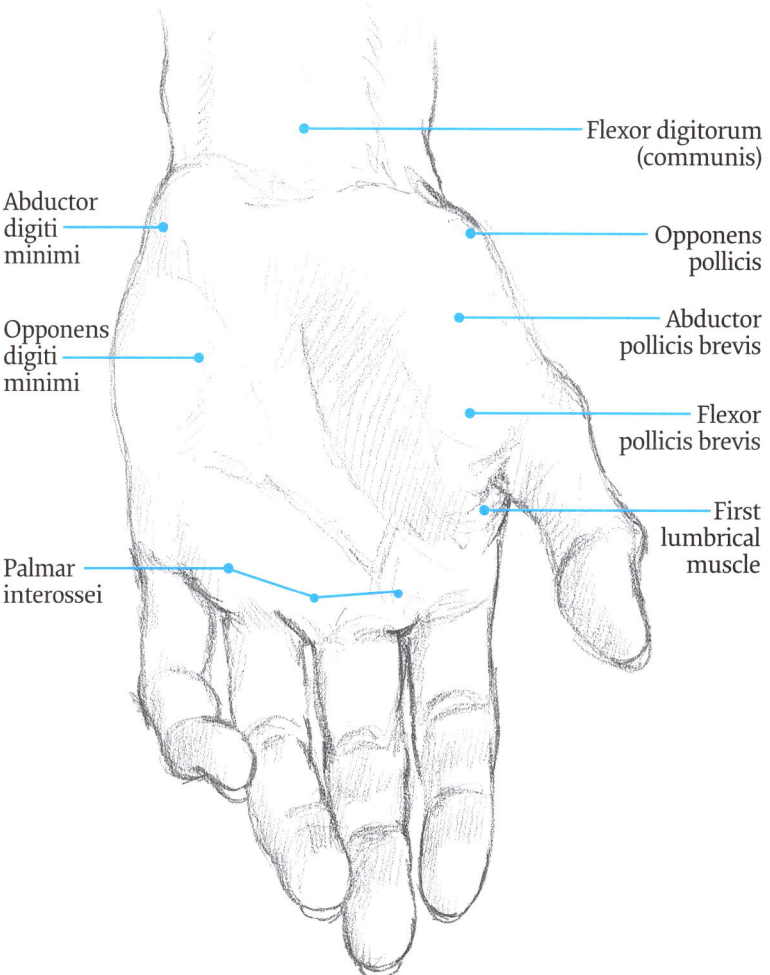

THE ARMS AND HANDS IN DETAIL 151

The hand in movement

Extension

Flexion

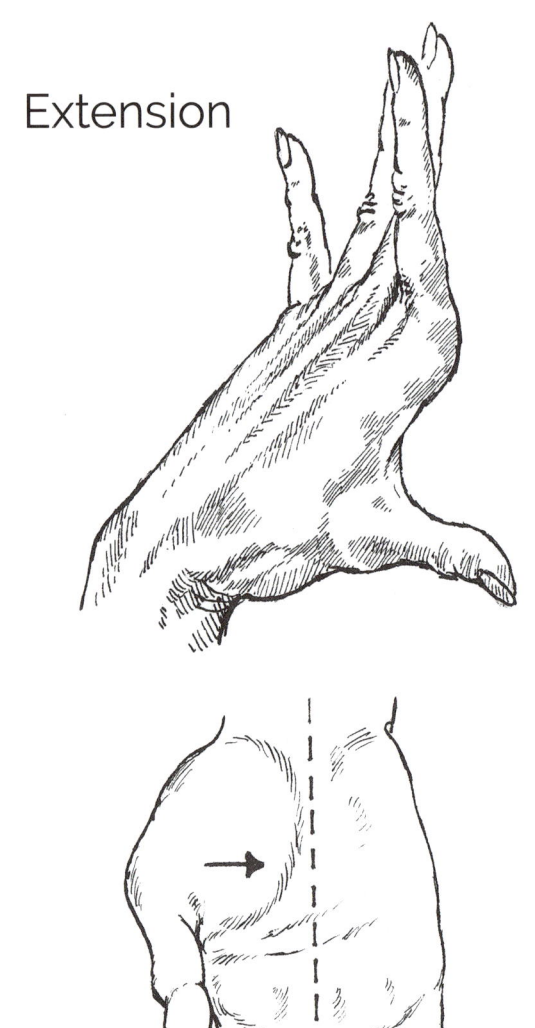

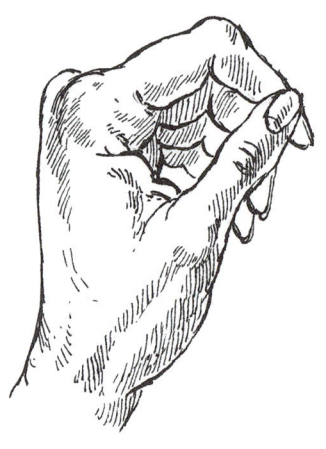

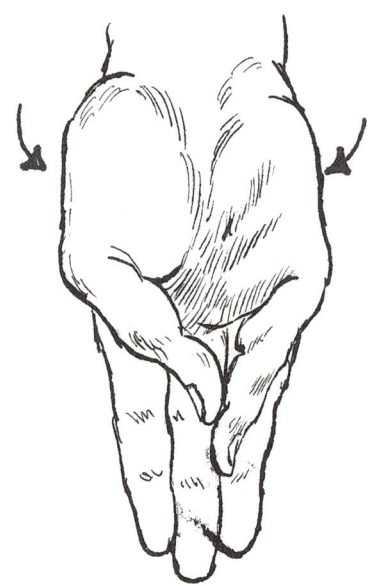

Adductor pollicis acting

The two opponens muscles acting

Range of hand movement

It is well worth studying the hand in detail, as its movements can be very expressive and capturing them accurately will add a lot to your drawing.

The movements of the hand are mainly produced higher up the arm, the hand itself only having a few muscles. When you move your hand, notice the movements in the muscles of your forearm or upper arm where the action originates.

Look out for details, like the pads on the palm of the hand and the front of the fingers which push out when the hand is closed into a fist.

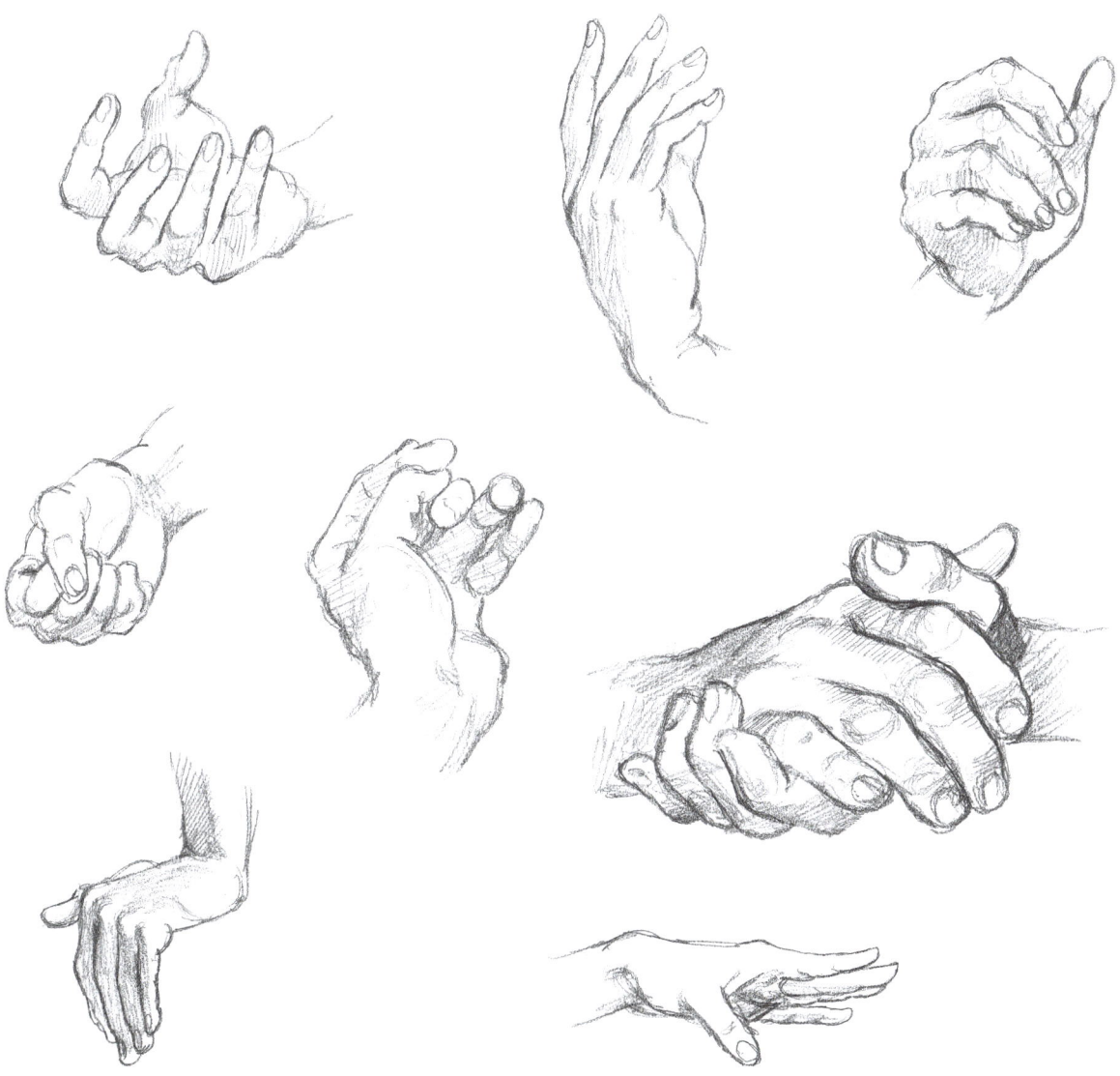

THE ARMS AND HANDS IN DETAIL

More precise hand movements

What is clear is how flexible and sensitive the hands are, being able to make large, strong movements and detailed, precise ones.

The following range of movements are just a few of the hundreds of actions the hand can perform.

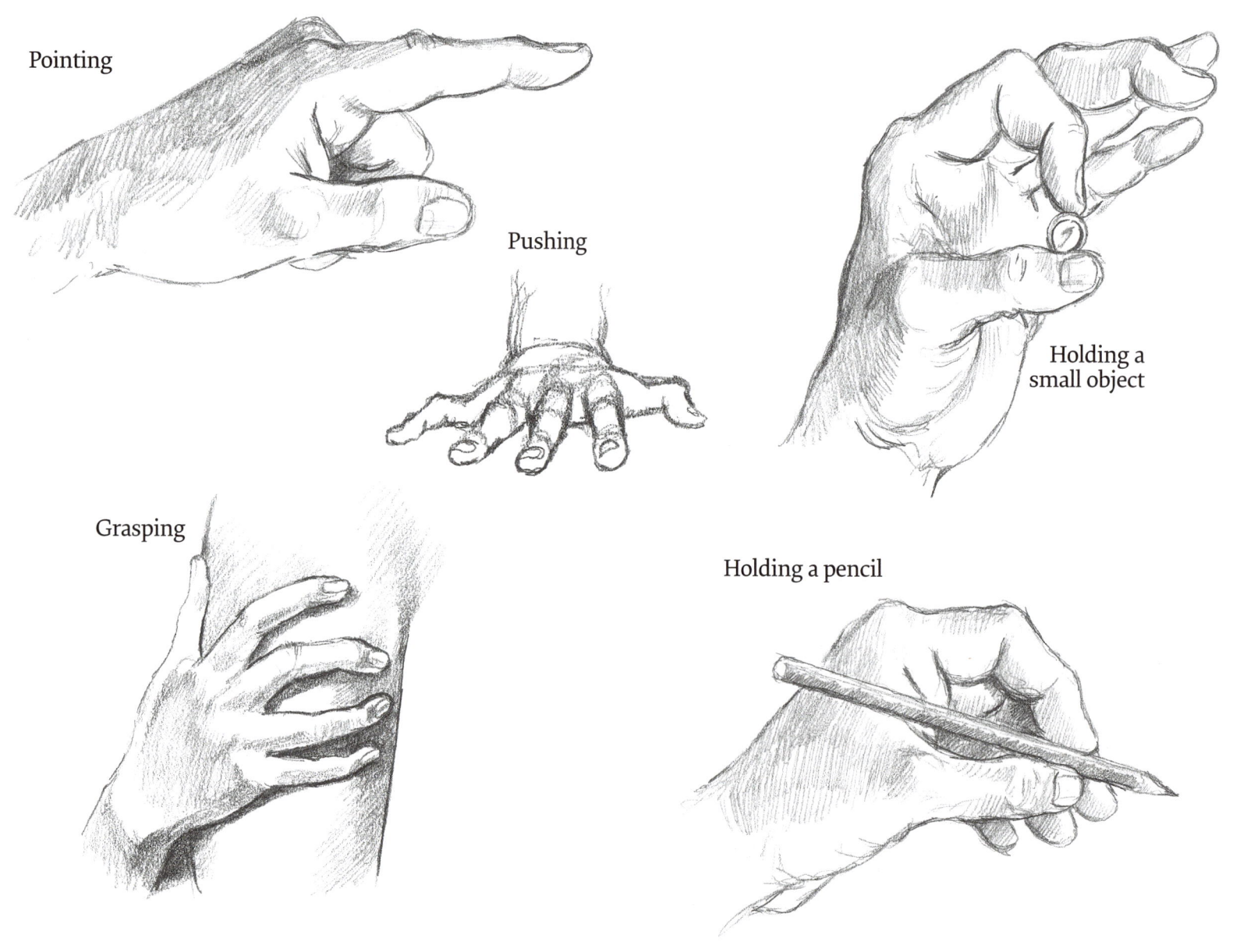

Pointing

Pushing

Holding a small object

Grasping

Holding a pencil

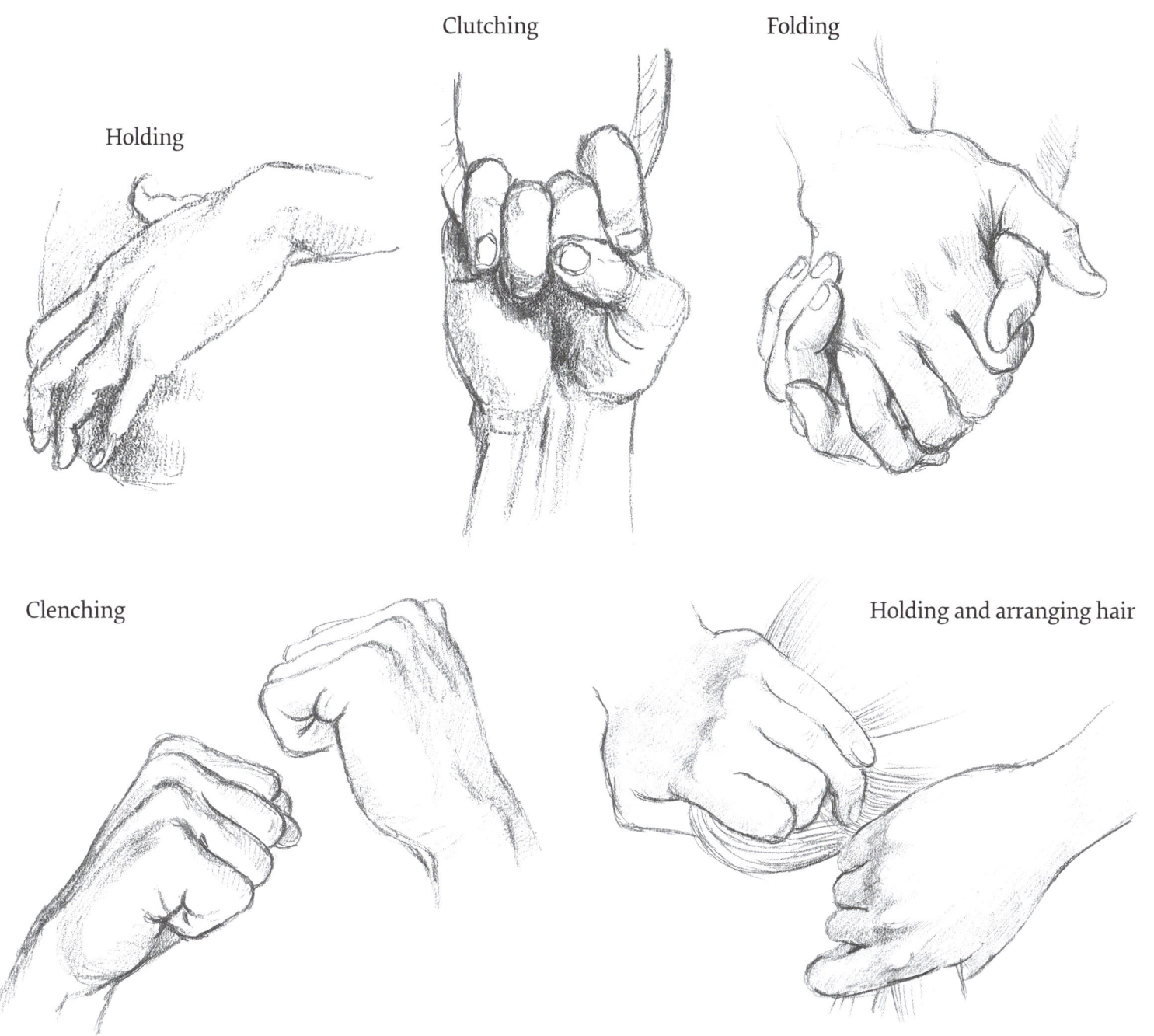

Surface views of arms and hands

When the arm is stretched out horizontally, we can see the shapes of the larger muscles at the surface of the limb. Here we look at the outstretched arm from two angles: with the palm facing up (supine view) and with the palm facing down (prone view).

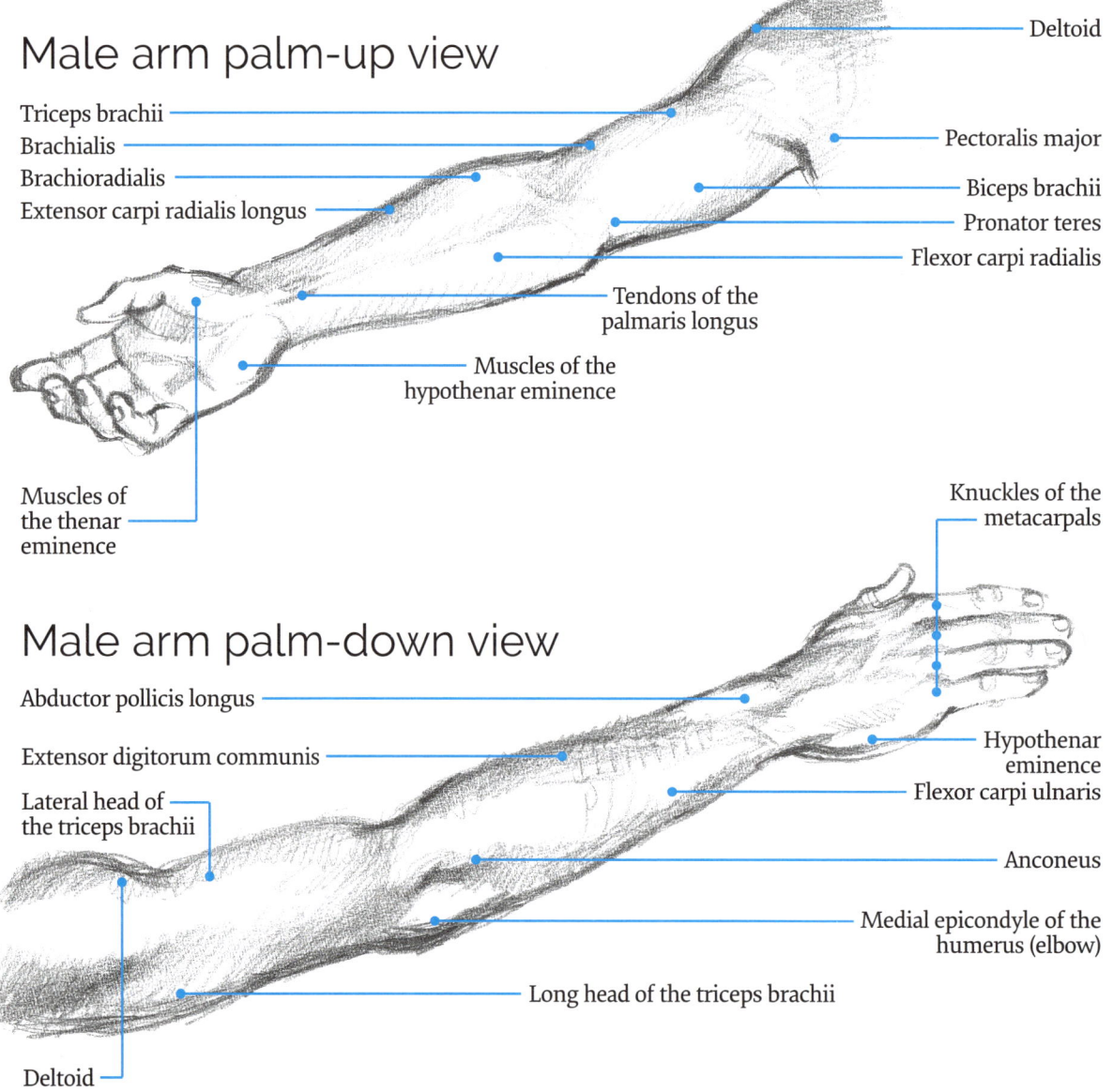

Male arm palm-up view

- Triceps brachii
- Brachialis
- Brachioradialis
- Extensor carpi radialis longus
- Muscles of the thenar eminence
- Muscles of the hypothenar eminence
- Tendons of the palmaris longus
- Flexor carpi radialis
- Pronator teres
- Biceps brachii
- Pectoralis major
- Deltoid

Male arm palm-down view

- Abductor pollicis longus
- Extensor digitorum communis
- Lateral head of the triceps brachii
- Deltoid
- Long head of the triceps brachii
- Medial epicondyle of the humerus (elbow)
- Anconeus
- Flexor carpi ulnaris
- Hypothenar eminence
- Knuckles of the metacarpals

156 THE ARMS AND HANDS IN DETAIL

Female arm palm-up view

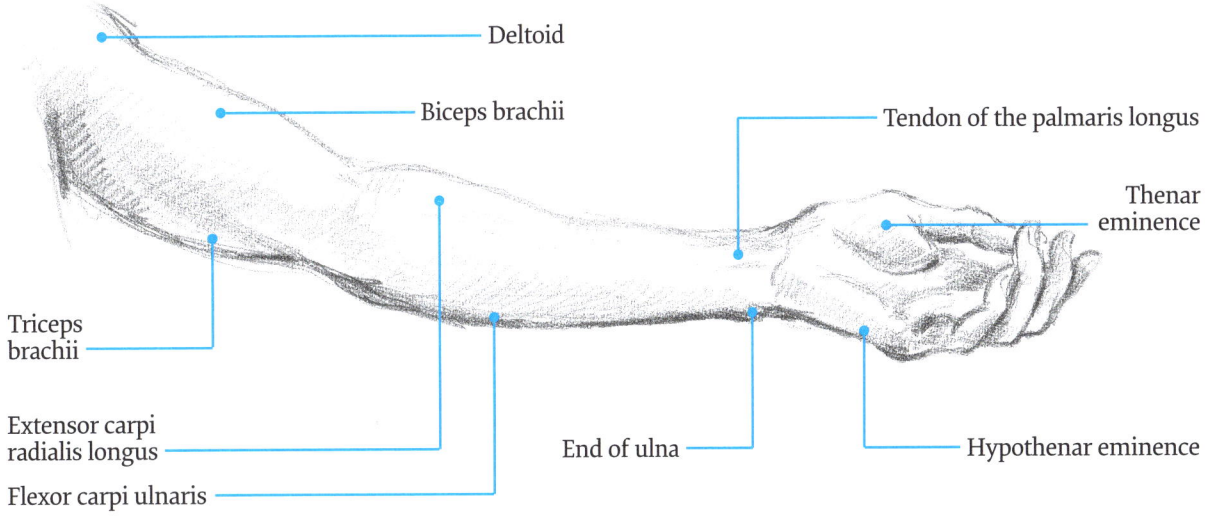

Female arm palm-down view

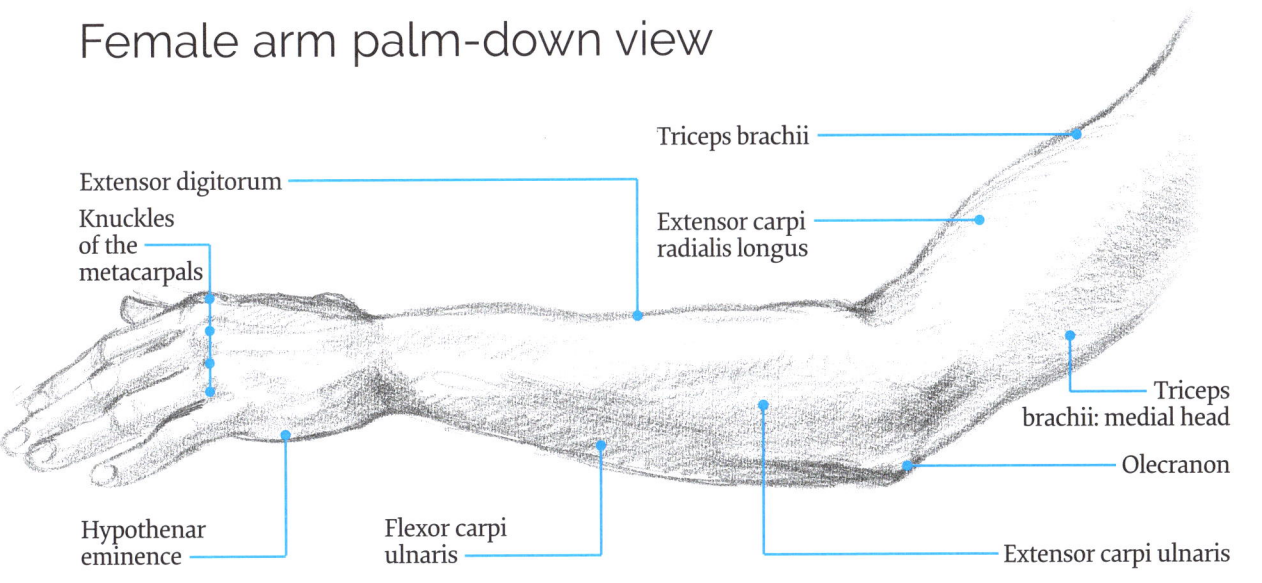

THE ARMS AND HANDS IN DETAIL

Arms and hands drawn by master artists

Over the following pages I have drawn several images of the arm and hand after master artists. Note the difference in muscularity between portrayals of the male and female arm.

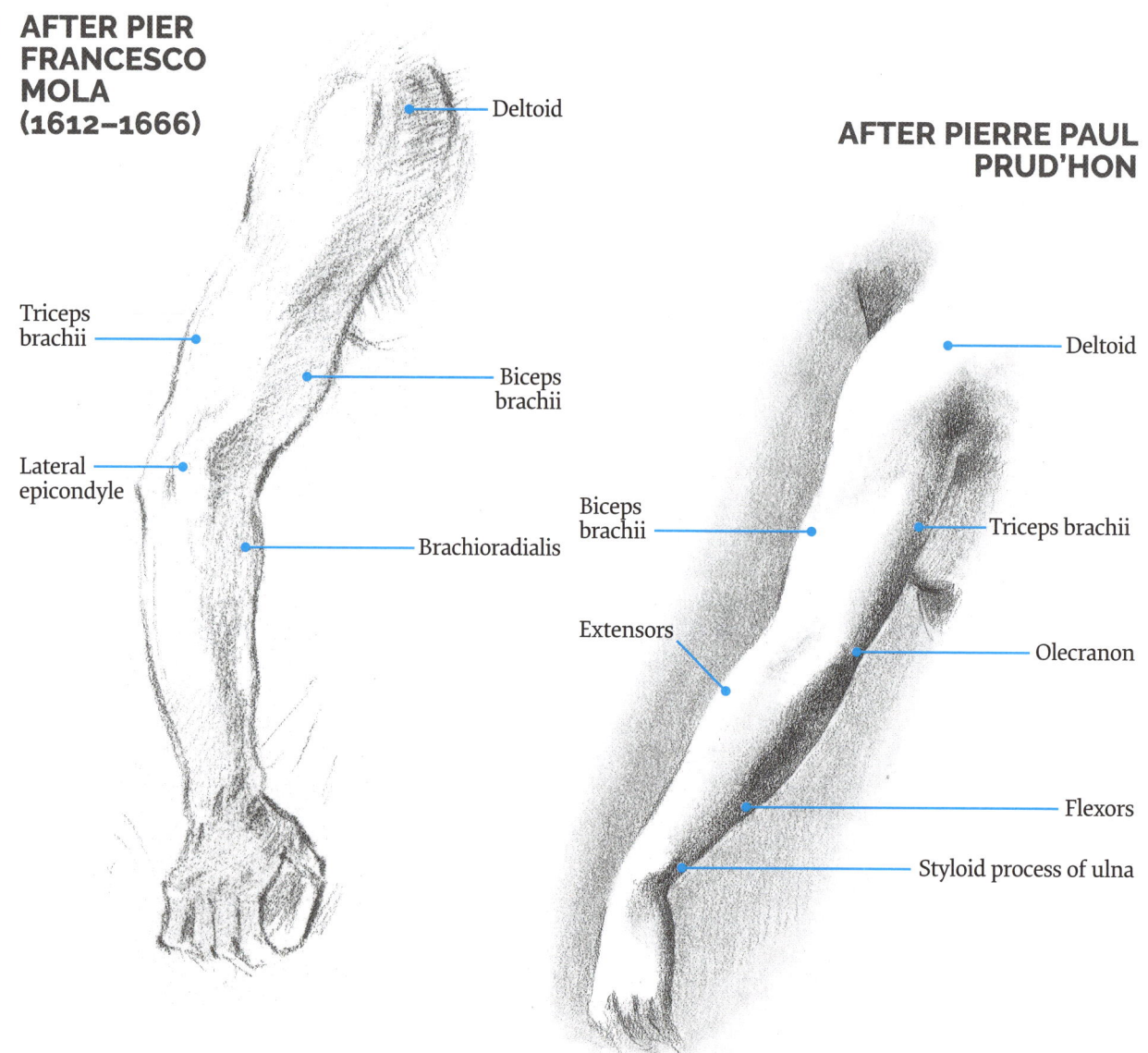

AFTER PIER FRANCESCO MOLA (1612–1666)

- Deltoid
- Triceps brachii
- Biceps brachii
- Lateral epicondyle
- Brachioradialis

AFTER PIERRE PAUL PRUD'HON

- Deltoid
- Biceps brachii
- Triceps brachii
- Extensors
- Olecranon
- Flexors
- Styloid process of ulna

158 THE ARMS AND HANDS IN DETAIL

FOUR DRAWINGS AFTER MICHELANGELO BUONARROTI

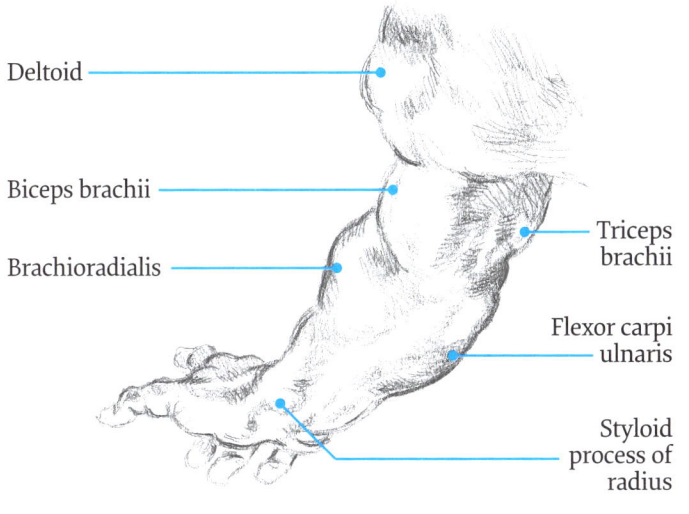
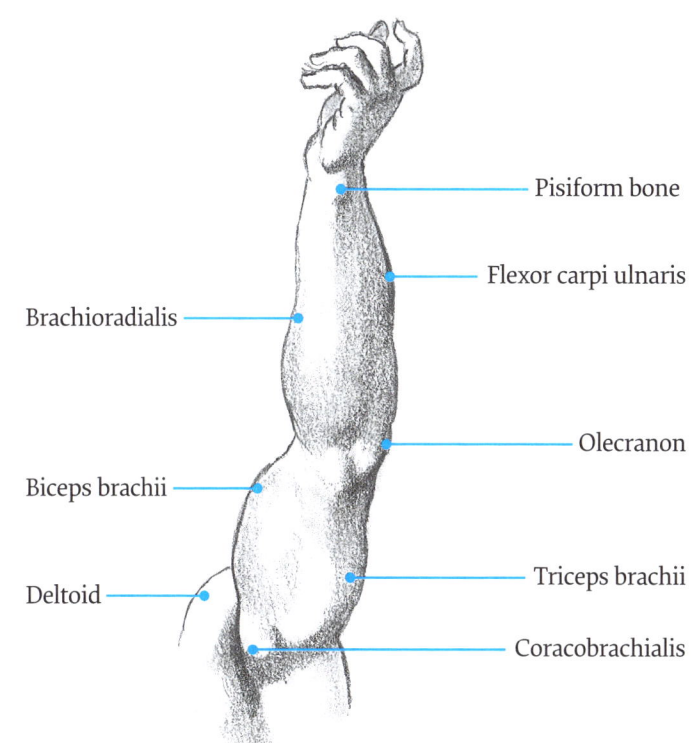
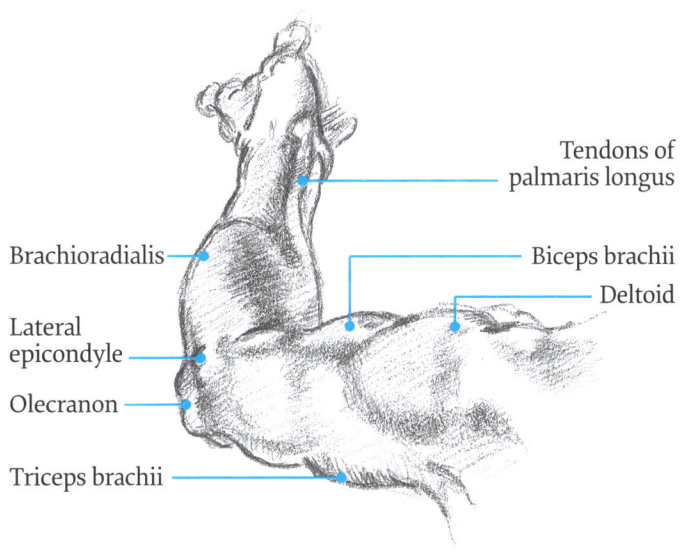
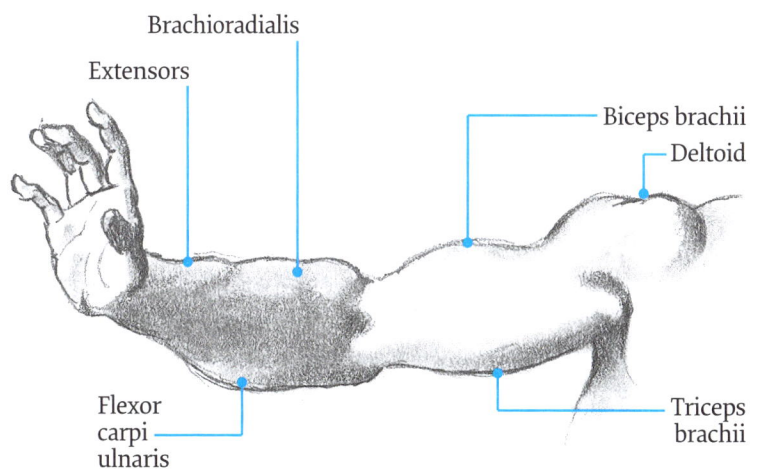

THE ARMS AND HANDS IN DETAIL

AFTER ANTONIO DE PEREDA Y SALGADO (1611–1678)

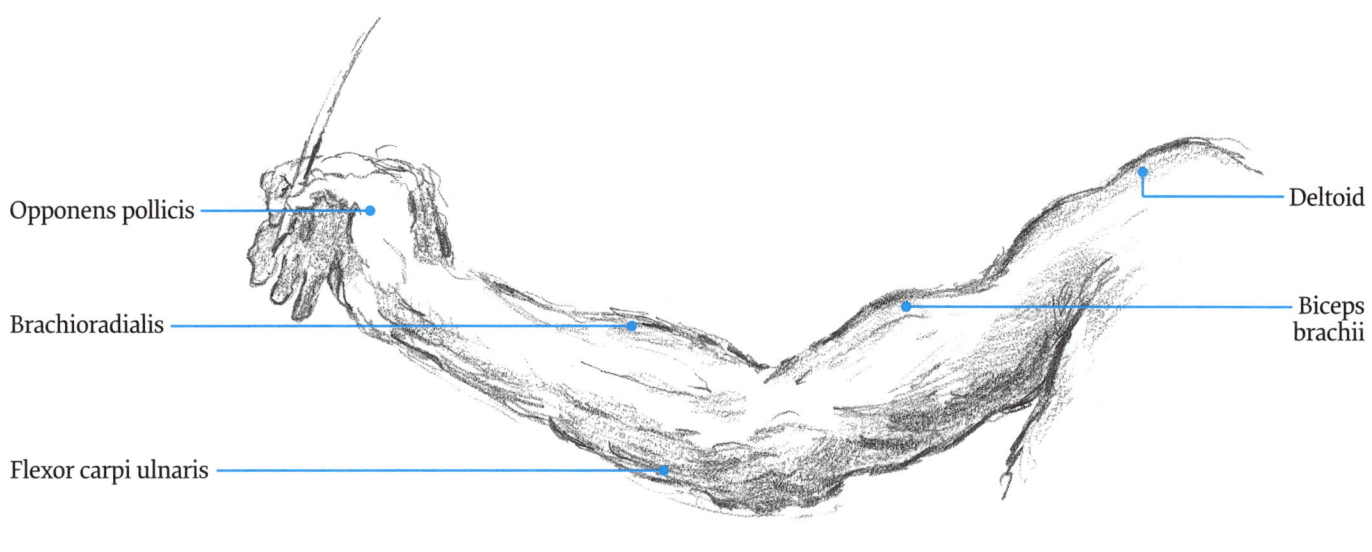

AFTER JEAN-ANTOINE WATTEAU (1684–1721)

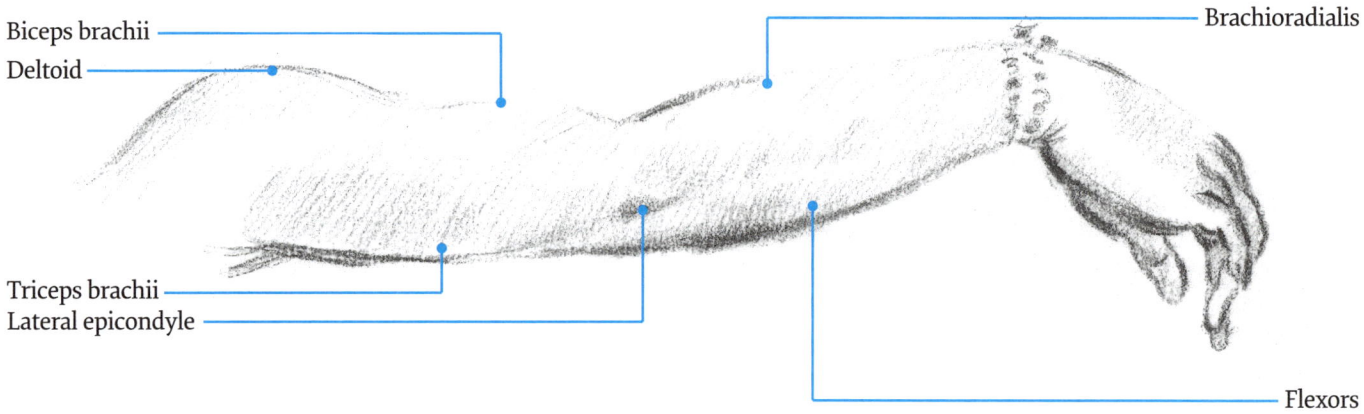

AFTER CHARLES-JOSEPH NATOIRE (1700–1777)

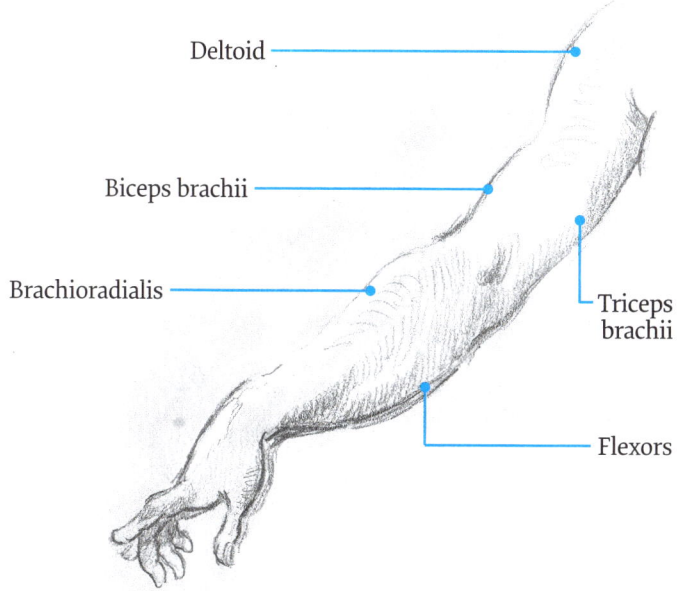

AFTER RAPHAEL

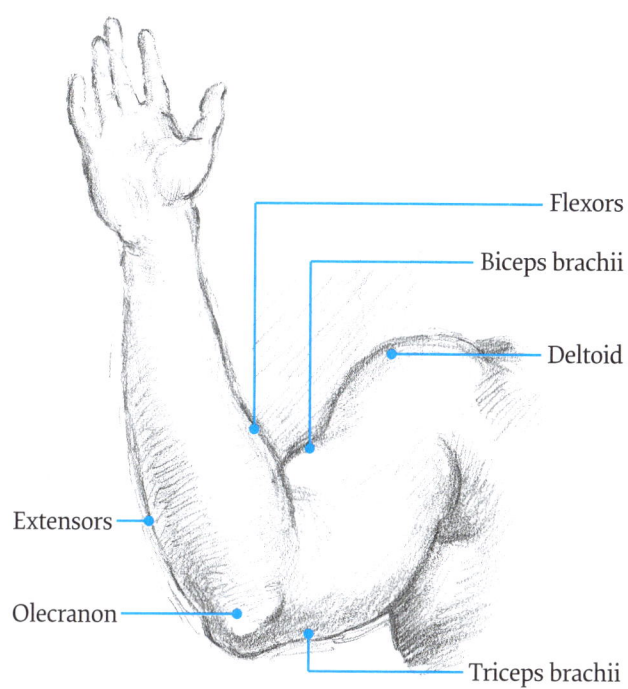

AFTER RAPHAEL

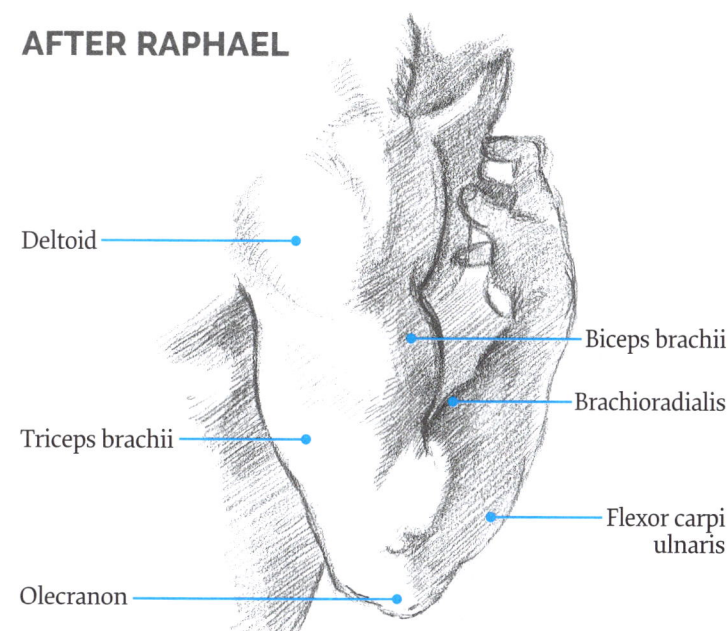

THE ARMS AND HANDS IN DETAIL

AFTER RAPHAEL

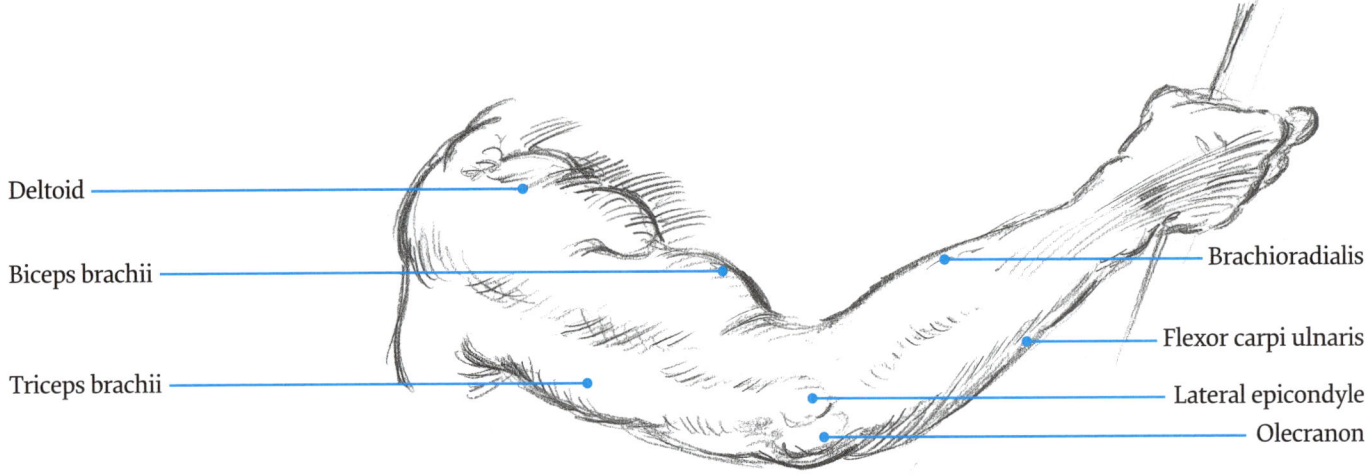

- Deltoid
- Biceps brachii
- Triceps brachii
- Brachioradialis
- Flexor carpi ulnaris
- Lateral epicondyle
- Olecranon

AFTER DANIELE RICCIARELLI DA VOLTERRA (1509–1566)

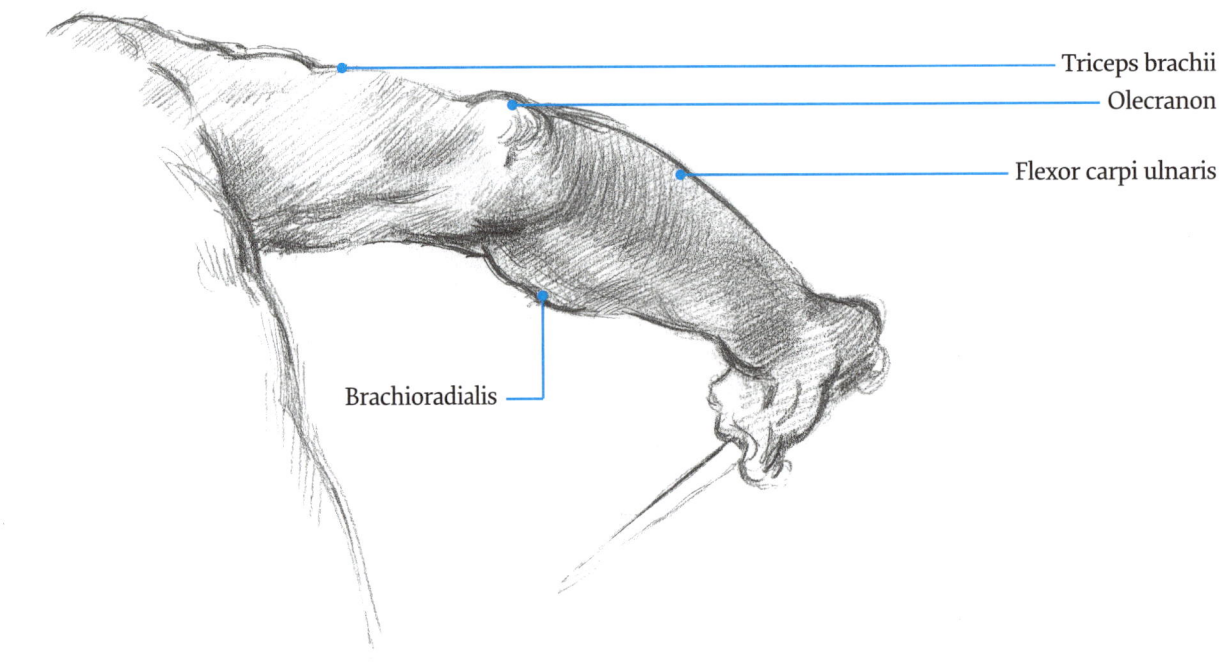

- Triceps brachii
- Olecranon
- Flexor carpi ulnaris
- Brachioradialis

Test your knowledge

Here are some more examples of very clearly drawn musculature, which I have not annotated. See if you can identify the various muscles shown. Refer to the detailed diagrams of muscles and the drawings on the previous pages to check your results. Pencil in your ideas before checking and see how many you get correct. This exercise is well worth doing.

AFTER PETER PAUL RUBENS

AFTER EUGÈNE DELACROIX (1798–1863)

AFTER FRANÇOIS BOUCHER (1703–1770)

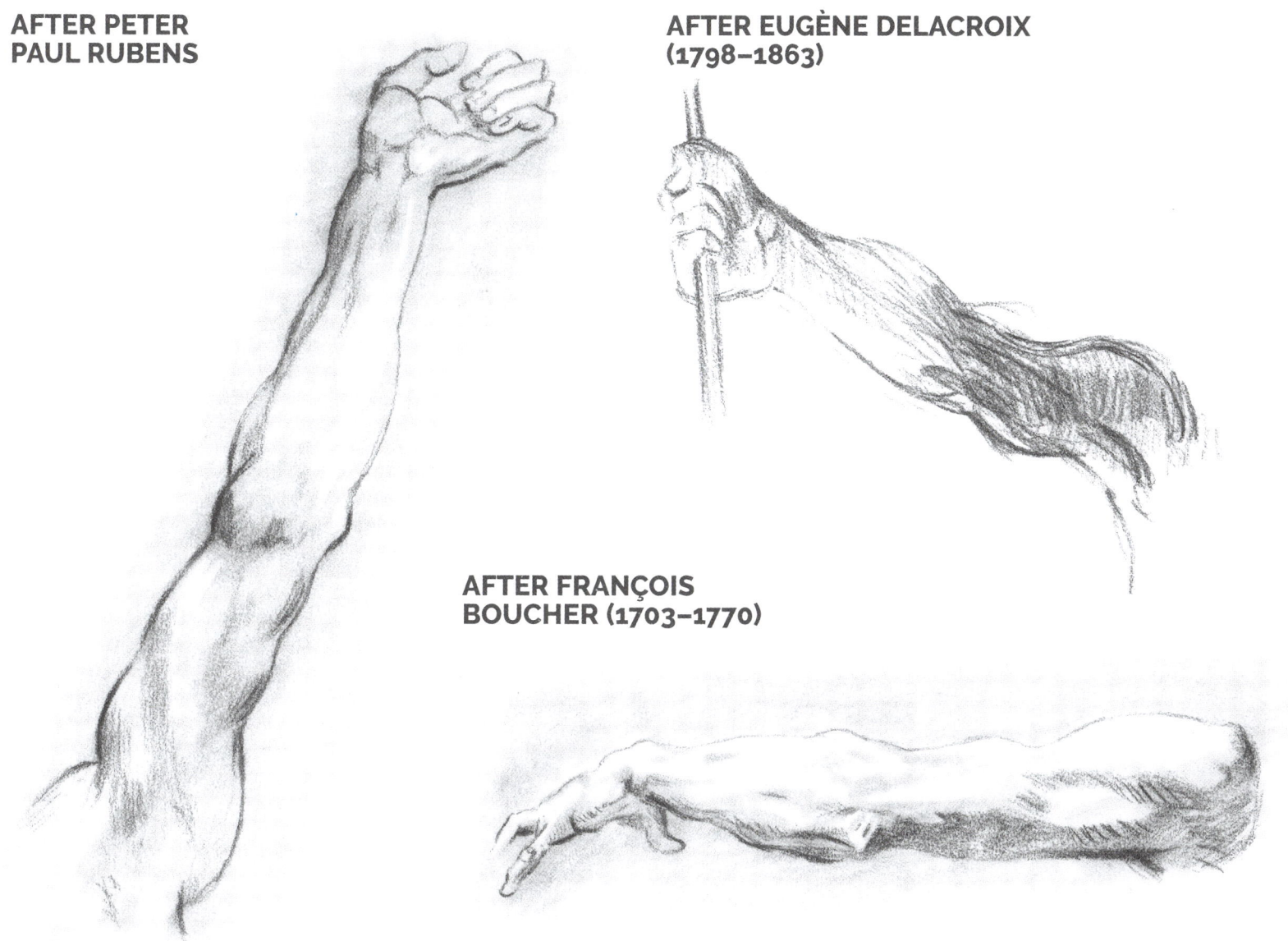

THE ARMS AND HANDS IN DETAIL

Studies of hands after master artists

AFTER LEONARDO DA VINCI (1452–1519)

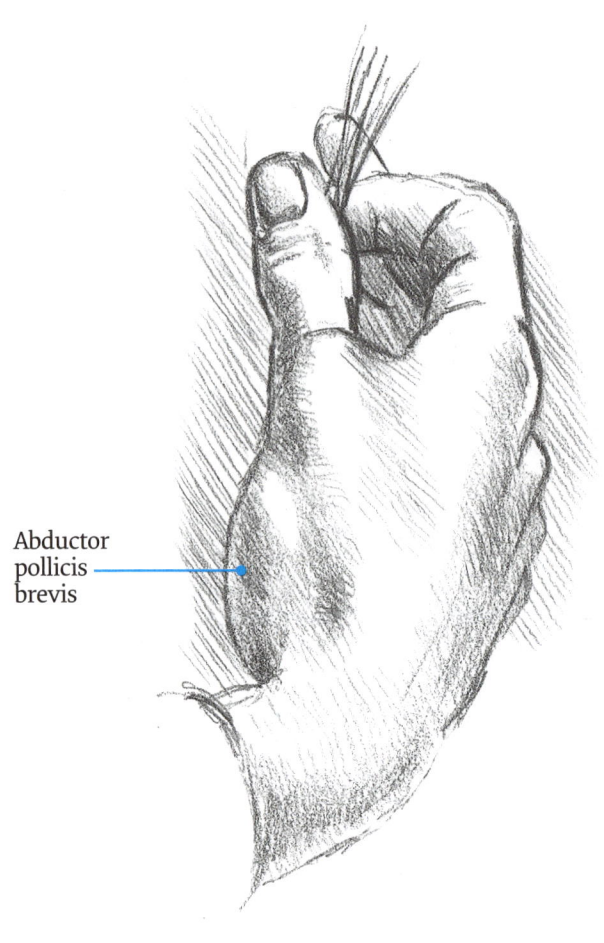

Abductor pollicis brevis

AFTER MICHELANGELO BUONARROTI

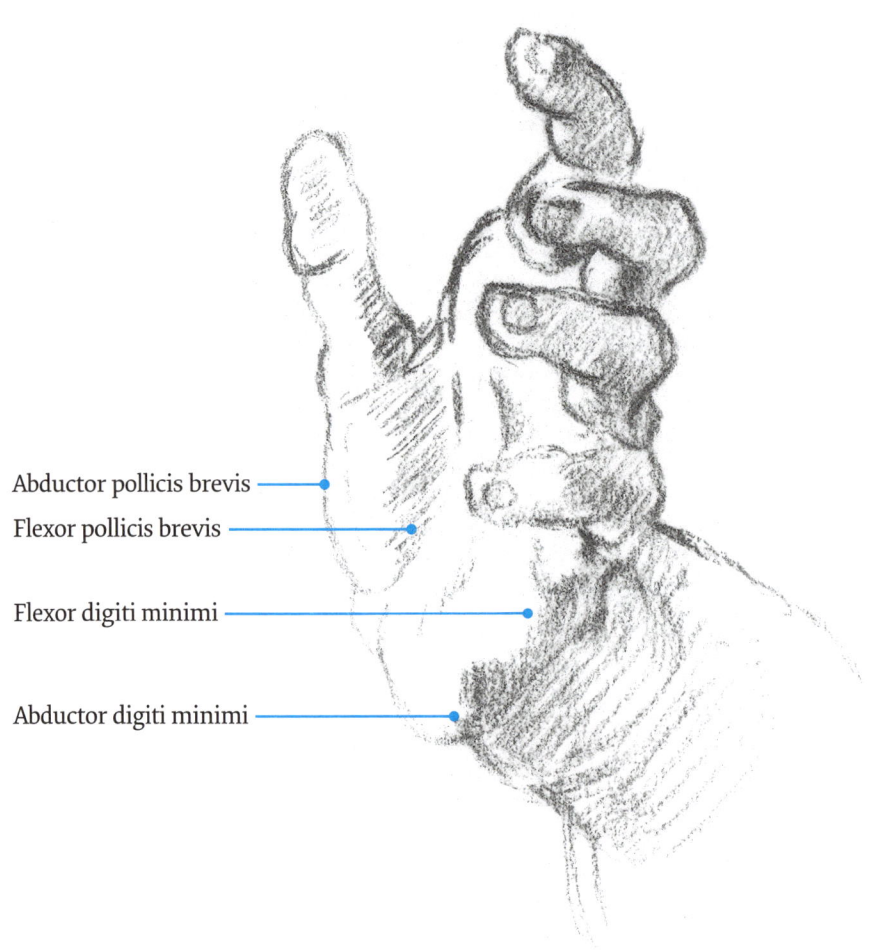

Abductor pollicis brevis
Flexor pollicis brevis
Flexor digiti minimi
Abductor digiti minimi

AFTER PETER PAUL RUBENS

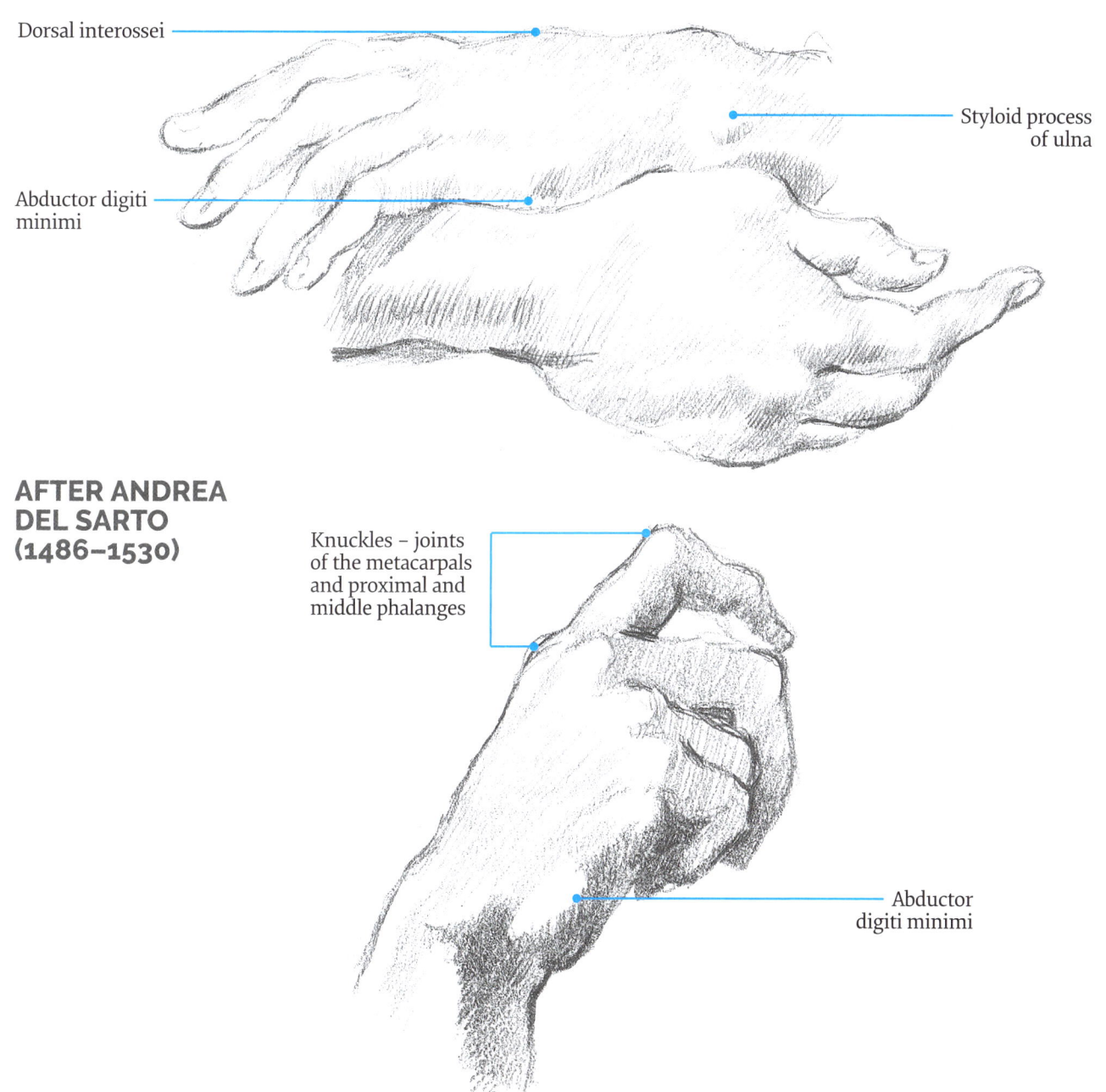

AFTER ANDREA DEL SARTO (1486–1530)

THE ARMS AND HANDS IN DETAIL

Draw your own hand

The advantage of studying hands is that you can always draw your own. This exercise starts with the simple task of drawing around the outline of your own hand, before adding detail.

1. Start by placing your hand flat on the paper and then carefully draw all around the shape, making sure that the pencil point does not get too far away from, or too much under, the edge of your hand.
2. Lift your hand carefully off the paper, keeping it flat and in the same position as before, then draw in all the wrinkles, bumps and hollows that you can see in the simplest way possible, and of course the fingernails too. You will have a fairly good representation of your own hand, matching it for size and shape.

Now have a go at drawing it in the same position but without tracing around the edge of it. Does the second drawing look as good as the first one?

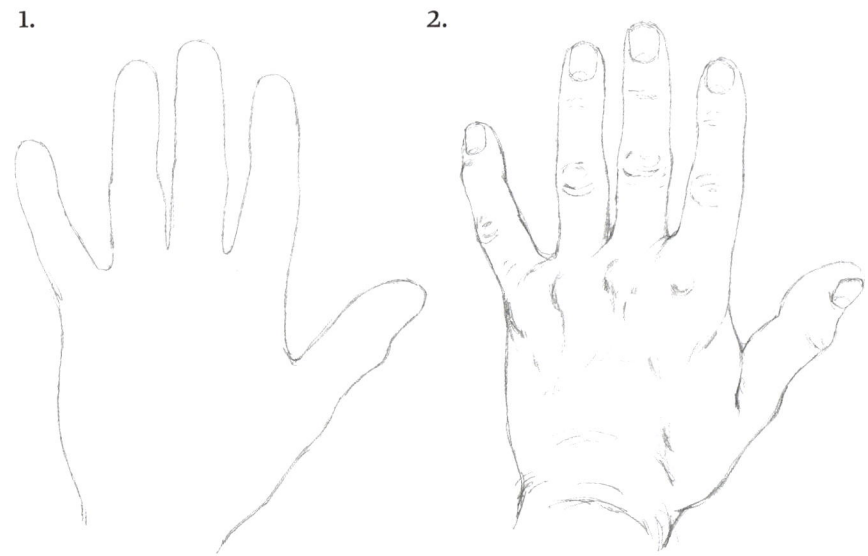

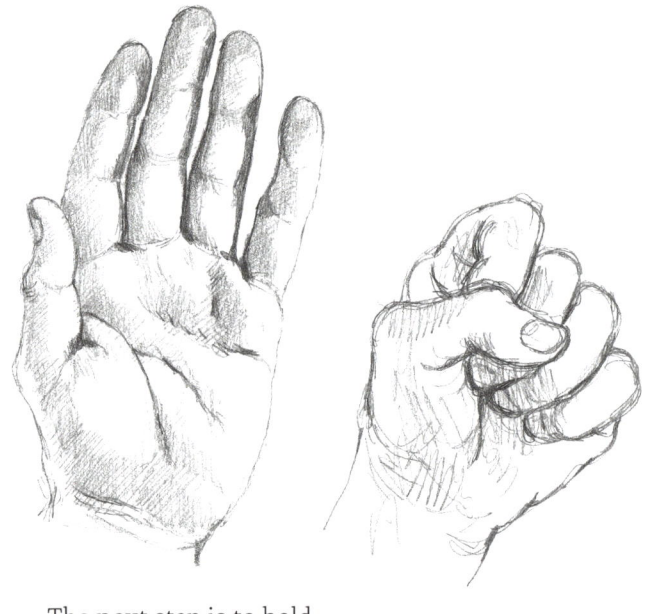

The next step is to hold your hand in a different shape, for example showing the palm instead of the back, or with a pointing finger, a clenched fist or any other shape you wish to try out. Refer back to pages 152–55 to remind yourself of the range of hand movements you can draw.

Experiment with different materials

When it comes to practicing the whole arm and hand, you will need to use a model or a photograph.

For these color studies I used conté pencils, which give a soft quality to drawing, well suited to skin. Whereas the two studies at the top are quite loosely drawn, the crossed arms show a more precise technique using carefully modulated brown and dark blue tones to give a smoother effect.

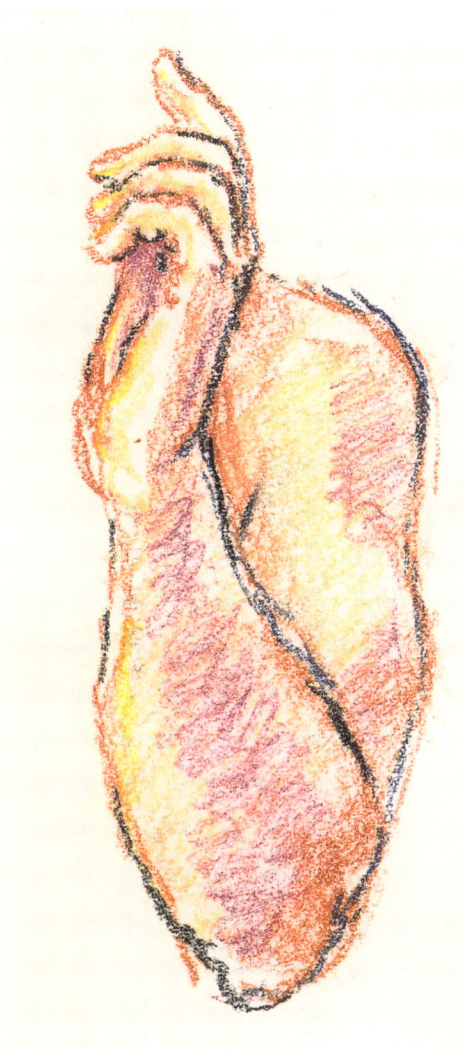
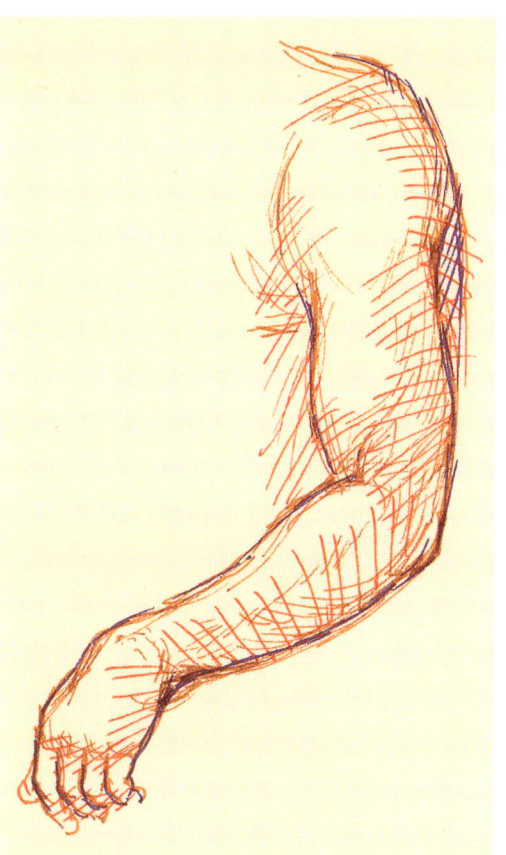
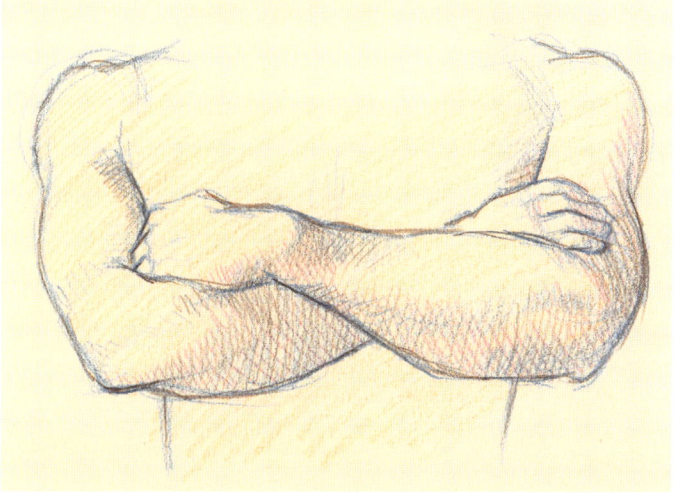

THE ARMS AND HANDS IN DETAIL

Chapter Five

THE LEGS AND FEET IN DETAIL

Our lower limbs are probably the most powerful parts of the body, having the largest bones and the strongest muscles. This is no surprise, since the legs not only support the total body weight but also have to propel it along in the world.

The hingeing of the legs on to the torso is very strongly supported, both in the shape and construction of the skeletal structure, and in the completeness of the muscle system that holds it all together and allows it to move.

Despite the lower and upper limbs being basically similar in form, the feet are more solid and their movements less subtle than the hands, which have to perform so many more complex tasks. Nor does the knee joint have quite the same range as the elbow, or the ankle as the wrist. The toes are clearly less dexterous than the fingers, despite being constructed along similar lines, but they are also considerably stronger.

As in previous chapters we will follow the anatomical diagrams with a series of surface views of the legs and feet, including examples after master artists.

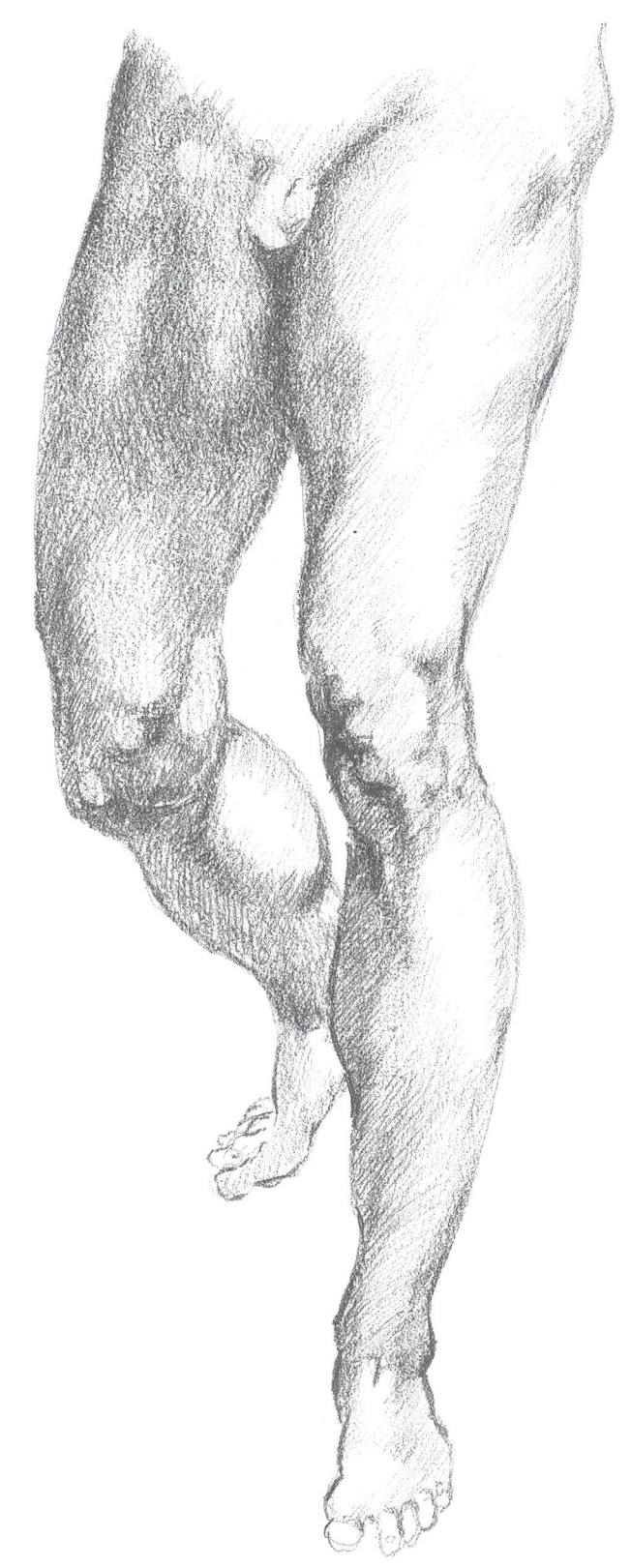

Views of legs and feet

The legs are not quite so flexible as the arms, but they are much more powerful, and so are much more powerfully built. The large muscles in the thigh and the strong, bony knee give the leg a similarity to the trunk of a small tree, so we understand connotations of strength and solidity. Remember that any part of the limb nearer to the torso is wider than the part further away, therefore calves are smaller than thighs and ankles are smaller than knees.

Notice how the foot compares in proportion with the length of the leg. Also note how easy it is to see the muscles on the leg because it has to support the weight of the body: the muscles are that much more powerful than those in the arm and so are more defined in the leg.

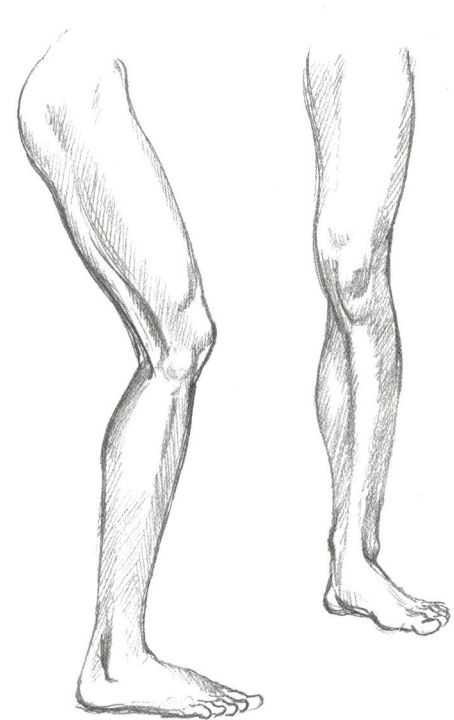

THE LEGS AND FEET IN DETAIL

THE LEGS AND FEET IN DETAIL

Skeleton of the leg and foot

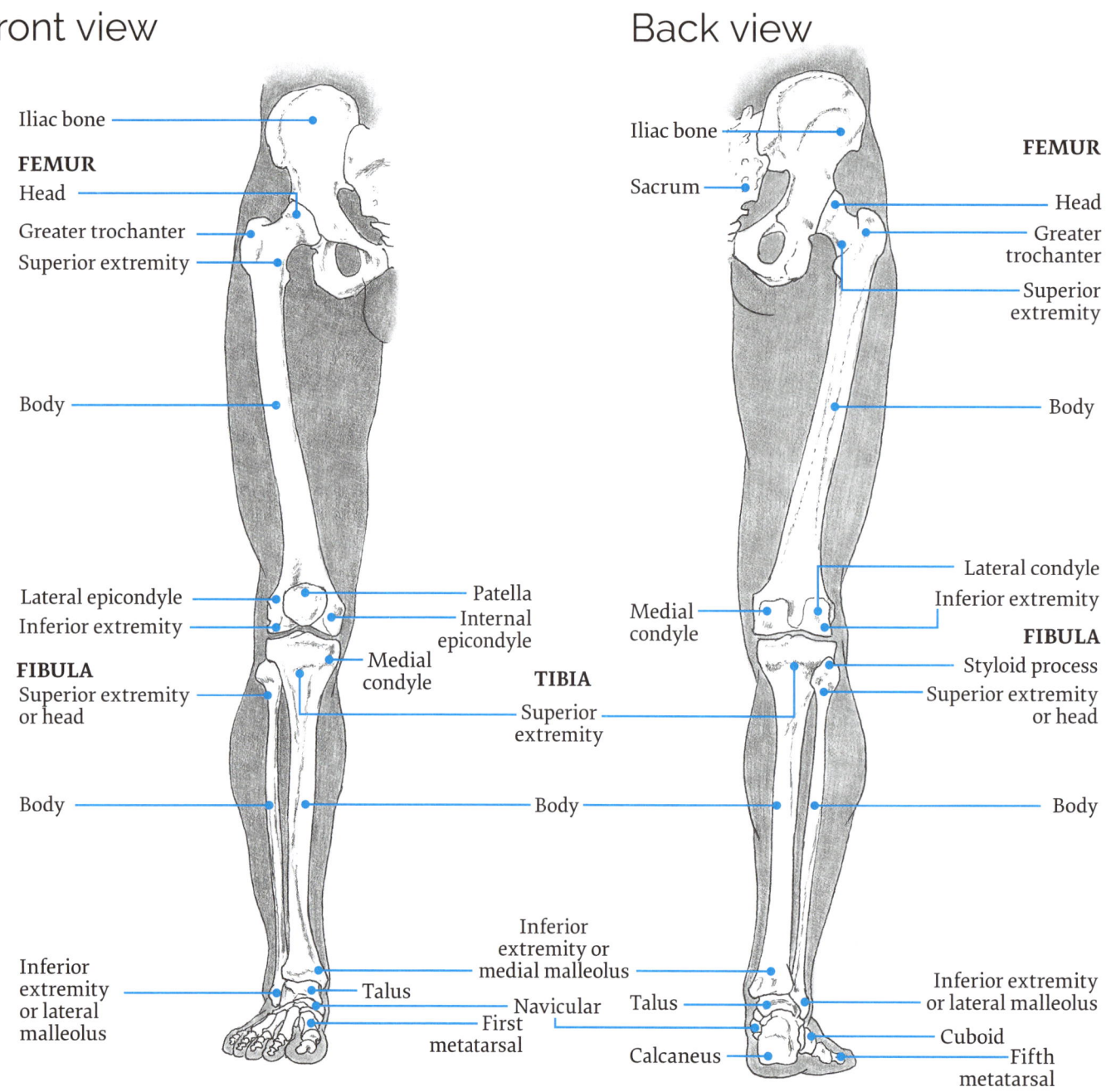

Side View

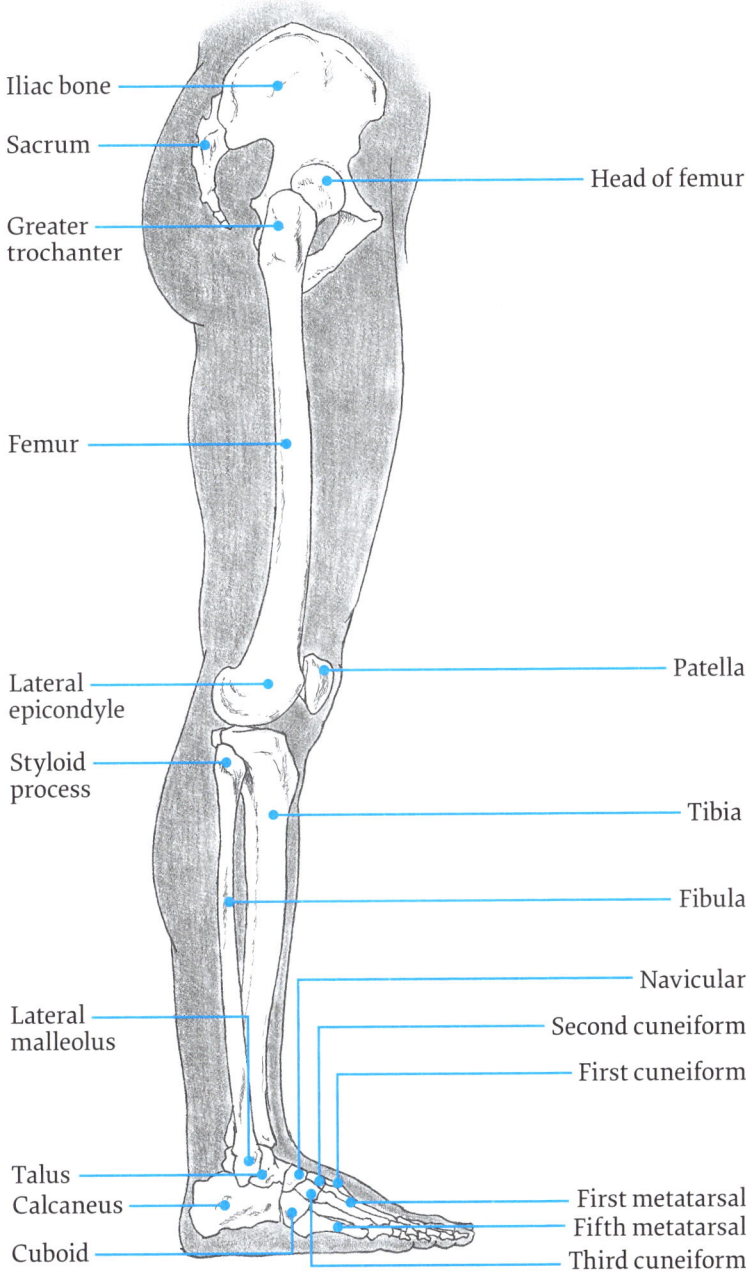

THE LEGS AND FEET IN DETAIL

Muscles of the leg and foot
Front view

Like the upper limbs, the legs are wrapped in long, layered muscles that help to give flexibility. However, because of the increased strength needed to support the rest of the body's weight, the leg muscles tend to be longer and bigger. I have included the band of fascia running down the side of the leg over the muscles (the fascia lata and the iliotibial band).

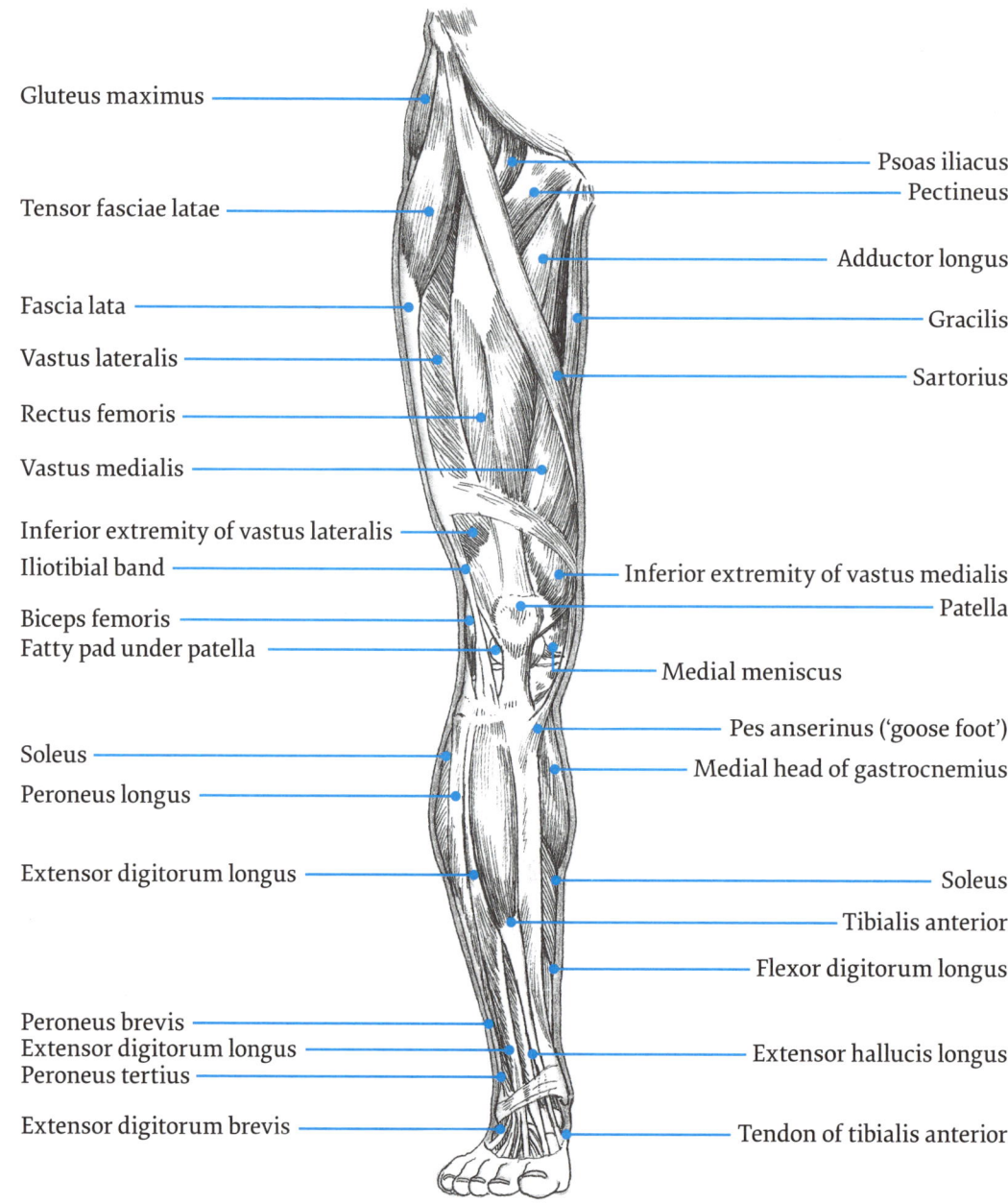

- Gluteus maximus
- Psoas iliacus
- Pectineus
- Tensor fasciae latae
- Adductor longus
- Fascia lata
- Gracilis
- Vastus lateralis
- Sartorius
- Rectus femoris
- Vastus medialis
- Inferior extremity of vastus lateralis
- Iliotibial band
- Inferior extremity of vastus medialis
- Biceps femoris
- Patella
- Fatty pad under patella
- Medial meniscus
- Pes anserinus ('goose foot')
- Soleus
- Medial head of gastrocnemius
- Peroneus longus
- Extensor digitorum longus
- Soleus
- Tibialis anterior
- Flexor digitorum longus
- Peroneus brevis
- Extensor digitorum longus
- Peroneus tertius
- Extensor hallucis longus
- Extensor digitorum brevis
- Tendon of tibialis anterior

174 THE LEGS AND FEET IN DETAIL

The group of tendons that run down the back of the leg to the knee are collectively known as the hamstrings. These are the tendons of the biceps femoris, the semitendinosus and the semimembranosus.

Back view

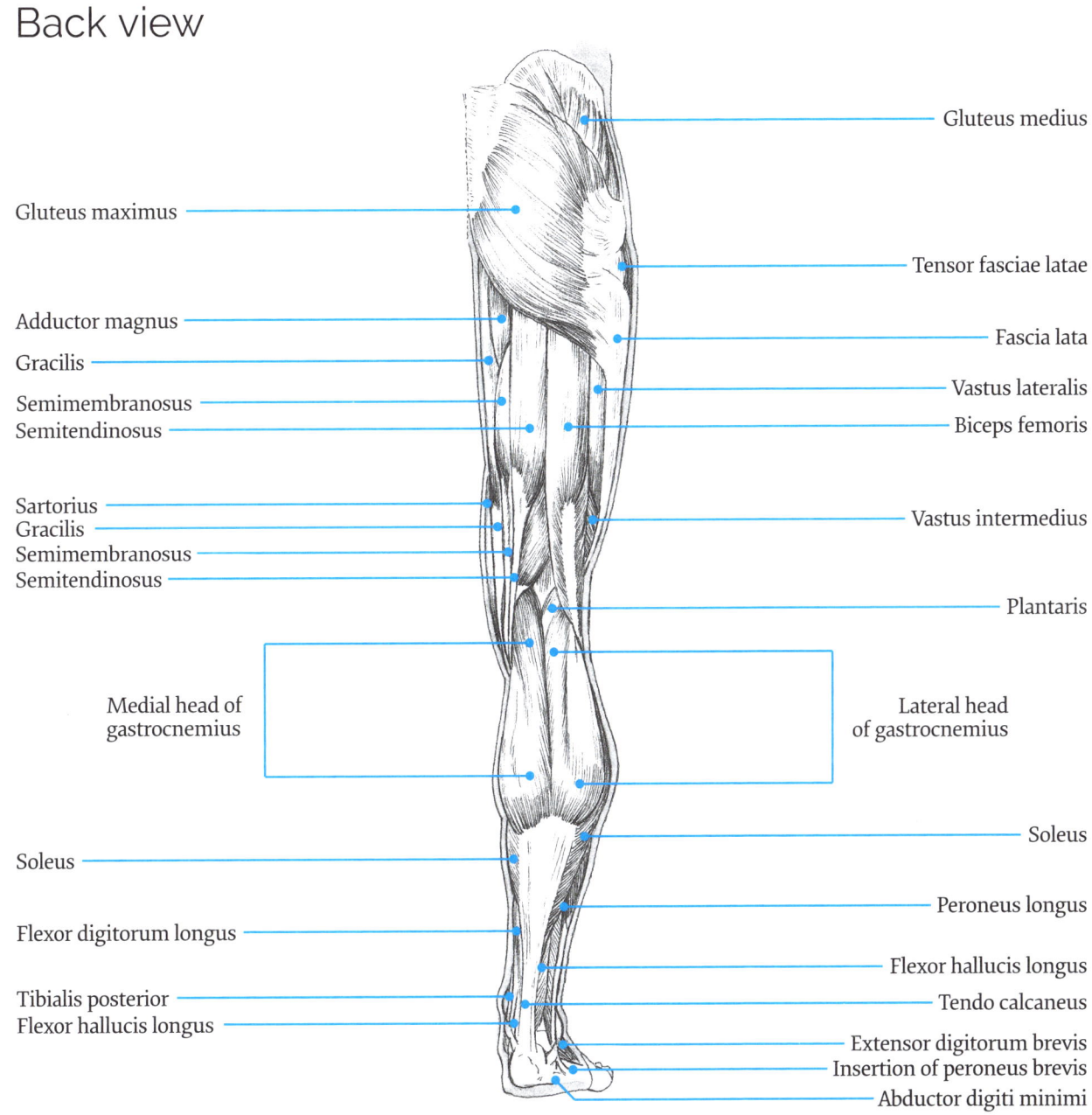

- Gluteus maximus
- Adductor magnus
- Gracilis
- Semimembranosus
- Semitendinosus
- Sartorius
- Gracilis
- Semimembranosus
- Semitendinosus
- Medial head of gastrocnemius
- Soleus
- Flexor digitorum longus
- Tibialis posterior
- Flexor hallucis longus
- Gluteus medius
- Tensor fasciae latae
- Fascia lata
- Vastus lateralis
- Biceps femoris
- Vastus intermedius
- Plantaris
- Lateral head of gastrocnemius
- Soleus
- Peroneus longus
- Flexor hallucis longus
- Tendo calcaneus
- Extensor digitorum brevis
- Insertion of peroneus brevis
- Abductor digiti minimi

THE LEGS AND FEET IN DETAIL 175

Side view, external aspect

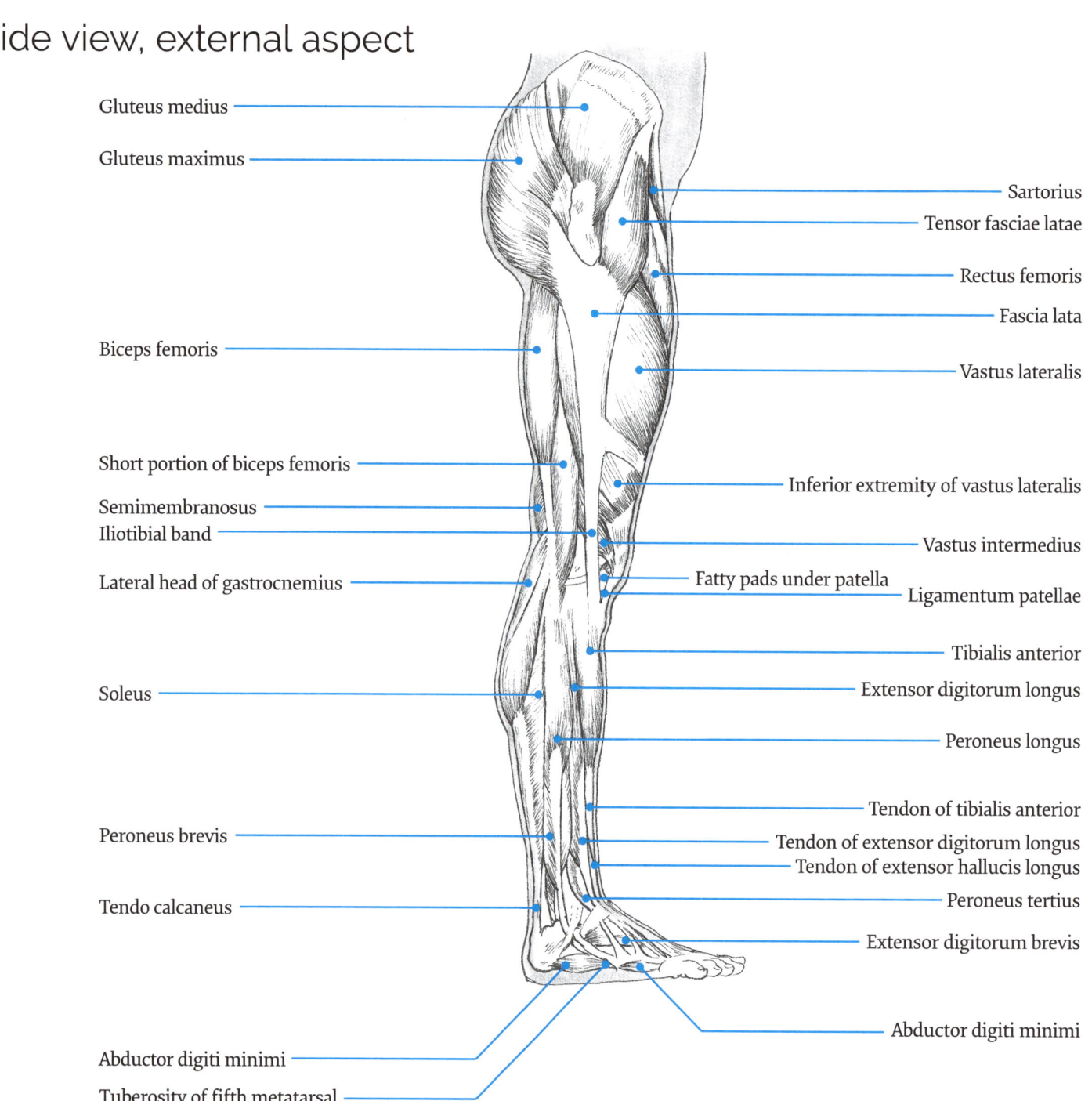

Side view, internal aspect

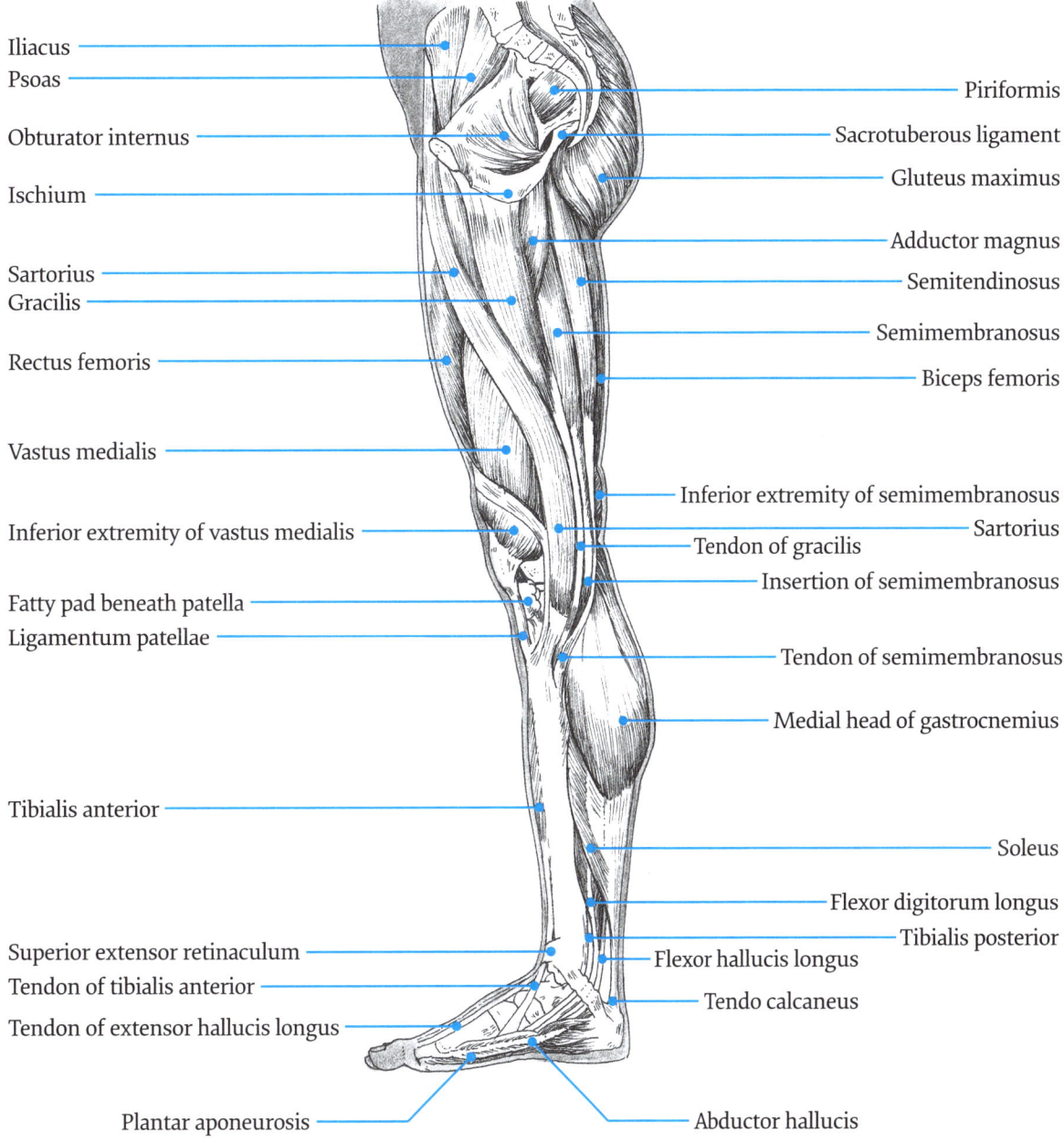

THE LEGS AND FEET IN DETAIL 177

Muscles of the hip and thigh

Front view, deep muscles: adductors

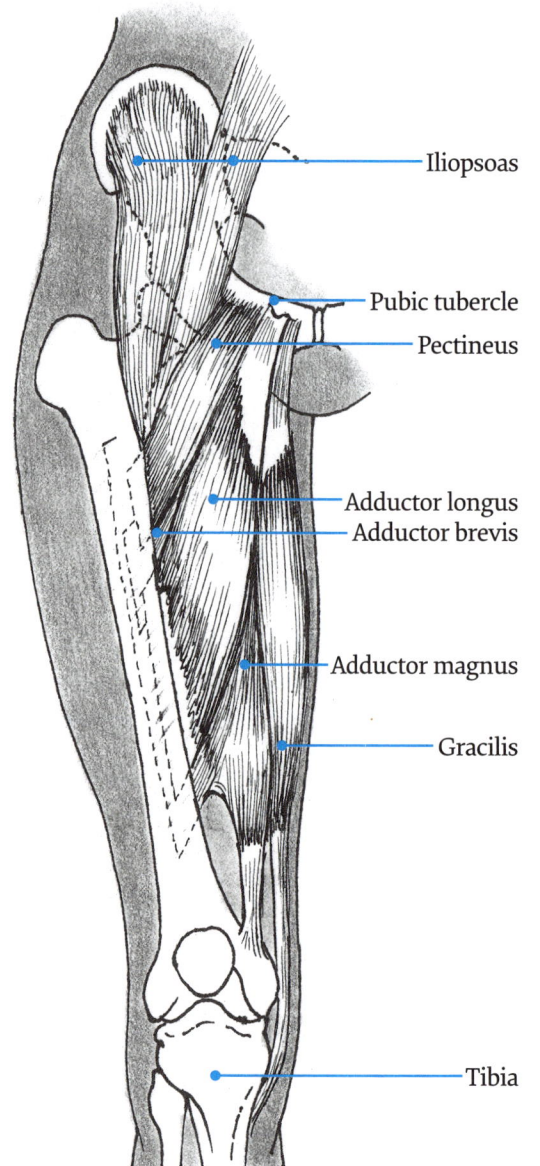

ADDUCTOR MAGNUS, ADDUCTOR BREVIS and ADDUCTOR LONGUS: simultaneous contraction of these muscles results in moving thigh towards centre line.
BICEPS FEMORIS flexes and then rotates leg towards centre line.
GEMELLUS SUPERIOR and GEMELLUS INFERIOR rotate thigh outwards.
GLUTEUS MAXIMUS extends from thigh onto fixed trunk. When leg is fixed, trunk is bent backwards by its contraction. It extends hip joint when subject climbs stairs or rises to erect posture after stooping.
GLUTEUS MEDIUS rotates thigh inwards and outwards.
GLUTEUS MINIMUS rotates thigh inwards and outwards.
GRACILIS flexes and rotates leg towards centre line.
ILIOPSOAS when trunk is fixed, flexes and rotates femur inwards; when leg is fixed, flexes trunk.
PECTINEUS moves thigh towards centre line and flexes it.
QUADRATUS FEMORIS rotates thigh outwards.
QUADRICEPS MUSCLES these are the VASTUS INTERMEDIUS/ LATERALIS/ MEDIALIS and the RECTUS FEMORIS; they extend and flex the knee.
TENSOR FASCIAE LATAE stretches fascia, elevates and moves thigh outwards.
RECTUS FEMORIS (see quadriceps) extends knee joint.
SARTORIUS moves thigh away from body and rotates it sideways, and flexes leg at knee joint.
SEMIMEMBRANOSUS flexes and then rotates leg towards centre line.
SEMITENDINOSUS flexes and then rotates leg towards centre line.
VASTUS MUSCLES (see quadriceps) extend and flex the knee.

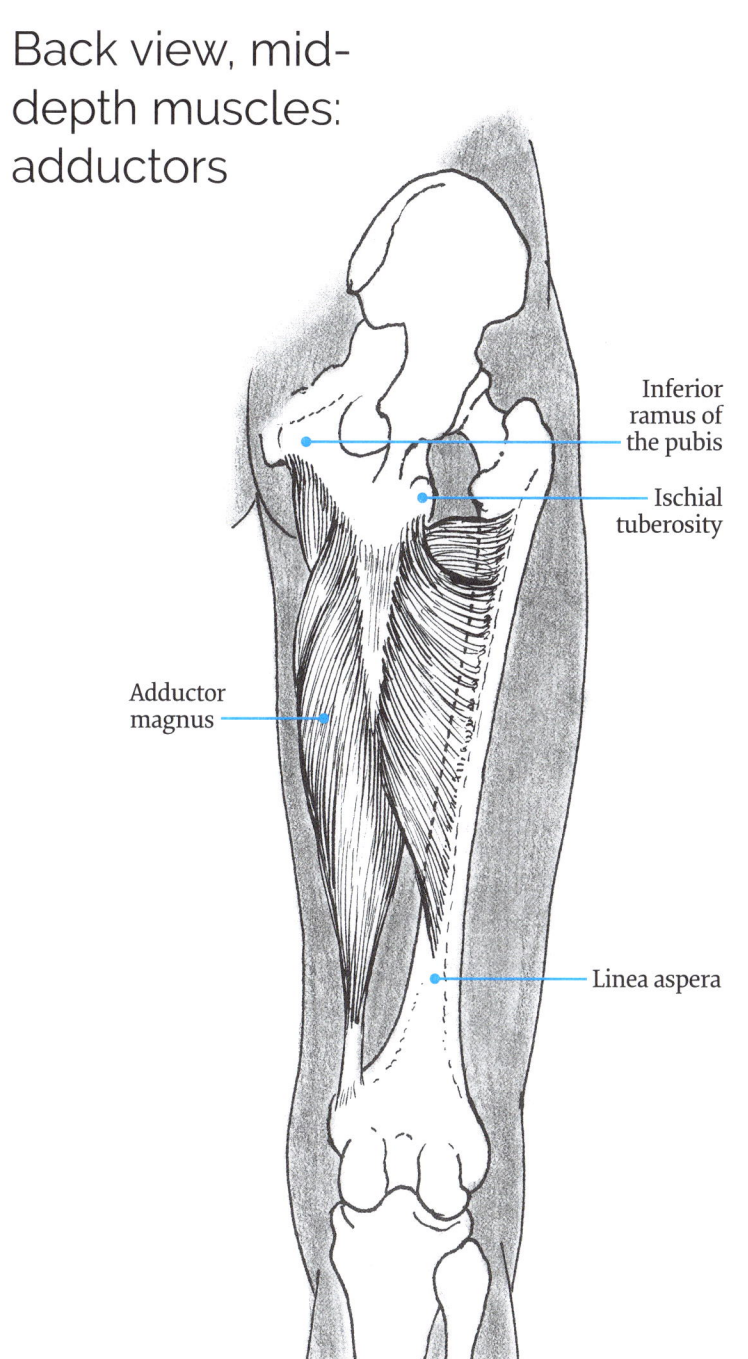

Back view, mid-depth muscles: adductors

- Inferior ramus of the pubis
- Ischial tuberosity
- Adductor magnus
- Linea aspera

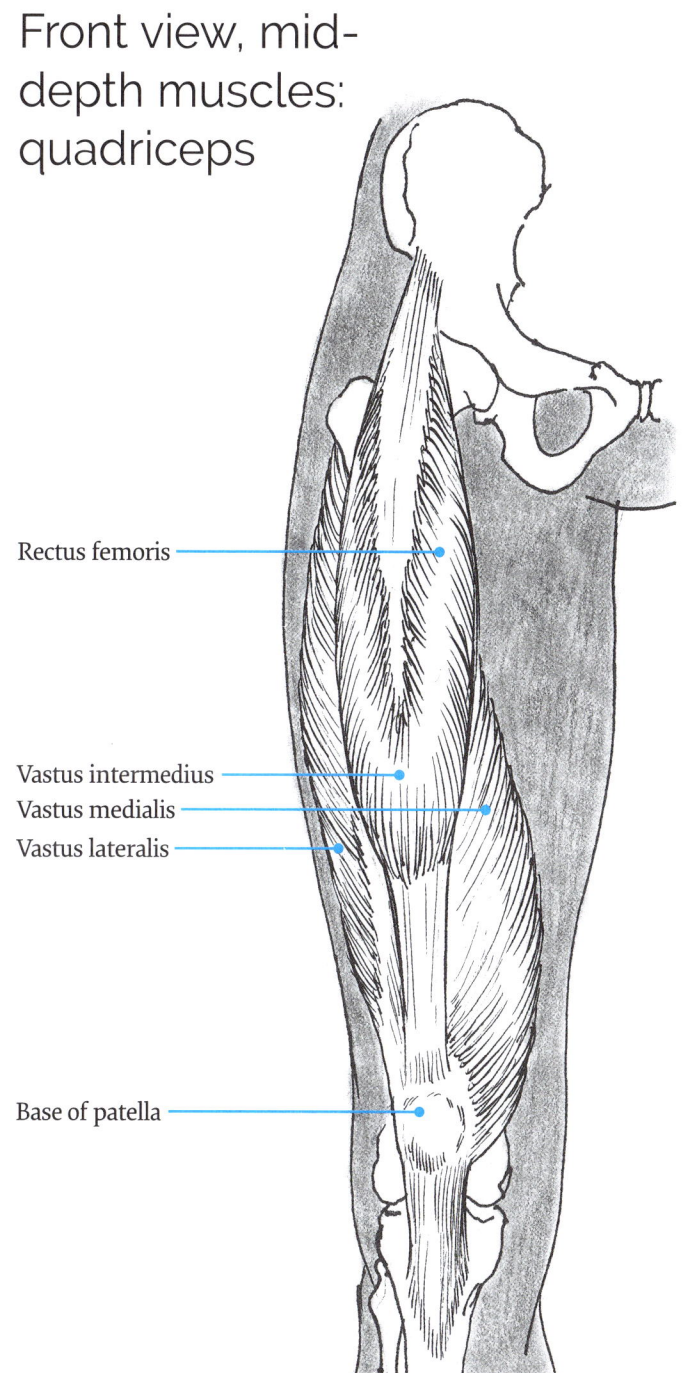

Front view, mid-depth muscles: quadriceps

- Rectus femoris
- Vastus intermedius
- Vastus medialis
- Vastus lateralis
- Base of patella

THE LEGS AND FEET IN DETAIL

Mid-depth view from the back

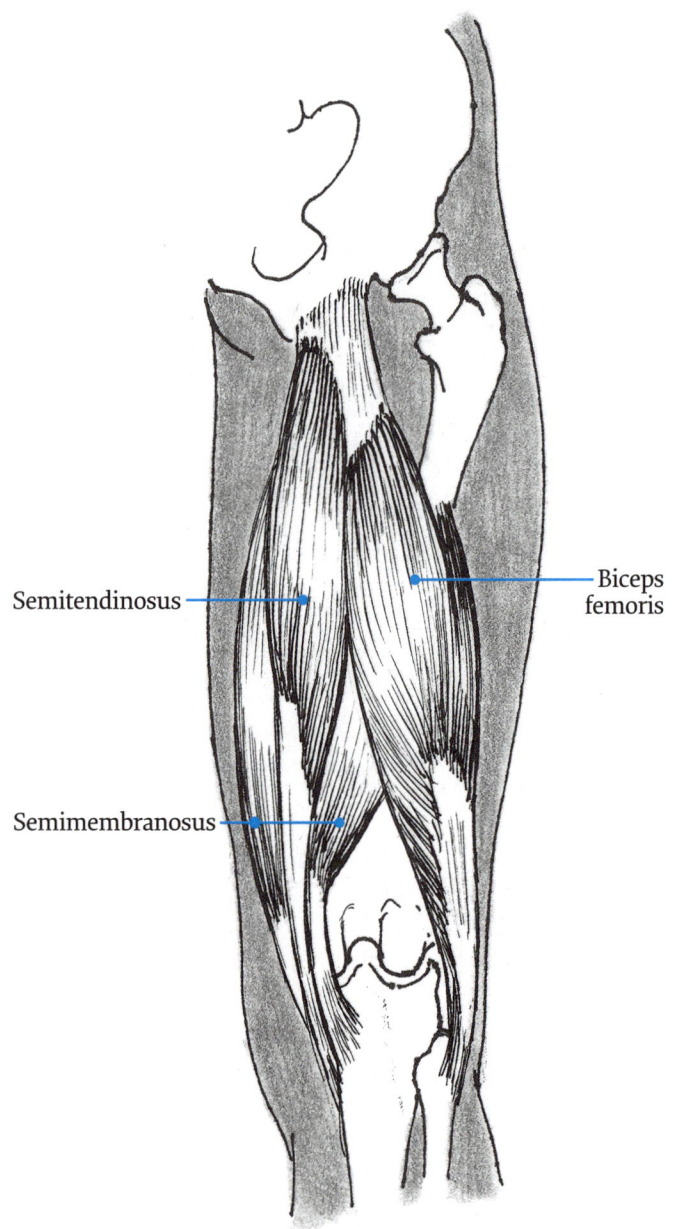

Superficial muscles from the front

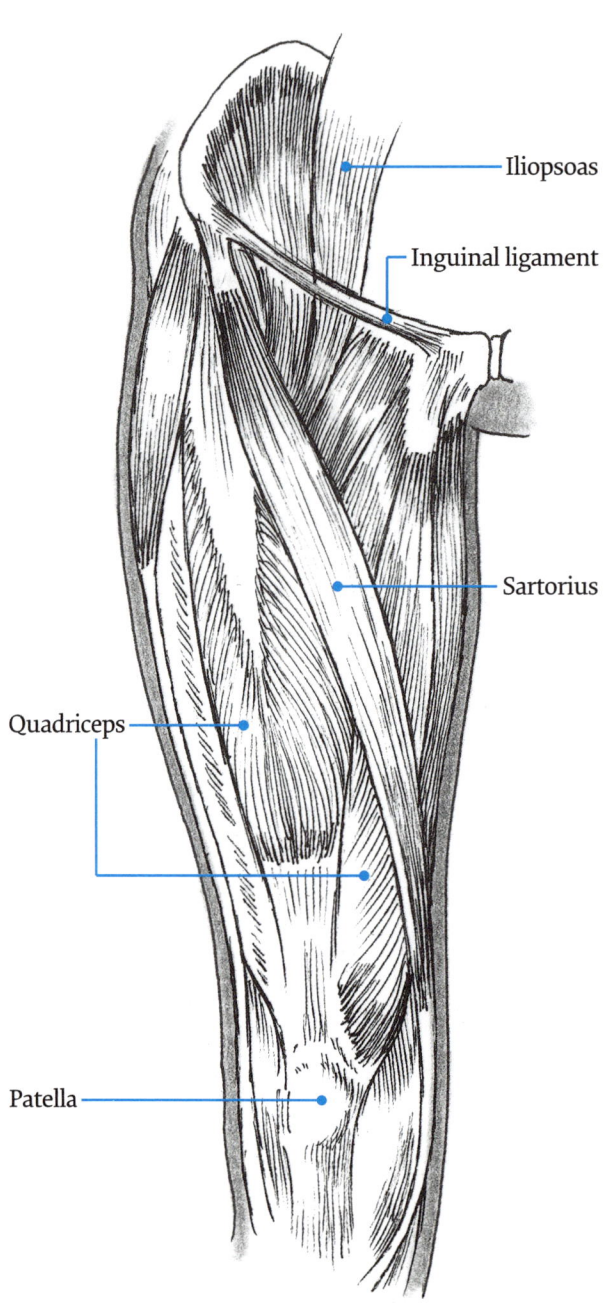

Muscles of the thigh, flexed

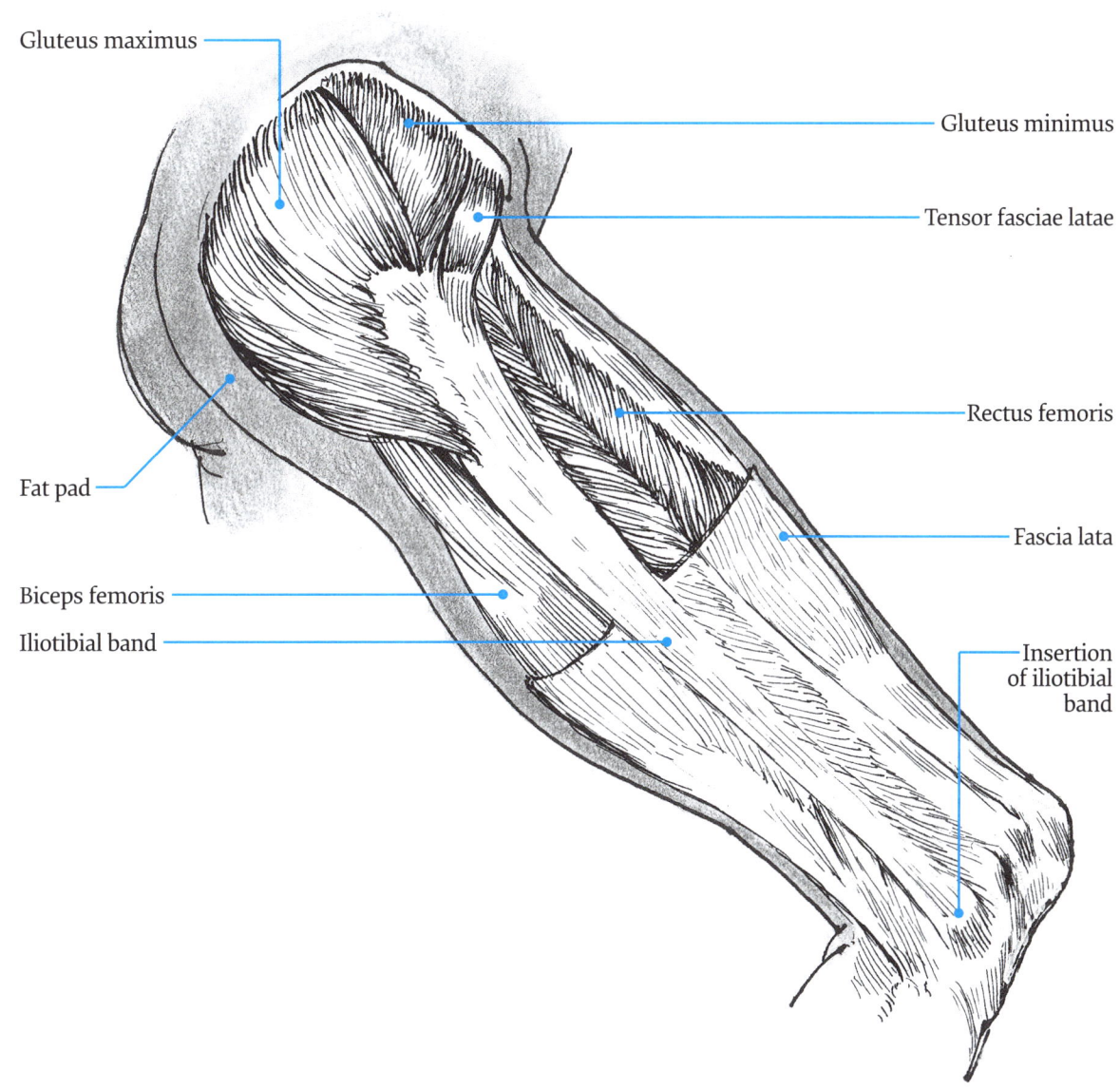

Gluteal muscles

Deep view from the back

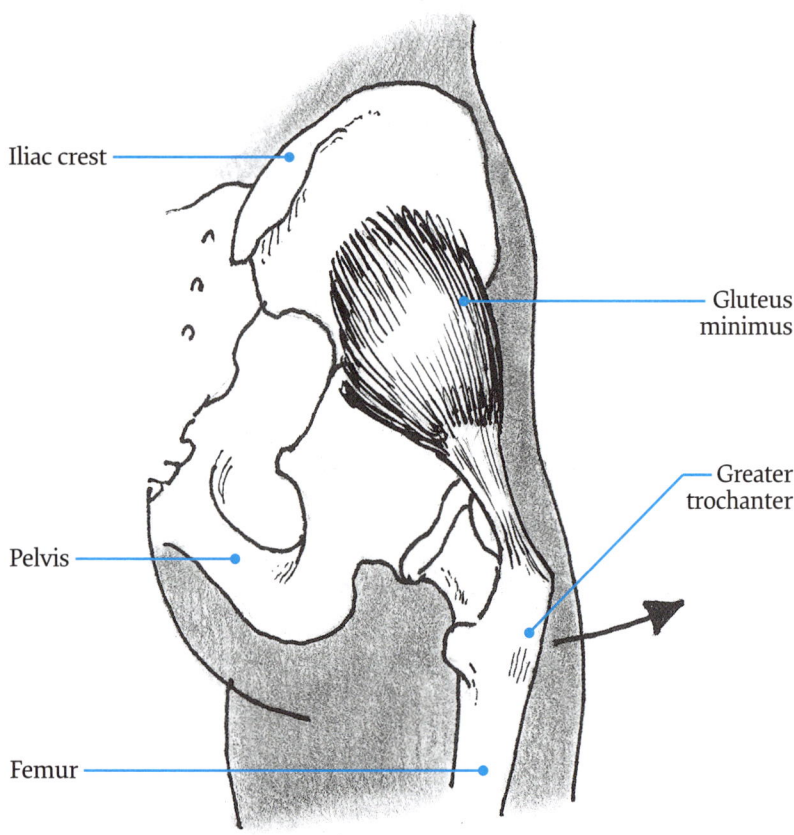

Mid-depth view from the back

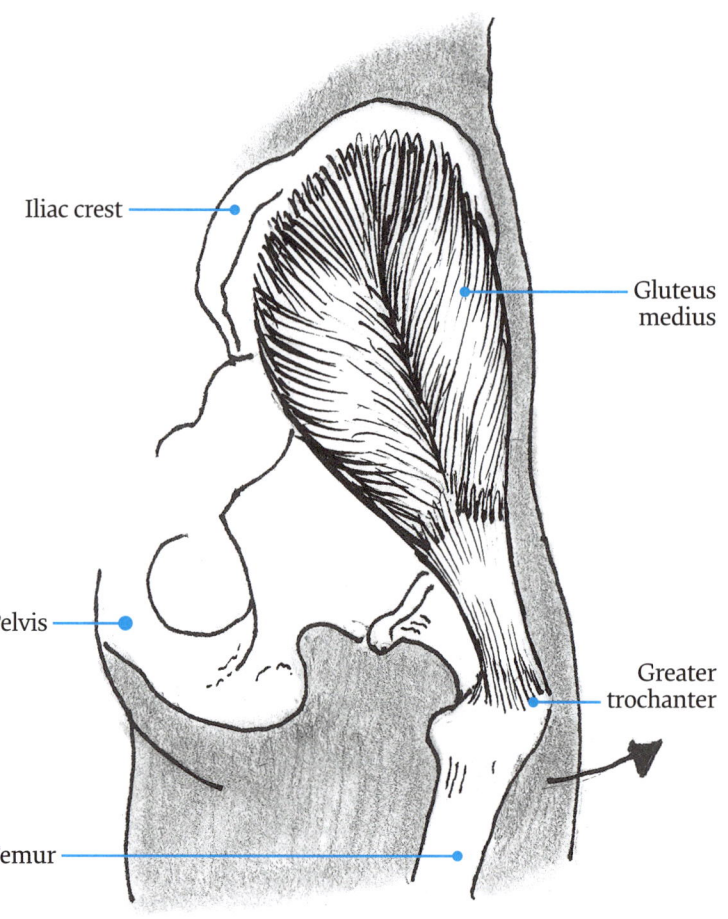

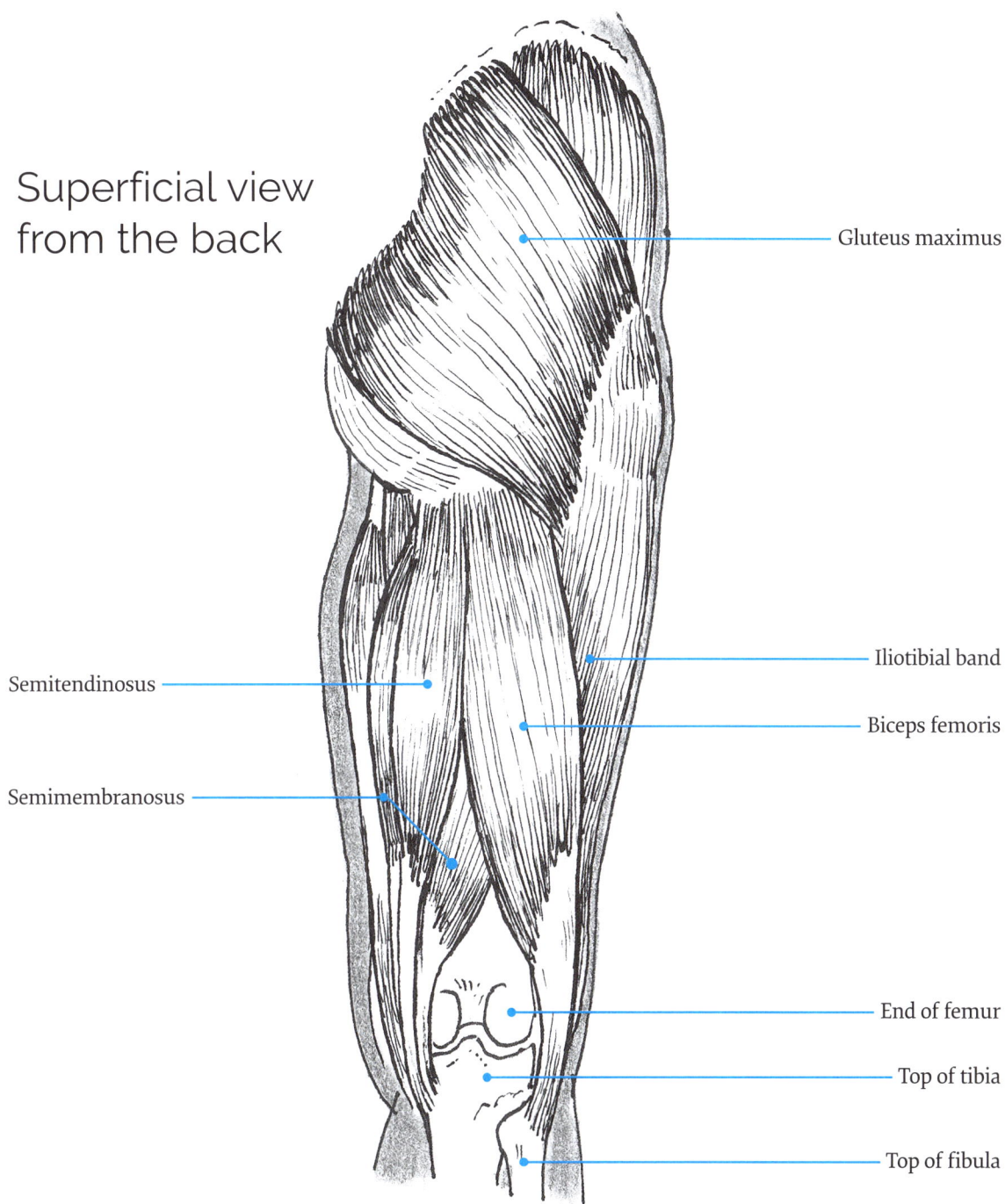

THE LEGS AND FEET IN DETAIL

Knee joint movement

Flexed

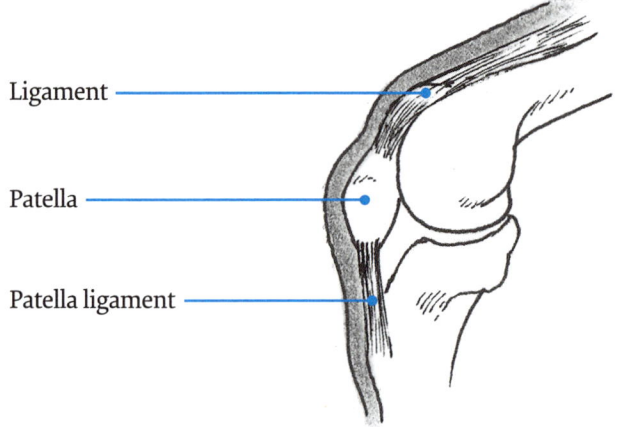

- Ligament
- Patella
- Patella ligament

Unflexed

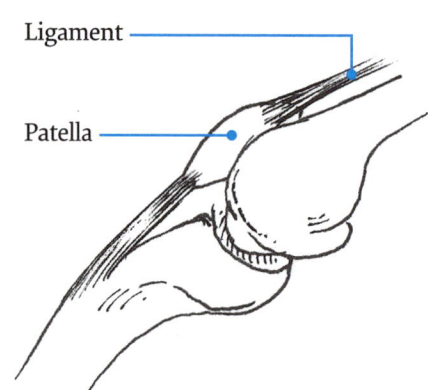

- Ligament
- Patella

Knee joint: patella removed showing ligaments

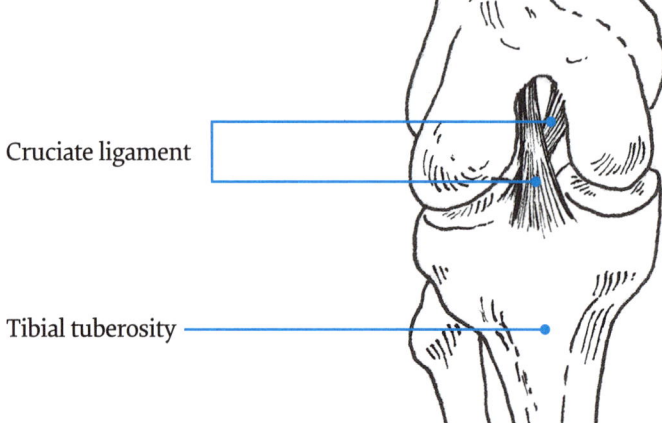

- Cruciate ligament
- Tibial tuberosity

Four quadriceps tendons: action of patella ligament to extend leg

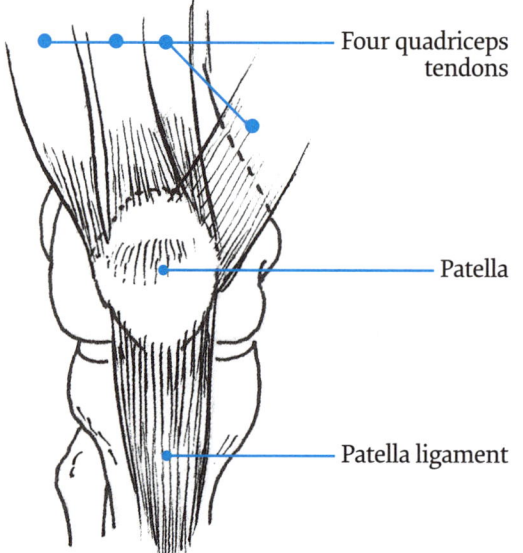

- Four quadriceps tendons
- Patella
- Patella ligament

184 THE LEGS AND FEET IN DETAIL

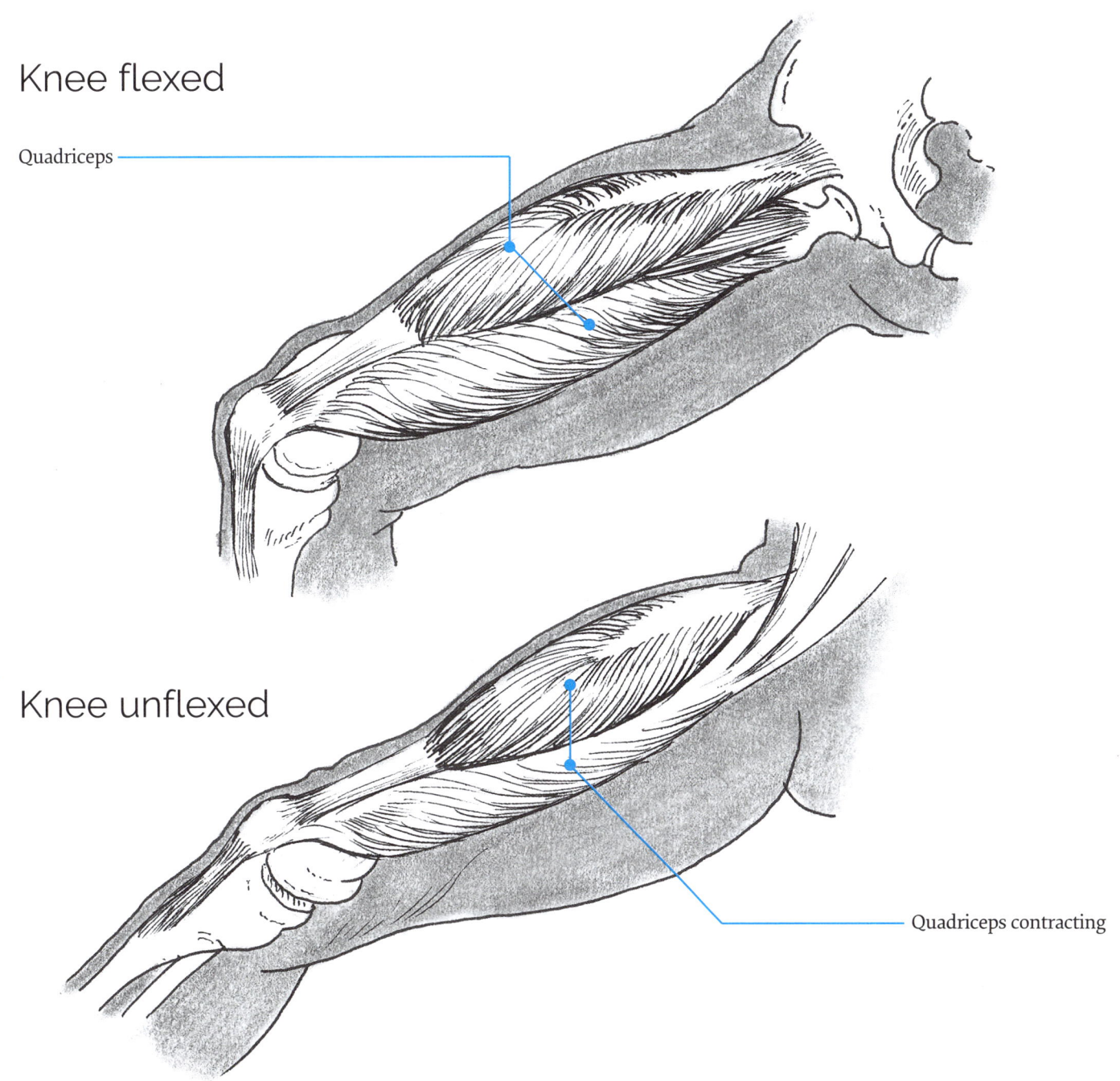

THE LEGS AND FEET IN DETAIL

Muscles of the lower leg
Front view

EXTENSOR DIGITORUM LONGUS straightens four lesser toes.
EXTENSOR HALLUCIS LONGUS straightens great toe.
EXTENSOR RETINACULUM, SUPERIOR AND INFERIOR enable tendons of the foot to change direction at the ankle.
FLEXOR DIGITORUM LONGUS bends second to fifth toes, helps in bending foot.
FLEXOR HALLUCIS LONGUS bends big toe (hallux) and through this the foot. Takes part in rotation of foot.
GASTROCNEMIUS extends foot downwards.
PERONEUS BREVIS raises outside edge of foot.
PERONEUS LONGUS bends and turns foot outwards, supports lateral side of arch, steadies leg on the foot, especially when standing on one leg.
PERONEUS TERTIUS raises the foot upwards and outwards.
PLANTARIS weakly flexes ankle and knee joint.
POPLITEUS bends and then, rotates leg towards centre line.
SOLEUS extends foot downwards.
TIBIALIS LONGUS (ANTERIOR) straightens foot, raises foot arch.
TIBIALIS POSTERIOR straightens foot, turns foot inwards, supports foot arch.

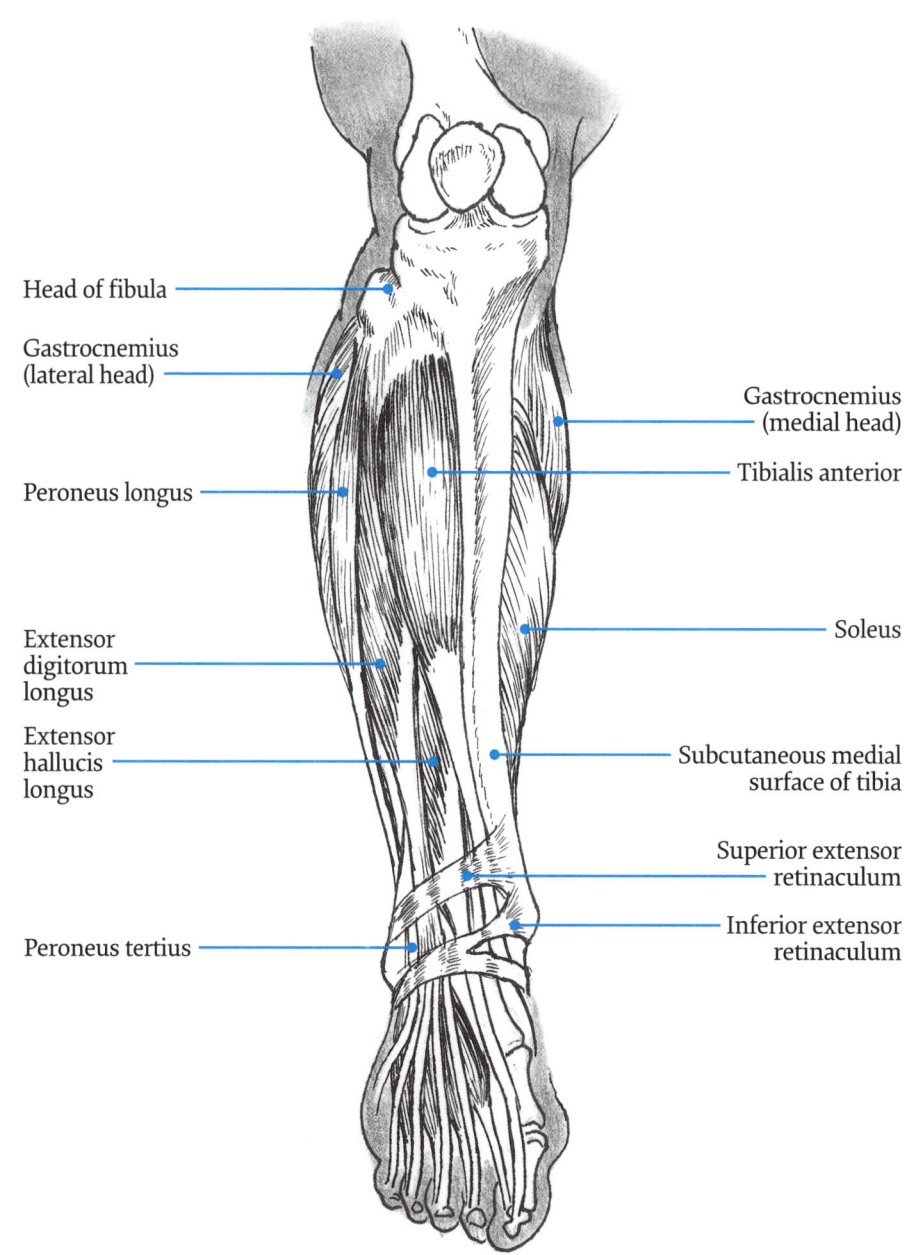

Inside view

- Sartorius
- Gracilis
- Hamstrings
- Tibialis anterior
- Gastrocnemius
- Subcutaneous medial surface of tibia
- Soleus
- Achilles tendon
- Insertion of tibialis anterior
- Medial malleolus
- Extensor hallucis longus

Outside view: bending

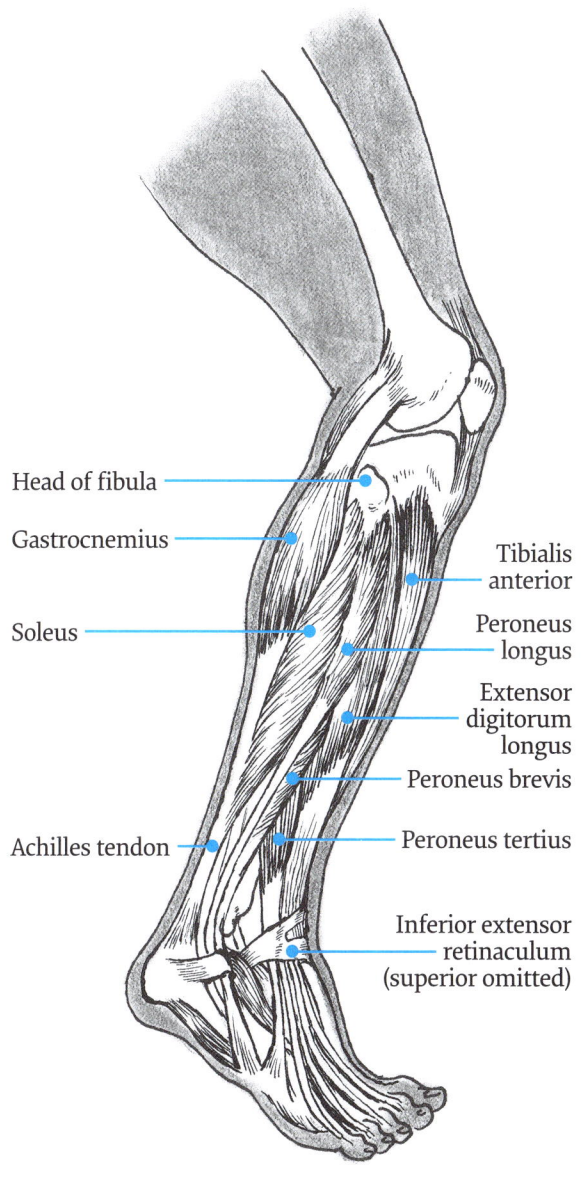

- Head of fibula
- Gastrocnemius
- Soleus
- Achilles tendon
- Tibialis anterior
- Peroneus longus
- Extensor digitorum longus
- Peroneus brevis
- Peroneus tertius
- Inferior extensor retinaculum (superior omitted)

THE LEGS AND FEET IN DETAIL

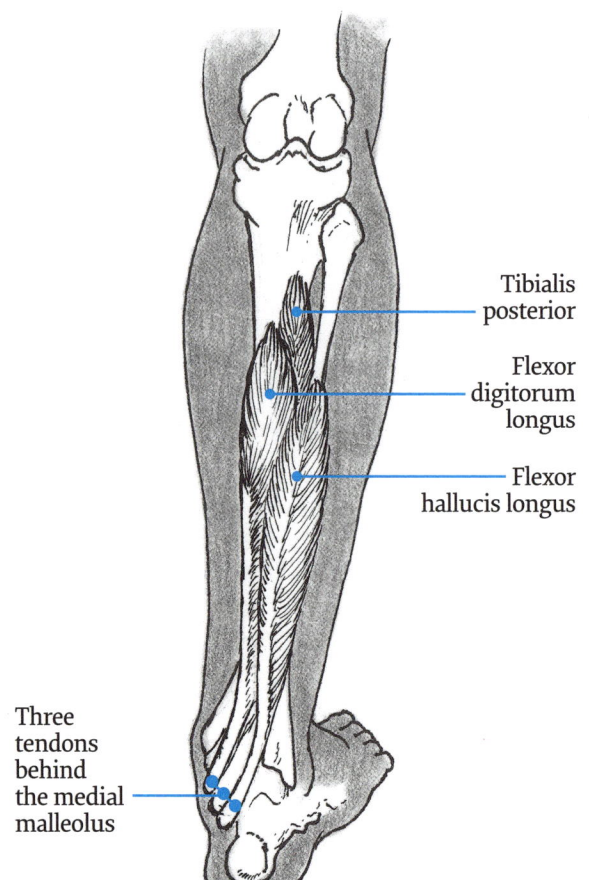

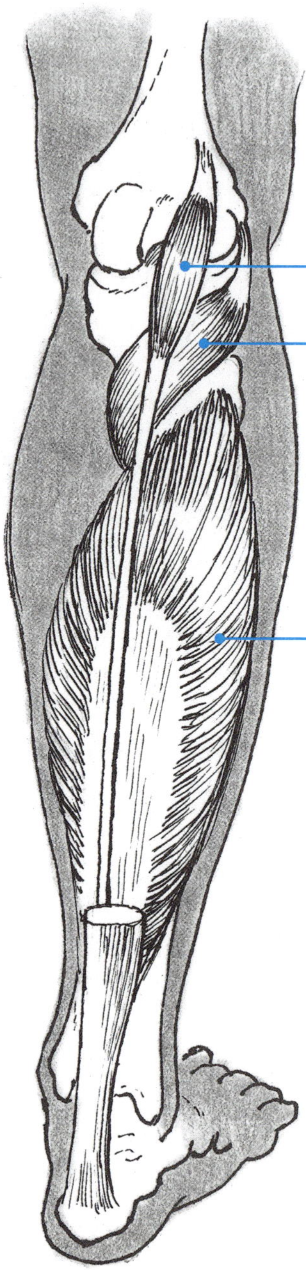

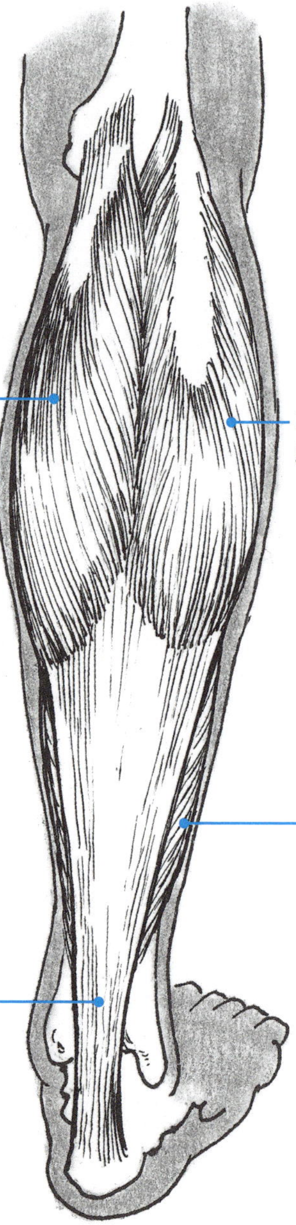

Muscle and bone structure of the foot

Like the hand, the foot is a complex structure of overlapping bone, muscle and tendons. The foot is less flexible than the hand but stronger, and the area around the ankle and heel has much larger bones than the wrist. Most of the muscles are found underneath the bones of the foot, and the toes are mainly bone and fatty pads.

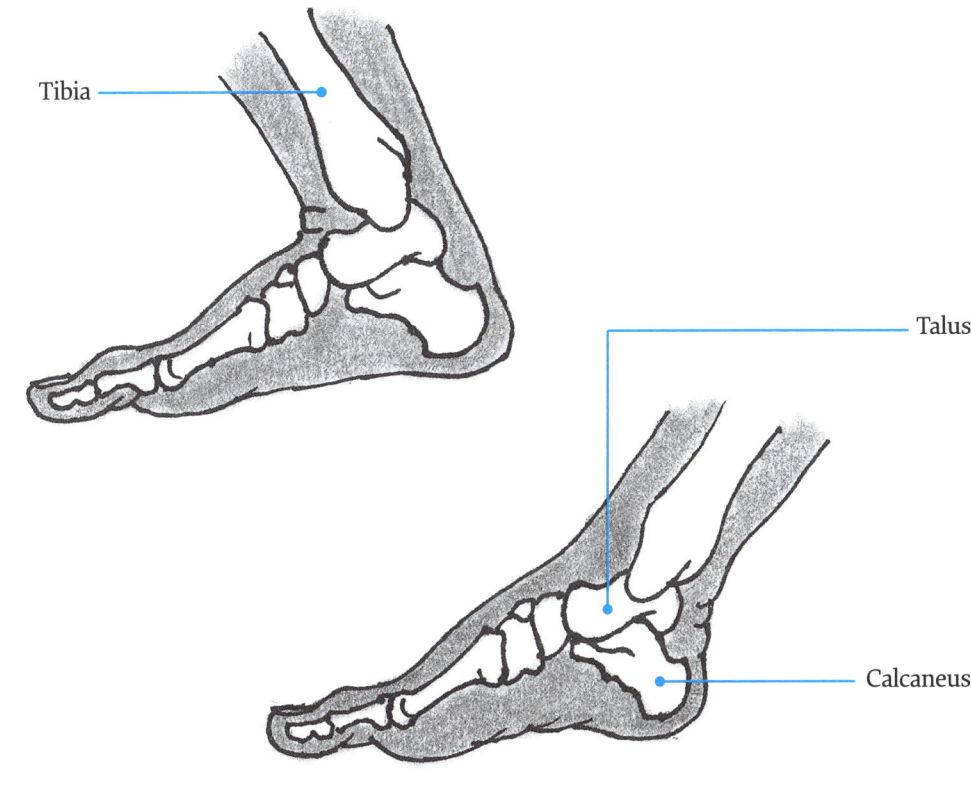

ABDUCTOR HALLUCIS moves big toe outwards.
ABDUCTOR DIGITI MINIMI moves little toe outwards.
ADDUCTOR HALLUCIS moves big toe inwards.
EXTENSOR DIGITORUM BREVIS straightens toes.
EXTENSOR RETINACULUM, SUPERIOR AND INFERIOR enable tendons of the foot to change direction at the ankle.
DORSAL INTEROSSEI Deep-seated muscles that move the toes apart.
FLEXOR DIGITI MINIMI BREVIS flexes little toe.
FLEXOR DIGITORUM BREVIS flexes second to fifth toes.
FLEXOR DIGITORUM LONGUS flexes second to fifth toes.
FLEXOR HALLUCIS BREVIS flexes big toe.
FLEXOR HALLUCIS LONGUS flexes big toe.
LUMBRICALES flex proximal phalanges. Invisible from surface.
OPPONENS DIGITI MINIMI pulls fifth metatarsal bone towards sole.
PLANTAR INTEROSSEI are deep muscles that move third, fourth and fifth toes towards second toe, and flex proximal phalanges.
QUADRATUS PLANTAE (FLEXOR DIGITORUM ACCESSORIUS) helps in flexing toes.

THE LEGS AND FEET IN DETAIL

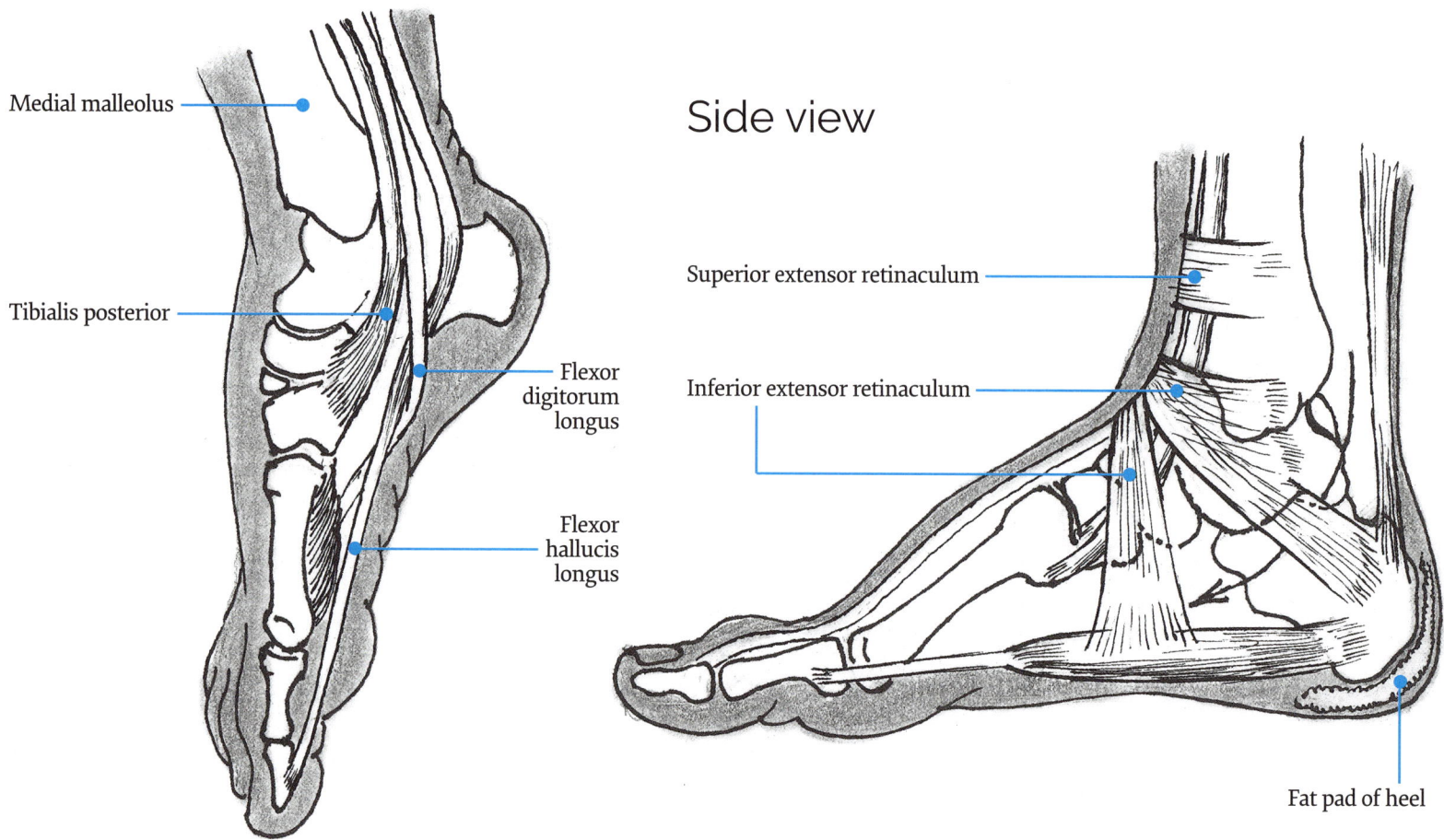

Views from beneath

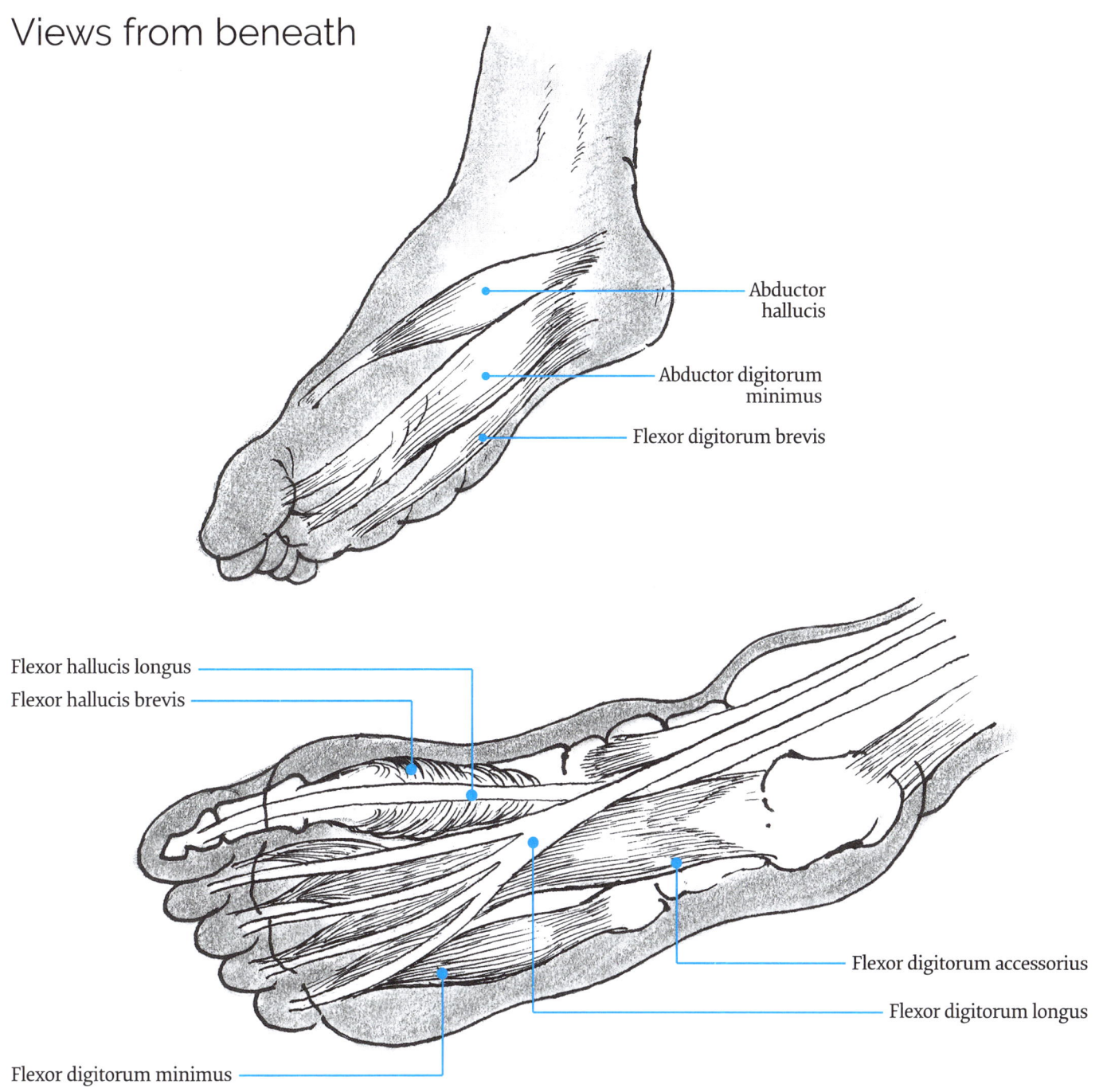

THE LEGS AND FEET IN DETAIL

Surface views of the foot
Flexing and extending

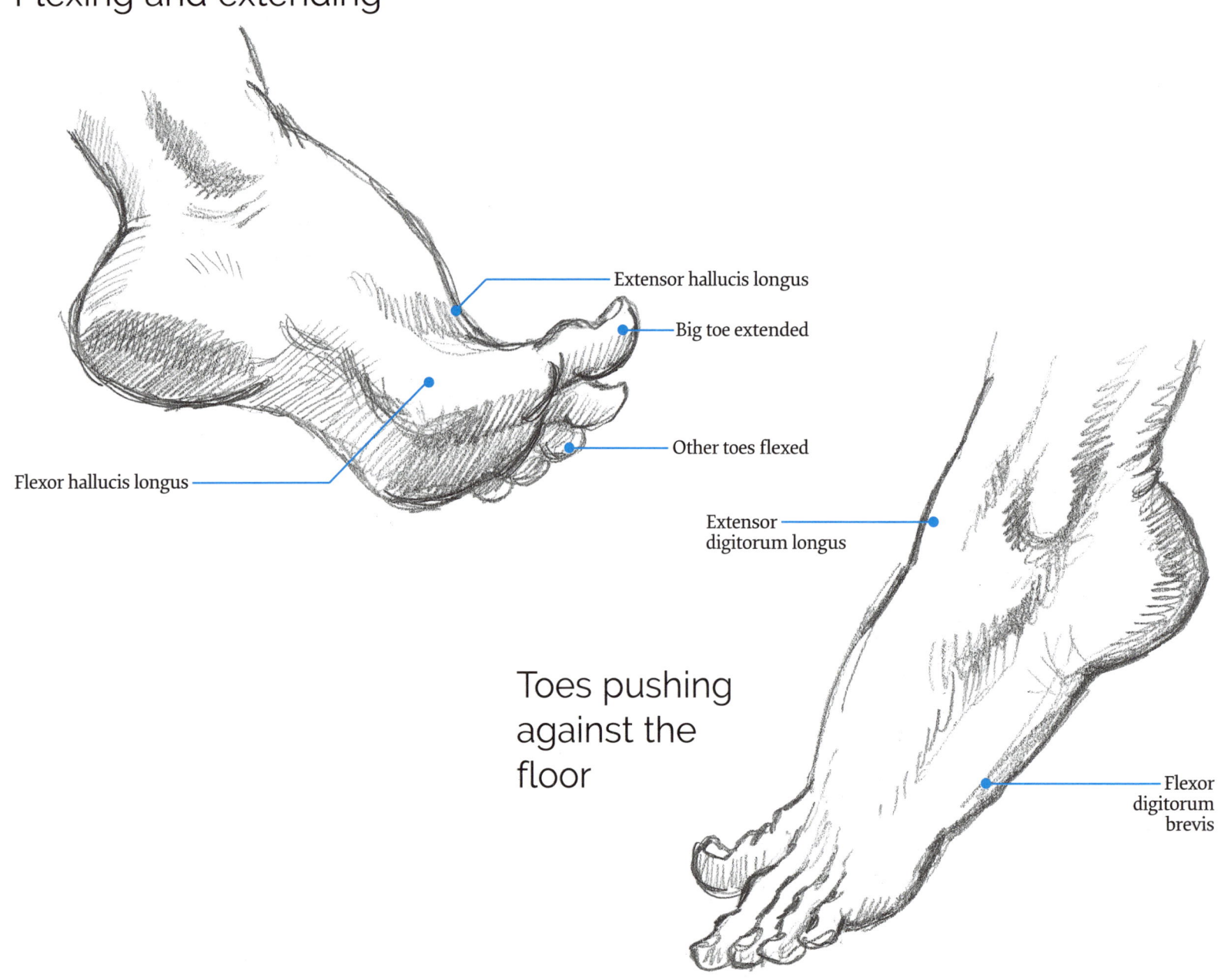

Extensor hallucis longus

Big toe extended

Other toes flexed

Flexor hallucis longus

Extensor digitorum longus

Toes pushing against the floor

Flexor digitorum brevis

Views after master artists

AFTER MICHELANGELO BUONARROTI

AFTER PETER PAUL RUBENS

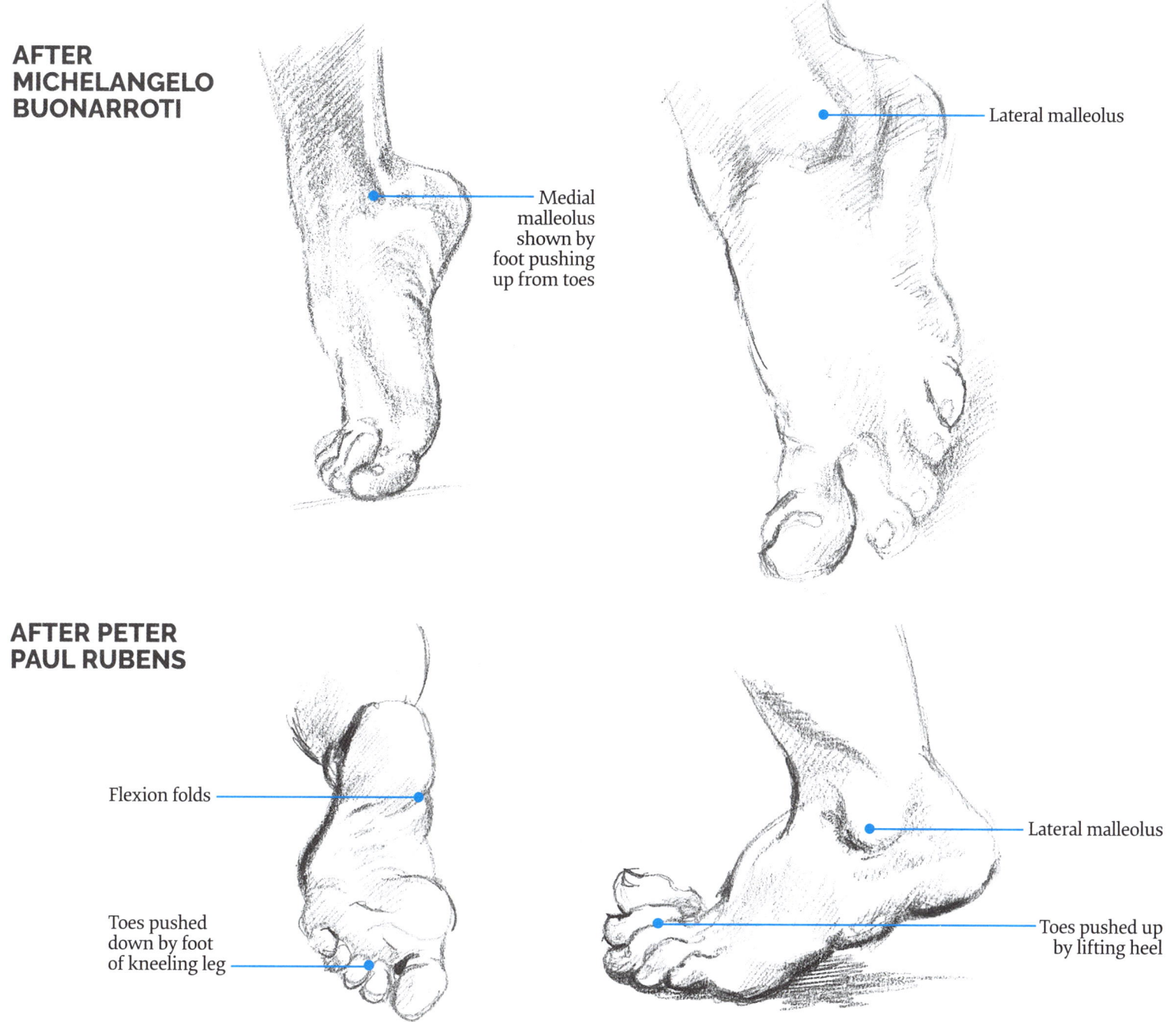

Medial malleolus shown by foot pushing up from toes

Lateral malleolus

Flexion folds

Toes pushed down by foot of kneeling leg

Lateral malleolus

Toes pushed up by lifting heel

THE LEGS AND FEET IN DETAIL

Surface views of legs and feet

Seeing the leg from the surface gives no real hint of its complexity beneath the skin. On the whole, the larger muscles are the only ones easily seen and the only bone structure visible is at the knee and the ankles. However the tibia (shin bone) creates a long, smooth surface at the front of the lower leg that is clearly noticeable.

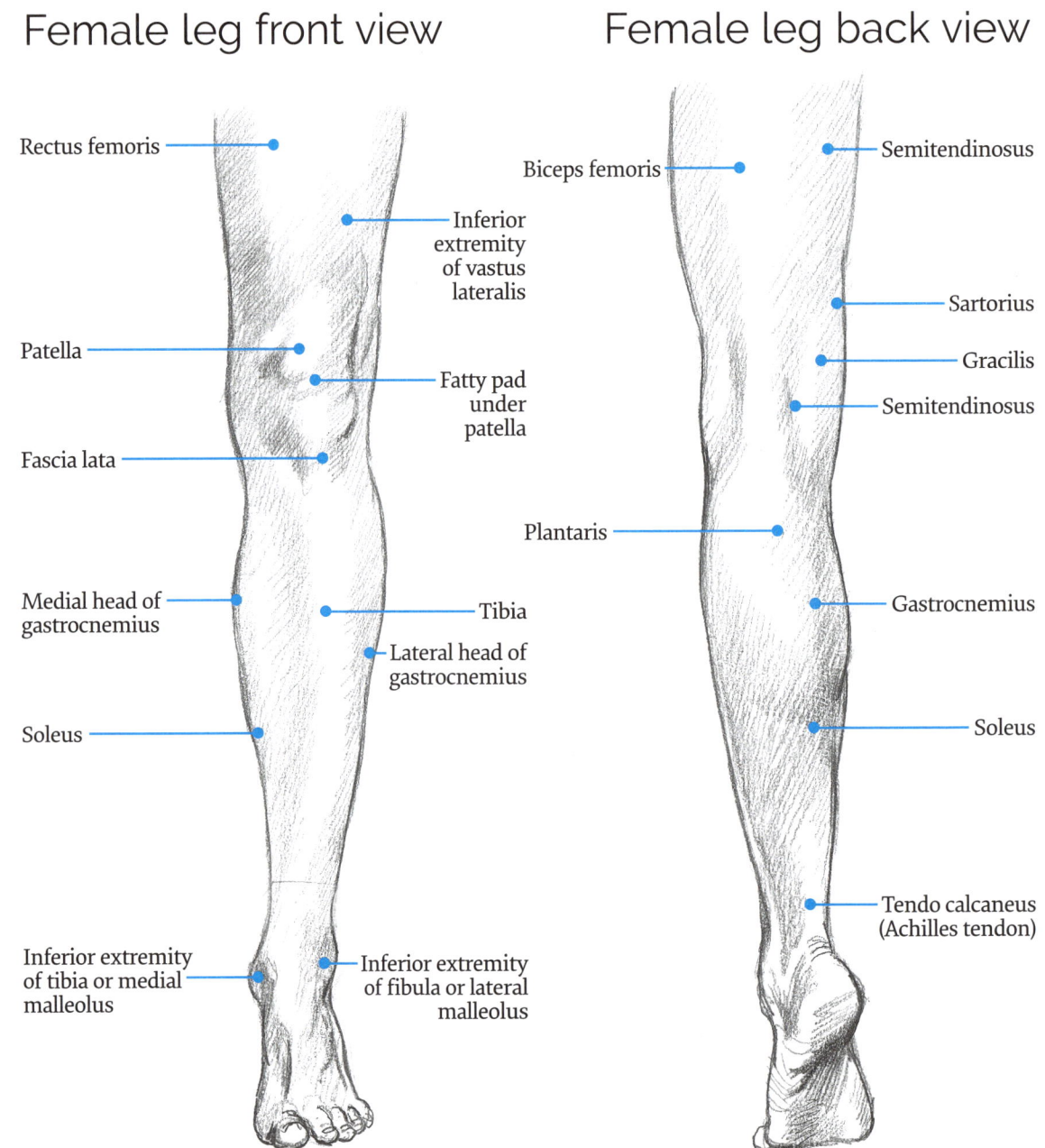

Female leg front view — Rectus femoris, Inferior extremity of vastus lateralis, Patella, Fatty pad under patella, Fascia lata, Medial head of gastrocnemius, Tibia, Lateral head of gastrocnemius, Soleus, Inferior extremity of tibia or medial malleolus, Inferior extremity of fibula or lateral malleolus

Female leg back view — Biceps femoris, Semitendinosus, Sartorius, Gracilis, Semitendinosus, Plantaris, Gastrocnemius, Soleus, Tendo calcaneus (Achilles tendon)

THE LEGS AND FEET IN DETAIL

Male leg back view

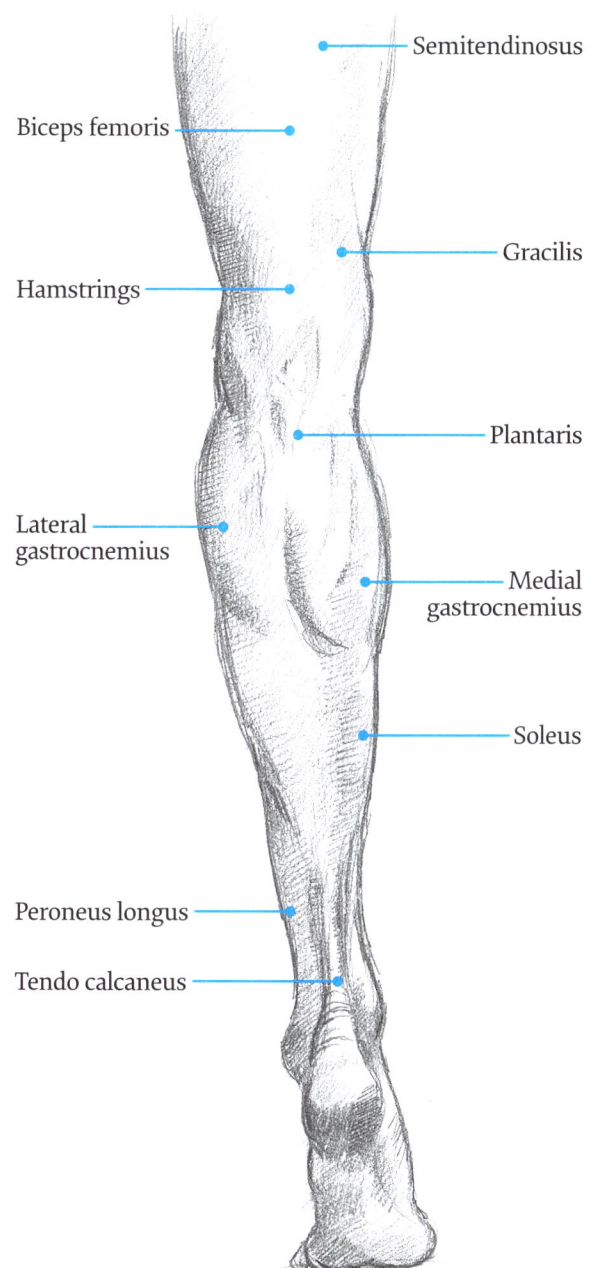

- Biceps femoris
- Semitendinosus
- Hamstrings
- Gracilis
- Plantaris
- Lateral gastrocnemius
- Medial gastrocnemius
- Soleus
- Peroneus longus
- Tendo calcaneus

Male leg front view

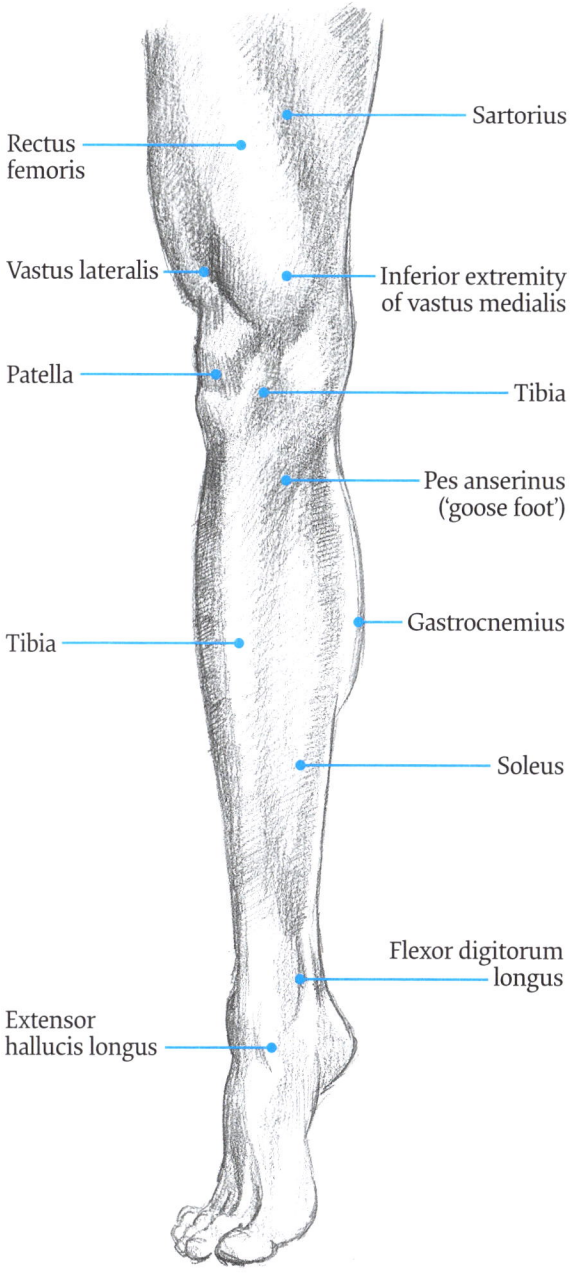

- Rectus femoris
- Sartorius
- Vastus lateralis
- Inferior extremity of vastus medialis
- Patella
- Tibia
- Pes anserinus ('goose foot')
- Tibia
- Gastrocnemius
- Soleus
- Extensor hallucis longus
- Flexor digitorum longus

THE LEGS AND FEET IN DETAIL

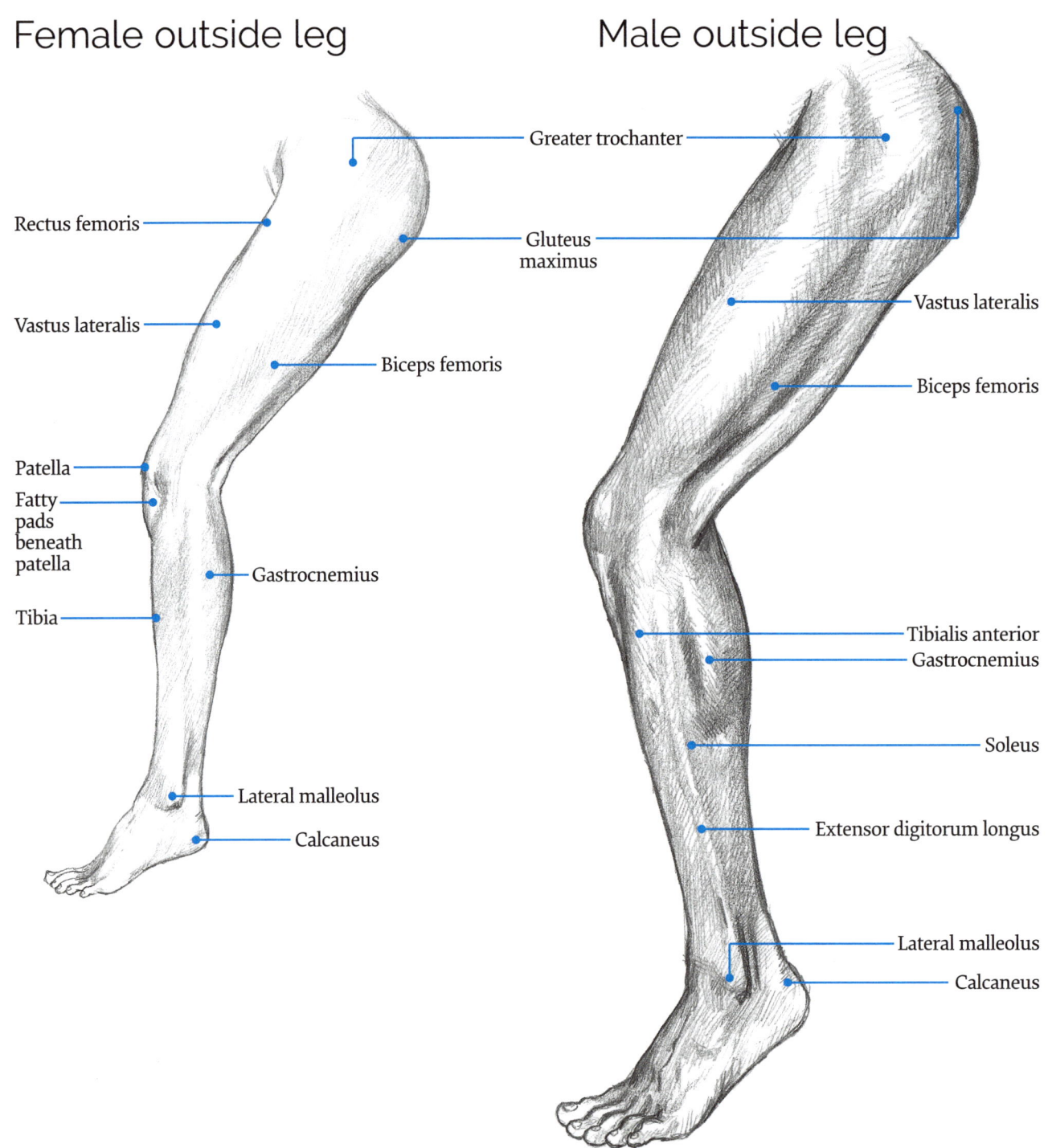

Female inside leg

- Long head of biceps femoris
- Vastus medialis
- Short portion of biceps femoris
- Vastus medialis
- Patella
- Gastrocnemius
- Tibia
- Medial malleolus

Male inside leg

- Biceps femoris
- Sartorius
- Gastrocnemius
- Tendo calcaneus
- Calcaneus

THE LEGS AND FEET IN DETAIL

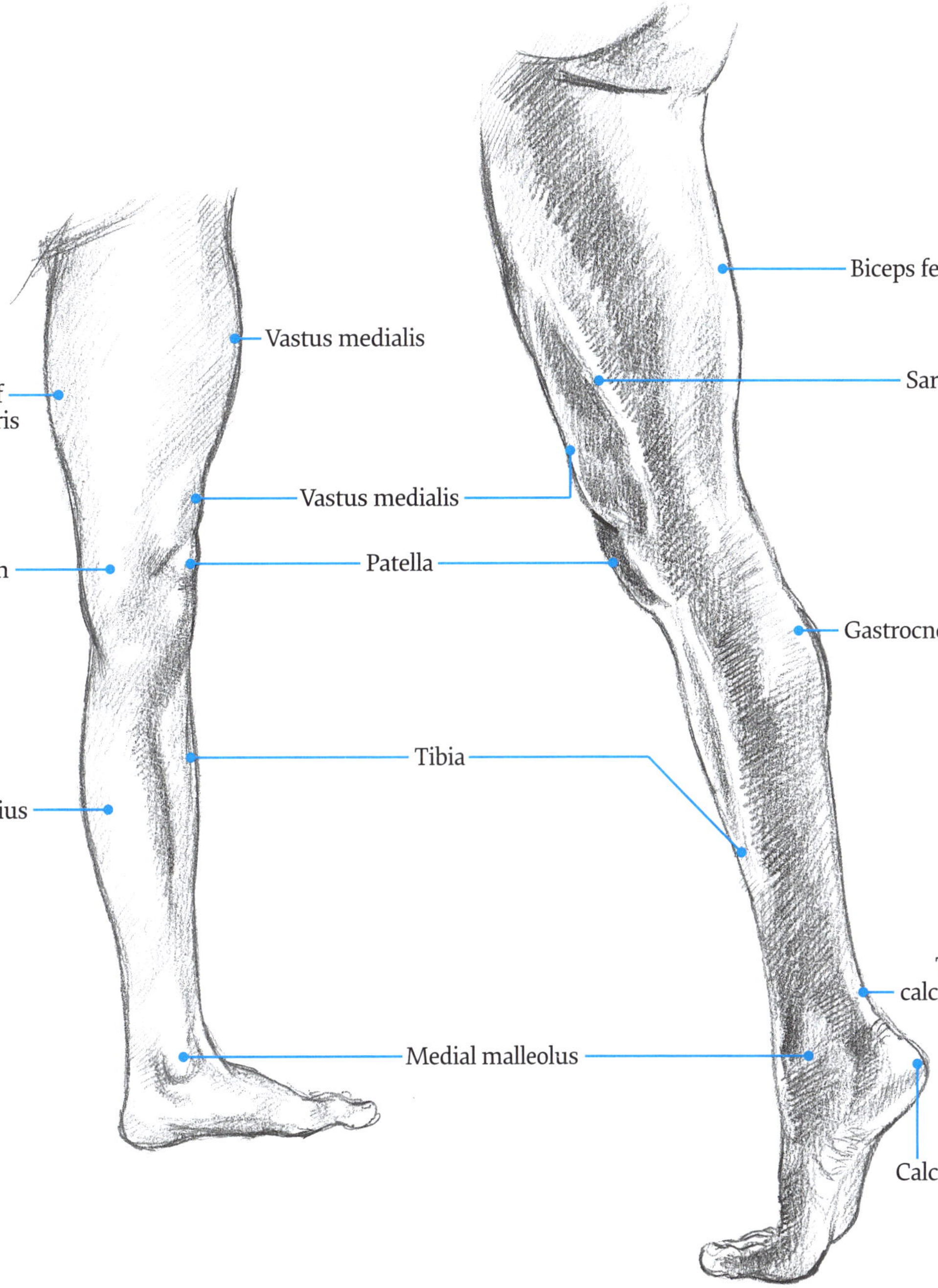

Female leg: side view, flexed

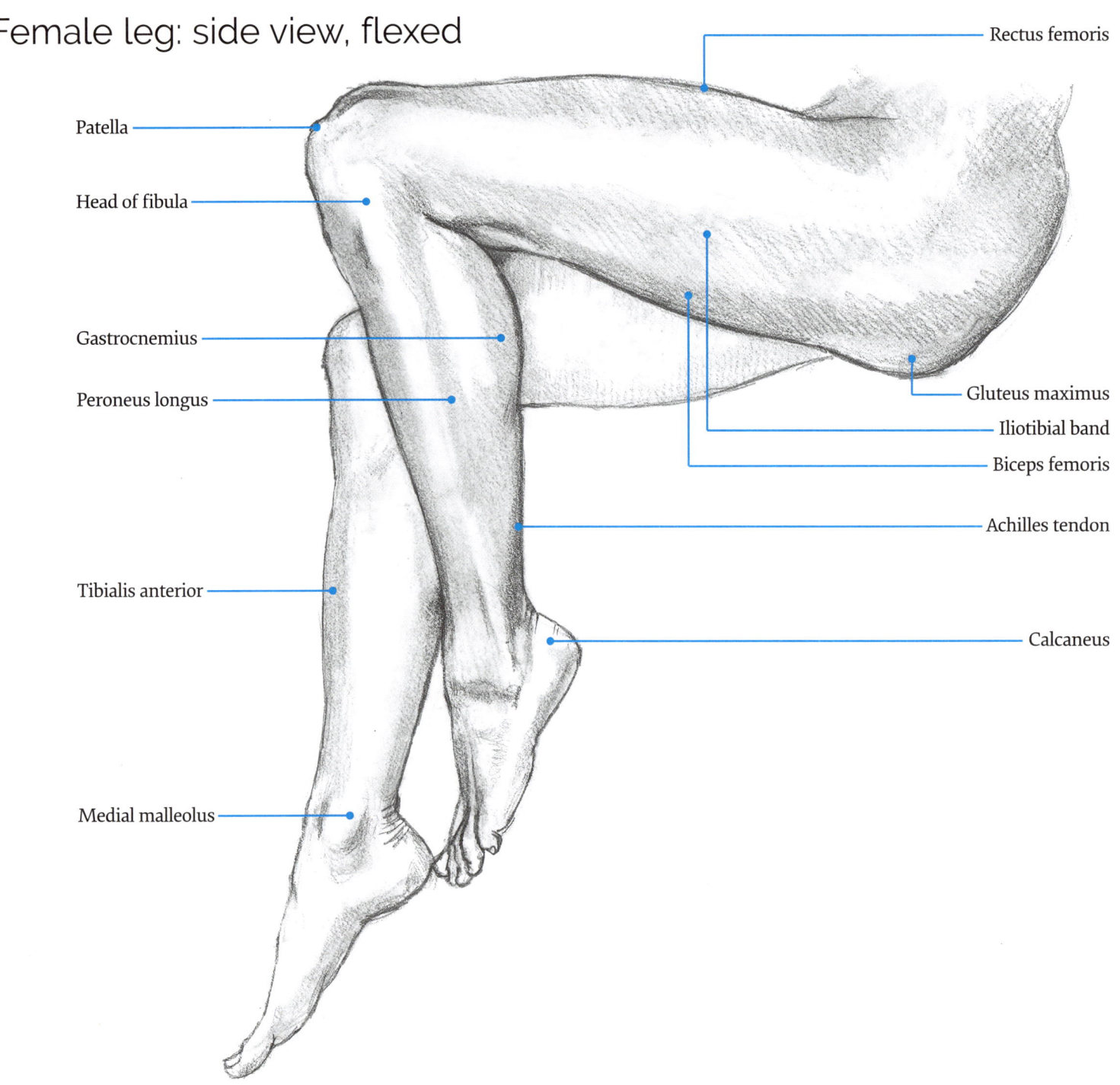

- Rectus femoris
- Patella
- Head of fibula
- Gastrocnemius
- Peroneus longus
- Gluteus maximus
- Iliotibial band
- Biceps femoris
- Achilles tendon
- Tibialis anterior
- Calcaneus
- Medial malleolus

Female leg: front view, flexed

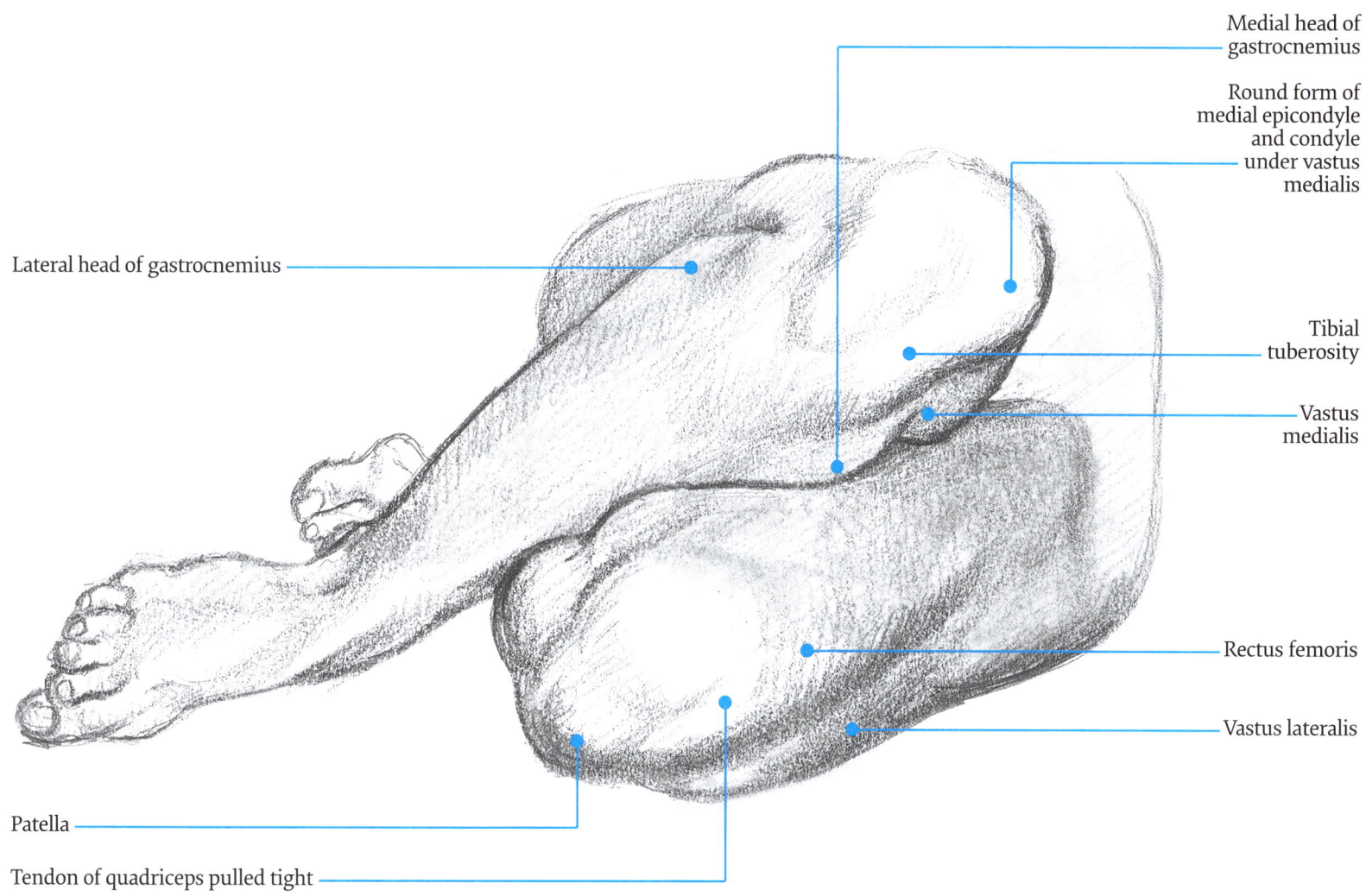

THE LEGS AND FEET IN DETAIL

Male leg: front view, flexed

Male leg: back view, flexed

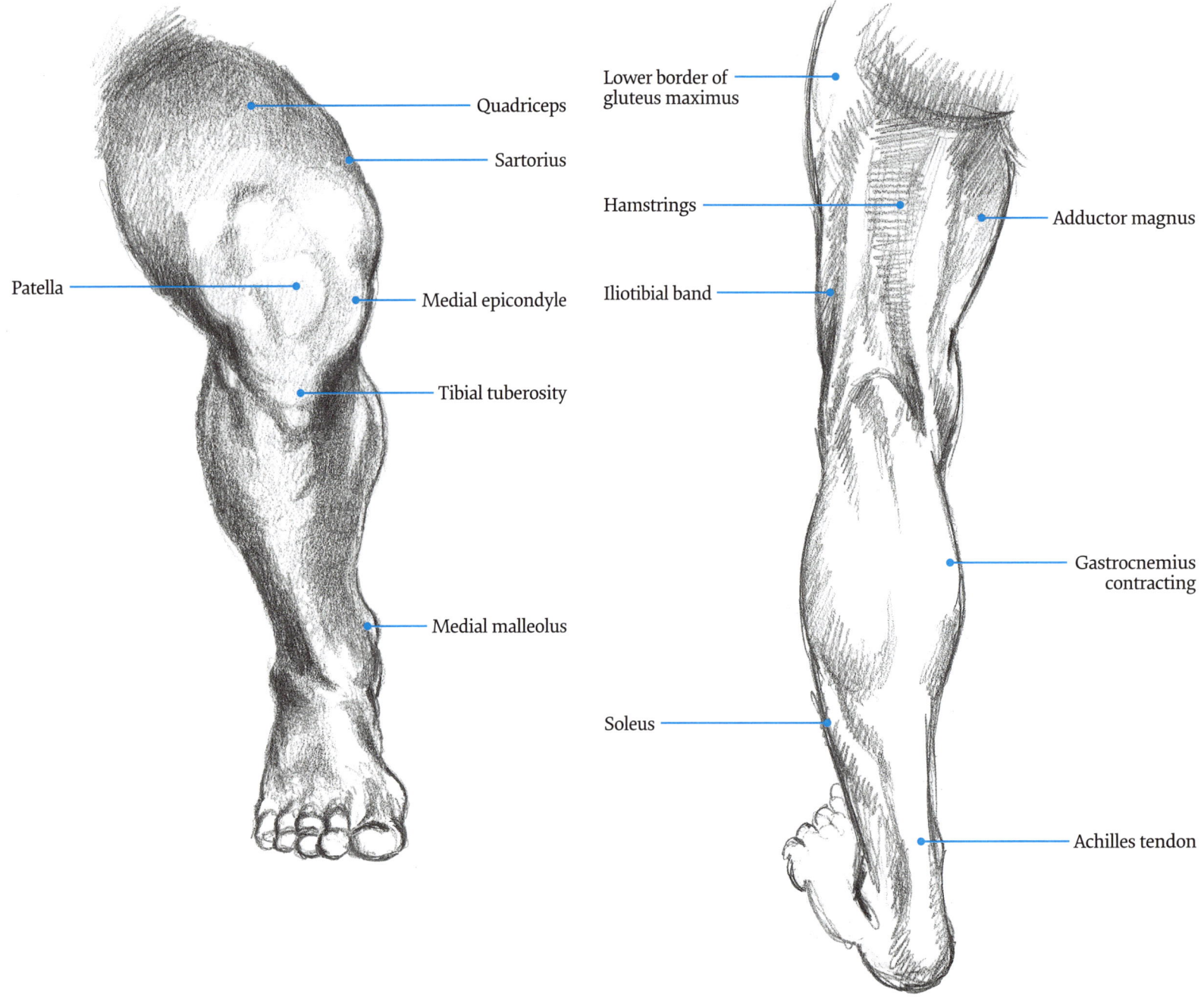

Male lower leg: side view, toes turned up

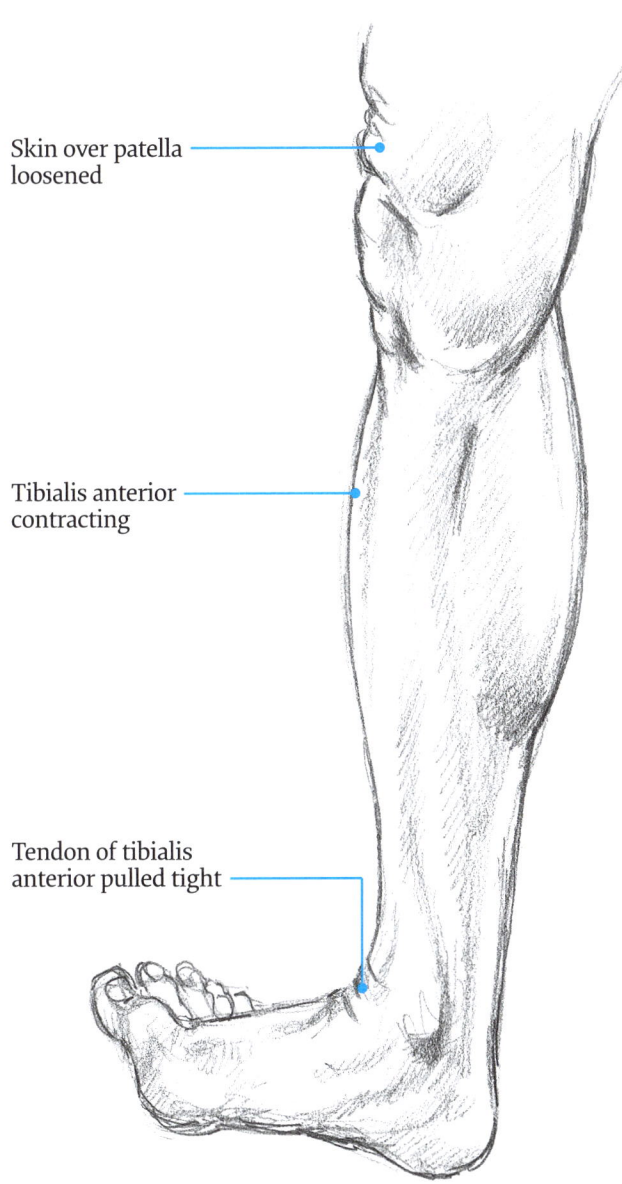

- Skin over patella loosened
- Tibialis anterior contracting
- Tendon of tibialis anterior pulled tight

Male lower leg: side view, flexed

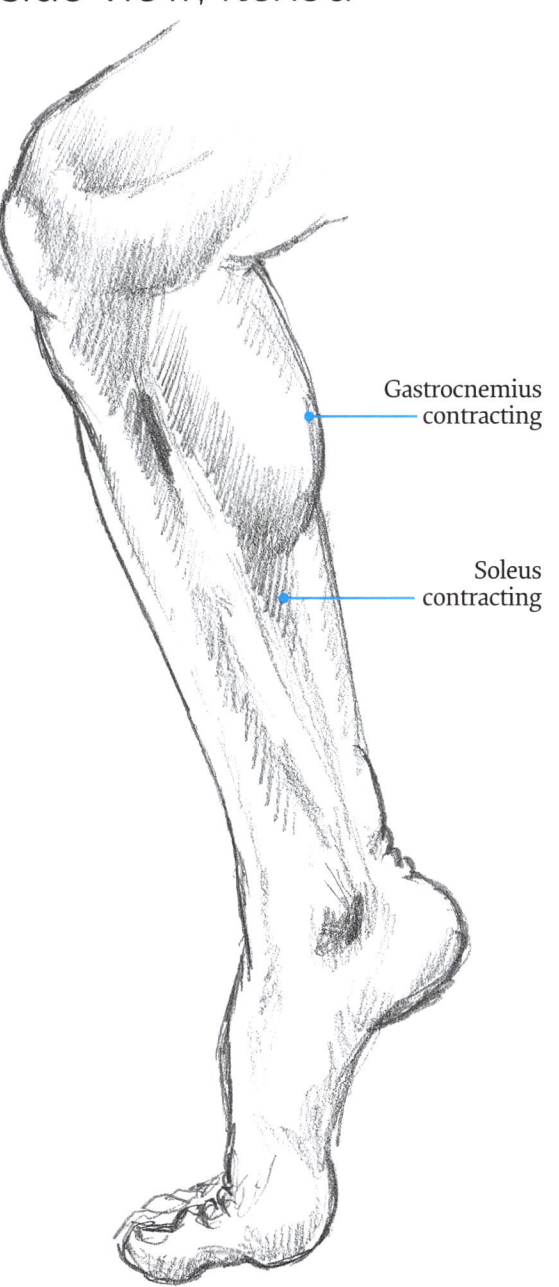

- Gastrocnemius contracting
- Soleus contracting

THE LEGS AND FEET IN DETAIL | 201

Legs and feet drawn by master artists

AFTER CHARLES-JOSEPH NATOIRE

In these drawings after master artists, I have only given the names of some of the visible muscles and bone structure. It would be a good exercise to see what others you can identify, using the diagrammatic information in the previous pages. This will help you to memorize the terms.

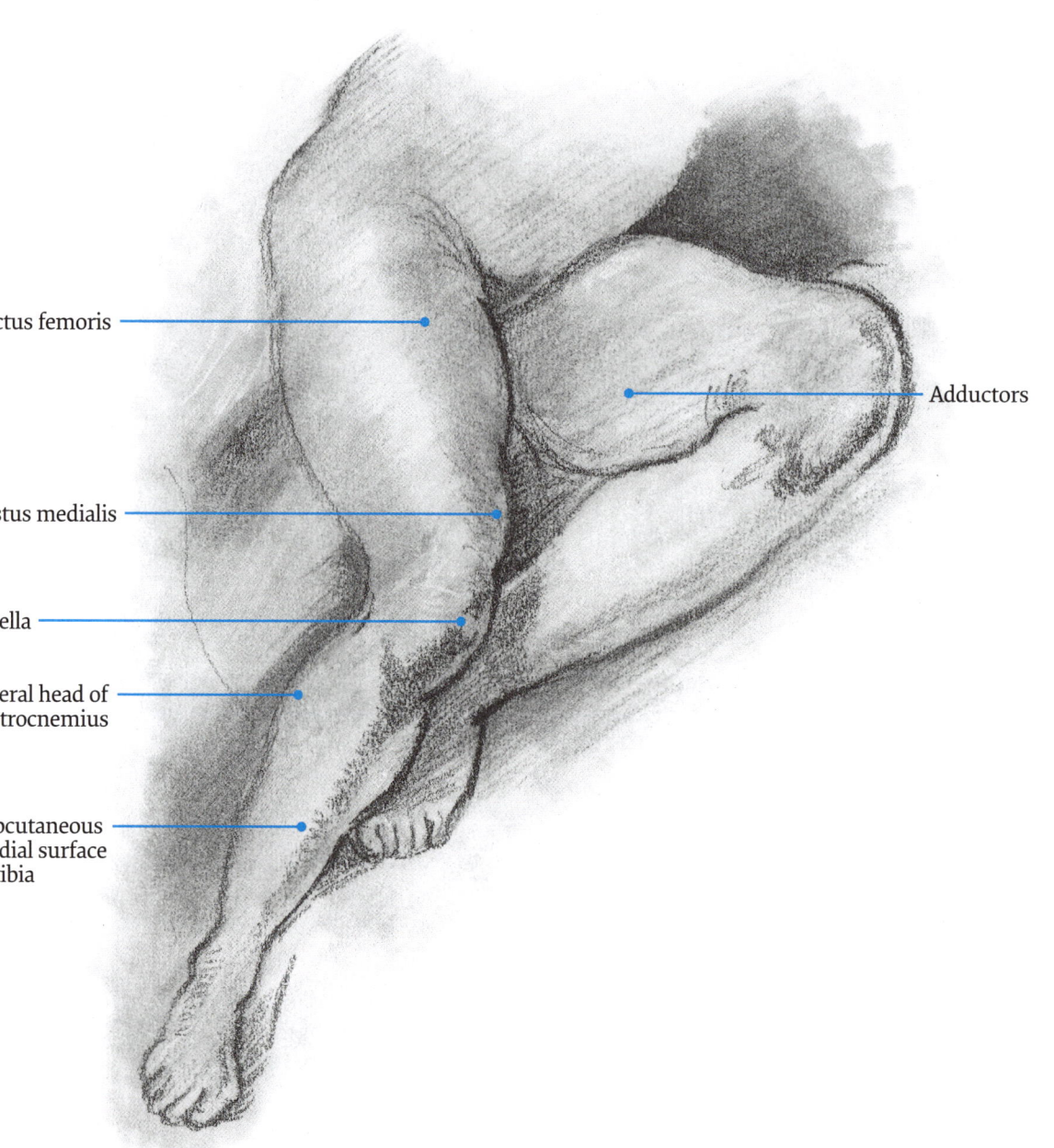

- Rectus femoris
- Adductors
- Vastus medialis
- Patella
- Lateral head of gastrocnemius
- Subcutaneous medial surface of tibia

AFTER ANNIBALE CARRACCI (1560–1609)

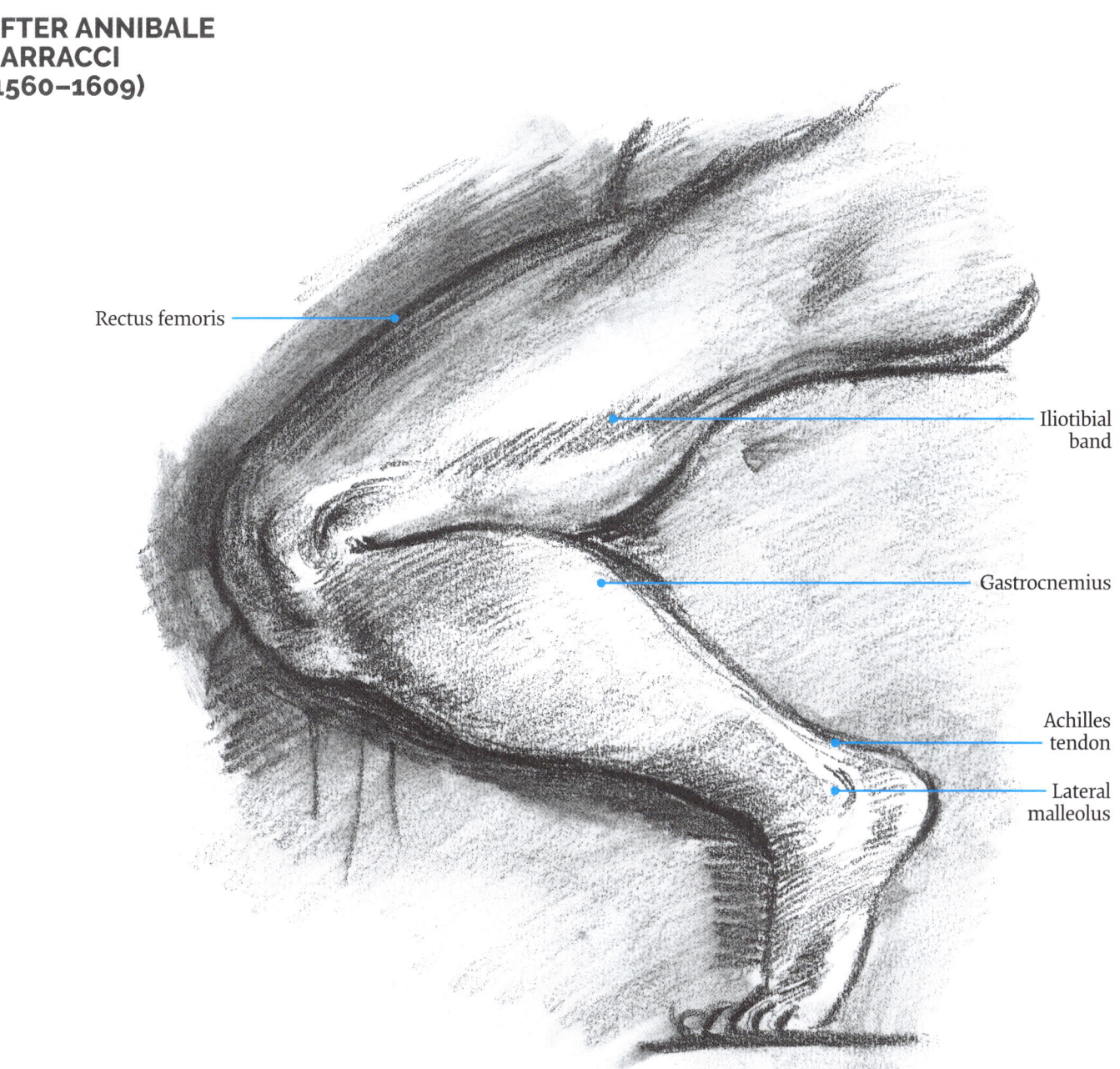

THE LEGS AND FEET IN DETAIL

AFTER MICHELANGELO BUONARROTI

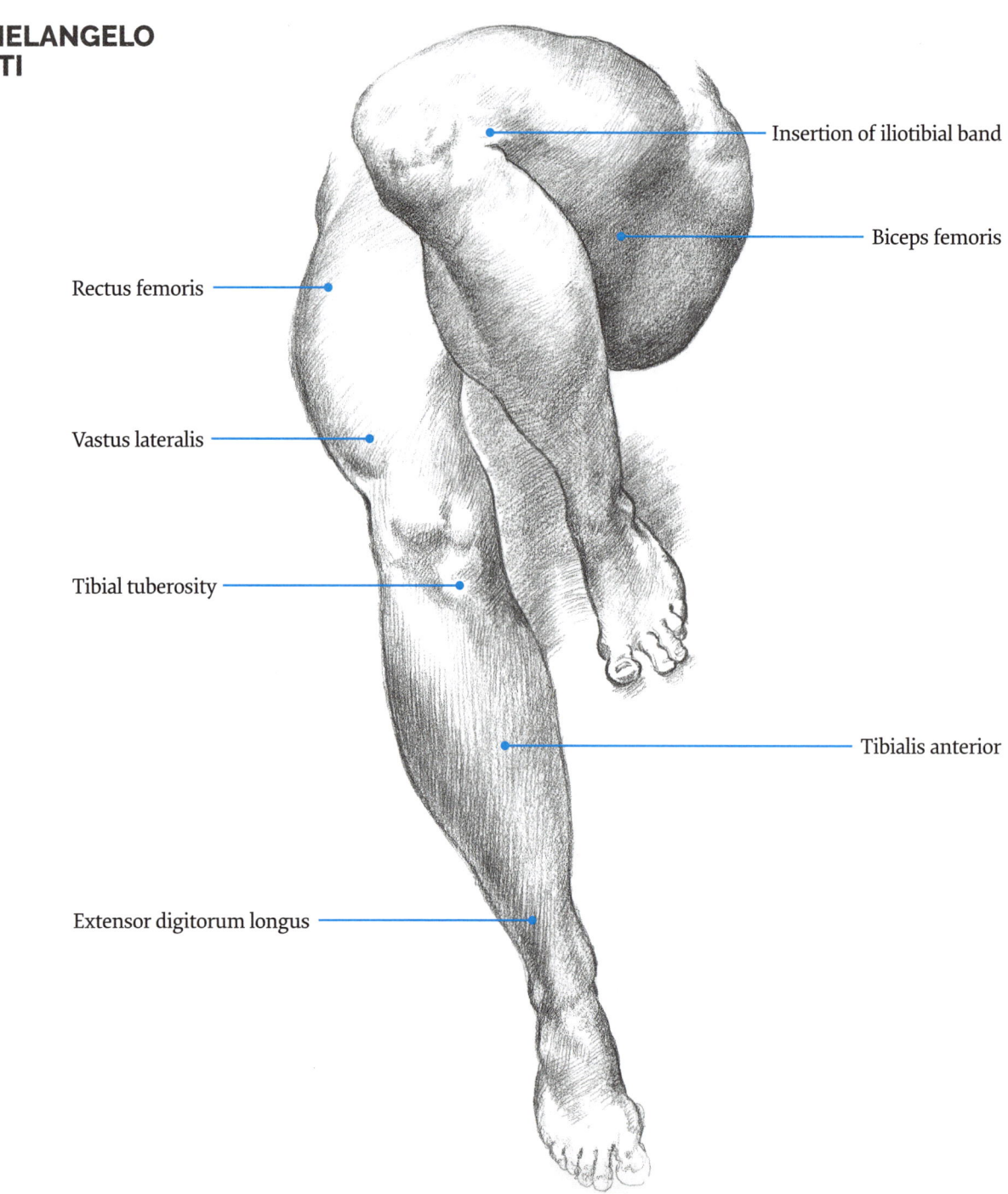

- Insertion of iliotibial band
- Biceps femoris
- Rectus femoris
- Vastus lateralis
- Tibial tuberosity
- Tibialis anterior
- Extensor digitorum longus

THE LEGS AND FEET IN DETAIL

AFTER PETER PAUL RUBENS

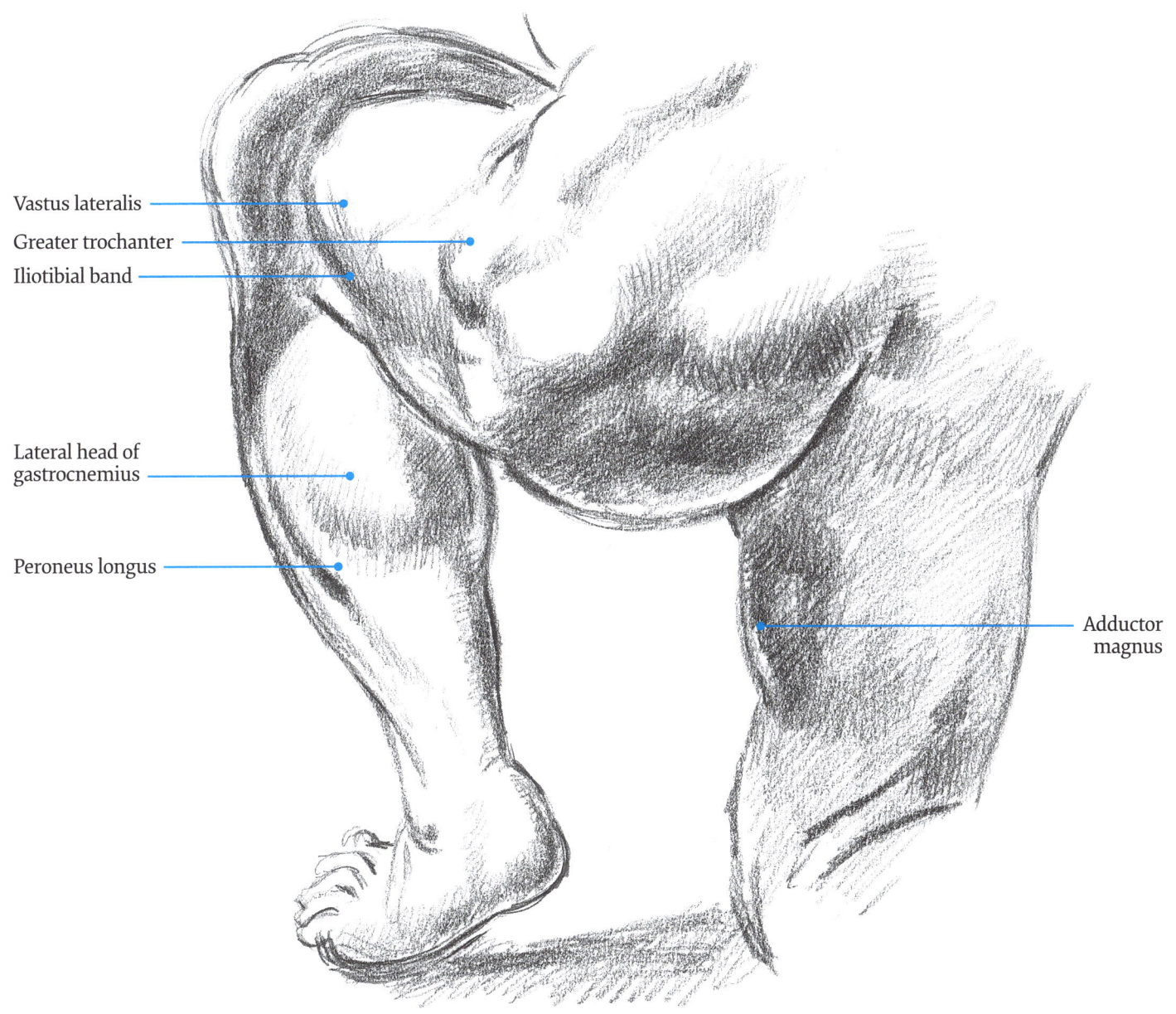

- Vastus lateralis
- Greater trochanter
- Iliotibial band
- Lateral head of gastrocnemius
- Peroneus longus
- Adductor magnus

THE LEGS AND FEET IN DETAIL

AFTER LOUIS DE BOULOGNE (1654–1733)

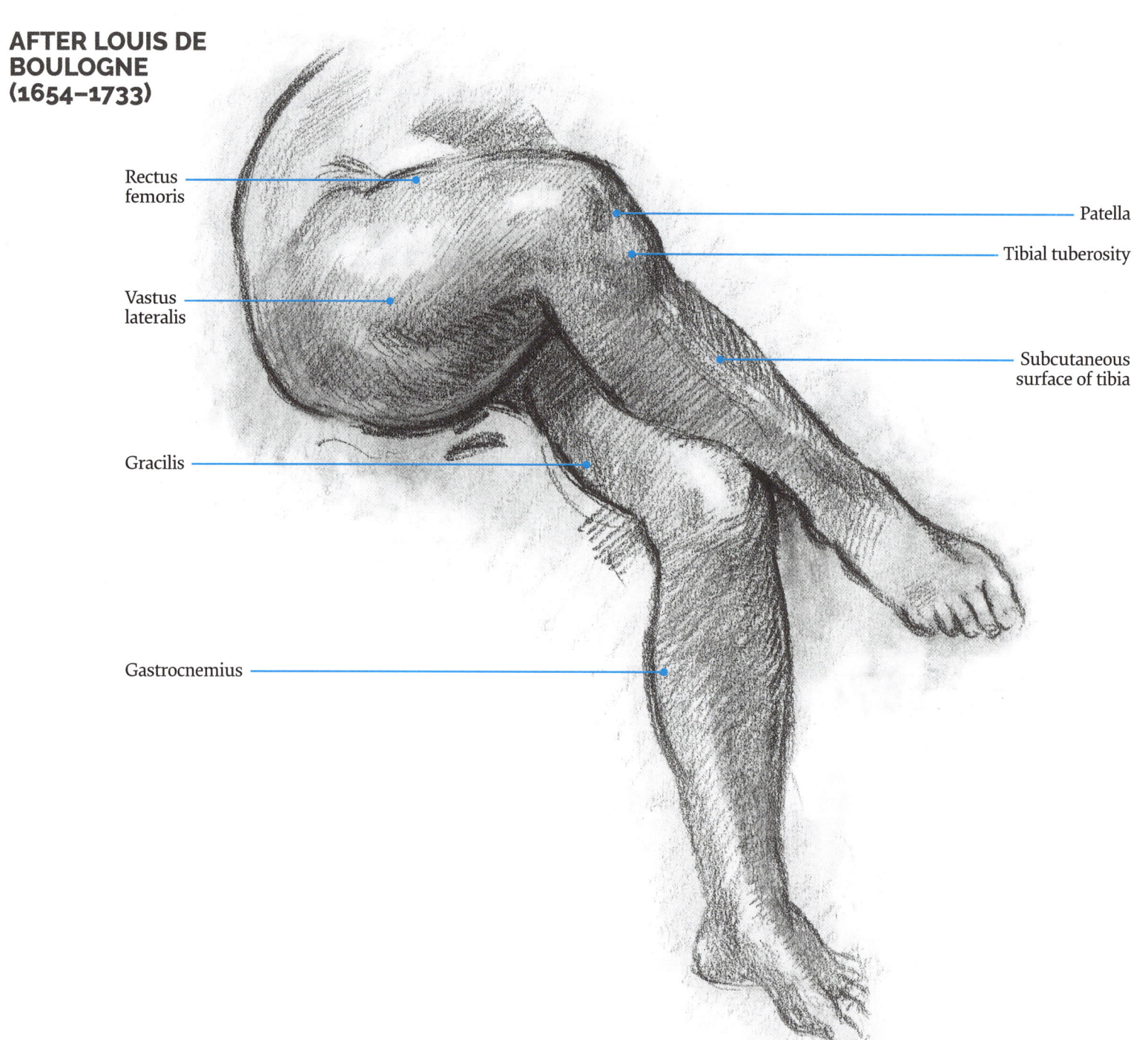

- Rectus femoris
- Vastus lateralis
- Gracilis
- Gastrocnemius
- Patella
- Tibial tuberosity
- Subcutaneous surface of tibia

THE LEGS AND FEET IN DETAIL

AFTER AN UNKNOWN ITALIAN MASTER (c. 1700)

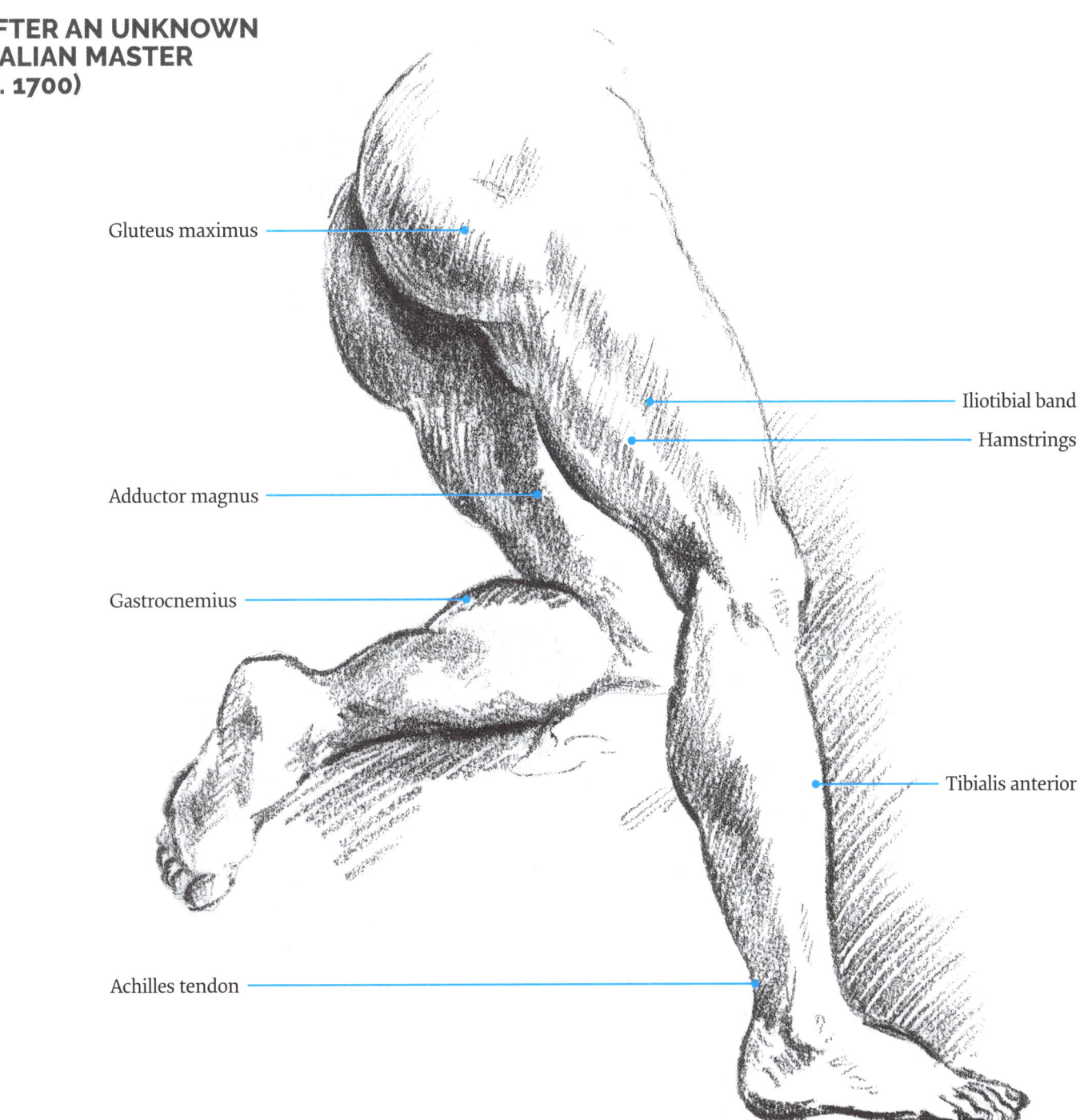

- Gluteus maximus
- Iliotibial band
- Hamstrings
- Adductor magnus
- Gastrocnemius
- Tibialis anterior
- Achilles tendon

THE LEGS AND FEET IN DETAIL

Practice perspective views of legs and feet

One of the most difficult problems with drawing the human figure (or any other figure for that matter) arises when the body or the limbs of the figure being drawn are foreshortened by perspective (see also pages 32–3); an example might be when a leg or arm is projecting towards your viewpoint. Instead of the expected shape of the limb you get an oddly distorted proportion that the mind often wants to correct. However, if you are going to draw accurately, you have to discount what the mind is telling you and observe directly, measuring if necessary to make sure that these rather odd proportions are adhered to. In this way, a limb seen from the end on will carry real conviction with the viewer.

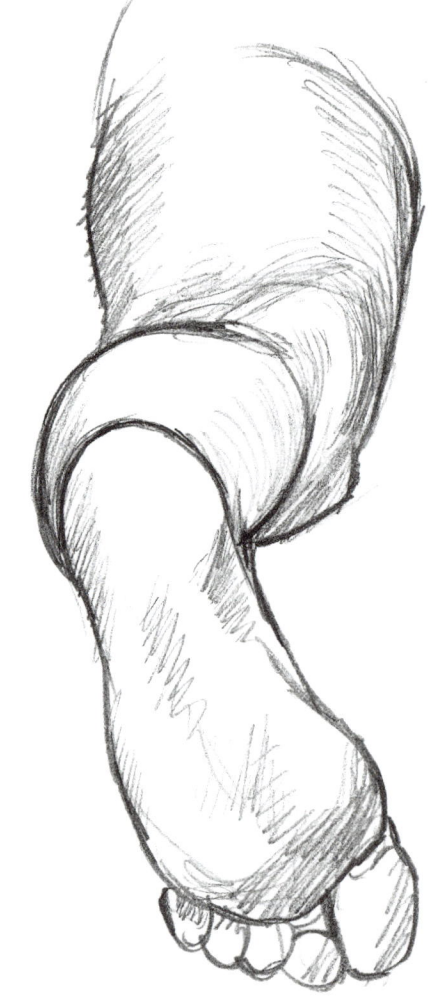

When viewing the leg from the foot end, notice how large the sole of foot looks in comparison with the apparent length of the leg. The muscles and the knee project outwards, their roundness and angularity very pronounced, while their length is reduced to almost nil. If you observe the shapes produced by this view, you shouldn't have any problem. Don't tell yourself that it looks wrong, because it's not; it's just an unusual point of view.

Experiment with different materials

These two color studies of folded legs show some different approaches with color. In the drawing of male legs (left) I used a black chalk outline in combination with soft color pastels, smudging the pigment in places to give the smooth effect of muscles under skin. The female legs were drawn in colored pencil, with a strong outline to denote the unusual shapes produced in this view.

> ### Artist's Note
> Drawing the individual parts of the human body is never a waste of your artistic time. It is at one and the same time the most difficult and the most satisfying exercise and will help you to become an efficient draughtsman quicker than any other kind of work.

Chapter Six
DRAWING THE BODY

This final chapter explores the benefits of practicing life drawing for artists, showing the variety of poses you might encounter and methods for conveying form and movement. There are exercises in working at speed, studying body language, and the effects of lighting on the appearance of your model. The chapter concludes with a selection of drawings showing how master artists have approached the human form using different styles and techniques.

Although a book like this will give you a lot of information about the human body, it is essential for really good results to draw from life as often as possible, in order to become familiar with what happens to the muscles and bone structure of the body in different circumstances. It used to be permitted for artists to attend medical dissections of bodies in order to understand the inner workings, but that is rather difficult now and will not be necessary, unless you intend to investigate anatomy in some depth.

If you join a life class at your local art institute or adult education centre, you will have the chance to draw all kinds of models using a variety of techniques. The tutors are generally well qualified to give you an effective course in drawing the human body, so your time will not be wasted. And after reading this book, you will be able to identify many of the bony parts and the visible muscles of the body, when you see it in its natural state.

Life drawing

When it comes to drawing the human figure, you can learn a lot from diagrams and examples but there is no substitute for drawing a model from life. This set of figure studies, all from life models, is to give you some idea of the variety of ways that you can show a figure to convincing effect. They use different techniques, attempting to echo the feeling of the particular pose or model.

The next drawing is more tentative in one way, but also very definite when the main shape has been detected. The wiry pen line sometimes suggests that an edge has not yet been clearly seen, and at other times is put down so strongly that there is no doubting its position. This results in a certain assurance, because we do actually tend to view things like that, sometimes sure about the image and sometimes uncertain.

The first model is drawn in pencil and the approach has been fairly fluid – meaning that although there are some strong lines, the way they have been repeatedly sketched around, in order to find the best line to describe the model's pose, gives a very soft feel to the edge of the figure.

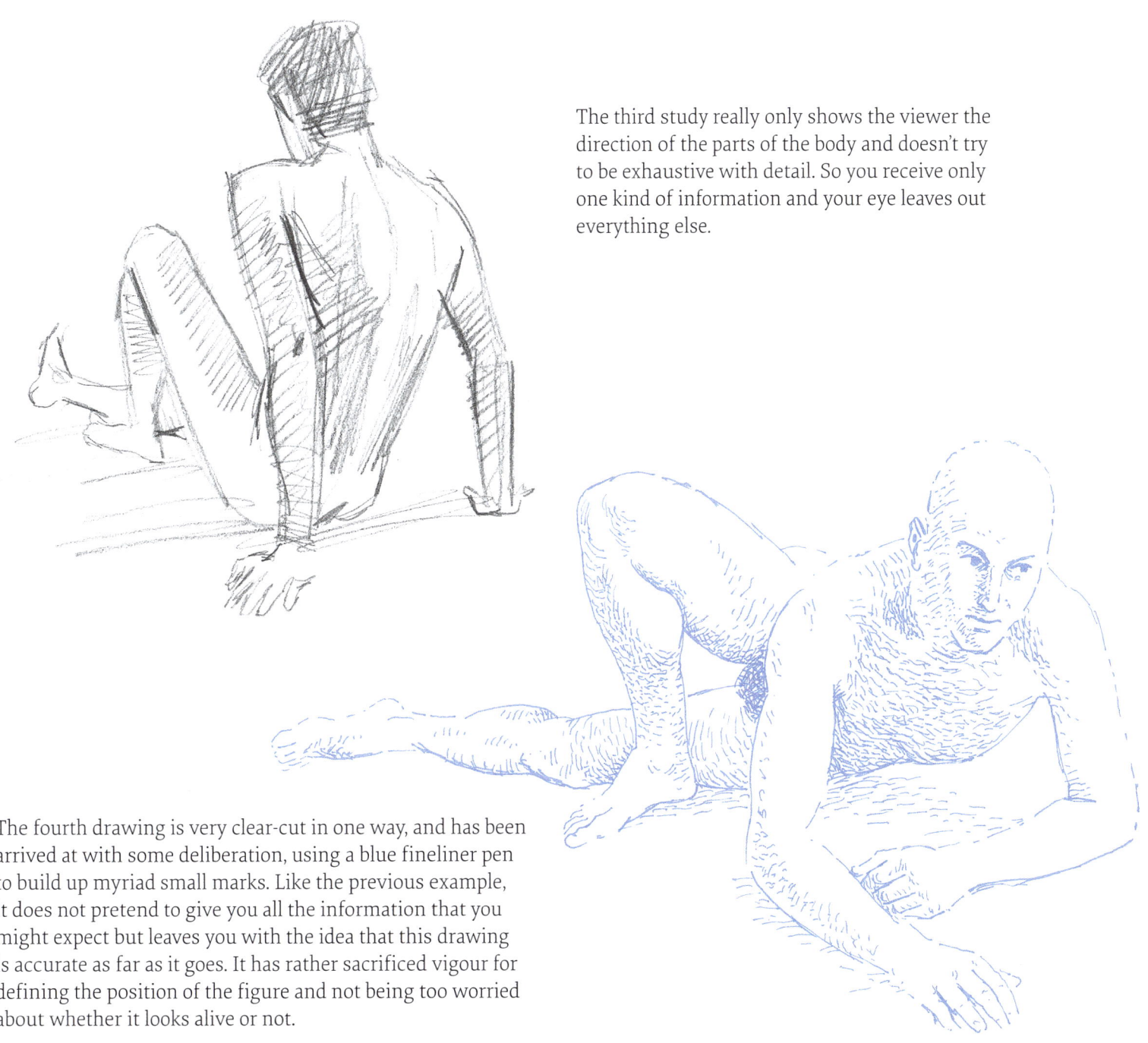

The third study really only shows the viewer the direction of the parts of the body and doesn't try to be exhaustive with detail. So you receive only one kind of information and your eye leaves out everything else.

The fourth drawing is very clear-cut in one way, and has been arrived at with some deliberation, using a blue fineliner pen to build up myriad small marks. Like the previous example, it does not pretend to give you all the information that you might expect but leaves you with the idea that this drawing is accurate as far as it goes. It has rather sacrificed vigour for defining the position of the figure and not being too worried about whether it looks alive or not.

This standing figure of a woman with hands behind her back is a simple combination of a straight line of leg, a forward bend of torso with shoulders and elbow acting as a line cutting across, and the general curve of the front shape of the figure.

Looking at a full-length reclining figure, the first thing I noticed was the angle of the upper half in contrast to the horizontal bias of the lower part. So first I drew a square to contain the hips and buttocks and then a longer, narrower rectangle for the rest of the legs. For the area above the waist I drew in a quadrilateral that is uneven, but projecting at the correct angle from the central square. Above this was a vague rectangular shape that took in the head and hair. It was interesting that the length of the two rectangles that contained the upper body and the legs were both about the same length either side of the central square.

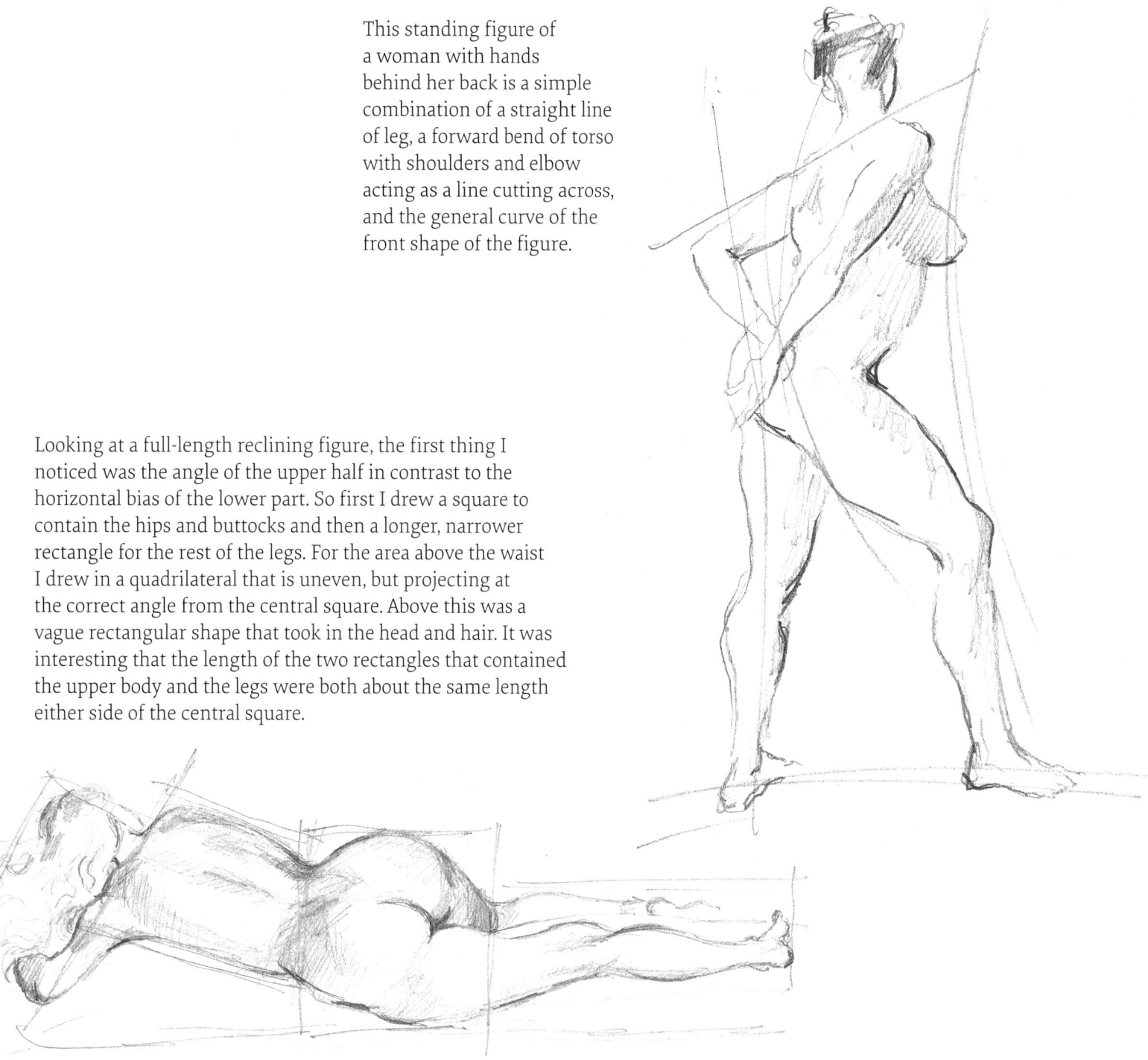

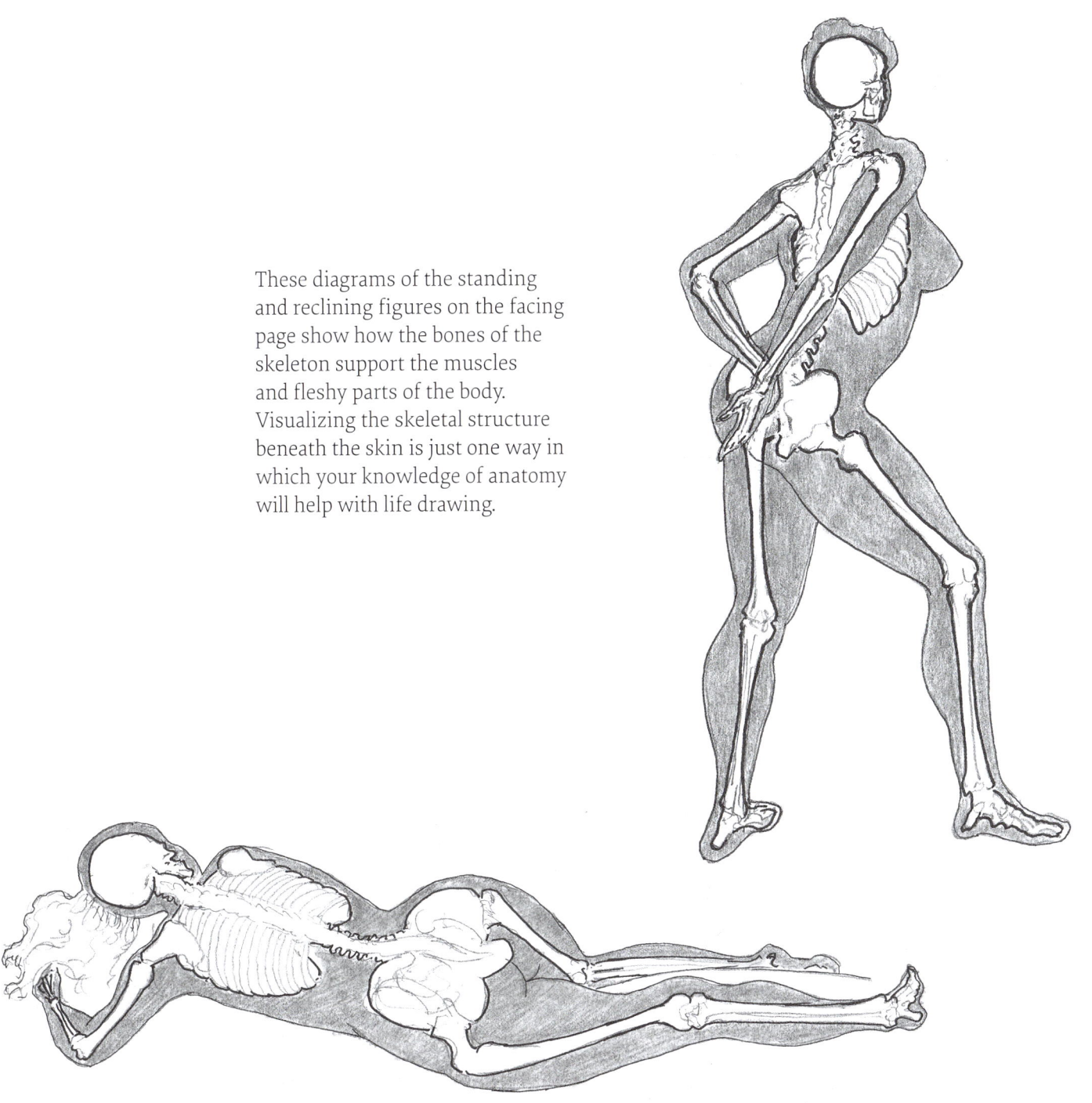

These diagrams of the standing and reclining figures on the facing page show how the bones of the skeleton support the muscles and fleshy parts of the body. Visualizing the skeletal structure beneath the skin is just one way in which your knowledge of anatomy will help with life drawing.

Dynamic poses

The next drawings show some dynamic life class poses. These are poses that the model obviously cannot hold for long, so you have to get down the main shapes of the body before adding detail.

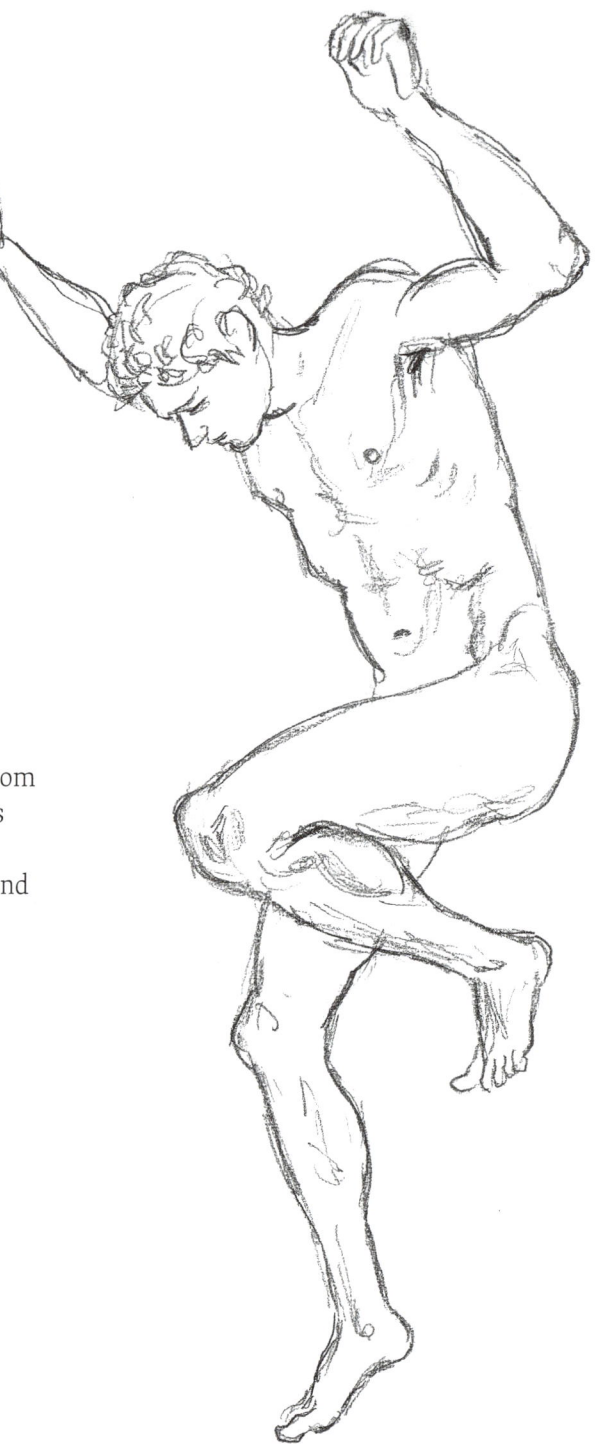

The leaping man is obviously on his way down from a higher level or a very high jump. Note how he is concentrating on his landing place. The muscles most noticeable here are those in the lower legs and along the front and side of the torso.

The woman bending over to touch the floor at her feet is stretching both her leg muscles and those of her back. This kind of detailed cross-hatching can be very effective in giving substance to your figure. It is time-consuming, so this shading was finished after the model had abandoned her pose.

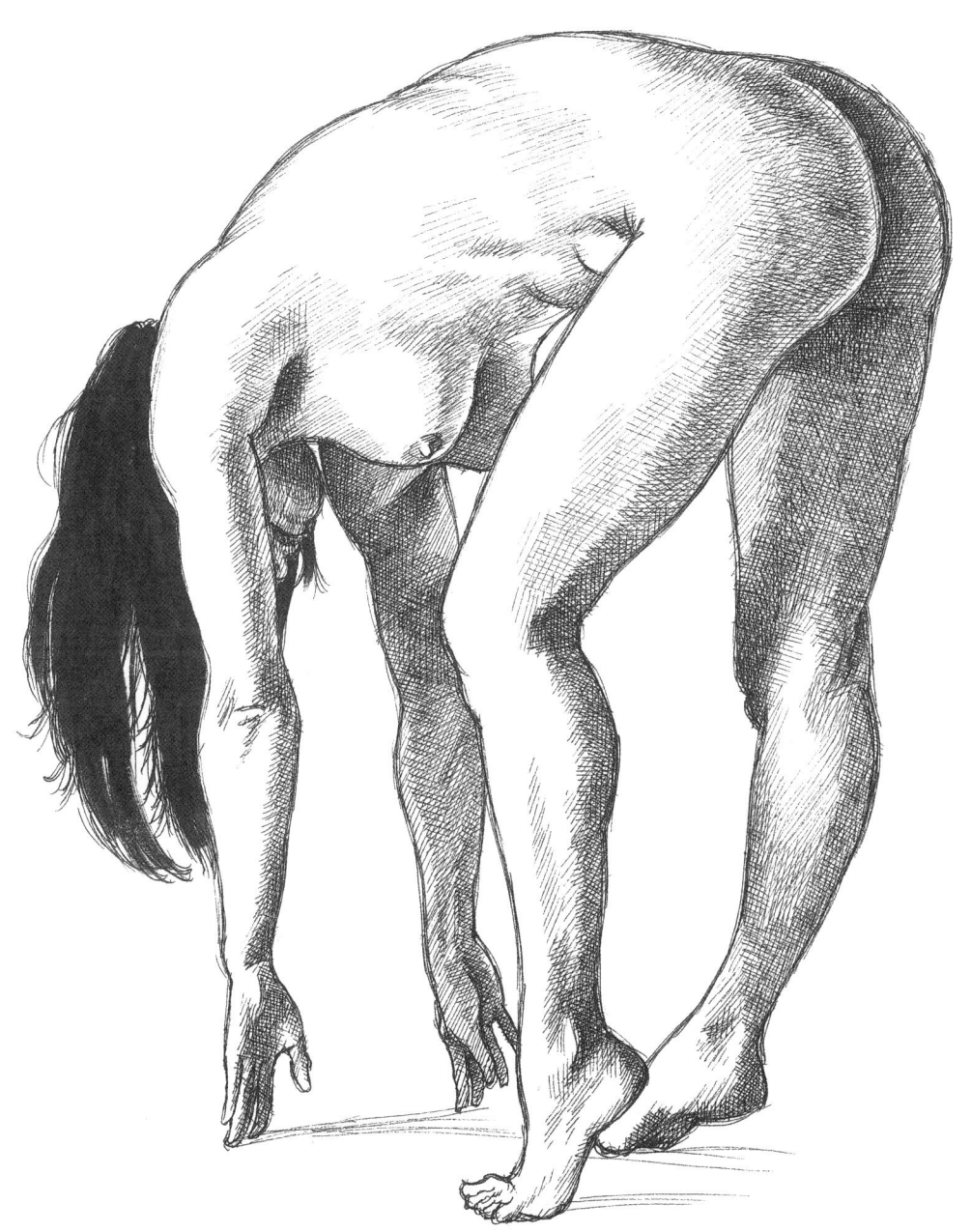

The model sitting cross-legged and stretching her arms above her head is showing very clearly the bony ribcage and her knee joints.

This pose makes the most of the opposition of the arms and legs. The model's torso is also turned to show how the muscles are being used. Normally the body wouldn't be worked as thoroughly as this. The heavier marker pen lines give emphasis to the areas of the body's outline that need to be expressed with a little more force. This helps to give an impression of dimension and lend the drawing a strength to match the pose.

Changing ends

You will encounter the effects of foreshortening at a life class, especially if your viewpoint is at one end of a reclining figure, as in these examples.

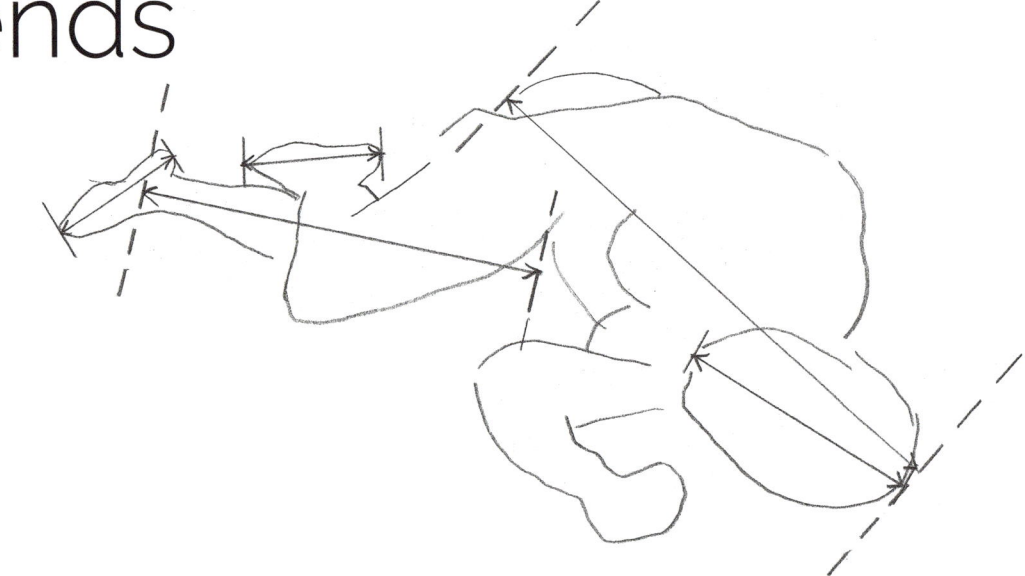

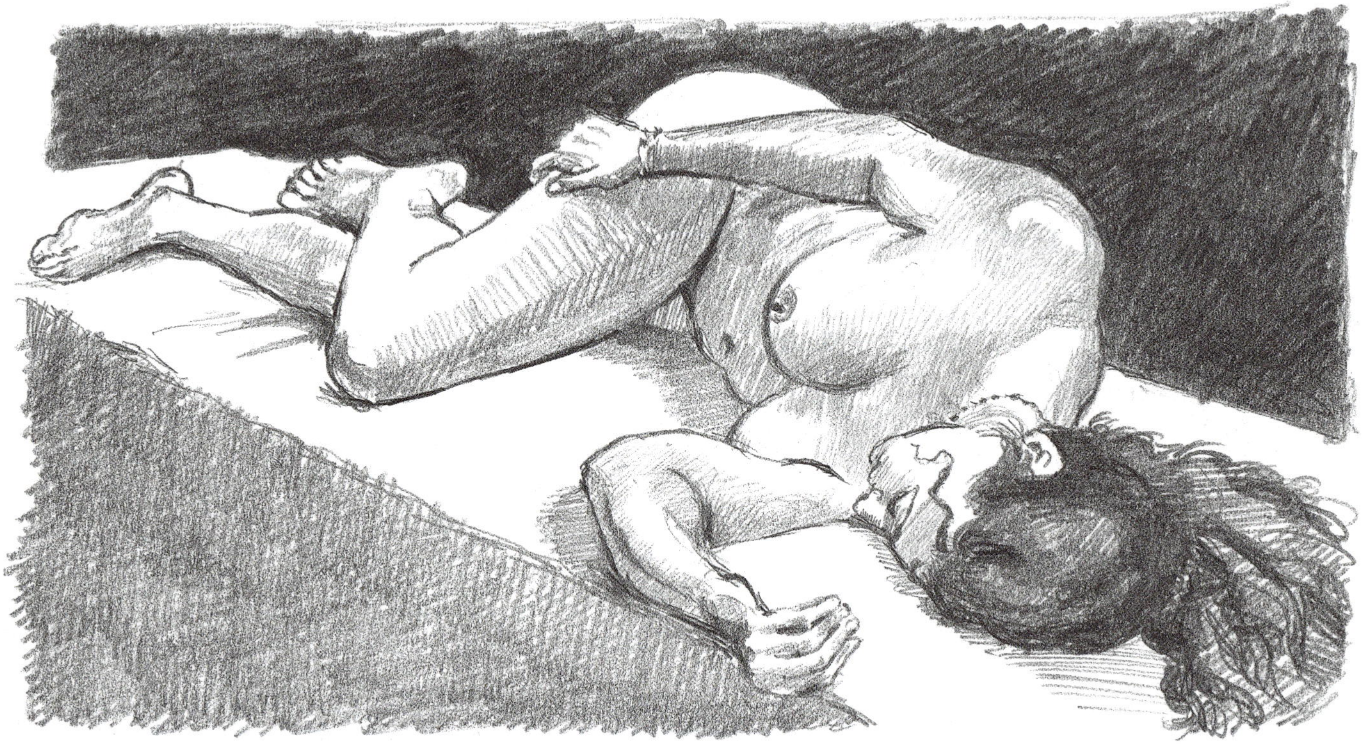

The examples on these pages show the same model reclining on her side from both the head end (opposite page) and the foot end (this page). You can see how the size of the feet in relation to the size of the head, and the length of the torso and head in relation to the length of the legs, is quite different in each.

Working at speed

Another practice always useful for life drawing is to draw extremely quickly with just a few fluid lines to see how fast the whole figure can be sketched in. This is encouraged by many life class tutors as it teaches students to look for the essential lines of the pose. Practice a dozen or so drawings like these of the model, taking various one- or two-minute poses and putting in the absolute minimum. You should be working so quickly you have no time to correct errors.

Describing form

One of the greatest challenges of life drawing is the need to indicate the three-dimensional qualities of the figure, so that the eye is convinced that what it is seeing has mass and volume. There is no fixed methodology for this and artists down the ages have tackled the question in many different ways. Over the next pages we look at a few approaches.

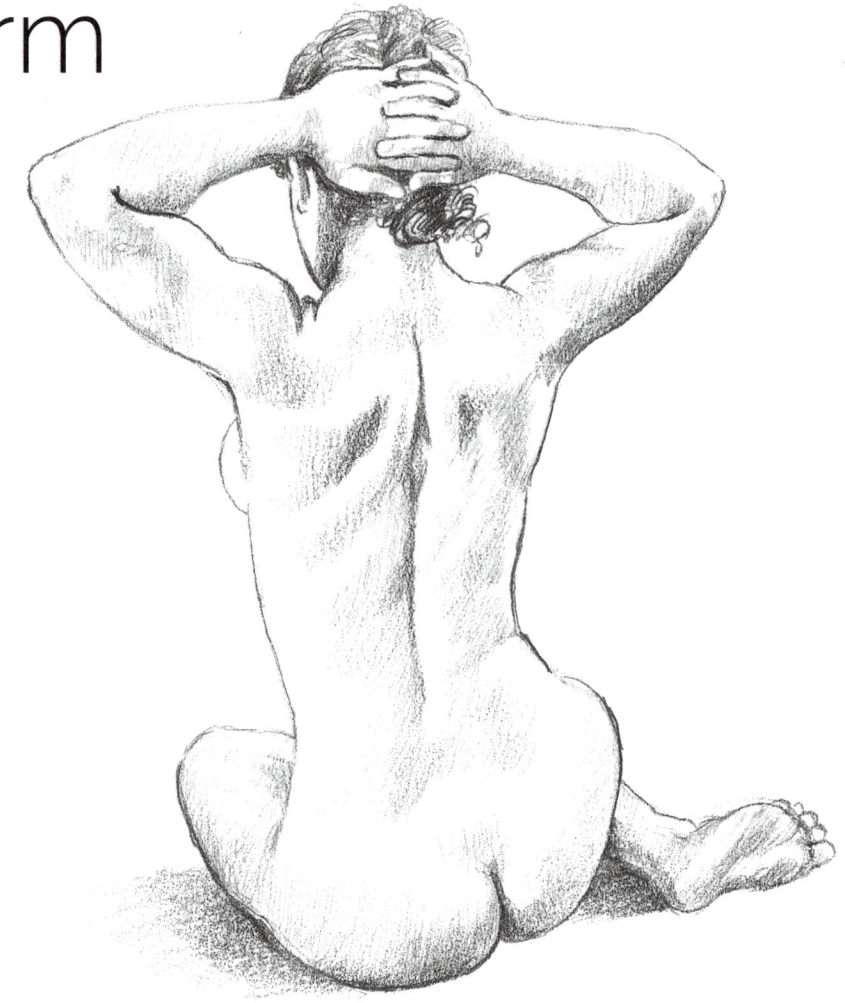

The first example shows the classic method of shading in pencil, which the majority of artists use at some time or another, and it is probably one of the most effective methods of showing solidity. What artists rely upon here is the fact that we cannot see anything without sufficient light both to illuminate one surface and throw another in the shade. Traditionally, the way to illustrate light and shade is to move your pencil across the paper in regular, close-set lines to affect an area of shadow. This has to be done in a fairly controlled way and the better you become at it, the more convincing is the result. Leonardo da Vinci was famous for laying on shadow in this way, using a technique called *sfumato*, meaning that the result was so subtle and soft that the gradation of tone looked almost like smoke. Our example doesn't claim to be as expert as Leonardo's, nevertheless you can see how by very careful progression with the shading, the impression of a solid body with the light falling on it from one side is convincing, and gives roundness to the limbs and torso of the model.

The second example is more drastic and less lifelike but does indicate the solidity of the figure quite clearly. The style is rather like the lines that a chisel makes around a piece of wood that is being carved.

The third one is simplified and rather angular; it works by describing the planes of the body in very clear-cut terms. This method has the tendency to sacrifice subtlety for the conviction of the main shapes and surfaces. It can give a dramatically strong look to a drawing but might well miss out on the detail.

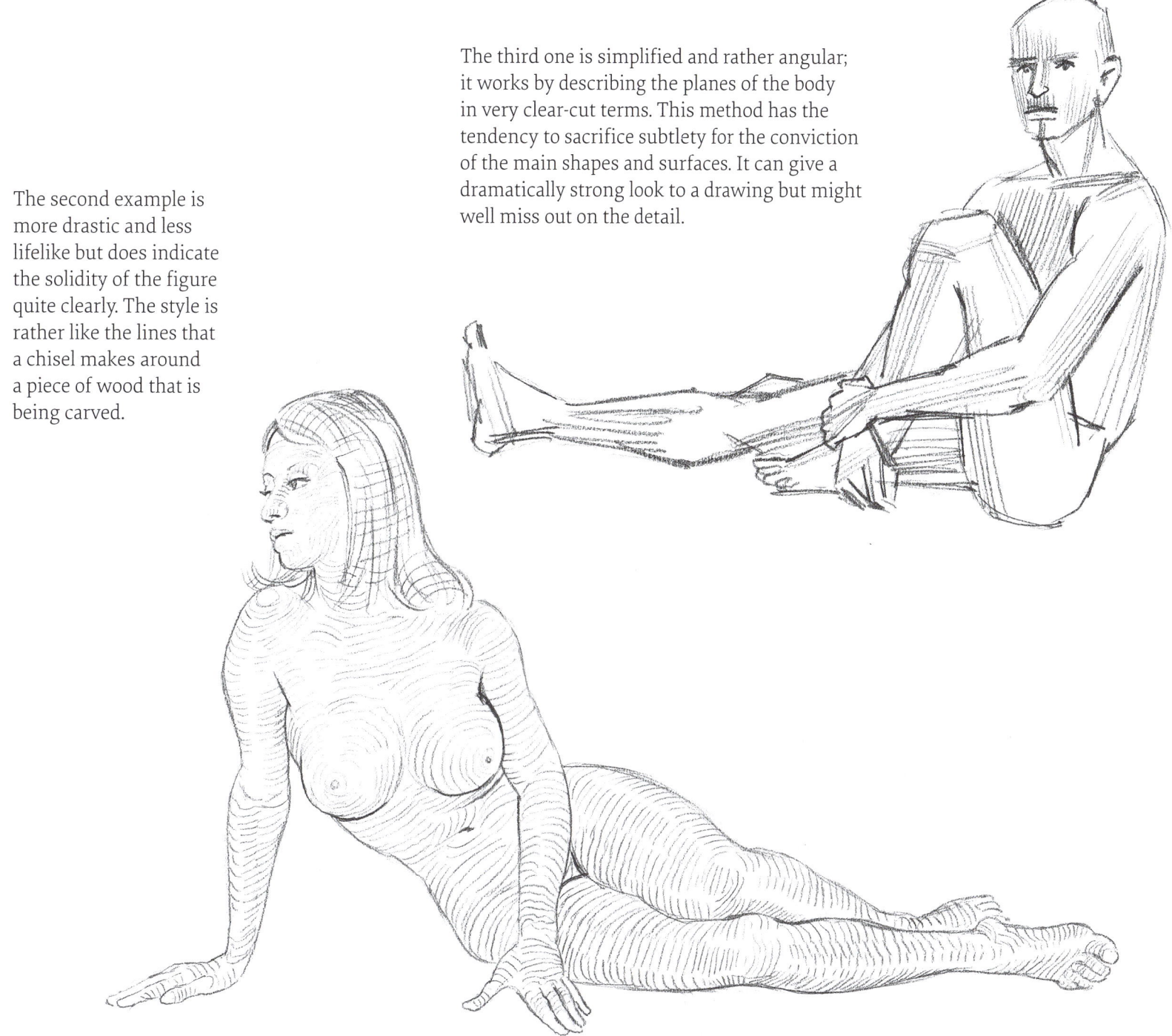

DRAWING THE BODY | 225

Showing the volume of the figure will make your drawings convincingly solid. After drawing in a very simple outline shape of the figure, the form is shown by a series of blocked-out areas of tone with the hatching going in different directions. You can see how this produces an effect as if the figure has been carved out of stone, with large facets of surface which give a monumental feeling.

In this similar pose, the focus is less on creating volume and more on an overall spatial effect and subtle use of color. The model is drawn in pen and ink on cream, almost flesh-colored paper. I used sparse lines to indicate the outline of the figure and added some color washes to give a sense of form. In the areas where the figure caught the light around the breasts, thigh and lower leg, I left mainly blank paper. Where the tones and shadows were darker I added more color to the wash. The addition of washes of color shows how much even limited color can achieve.

DRAWING THE BODY

Hard and soft lines

Even in a line drawing with no attempt at tone you can influence the way the viewer will see and understand your figure. Producing a hard, definite line requires a steadier nerve on the part of the artist than a softer, more tentative line, but both are an equally valid way of describing the human form and lending feeling to the image.

With the minimal approach shown in the example on this page, you will have to make up your mind about a whole passage of the figure and then, as simply and accurately as you can, draw a strong, clear line without any corrections. Only the very least detail should be shown, just enough to give the effect of the human figure you see in front of you. This requires a bold approach and either works first go or not, but of course you can have as many shots at it as you have time for. It really teaches economy of both line and effect and also makes you look very carefully at the figure.

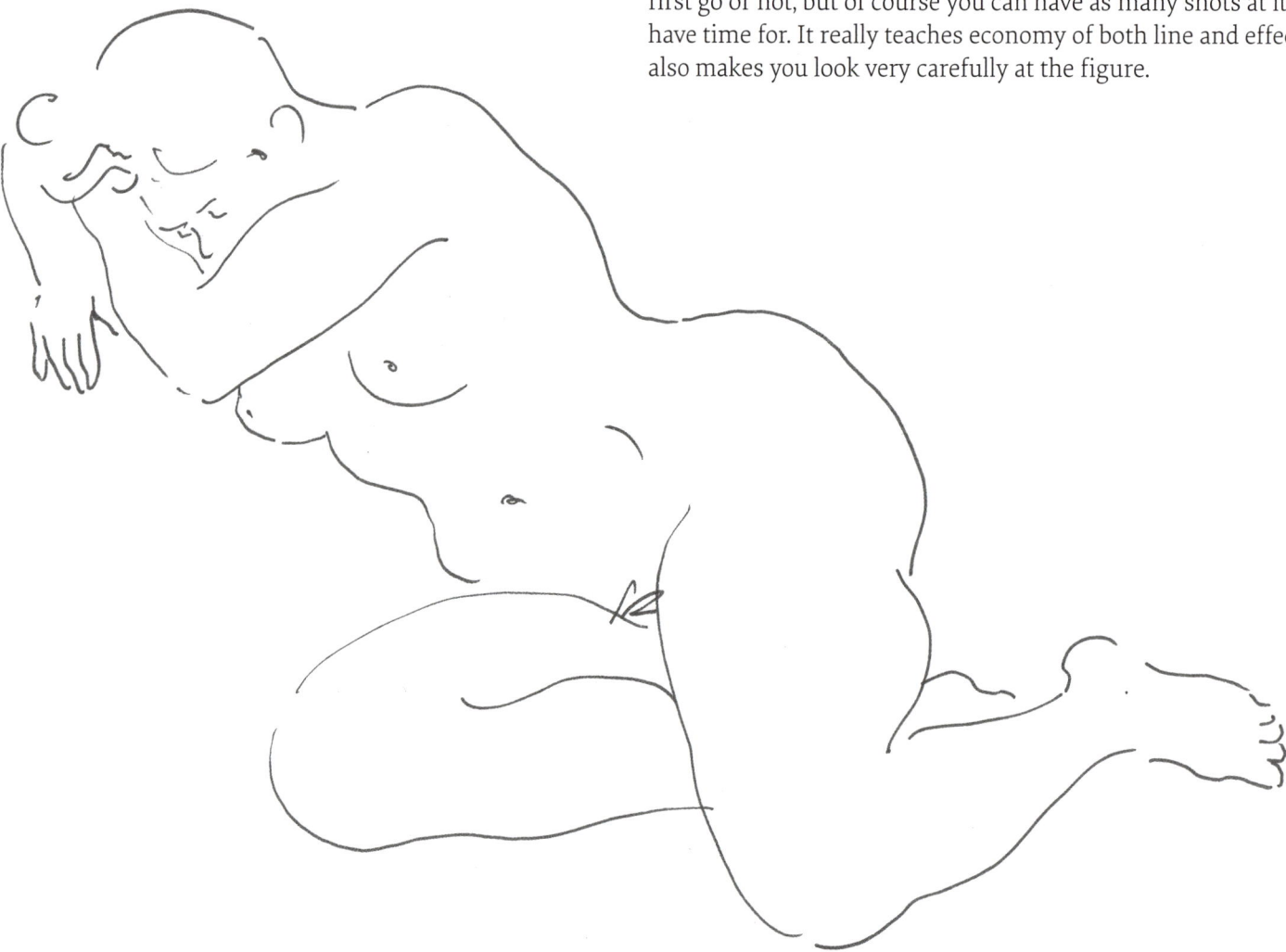

Allowing your pencil or pen to loosely follow the model's form in such a way that you produce a mass of weaving lines around the main shapes helps to express the softness and fluidity of the figure. This allows you to gradually discover the shape by a series of loosely felt lines that don't pin you down too tightly. What it loses in sharpness it gains in movement and flow of form.

Form in movement

Now let us explore what happens when trying to show the human body in motion, which is by no means easy considering that you are working on a static image. Even so, artists have always found ways of conveying the idea of movement and there are several stratagems designed to bring action drawings to life.

The first uses two artistic devices, one of which is based on a photographic technique. When photographing a moving figure at a slow shutter speed, the result is a deliberate blur. In the drawing on the left, the artist has blurred the form significantly in order to produce the same effect. Not only that, he has chosen a pose that, from the positions of the legs and arms, suggests that the model must be jumping in the air; hair does not look like this otherwise, and even the expression on her face adds to the illusion.

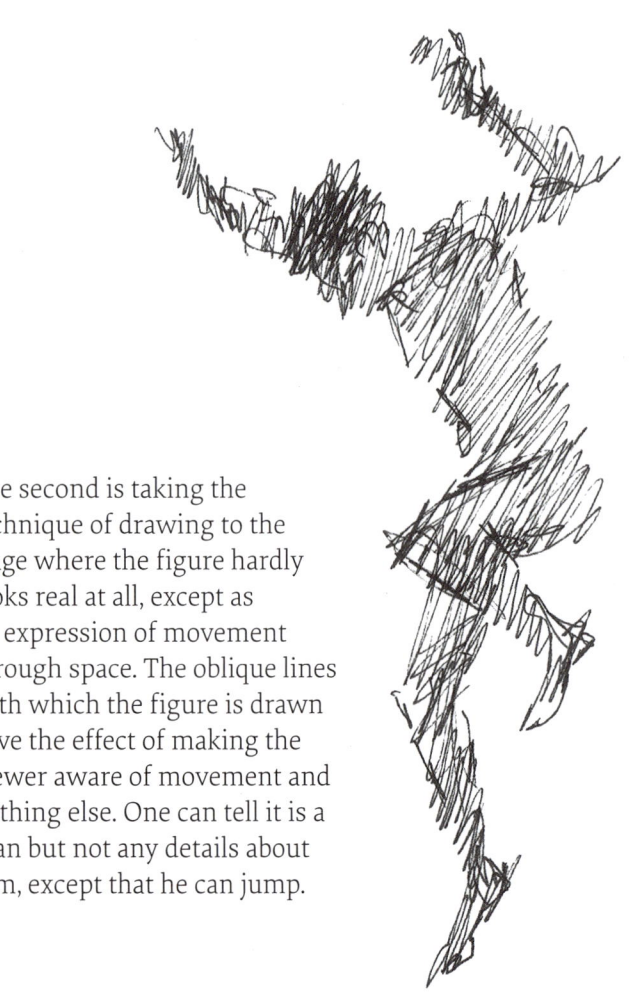

The second is taking the technique of drawing to the stage where the figure hardly looks real at all, except as an expression of movement through space. The oblique lines with which the figure is drawn have the effect of making the viewer aware of movement and nothing else. One can tell it is a man but not any details about him, except that he can jump.

230 DRAWING THE BODY

The Michelangelo drawing of the risen Christ is very clever in the way that he manages to suggest movement. He has drawn the figure with a rather meandering line at the edges that suggests the figure is in constant motion, and furthermore the pose is such that you cannot help associating it with a body that is rising upwards. This effect is partly due to Michelangelo's technique and partly to the actual balance of the pose. The successful evocation of movement is what you might expect from one of the most brilliant artists of all time.

Dancing figures

The figures here show what happens when the body is projected off the ground with necessary vigour; in some cases informally and in others in more stylized poses.

The woman in a ballet leap shows how she has extended her legs as far as she can in both directions, pointing the toes, arching the back with the arms extended and the head back creating a typical dance pose in mid-air.

This drawing of a leaping man shows how the left leg is bent as much as possible while the right leg is extended. The torso is leaning forward, as is the head, and the arms are lifted above the shoulders to help increase his elevation.

The next two figures of a woman leaping in dance mode show extreme extension of the legs and arms in order to create a balanced figure in mid-air. Notice how the muscles, particularly in the thighs, are very evident because of the effort involved in the action.

Notice how the pencilling reflects the energy and sense of urgency in the subject matter.

DRAWING THE BODY

Body language

The human figure will usually bring some emotional context to a picture. For example, a figure waving its fists in the air and confronting a cowering figure would obviously suggest some disagreement or aggression going on. However, the moods indicated are usually more subtle than this and, particularly when there is only one figure present, the artist has to understand and master the conventions of body-language before the picture will tell the desired story. On these pages you will find some examples of the moods that different poses evoke.

A. The pose of this masculine figure suggests some effort possibly related to pulling or pushing, shown by the braced legs, straight arm and twisted spine.
B. The female figure seems to stretch out in dreamy languor, emphasized by the sinuous quality of her arms and legs.
C. Another female figure, this time one who looks startled by something behind her, with a slightly theatrical gesture.
D. This male figure is obviously aggressive, with his pulled-back fist and fighting stance, reinforced by his heavily muscled form.

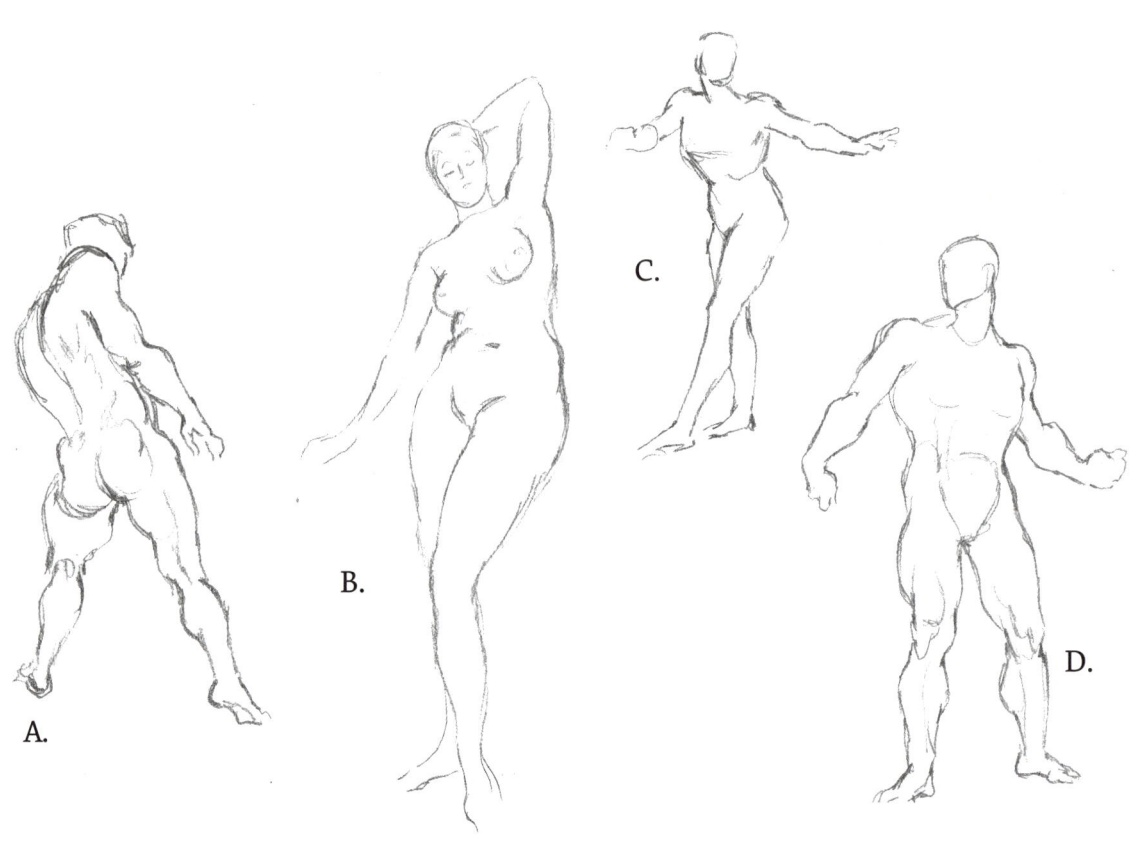

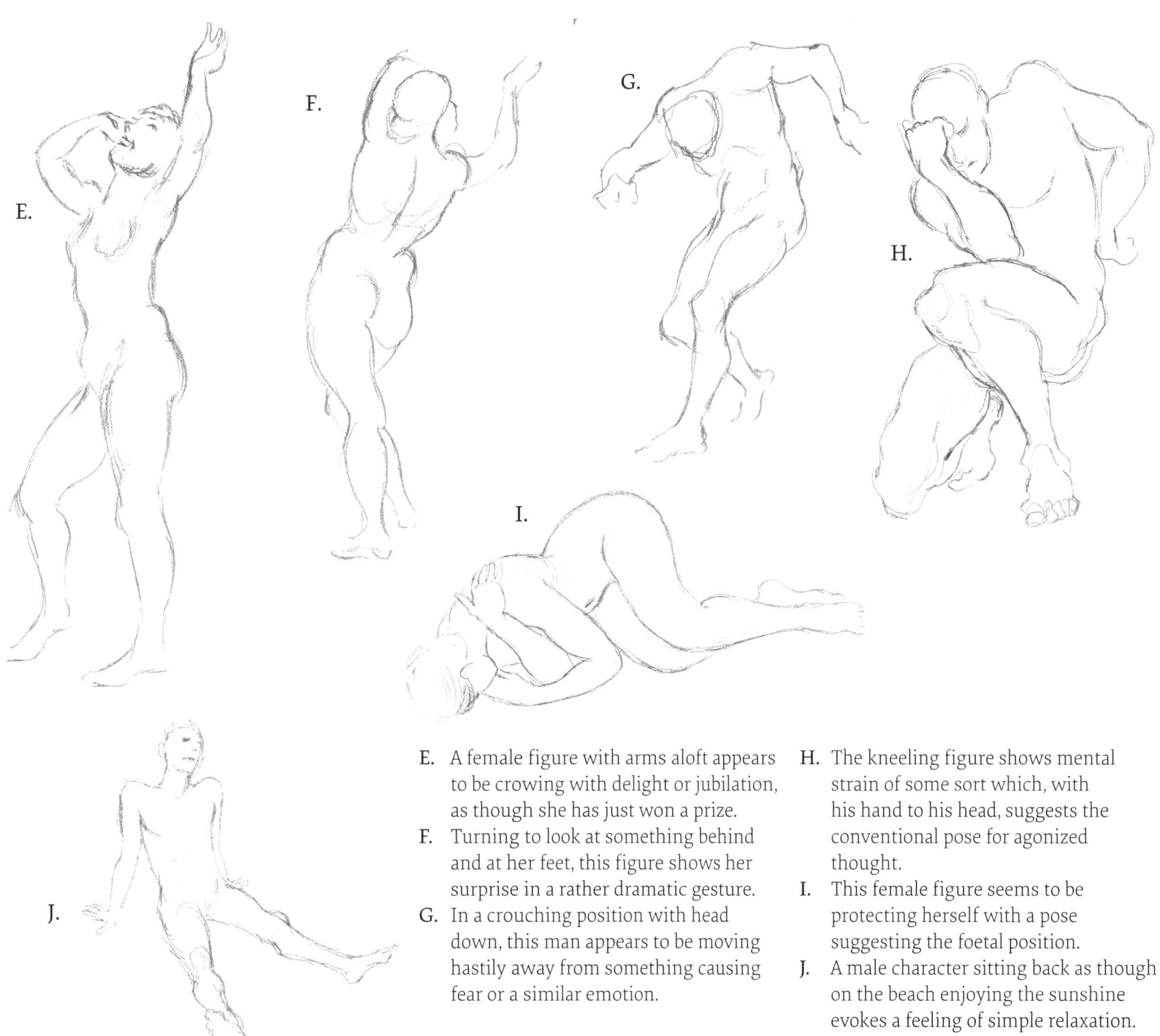

E. A female figure with arms aloft appears to be crowing with delight or jubilation, as though she has just won a prize.//
F. Turning to look at something behind and at her feet, this figure shows her surprise in a rather dramatic gesture.//
G. In a crouching position with head down, this man appears to be moving hastily away from something causing fear or a similar emotion.//
H. The kneeling figure shows mental strain of some sort which, with his hand to his head, suggests the conventional pose for agonized thought.//
I. This female figure seems to be protecting herself with a pose suggesting the foetal position.//
J. A male character sitting back as though on the beach enjoying the sunshine evokes a feeling of simple relaxation.

DRAWING THE BODY 235

Lighting the model

In order to make your drawing work more effectively it is necessary to take the way the light falls onto the figure in to consideration. Natural light is the norm in life drawing, except in winter when it may not be available for sufficient hours in the day. Most artists' studios have north-facing windows because they give light, without the harsh shadows caused by sunshine. With north light the shadows tend to be even and soft, showing very clearly quite small graduations in tone so that the changes of surface direction can be quite easily seen.

In this drawing of a model in a north-lit studio, a typical even light is spread across the space, giving wide gradations in the tonal quality of the shadows on the form. Note how the angle of the light causes the shadows to fall on the left side of her body and beneath her chin and breasts.

Lighting from the side

This picture gives a clear indication of how strong directional light produces harsh shadows and very brightly lit areas. This can produce very dramatic pictures: the Italian artist Caravaggio, for example, was known to have had massive arrays of candlepower to light his models in order to produce his very dramatic contrasts in light and shade, known as chiaroscuro.

Lighting from above

In most cases even light is the best for accurate drawing, and if you can achieve it, is very useful. However, there may be occasions when this is not what you want and then you will either have to wait for sunlight to give you sharp clean-cut shadows and very brightly lit surfaces or invest in some powerful directional lamps which you can adjust to suit your purpose.

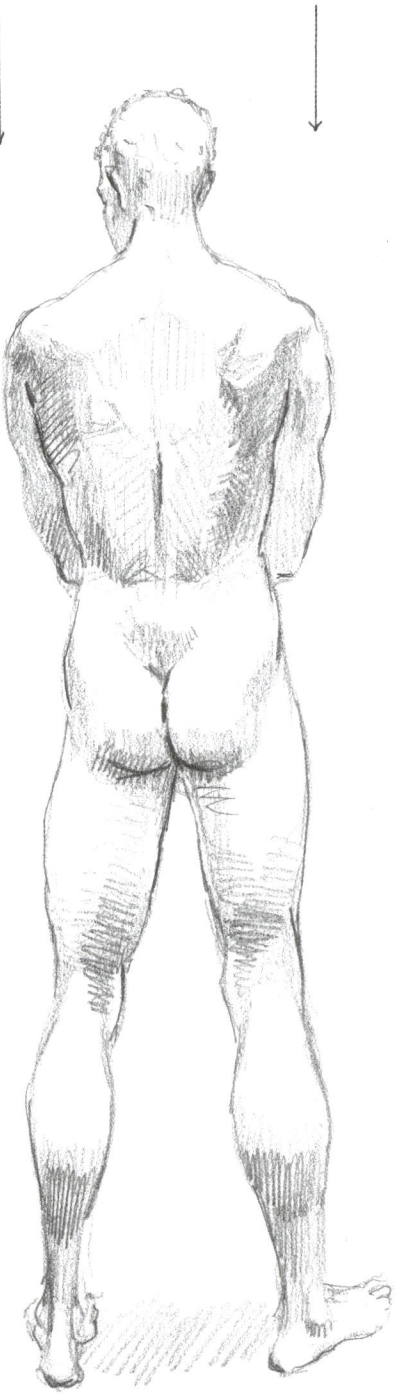

Light from directly above the model has a very strong dynamic, but when the model is standing heavy shadows form under the shoulder blades and down the length of the back, under the buttocks and on the lower thighs and calves of the legs. Light coming only from above does not occur frequently, so the standing figure will also look unfamiliar. When the model is lying down the effect is not quite so dramatic and looks more natural.

Lighting from below

Lamps will give you the chance to explore dramatic lighting effects that strongly influence the mood of your drawings, but light that is diffused shows more graduation of tone than direct light. Soft candlelight gives a very different effect from floodlight. Explore a range of different light sources, using different angles and strengths of light, and noting how they affect how the shadows appear on the model's body.

Lighting from below is very unusual and looks rather unnatural. The calves, buttocks and middle back get most of the light, but it also falls on the back of the head and, at the front, the lower belly, ribcage and breasts. There is also a lot of light under the chin, which gives a rather ghostly look. This kind of dramatic lighting from below was often used for the demonic characters in old horror films.

Front and back lighting

Light sources coming from behind or in front of the model present the most difficult challenge to the artist in terms of drawing the form and substance of the figure. When the light is directly in front of the model the effect is to flatten the form so that the obvious planes of light and shade tend to disappear into the overall light tone. Consequently, this lighting will result in a drawing that is more of an outline, with just a few subtle tonal areas shown. Lighting from behind has a similar effect, but in reverse. This time the only area with light shining on it is the edge of the form – usually the top edge.

With the model lit from the front, there is a large area of light tone with a few tiny edges of darker tone where a curve of the body turns away from the light.

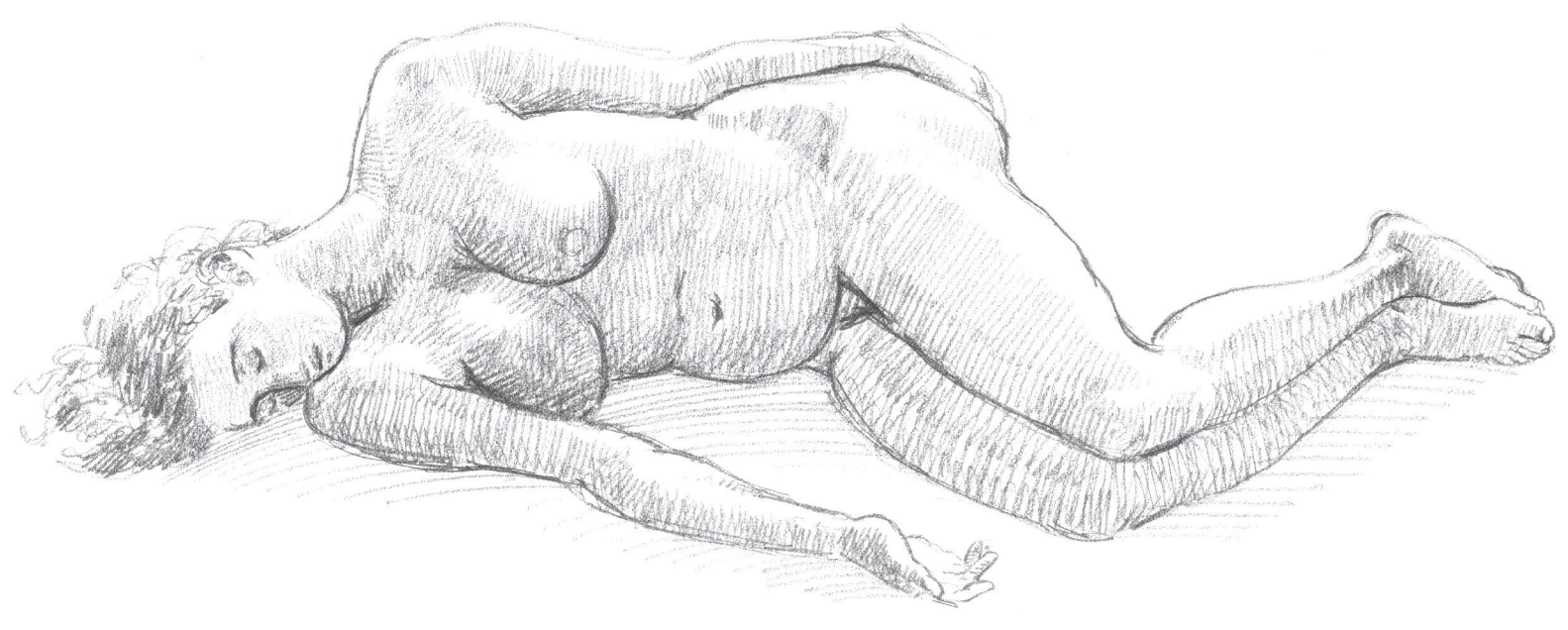

In this reclining model I have depicted slightly more line along the edge than you might see when the drawing is entirely *contre jour* (against the light) so that it is easier to understand the point. Sometimes you might only see an outline silhouette with bright light all around. The effect is exactly the opposite of frontal lighting in that the large area is of a dark tone with light edges appearing where the light hits. With both types of lighting the outline drawing is the key, so it is important to get the outline shape as accurate as is possible.

Light and dark tones

Here are some examples of figures drawn in color which demonstrate how to balance out your tonal range. The problem with drawing a figure in color is the risk that you run of making the final result look too melodramatic. The range of tones on the human body is quite subtle, but they do go from cool or cold colors to warm, rich tones. The sort of light that is used makes a difference – sunlight being so strong that it often washes out contrasts of color, and artificial light being restricted and therefore changing the natural color of the body.

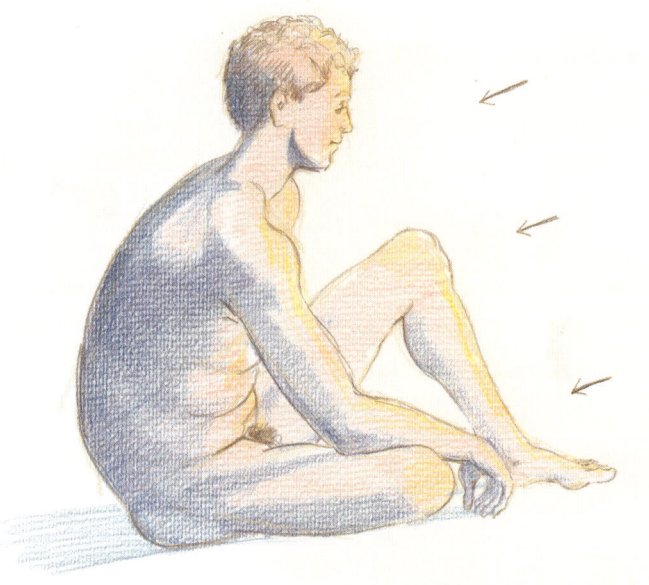

The man is seated, facing the source of light and since he is drawn in colored pencil, there is no great contrast between the very darkest tone and the very lightest. Note how the shadowed area is mostly in cool blue tones, and a warm yellow has been used in the areas where the light is falling on the figure. The numbered patches show the colors used.

Artist's Note

When drawing the human form, the simple understanding of the geometric shapes and the overall tones are far more important than the details. Without this care in the main shapes and colors, the details won't work to your advantage. So, take immense care with the large, main shapes and colors of the body, and then the details will really take off.

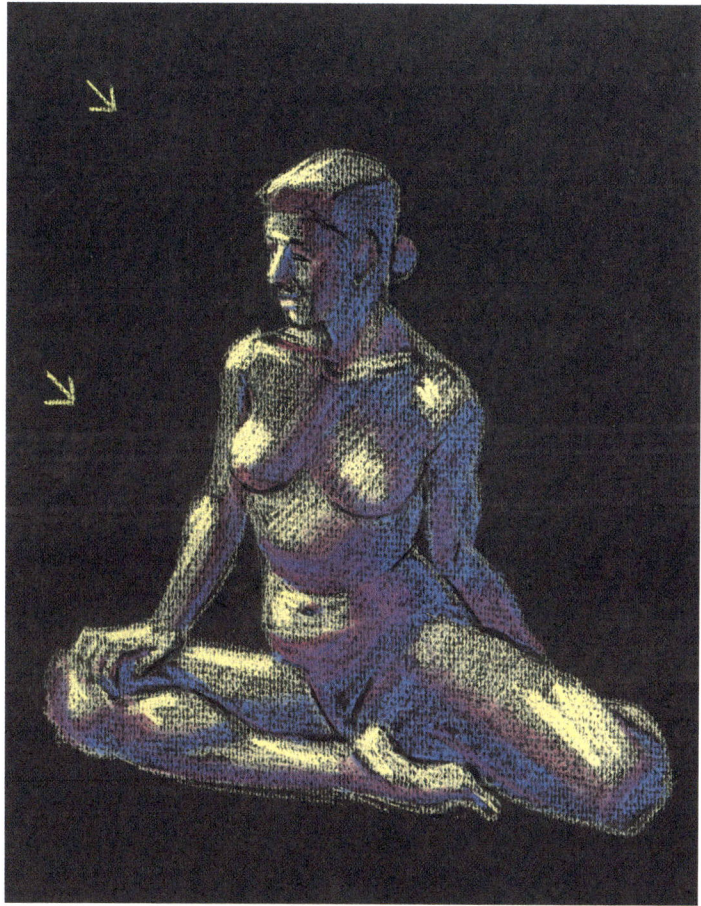

For maximum contrast on the black background, I have used pastels. Note the use of warm and cool colors for the light and dark areas; and to add a touch more warmth to the picture I've put in a rich reddy-purple to prevent the blue from becoming too dominant. When working like this you should do the initial drawing in a single color first, to establish the overall shape of the figure.

This dark, densely sketched background in deep blues has the effect of throwing the lighter, yellow-toned body forward into relief.

DRAWING THE BODY 243

Life drawing step by step

This step-by-step exercise takes a fairly classic approach to portraying a model and demonstrates how you can build up form during a longer pose at a life class. I used colored pencils for this study, starting with a faint ochre line and adding more color as I developed the figure.

STEP 1

First, make a few swift, light marks, just to give an idea of the proportions and shapes of the main figure. At this stage you only need to get a feel of the overall shape of the whole body in space.

STEP 2

Next, start to define the figure more fully, getting the shapes of the limbs and head and torso as accurate as possible. Keep drawing lightly so that you can correct any mistakes easily. This stage is extremely important to help produce a good drawing.

STEP 3

Now you can start to define the forms with clear edges and darker tones. At this stage I used a much darker brown, and if you are working in pencil you can apply greater pressure for more definite marks. With a lighter tone, I outlined the areas of tonal shading on the body, to guide me at the next stage when tone will be added. Look carefully at your model to get these areas accurate.

STEP 4

Now at last you can begin to build up the tone with careful, light marks to get a good even area of shading which appears to indicate the roundness of the limbs and torso. If you are working in color you can also put in a touch of a warm fleshy color for the skin and a bit of yellow ocher for the hair. Note where the darkest parts of the shadows are and increase their density. It also helps to put in the surface the model is sitting on. I used a blue tone for this, to give some basis for the whole figure.

Whatever the shape or pose of your model, by following these steps you should end up with a fairly solid-looking figure.

DRAWING THE BODY

Examples by master artists

To develop an individual style of portraying the human form, you will have to experiment with your style and materials. Over the next pages we look at some very different approaches to life drawing taken by master artists, considering why each is successful.

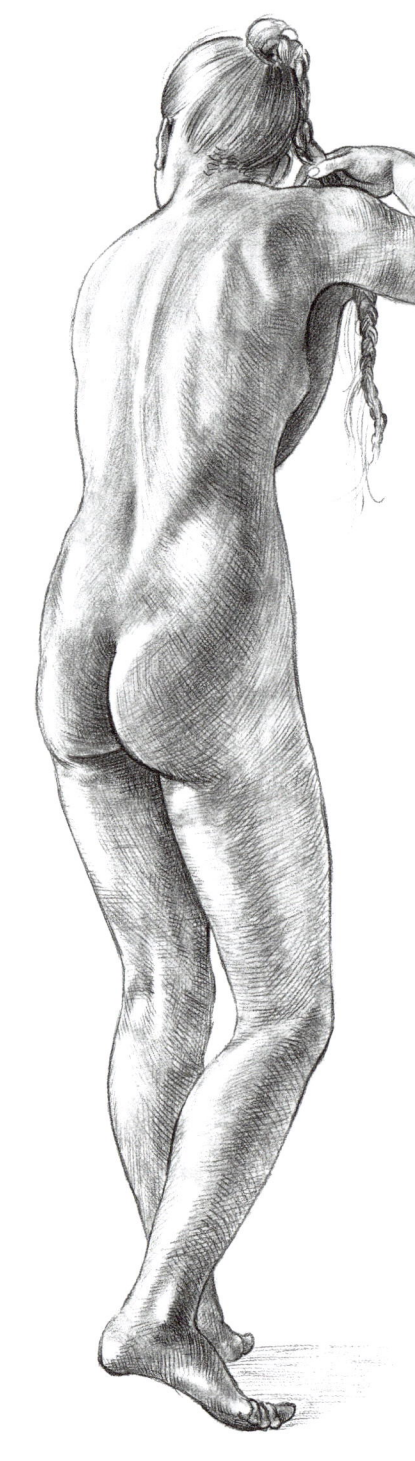

AFTER JULIUS SCHNORR VON CAROLSFELD (1794–1872)

In this example the pencil is used almost scientifically with the line taking pre-eminence. It is one of the most perfect drawings I've ever seen in this meticulous pencil style. The result is quite stupendous, even though this is just a copy and probably doesn't have the precision of the original. Every line is visible. The tonal shading which follows the contours of the limbs is exquisitely observed. This is not at all easy to do and getting the repeated marks to line up correctly requires great discipline. It is worth practicing this kind of drawing because it will increase your skill at manipulating the pencil and test your ability to concentrate.

AFTER GUERCINO (1591–1666)

Rarely have I seen such brilliant line drawings in ink of the human figure as those of the painter Guercino. In this example the line is extremely economical and looks as though it has been drawn from life very rapidly. The flowing lines seem to produce the effect of a solid body in space, but they also have a marvellous lyrical quality of their own. Try drawing like this, quickly without worrying about anything except the most significant details, but getting the feel of the subject in as few lines as possible. You will have to draw something directly from life in order to get an understanding of how this technique works.

AFTER TINTORETTO (c.1518–1594)

In his masterly original of this drawing in line (and ink), Tintoretto was careful to get the whole outline of the figure. The curvy interior lines suggest the muscularity of the form. There is not too much detail but just enough to convince the eye of the powerful body; every muscle here appears to ripple under the skin. The barest of shading suggests the form.

Moving figures

In all these drawings after Ingres, the figures show a fluid line which makes them look very mobile. Ingres doesn't define the muscles very sharply, preferring a smoother overall look to his figures. Nevertheless, it is obvious enough which muscles are being indicated in these drawings.

AFTER JEAN-AUGUSTE DOMINIQUE INGRES (1780–1867)

The first drawing is of a young man bending dramatically down to gather something up, while looking backwards.

The second drawing is of a nymph stretching upwards, showing the tension in her body as she does so.

The next drawing shows a man lifting a chair above his shoulder as he walks forward. The arm muscles are particularly obvious.

The final Ingres life study shows a man reaching down to lift something from the ground. The stretching of the legs and arms brings into play all the muscles of the limbs.

As happens in many life drawings by accomplished artists, Ingres has drawn extra definitions of the feet in the standing pose and the stretched arm in the drawing below. These workings help to clarify what is actually happening in a complex part of the pose.

Examples using different materials

Here I look at a series of drawings in different mediums by great artists showing how they used their chosen materials to great effect.

AFTER REMBRANDT VAN RIJN (1606–1669)

This drawing of a reclining nude woman by Rembrandt in 1658 shows how brilliant he was with the use of a brush. The economy of the line and the handling of the very light tonal areas give maximum effect with very little drawing.

AFTER RAPHAEL

In this drawing the great Renaissance artist Raphael Sanzio used a very particular technique of the time which was probably influenced by Michelangelo's drawings. The use of ink in clearly defined lines, some heavier than others, gives a very precise result in which there is no doubt about the shape and bulk of the figure. It is a good, albeit rather difficult, method for a beginner that is worth practicing and persisting with.

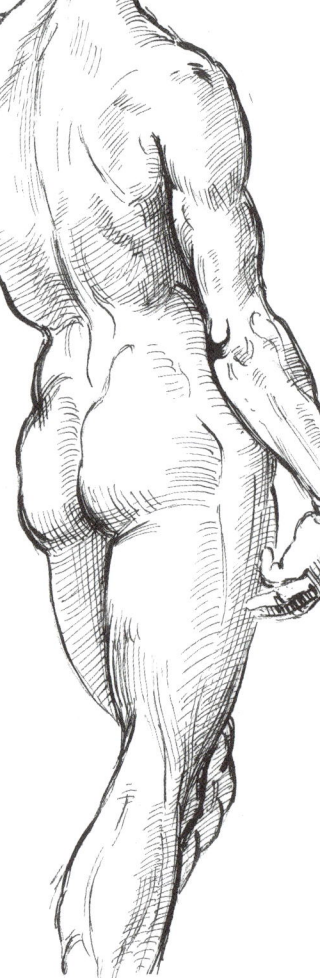

AFTER ARISTIDE MAILLOL (1861–1944)

This beautiful line drawing of a crouching woman by the great French sculptor Aristide Maillol, drawn at the beginning of the 20th century, shows how the soft smoky texture of the chalk line gives a feeling of the roundness of the limbs and the soft quality of the flesh. A line drawing like this is quite difficult to achieve with any degree of quality because you need to get it more or less right first time. However, it is worth trying because of the discipline which it imposes on the artist not to make too many mistakes.

DRAWING THE BODY

PIERRE PAUL PRUD'HON

The French neo-classicist master Pierre Paul Prud'hon was a brilliant worker in the medium of chalk on toned paper. In these copies of examples of his work, he shows us two very effective ways of using light and dark tones to suggest form.

In this drawing of Psyche, marks have been made with dark and light chalk, creating a texture of light which is rather Impressionistic in flavor. The lines, which are mostly quite short, go in all directions. The impression created is of a figure in the dark. This is helped by the medium tone of the paper, which almost disappears under the pattern of the mark making.

The chalk marks in this close up are very disciplined. A whole range of tones is built from the carefully controlled marks, which show up the form as though lit from above. Here, too, the middle tone is mostly covered over with gradations of black and white.

Practice: the 'Rokeby Venus'

In this final exercise, try drawing from a famous classical figure painting, the *Rokeby Venus*, by Diego Velázquez (1599–1660), using tone to increase the dimensional qualities of your drawing. Pay attention to the direction of the light source, as this will tell you what is happening to the shape of the body. Keep everything very simple to start with and don't concern yourself with producing a 'beautiful' drawing. Really beautiful drawings express the truth of what you see.

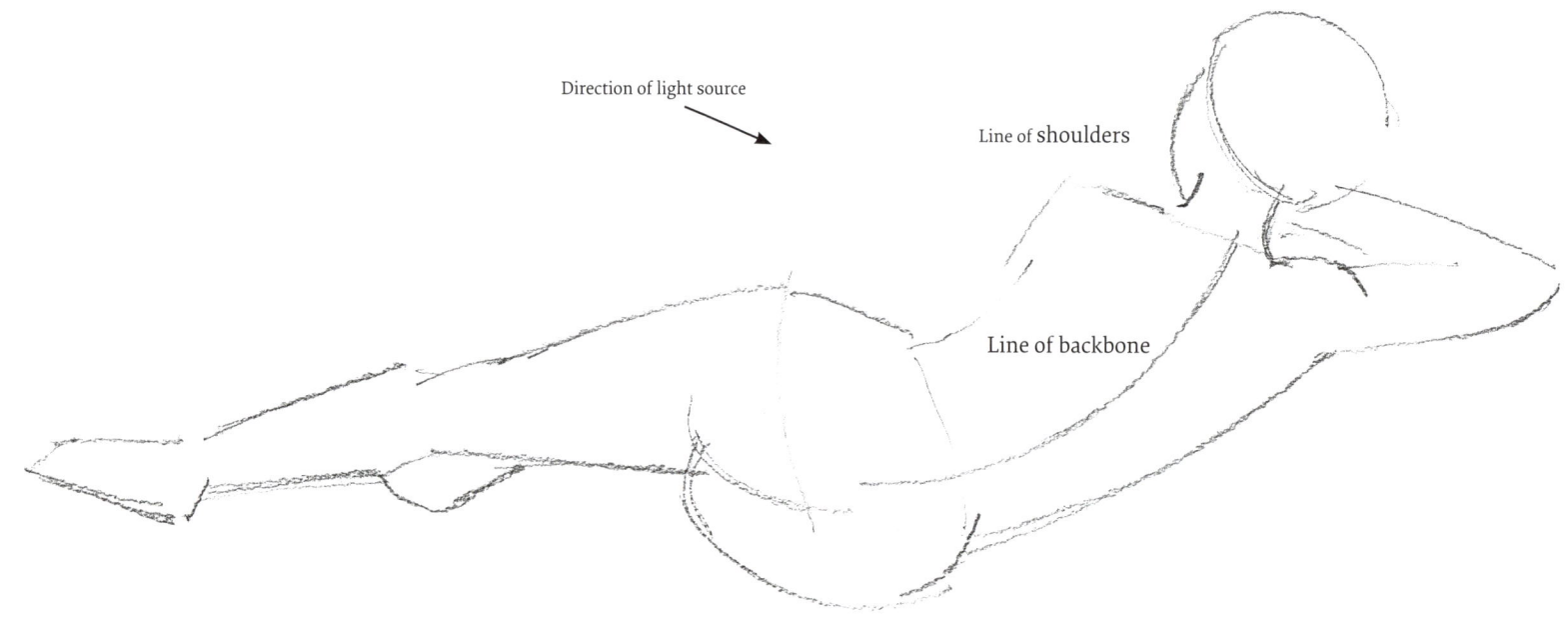

STEP 1

Sketch in the main outline, ensuring that the proportions are correct. Note the lines of the backbone, shoulders and hips. Check the body width in relation to the length and the size of the head in relation to the body length. Pay special attention also to the thickness of the neck, wrists, ankles and knees. All of them should be narrower than the parts either side of them.

DRAWING THE BODY

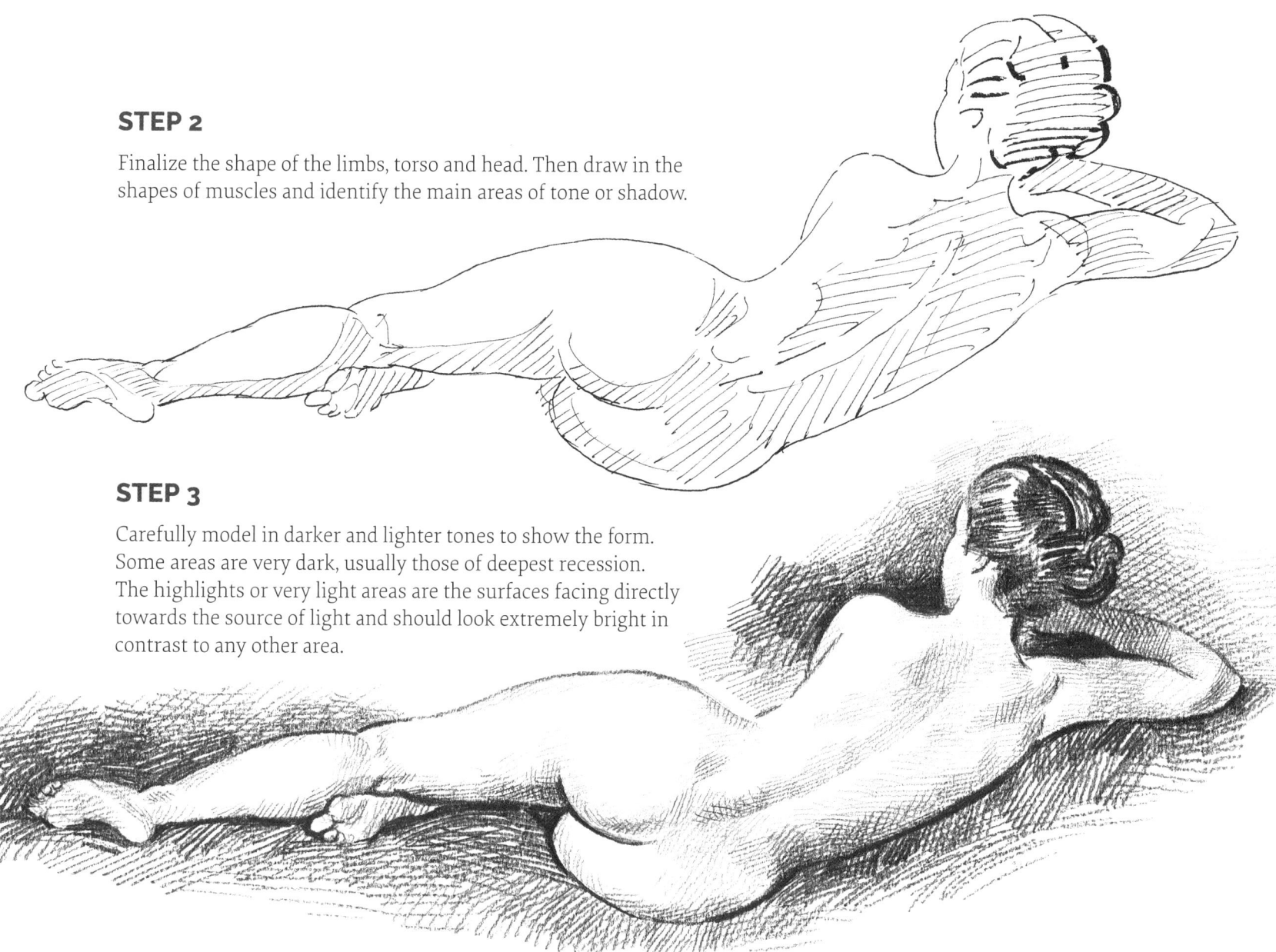

STEP 2

Finalize the shape of the limbs, torso and head. Then draw in the shapes of muscles and identify the main areas of tone or shadow.

STEP 3

Carefully model in darker and lighter tones to show the form. Some areas are very dark, usually those of deepest recession. The highlights or very light areas are the surfaces facing directly towards the source of light and should look extremely bright in contrast to any other area.

When you have finished applying tone, give your figure a place to exist in by adding tones to the background. These will enhance your drawing by throwing the strongly defined areas of light forwards, thereby increasing the three-dimensional effect.

DRAWING THE BODY

Index

ageing 66–7
anatomical terminology 11–13
aponeuroses 9
arms
   bones 124–5, 130, 136–7, 140
   female 157
   flexed arm 142–3
   lower arm 138–40
   male 156
   master artists 158–63
   muscles 126–9, 130–43
   skeleton 124–5
   surface of 156–7
   turning 136–7
   upper arm 130, 132–5
   views of 122–3
back 99–100
body language 234–5
bones 8, 12
   arms 124–5, 130, 136–7, 140
   feet 172–3, 189–91
   hands 124–5, 144–5, 148–9
   legs 172–3
   shoulders 130–1
   torso 94–5
Boucher, François 163
Boulogne, Louis de 206
brushes 16
Carolsfeld, Julius Schnorr von 246
Carracci, Annibale 203
cartilage 10
charcoal 14
children
   heads 38
   proportions 31
colored pencils 17
Da Vinci, Leonardo 164, 224
De Peters, Johann 118
Del Piombo, Sebastiano 109
Del Sarto, Andrea 165
Delacroix, Eugéne 163
drawing materials 14–17

dynamic poses 216–20
ears 64
epidermis 10
erasers 16
eyes 58–60
facial expressions 54–7
fasciae 10
fat 10
feet
   bones 172–3, 189–91
   master artists 193, 202–7
   muscles 174–7, 189–91
   perspective 208
   skeleton 172–3
   surface of 192–201
   views of 170–1
felt tips 15, 17
foreshortening 220–1
gluteal muscles 182–3
Gossaert, Jan 112
graphite stick 14
Guernico 247
hair 65
hands
   bones 124–5, 144–5, 148–9
   drawing own 166–7
   female 151, 157
   male 150, 156
   master artists 158–65
   movement 152–5
   muscles 126–9, 146–9
   skeleton 124–5, 144–5
   surface of 150–1, 156–7
   views of 122–3
head
   ageing 66–7
   approaches to drawing 72–7
   different angles 39–41
   lighting 78–9
   master artists 52
   muscles 46–8, 51
   proportions 36–8, 68–9

   skeleton 86–8
   steps to drawing 80–3
   tilted 70–1
hips 178–80
human figure
   approaches to 224–7
   body language 234–5
   form in 224–33
   drawing materials 250–3
   hard and soft lines 228–9
   life drawing 244–5
   master artists 246–55
   movement 230–3, 248–9
   proportions 28–31
illuminators 17
Ingres, Jean-Auguste 248–9
inks 15
joints 10–11, 137, 184–5
knees 184–5
legs
   bones 172–3
   drawing materials 209
   female 194, 196, 197, 198–9
   lower legs 186–8
   male 195, 196, 197, 200–1
   master artists 202–7
   muscles 174–7, 178–83, 186–8
   perspective 208
   skeleton 172–3
   surface of 192–201
   views of 170–1
life drawing 212–15, 244–5
ligaments 10
lighting 78–9, 236–41
lines, hard and soft 228–9
marker pens 15
Michelangelo Buonarroti 113, 159, 164, 193, 204
Mignard, Pierre 115
Mola, Francesco 158
mouths 62–3
muscles 8–9, 13

arm 126–9, 130–43
back 99–100
back view 24
feet 174–7, 189–91
front view 23
hand 126–9, 146–9
head 46–8, 51
legs 174–7, 178–83, 186–8
neck 49–50, 91–3
shoulders 130–1
side view 25
spine 98
torso 91–3, 94–100
Natoire, Charles-Joseph 161, 202
neck
   muscles 49–50, 91–3
noses 61
Orpen, William 53
Passarotti, Bartolommeo 116
pastels 17
pelvis 90
pencils 14
pens 15
perspective
   foreshortening 220–1
   legs and feet 208
   life drawing 220–1
   and proportions 32
Pontormo, Jacopo 114
proportions
   head 36–8, 68–9
   human figure 28–31
   and perspective 32
Prud'hon, Pierre Paul 111, 158, 252–3
Raphael 108, 110, 161, 162
rectus abdominis 97
ribcage 97
Rokeby Venus (Velázquez) 254–5
Rubens, Peter Paul 52, 119, 163, 165, 193, 205

Salgado, Antonio de Pereda y 160
sharpeners 16
shoulders 130–1
skeleton
   arms 124–5
   back view 21
   feet 172–3
   female 27
   front view 20
   hands 124–5, 144–5
   head 86–8
   legs 172–3
   male 26
   side view 22
   torso 86–8
skin 10
skull
   back view 44
   front view 42
   male and female 45
   side view 43
   top view 44
speed drawing 222–3
spine 89, 98
tendinous arches 9
tendons 9
thighs 178–81
Tintoretto 247
tones 242–3
torso
   bones 94–100
   female 103–4, 107
   male 101–2, 105–6
   master artists 108–19
   muscles 91–3, 94–100
   skeleton 86–8
Velázquez, Diego 254–5
Volterra, Daniele Ricciarelli da 162
Von Stuck, Franz 117
watercolors 17
Watteau, Jean-Antoine 160